REVOLT OF THE TAR HEELS

REVOLT OF THE TAR HEELS

The North Carolina Populist Movement, 1890–1901

James M. Beeby

UNIVERSITY PRESS OF MISSISSIPPI
JACKSON

www.upress.state.ms.us

The University Press of Mississippi is a member of the Association of
American University Presses.

Copyright © 2008 by University Press of Mississippi
All rights reserved
Manufactured in the United States of America

First printing 2008

∞

Library of Congress Cataloging-in-Publication Data
Beeby, James M., 1969–
Revolt of the Tar Heels: the North Carolina populist movement,
1890–1901 / James M. Beeby.
p. cm.
Includes bibliographical references and index.
ISBN 978-1-60473-001-2 (cloth : alk. paper) 1. Populism—North
Carolina—History. 2. Populist Party (N.C.)—History. 3. North
Carolina—Politics and government—1865–1950. 4. North Carolina—
History—1865– 5. Racism—North Carolina—History. I. Title.
JK2374.N85B44 2008
324.2756'02—dc22   2007039275

British Library Cataloging-in-Publication Data available

For my partner, Robin, with love

CONTENTS

Contents

ACKNOWLEDGMENTS

This book is the culmination of many years of work and the help and assistance of so many people, institutions, and award committees that it is almost impossible to know where to begin really. My research was funded by grants and fellowships from Bowling Green State University, an Archie K. Davis Fellowship from the North Caroliniana Society, a Faculty Improvement Grant from West Virginia Wesleyan College, and, finally, a Summer Faculty Fellowship from Indiana University Southeast. These examples of institutional support gave me the time and intellectual space to gather vast quantities of materials and to write. I am sincerely grateful to all of those people on the respective institutional committees who believed in my work and supported my academic career, not least because without it I could not have completed this book.

The staff at the Southern Historical Collection and the North Carolina Collection at the University of North Carolina at Chapel Hill, the staff at the Duke Library Manuscript Collection, and the staff at the Raleigh Division of Archives and History in Raleigh were all so very generous in helping me to locate obscure primary sources and so terribly nice and helpful. It was a great pleasure to research in such hospitable and pleasant surroundings during the long hot North Carolina summer days. It would have been impossible for me to spend time at these institutions without the generosity, kindness, and friendship of Caroline Weaver and Tony Reevy, who opened their Durham home to me for two summers as I beavered away in the archives—the hours spent talking all things North Carolina, visiting small towns in the state, and discussing Tar Heel politics and culture have influenced me beyond measure. I thank you both from the bottom of my heart.

In the course of researching and writing this book, I have benefited from the advice, insights, critiques, and friendship of many people, including David Wall, Jo Mead, Adam Fairclough, Liette Gidlow, Christelle Dhugues, Chip Keating, Stephen Cresswell, Devon McNamara, John Saunders, Kelvin Mason,

Bill Mahoney, Marge Trusler, Judy Martin, Arthur and Jolanda Holmes, Carol Pelletier, Maya Mei-Tal, John Toth, John Turner, Mary Jo Sims, the late Djisovi Eason, Lewie Reece, Don McQuarie, Phil Terrie, Bill Grant, Scott Martin, E. San Juan Jr., Alicia Rodriquez, Joe Creech, Omar Ali, John Hinshaw, Gregg Cantrell, Rebecca Edwards, Jeffrey Crow, Jeff Abernathy, Yu Shen, Stephanie Bower, and Debbie Finkel. I hope each of you realize how much I appreciate your interest in my research on southern history, Populism, and African American history. Commentators and audience members at my conference presentations at the Southern Historical Society, the British Association of American Studies, the Organization of American Historians, and the Salzburg Seminar also sharpened my arguments and improved my writing. My colleagues, librarians, and students at West Virginia Wesleyan College and now at Indiana University Southeast have also assisted me in so many ways in this project—not least in sustaining my passion for history, research, and writing and striving for excellence in the classroom.

I would also like to thank everyone at the University Press of Mississippi who contributed their time and effort into the production of this book and made this a pleasurable experience from start to finish. In particular, I appreciate the enthusiasm and guidance of my editor, Craig Gill, throughout the whole process. I would also like to thank the anonymous readers who gave helpful, insightful comments that ultimately improved this book.

Two individuals deserve special mention. My dissertation advisor, Don Nieman, supervised this study from start to finish; and he helped me to ask the right questions, discern key themes, hone my writing, and clarify my arguments. Don's expertise in southern history informs this work on every page, and he gives me the space to form my own interpretations. Don also stands as a role model to me as the consummate historian, scholar, university citizen, and friend—thank you, Don. My dear friend and mentor Lillian Ashcraft-Eason warrants particular appreciation. Lillian is quite simply a wonderful person, a top-notch academic, and a scholar par excellence of African American history. Over the past fourteen years, I have benefited in numerous ways from her support, friendship, and warmth of spirit. Lillian's classes were the most challenging and satisfying of my graduate career, and she enabled me to become the teacher I am today.

My family helped me enormously over the years, especially with supporting me as I moved to a new country. My father, Paul, his partner, Jane, and my sisters, Sarah and Laura, made my transition much easier than I ever thought possible by championing my academic career and life in the United States and remaining close despite the distance apart. As I set up home in Louisville, Kentucky, I now realize that my home is here and also in England. Finally, I would like to thank my partner, Robin Wallace, for her love and friendship. She is wonderful and I am a very fortunate person, indeed.

REVOLT OF THE TAR HEELS

INTRODUCTION

In the summer of 1892, the first state chairman of the People's Party in North Carolina, William R. Lindsey, wrote a stirring call to those who favored the formation of the Populist Party after the state Democratic Party refused to respond to the problems facing small farmers in North Carolina and in the South. Lindsey exclaimed, "If the people believed . . . that they could speak through the party to the throne of power not a single Allianceman would desert its banner." But, Lindsey asked, "What do we see? Not a single Alliance measure has been gained in the Democratic conventions or legislatures except under the smoke of political opposition." He then warned the Bourbon Democrats that Alliancemen meant business:

> They longed for freedom of olden time and they are going to have it. They are not going to be chained to the rock on the side of the sea to be plucked by the vultures at will. There is mutiny in camp. There is revolt among the soldiers. There is pent up wrath in the breast of manhood. The people have taken up their march in the middle of the road, pressing down and trampling under foot all opposition. On the banner is inscribed "death to plutocracy" "Equal rights to all men." . . . If they cannot pull down disobedient parties, establish one of their own, open the road to moral progress and Christian civilization, they will confess their weaknesses and bow to the inevitable.[1]

In this address Lindsey evoked all the hallmarks of Populism in North Carolina. The reformers had tried to change the policy of the Democrats but time and time again they met defeat. Now was the time for a new party to throw out the machine rule of the oligarchical Redeemers, for the good of all classes in North Carolina. Populists saw this fight as noble crusade of the forces of good against the forces of evil, and Lindsey's address served as a rallying cry for those who demanded immediate and independent political action to rectify the economic and political ills facing the common folk of North Carolina.

What led a former Democratic state legislator and member of the Farmers' Alliance to oppose the Democrats so vehemently in 1892? Why did tens of thousands of small farmers risk social ostracism and calls of selling out the white race by forming a new and independent political party? How did this mass movement organize itself into a coherent political party and organization that defeated the Bourbon Democrats in 1894, and again in 1896, in a cooperative movement with the Republican Party? To what extent did the People's Party enact socioeconomic and political change in North Carolina and what role did the rank and file play in sustaining the Populist movement? This book seeks to answer these questions and to suggest that the "Solid South" was never completely solid after the end of Reconstruction.

From Reconstruction until the mid-twentieth century, southern states elected Democratic senators, congressmen, governors, and thousands of state legislators, but Democratic success during the nineteenth century was not without stiff opposition. In his classic work on the emergence of the New South, C. Vann Woodward argued that a whole series of opposition groups, organizations, and political parties struggled against the Democratic leadership in the South. For Woodward, the Populists were the last and most powerful group to oppose the Democrats. In his famous analysis of race relations in the post-Reconstruction era, he argued there were "forgotten alternatives" to the rule of the Redeemers between the end of Reconstruction and the emergence of disfranchisement and Jim Crow legislation in the 1890s. In recent years several studies have explored in more detail these "forgotten alternatives." Political dissent against Democrats reached its height in the Populist movement in the 1890s, and historians have engaged in a series of studies of Populism in several southern states.[2]

Interestingly, however, little work has focused on the two southern states where Democrats actually lost power between the end of Reconstruction and the mid-twentieth century. The first was in Virginia, where a coalition of Republicans and disaffected Democrats called the Readjusters gained power in the state and passed reform legislation between 1879 and 1883. The second was in North Carolina, where a coalition of Populists and Republicans gained control of the state legislature in 1894 and 1896, elected a governor in 1896, elected U.S. congressmen in 1894, 1896, and 1898, two U.S. senators, and scores of local officials. This coalition also enacted sweeping reform legislation and increased spending on education in the midst of a terrible financial depression. For a brief period of three years, the cooperation partners changed the political landscape of North Carolina, opened up the election process, reformed county government, and ended the machine rule of the local Democratic elite. This success provoked a well-funded, coordinated, and violent white supremacy campaign in 1898, which restored the Democrats to power for the next generation. In just two years Democrats pushed through a constitutional amendment that disfranchised most African Americans as well as many thousands of illiterate white voters, and they also overturned all the reform legislation passed by the Populist-Republican legislatures of 1895 and 1897.[3]

The cooperation period in North Carolina has attracted some scholarly attention. J. G. de Roulhac Hamilton published the first scholarly treatment of the cooperation period as part of larger study of North Carolina after 1860. Although Hamilton argued that the Democratic howls of "negro domination" only reflected conditions in some (not all) counties in the eastern section of the state, he did postulate that the cooperation government was incompetent, that the GOP (Grand Old Party, Republican) dominated Populists, and that African American control in the east meant "sometimes violence, injustice, dishonesty, always inefficiency, incompetence, and partisanship, accompanied by a deadly blight upon all progress." In Hamilton's analysis the cooperation experiment was a disaster for North Carolina.[4]

The first real challenge to Hamilton's thesis came with the publication of Helen G. Edmonds's groundbreaking work on African Americans in the cooperationist period. Edmonds carefully analyzed black office-holding at the federal, state, county, and local level; and she successfully refuted the claim that African Americans had excessive political power, dominated the counties in the eastern section of the state, and threatened the liberties of law-abiding whites. She also argued that the cooperationists passed much-needed election and county government reforms that aided those at the lower end of the economic spectrum, black and white. In doing so Edmonds dealt a fatal blow to Hamilton's thesis that the cooperationists were incompetent, power hungry, and captives of black political assertiveness. After Edmonds's work many historians further elaborated on the thesis that the cooperation period led to both economic and political reforms that made North Carolina's experience in the 1890s very different compared to the vast majority of other southern states.[5]

Historical treatments of North Carolina's Populist Party have been relatively cursory and often misleading. Most historians focus on what they term the rather conservative nature of the People's Party in the Old North State. The most recent is Lawrence Goodwyn, who argues that Populism in North Carolina was unique because of its poor leadership and the overcautious attitude of the leaders in the North Carolina Alliance in building a cooperative movement that formed, according to Goodwyn, the crucial stage in the emergence of the third party. Goodwyn argues that these cautious attitudes prevented the People's Party from supplanting the Democratic Party in North Carolina; and the death of Leonidas Lafayette Polk left the "most reluctant Populist of them all," Marion Butler, at the head of the state's new party in 1892. According to Goodwyn, Butler's moves toward cooperation with Republicans and later with Democrats caused him to moderate the more radical elements of the Populist program in order to gain votes. This interpretation, however, fails to comprehend the complexities of the political world in North Carolina and the narrow set of options Populists faced in the Old North State to win power.[6]

Bruce Palmer's meticulous study of southern Populists' attitudes toward the financial policies of the 1890s and laissez-faire capitalism in the United States echoes Goodwyn's claims that North Carolina Populism was decidedly conservative. Palmer notes that after 1892 the People's Party of North Carolina moderated its goals and policies, including advocacy "of a poor white-poor black coalition." Palmer also contends that the weak leadership of the Populists failed to understand the "implications of antimonopoly greenbackism." Palmer and Goodwyn, as well as Woodward, believe that the southern Populists sought interracial cooperation and a reorientation of southern society in a progressive direction. Because they view the North Carolina Populists as deeply racist, however, they judge them as far more conservative than their counterparts in Georgia, Texas, and Alabama. However, recent studies have questioned the validity of these claims. Most historians now believe that Populists displayed, at best, contradictory attitudes toward African Americans depending on local factors, the strength of the Republican Party in a state, the response by the threatened Democrats, and the actions and attitudes of African Americans themselves toward Populists. In North Carolina the detailed work by Eric Anderson on the majority black congressional district has discredited the notion that the Populists sought meaningful alliances with African Americans and clearly demonstrated that they sought to defeat black candidates or prevent black voting in the 1898 and 1900 elections. Although Anderson's study is an excellent African American-centered work, it fails to grasp the complexities of the Populist movement in North Carolina, and one cannot draw conclusions on Populists' attitudes toward African Americans based on one, albeit important, congressional district in the eastern section of North Carolina.[7]

These scholarly treatments, however, do have something in common. They do not grasp the complexity of the history the Farmers' Alliance and People's Party in North Carolina and the challenges it faced. The leader of the North Carolina Farmers' Alliance, Leonidas Lafayette Polk, was a planter, as were the majority of the state Alliance's initial leaders, but these men *did* organize one of the best systems of cooperatives throughout the state and in the South. The Alliance was also full of divergent factions, but the leadership pressed the Democratic Party to support reform legislation to help struggling farmers. The failure of the Democrats to respond to these demands led many radical Alliancemen toward a third party. Lala Carr Steelman's excellent work on the political history of the Alliance in North Carolina casts doubts on the plausibility of Goodwyn's and Palmer's position on the conservative nature of the North Carolina Alliance. Indeed, the Alliance produced some well-respected leaders in the movement: Leonidas Lafayette Polk, Marion Butler, Cyrus Thompson, S. Otho Wilson, and many others. The People's Party in North Carolina was really no more conservative in its state policies and attitudes toward African Americans than the rest of the South. The only difference was that in North Carolina Populists gained power in an alliance with Republicans.[8]

In recent years several works have attempted to understand Populism in North Carolina. James Hunt's excellent biography of Marion Butler is the first major attempt to reassess the work of Woodward and Goodwyn on the Alliance and Populism and the work of Butler. Hunt successfully resuscitates the centrality and importance of Butler to the Populist movement in North Carolina, the South, and the nation as a whole. Hunt is correct to point out that if Butler was not a real Populist, it was not likely that he would have held virtually every high office in the state and national Populist Party, including that of national chairman for almost ten years. Butler was a Populist, he did understand Populist doctrine, and he never deserted the Omaha platform. The problem, however, is that Hunt does not analyze other leading Populists in North Carolina and their influence on the development of the People's Party. He also spends little time on the political culture of the party and the nature of the rank-and-file activism—because that is not the focus of his study. As a result, Hunt offers a depiction of the Populist movement as a top-down insurgency where Butler fights the Democratic leaders for control. There is, however, far more to the Populist insurgency in North Carolina than this.[9]

This book is the first full study of the Populist Party in the Old North State. It fills an important gap in the history of southern Populism and late-nineteenth-century political culture. Eschewing a top-down analysis of party leaders, it explicates the political culture of the Populist movement. It utilizes heretofore unused sources, namely, contested federal election testimony as well as letters, diaries, newspapers, pamphlets, and other primary source material, along with cultural theory, offering a complete picture of the stresses and strains within the party: the competing wings of the party, where Populism was strong and weak in North Carolina, the policy and strategies behind cooperation with the Republican Party, how Populists fought their campaigns, and the Populist response to the Democrats' use of the white supremacy issue in 1898 and 1900.[10]

This study explicates key themes and issues in the Populist Party that will address longstanding historiographical questions on southern Populism, North Carolina politics, Populists' attitudes toward African Americans and black voting, the long-term impact of the movement on the lives of small farmers in the Old North State, and the legacy for historians. In doing so, I analyze Populists on their *own* terms and offer the first systematic study of one of the most successful political insurgencies in the South prior to the civil rights movement in the 1950s and 1960s. The central theme of this study is the political culture of the Populist Party and the grassroots activism of its rank and file. Despite a few notable exceptions, the vast majority of studies of southern Populists revolve around the life of a significant leader, the political battles between elites in the Populist and Democratic parties, or the analysis of Populist ideology and the party's support of free coinage of silver. Although these issues are important, it is vital to place the rank and file of the party at the heart of the People's Party. The Populist Party was a *movement* of the people, it was the "people's party." Indeed, Populists saw their party as different from the other parties. Therefore, interwoven throughout this book is an analysis of local efforts at party organization, cooperation with Republicans, resistance to Democratic hostility, and the voices of rank-and-file Populists. For example, chapter 4 directly analyzes the nature of grassroots political culture and organization and the vitality and organizational subtleties of the rank and file. These sources of strength also contained kernels of weakness. A constant theme in the study of North Carolina Populism is the difficulty that party leaders, such as Marion Butler and Harry Skinner, had in keeping the rank and file in order and following their leaders on state policy and campaign strategy. Indeed, in many cases the rank and file pushed electoral policy in the state and the move toward cooperation at the local level, particularly in the eastern counties of the state, where Populists realized that only an alliance with Republicans could possibly end the machine rule of Democrats. This caused no end of problems for both Butler and his handpicked leadership team. In the short term the actions of the rank and file made for a vibrant mass movement that succeeded in joining with the GOP, overthrowing Democrats, and electing a progressive-minded state legislature that both reformed the election laws of the state and increased public spending in the notable areas of education, charity, and other state institutions. However, the independent actions of the rank and file caused consternation amongst the cadre of leaders in Raleigh and in the U.S. Congress. Marion Butler, the great political trickster of the North Carolina Populist Party, could not control the party during his complex cooperation negotiations with Democrats during the campaign of 1896 and again in 1898. Rank-and-file members in scores of counties refused to follow the edicts of Butler as he vainly sought an agreement with Democrats based on free silver and financial reform. As a result, two wings of the party developed: One followed Butler, with his moderate reform agenda and his attempts to align with the state Democratic Party. The second followed Harry Skinner, who favored a continued alliance with Republicans to preserve the life of Populism and to reinforce North Carolina's new election and county government laws. These tensions existed because by 1896 Populists had failed to supplant Democrats in the state and Republicans remained strong. These divisions in the People's Party began in 1896 as Butler moved Populists toward a national alliance with Democrats on silver, and later in North Carolina following the nomination of William Jennings Bryan. This crippled the People's Party for the remainder of its existence in North Carolina. As the national party died, the party in North Carolina floundered. Rank-and-file Populists and some leaders refused to align themselves with Democrats at the state and local level because they feared the return to the machine and ring rule of the Democratic Party, a situation Marion Butler and the rest of the party campaigned against in 1892 and 1894. This intraparty struggle and turmoil demoralized and disillusioned the rank and file of the People's Party at a time when unity was desperately needed. In short, the internal divisions and machinations of the leadership over electoral strategy precipitated the decline of the Populists *before* the 1898 white supremacy campaign. As a result, the racialized nature of that infamous campaign was the occasion, not the cause, of the decline of the Populist Party.

Concomitant with a discussion of the actions of the rank and file of the Populist Party, this study also analyzes the development of the People's Party in the early 1890s and details how the party in conjunction with the GOP defeated Democrats. Although the People's Party formed during the worst economic depression to hit the United States, the party in North Carolina was more than just a response to economic problems in the nation and in the South. Rather, the People's Party in North Carolina developed because Democrats refused to address the problems the depression wrought on small farmers in the Old North State and perpetuated an oligarchical system that offended the republican principles most Tar Heels held dear. Democratic intransigence forced many farmers first to form the North Carolina Farmers' Alliance in the late 1880s. For a time the Democrats did respond to the Farmers' Alliance's agenda. Indeed, for a short time, the Alliance managed to control state policy through the Democratic Party, but this did not last long. Once it was clear that Democrats would not really respond to the plight of farmers, many radical Alliancemen, led by Leonidas Lafayette Polk, chose to bolt the party of their fathers and form the People's Party in 1892. Most of the leadership in the People's Party came from the Alliance, and the majority were Democrats. After the party's debacle in its first campaign of 1892, Populists moved toward a cooperative arrangement with Republicans because both parties focused on the Democratic election law that prevented opposition parties from defeating the entrenched Bourbons. Republicans had long been victims of Democratic chicanery, and in the election of 1892 Populists were convinced that Democrats had counted out the People's Party in scores of local elections in the eastern section of the state. As the economic depression worsened in 1893 and Democratic president Grover Cleveland alienated more farmers from the party of their fathers, Marion Butler and the Populist leaders led an educational movement in 1893 and 1894 to convince rank-and-file Populists that the party must defeat the Democrats in order to overturn the "evils" of the unfair election law and the machine rule of Democrats and force them to respond to the economic crisis in the nation. In 1894 Populists succeeded beyond their wildest dreams, a victory that was repeated in 1896.[11]

Populist success, however, proved short-lived. Historians have tended to blame the Democrats' white supremacy campaign of 1898 for the demise of the cooperation movement and People's Party. Although this is true in part, it is only half the story. The Populist Party was fatally weakened in the battle over the U.S. senatorship in the 1897 state legislative session, a battle that came from the division of the party into two wings during the campaign of 1896. During the violent white supremacy campaign of 1898, the political leaders of the party, in particular, Marion Butler, spent as much time attacking the wing of the party that favored cooperation with Republicans as they did the resurgent Democrats. In the face of a divided People's Party, Democrats campaigned on the interlocking strategy of protecting white women and ending black rule. It was a brilliant campaign that virtually ended the political life of the People's Party just six years after Leonidas Lafayette Polk led the farmers into the Populist Party. Internal division and an internecine war in the leadership, coupled with independent rank-and-file activism, began to undermine Populists when they needed a united party.[12]

Another central concern of this study is the People's Party's relationship with African Americans. Populists' attitudes toward African Americans changed during the 1890s. In 1892 the Populist Party made overtures toward black voters in the state, and in some majority black counties the party even nominated African Americans for office. However, this appeal to African Americans remained short-lived. The party was made up principally of former Democrats who held racist attitudes toward African Americans. Believing that it would supplant the Democratic Party in the state, the party appealed to the core constituency of the Democratic Party—white men. Further complicating matters, the vast majority of African Americans remained loyal to the party of Lincoln. Throughout the 1890s, African Americans continued to vote for Republicans and gained scores of local offices. Thus, when the People's Party joined a cooperative movement with Republicans, Populists no longer had to appeal to the black vote. At the same time, however, cooperative arrangements led African Americans and whites to vote for one another in 1894, 1896, and even during the white supremacy campaign of 1898. When Democrats tried to focus on the race issue in 1894 and 1896, Populists responded quickly and strongly by accusing Democrats of using the "scarecrow" of race to obscure the real economic issues. This approach worked well for the People's Party for three years. However, in 1898, a united, resurgent, and well-financed Democratic Party mercilessly attacked the cooperationists' Achilles' heel, race, and forced Populists into the defensive for the remainder of the decade. Meaningful debate on economic reforms was drowned out by the Democratic howls on African American "outrages" against defenseless white women. Race triumphed over class precisely because Populists threatened the class interests of the wealthy elites in North Carolina and the hegemony of the Democratic Party. Although Populists were white supremacists who believed in the "natural superiority" of whites, they were far more enlightened on race issues and race relations than Democrats. This biracial political marriage of convenience could have led to a realignment of politics in the South, but it never had that chance. In 1900, Marion Butler and leading Populists campaigned to protect African Americans' right to vote in the disfranchisement election.

This study, therefore, seeks to place the People's Party at the heart of the analysis on the cooperation period in North Carolina. It seeks to understand the party from its origins to its eventual demise in 1900. Throughout this study the actions of the rank and file and the party leadership will illustrate the political upheaval that the People's Party brought to the Old North State for a brief period. Rejecting the notion that the Tar Heel Populist Party was purely a conservative manifestation of its southern counterparts, I shall highlight the extent to which the People's Party, a party of earnest activists, sought to reorient southern society in both a politically and economically progressive direction. The reform legislation passed by the 1895 state legislature and the party's commitment to universal manhood suffrage offered a new alternative to the do-nothing, machine rule, and white supremacist attitudes of the Bourbon Democrats. If there were "forgotten alternatives" to the Redeemers, as Woodward claims, it is now time to analyze one of the southern states where the alternative became a reality. This reality was due to the People's Party in North Carolina and the activism of the rank and file.

CHAPTER ONE

THE ALLIANCE BROTHERHOOD

The Origins of the Populist Party in North Carolina

During the decades following the Civil War, farmers across America faced economic decline due to a deflationary federal monetary policy and low commodity prices. Southern agriculture has been the focus of much scholarly discourse, with many commentators advancing reasons for the decline in subsistence farming, the attachment to a cash-crop economy, the growth of the crop lien, the emergence of a merchant class, and the expansion of tenancy and sharecropping in the late nineteenth century. What especially irritated the farmers were the high tariff and the credit squeeze, which, coupled with high railroad rates, hurt them both economically and psychologically. Economically, the farmers were now more dependent on the commercial market. Psychologically, the farmers felt a loss of social status and political power. Politicians in the South did little to help the lot of the farmer. As a result of the economic problems, social and political movements developed in an attempt to alleviate the farmers' grievances. The dominant agrarian organization in the 1880s and 1890s was the National Farmers' Alliance and Industrial Union. South of the Mason-Dixon line, this organization was the Southern Farmers' Alliance.[1]

Any study of Populism needs to take into account the forerunner of the People's Party, the Farmers' Alliance. Paramount to any study of the Alliance is an overview of the state of southern agriculture because small farmers of humble origins made up the bulk of the Alliance and, subsequently, the Populist Party. The Alliance movement formed as a response to the economic depression that was occurring all over the South. However, it would be too simplistic to view the Alliance and, ultimately, the Populists as solely a reaction to the agricultural situation. The Alliance had distinct ideological foundations. Economic issues may have been the catalyst that ignited the movement, but there were other issues involved, as one historian noted, "The mass of southern farmers lived in a state of economic, social and political dependency."[2]

The Alliance was not the first agricultural organization in the South. There were many farming organizations often with individual regional characteristics, differences in membership, agendas, and an animosity to other groups. However, they all aimed to improve the lot of the farmer. The Louisiana Farmers Union, the Southern Grange, and the radical Agricultural Wheel are all examples of farmers organizing themselves in the post-Reconstruction era. The Southern Farmers' Alliance originated in Texas and quickly spread throughout the South, ultimately engulfing all the aforementioned organizations. Thus, throughout its existence the Alliance consisted of many different groups and, consequently, had numerous inherent contradictions in its ideology and program. One historian correctly argues, "The Farmers' Alliance was as truly a grassroots movement as the nation produced, and represented the first attempt to synthesize an agrarian philosophy during an era of maturing industrial capitalism"; he adds, "The Alliance spearheaded the agricultural reform movement of the late nineteenth century, and in the spirit of a genuine reformer, it helped sow the seeds that the Progressives of succeeding generations reaped."[3]

Charles Macune, the president of the Alliance, was an astute leader. Macune advocated the establishment of cooperatives in order to counteract the power of the merchants, who were using crop-lien and tenancy agreements to impoverish the small farmers. Brought by traveling lecturers and educators, the promise of improved economic conditions was enough to attract thousands of dispirited farmers. For many small-holding farmers, this was a first encounter with the idea of collective action. By the end of 1888, the Alliance had perhaps as many as four hundred thousand members in ten thousand sub-alliances across the South. The Alliance's merger with the Agricultural Wheel in 1889 doubled the membership to almost one million. Now came the moment for concerted economic action. The cooperative idea now began at the state level, and "the dream of organizing the cotton belt was within reach, but the rapid expansion was so far based more on promises than on performances. By the end of 1888, the Alliance had the numerical strength to try to redeem its pledge of salvation through cooperation."[4]

The cooperative venture by the Southern Farmers' Alliance ultimately proved to be unsuccessful due to the power of the merchants and bankers and the inexperience of the farmers. However, the cooperative issue had initially proven attractive to the Alliance for several reasons. First, the cooperatives had attracted many farmers to the Alliance, and their initial successes in 1888 and 1889 had at least stimulated some kind of interest. Second, the exchanges and the agencies prevalent in the cooperatives gave the Alliance a much needed sense of focus, of internal cohesion and strength. This is extremely important if one remembers that the Alliance contained within itself disparate groups. The cooperative movement helped meld these groups together, a development that would stand the Populist Party in good stead in the 1890s. Third, the Alliance achieved success on a regional scale in the now-famous jute-bagging episode when it opposed the high prices for the bagging of cotton charged by the trusts that controlled jute, and in 1889 after some organizational problems the price of jute fell markedly. All of these showed the farmers that cooperation could lead to positive advancements for small farmers.[5]

As in other states, the Alliance proved successful in bringing Tar Heel farmers together to support economic and political change. The Alliance provided the social and economic organization necessary to mobilize small farmers into a powerful political force. Alliance farmers first attempted to persuade Democrats to change economic policy and to help the farmer. When this failed, some of the Alliance leadership and the radical rank-and-file members pushed for a third party. The Alliance also gave agrarian leadership opportunities to several key figures of the future Populist Party. Marion Butler, Cyrus Thompson, S. Otho Wilson, and William H. Worth got their start with the Alliance. Their activities in the Alliance gave them experience in organization and a degree of what we call today "name recognition" that proved vital to a fledgling party in 1892. Finally, the action of the Alliance splintered Democrats and caused friction and problems. As a result, the seeds of change were sown in the late 1880s for the demise of Democrats in the mid-1890s and the triumph of Populism.

In 1887, Leonidas Lafayette Polk and Syd Alexander organized the Farmers' Alliance in North Carolina. Polk's newspaper, the *Progressive Farmer*, put the problems facing farmers in North Carolina in a nutshell:

> There is something radically wrong in our industrial system. . . . There is a screw loose. The wheels have dropped out of balance. The railroads have never been so prosperous, and yet agriculture languishes. The banks have never done a better or more profitable business, and yet agriculture languishes. Manufacturing enterprises never made more money or were in a more flourishing condition, and yet agriculture languishes. Towns and cities flourish and "boom" and grow and "boom," and yet agriculture languishes. Salaries and fees were never so temptingly high and desirable, yet agriculture languishes.[6]

The main cause behind the organization of the Alliance in North Carolina and, for that matter, in the South was the significant decline in farm prices. For example, the staple crop of the South, cotton, saw a marked decline in price. In 1868, the average price per pound was 25 cents. This number decreased to 12 cents in the 1870s, and by 1887 the price of cotton was down to 8.7 cents a pound. Once prices dropped still further, Marion Butler's paper, the *Caucasian*, commented that his county "has not been blessed with a good crop since 1882." Although the decline in cotton prices and farm product prices in general was part of declining prices in all sectors of the economy, this did little to appease farmers, especially as the prices for their products declined more precipitously than the prices of most other commodities and the cost of supplies and transportation rates remained so high.[7]

Not only did cotton prices decline, farmers in North Carolina found it increasingly difficult to gain credit. Money was in short supply and the credit supply during the 1880s in North Carolina was at an all time low. Consequently, farmers turned to the crop-lien system to gain credit. In short, the crop-lien system rested on the small-town merchant supplying household goods and farm goods on credit to the farmer in return for a lien on the farmer's crop and the understanding that they could easily convert the crop into cash at harvest time to pay off the lien. As a result, farmers found that growing cotton and tobacco was the best way to ensure money to pay off the creditors and their high interest rates (sometimes as high as 40 percent). Ultimately, this system entrapped farmers as overproduction caused cash crop prices to decline throughout the 1880s, and many farmers found it impossible to even meet interest payments on their crop liens. A vicious circle ensnared farmers. They could not pay off their debts, and they could not diversify their crops from cotton and tobacco.[8]

North Carolina was an overwhelmingly agrarian state in the 1880s and 1890s. Large plantations existed in the eastern section of the state, where cotton dominated the economy and African Americans made up the large majority of the rural population. Small farmers were in the majority in the Piedmont and mountain regions of North Carolina as well as the northeastern section of the state along the Atlantic coast. The greatest concentration of small farmers (those who owned a farm of 100 acres or less) existed in the western section of the state and northeast. Middling farmers (those who owned farms between 100 and 499 acres) predominated in the middle section of the state and in a few counties in the eastern section of the state. As farming conditions deteriorated in the 1880s, the agrarian economy of North Carolina entered a transitional period. Of the 178,239 farm operators in the Old North State in 1890, two-thirds or 118,826 owned land. The economic downturn, the decline in farm prices, and the scarcity of credit hit farmers across the board. However, the impact was worse the smaller the farm size. Tenants and sharecroppers faced even more difficulties. In 1890, this group made up 34.1 percent of farm operators or 50,500 farmers, with a large majority living in the eastern section of the state and in the majority black counties.[9]

It is not necessary to go into all the complex details concerning the forces behind the formation of the North Carolina Farmers' Alliance for this study; what we must understand is that the farmers did not believe that they were receiving a fair hearing from the state legislature and the leadership of the state's dominant party, the Democrats. Therefore, although the North Carolina Alliance formed as a response to economic dislocation, it also organized because Democratic leaders seemed ambivalent if not outright hostile to the needs of the small farmer.

The farmers' clubs and granges in North Carolina did not know what had hit them. The Alliance seemed far more attractive to small farmers than the clubs or granges. Leonidas Polk quickly identified that the Alliance was the stronger organization and led the farmers' clubs into the Alliance. Thus, in 1887, as the farmers saw their demands for help and action ignored by Democrats, the Alliance movement swept across the state. By the end of 1887, there were twenty-one Alliance organizers active in North Carolina. Alexander gained election to the presidency of the North Carolina Farmers' Alliance; Polk was the secretary; and Polk's newspaper, the *Progressive Farmer*, became the organization's official state organ. The Alliance grew at an amazingly fast rate. By August 1888 there were 1,018 subordinate alliances in fifty-three counties with a membership of 42,000. In 1889 there were 1,816 subordinate alliances in eighty-nine counties with a membership of 72,000. At the height of Alliance membership in 1891, there were 2,147 subordinate alliances in ninety-six counties with 100,000 members.[10]

Landowners made up the majority of the Alliance. Reflecting the racial climate of nineteenth-century southern society, membership was restricted to white citizens, male and female of sixteen years or older. Farmers, farmer laborers, county teachers, country doctors, and country preachers made up the fraternal order. Excluded from membership were lawyers and merchants. Large or small planters such as Elias Carr, Polk, and Alexander tended to dominate the leadership positions in the Alliance in the early days. Although the leadership was from a higher social group than the rank-and-file Alliancemen, this does not necessarily point to an inherent contradiction in the movement. Leadership in social movements often comes from a higher social class than the rank and file. Despite the elite status, the nature of Alliance organization encouraged its leaders to espouse the views of the common farmer. To give the Alliance a more coherent organization and program, Charles Macune proposed organizing the Farmers' State Alliance and writing a constitution, and also employing salaried officials to encourage expansion. An executive committee of three would determine policy. The county and subordinate Alliances within a state would have the same structure. The counties would meet quarterly, and the subordinate Alliances in each locale met at least once a month. A membership fee of twenty-five cents a quarter would keep the sub-Alliances on a sound economic footing. Membership in the society was kept secret in an attempt to keep unity and guarantee confidentiality. Women had the same rights and privileges of men. Both men and women could vote and hold office in the Alliance. Mrs. Evangeline Usher of the Long Branch sub-Alliance felt that women Alliance members offered another useful role in the Alliance. In a letter to Polk, Usher argued that women should attend Alliance meetings regularly because "it encourages the brothers and attracts the younger brothers to attendance." Usher backed up her claim, arguing that one of the most successful sub-Alliances she knew was where women were in regular attendance. Usher pointed out, "[Men] like the ladies to manifest their appreciation of their effort by going and canvassing with them in something else beside asking fir a new dress or bonnet."[11]

The Alliance served a social function, organizing picnics, entertainment, cook-outs, and the like. Education also played a key role in the Alliance. At every level the Alliance had an official lecturer to disseminate information and provoke lively discussions on a host of issues important to farmers, from crop diversification and new farming methods to national economic policy and the subtreasury system. However, the main function of the Alliance was in the economic and business spheres. For example, it set up business agencies in order to secure goods for farmers at discounted prices. One cannot overemphasize the importance of the economic functions of the Alliance. Small farmers, entrapped in the crop-lien system, paid top dollar for agricultural supplies, such as fertilizer, from merchants. By buying in bulk the Alliance endeavored to purchase goods at a reduced rate and then pass the benefits on to Alliance members. At a time of economic dislocation small farmers looked to the Alliance to help them at least break even each year. Thus, the Alliance business agencies and local cotton and tobacco warehouses served a pivotal function in the lives of farmers. One farmer noted, "The farmers are getting poorer but very few are able to build the traders have all combined trusts + monopolies and all against the farmers' interests. An Alliance of farmers are formed here are more than 3,000,000 in the United States. I hope they have the power for good, time alone will tell."[12]

From its inception the Alliance engaged in non-partisan politics—it was simply too large and too important to ignore. As early as 1888, the *Progressive Farmer* called for farmers to stand for Congress and the state legislature, and Alexander stood for governor at the Democratic state convention in 1888.[13] Although the Alliance was not a political party, its leaders had aspirations for office and its rank-and-file members were politically conscious. In 1888, the Alliance was staunchly Democrat. The Alliance had realized that in order to get anything done that would relieve the economic problems facing the farmers, there must be a sympathetic state legislature. It did seem that the 1889 assembly was sympathetic to the needs of farmers, by targeting the powerful railroads, which were a symbol of the injustice in society. The railroads were exempt from taxation and practiced discriminatory tactics on freight rates, to the detriment of farmers. The state Alliance's primary goal was therefore to set up a regulatory commission with real authority. The new governor of North Carolina and the Democratic Party pledged themselves to a railroad commission in 1888. However, the inexperienced legislators found themselves outmaneuvered, and the railroad commission bill did not pass into law. This infuriated the Alliance, whose farmers badly needed a cut in railroad freight rates. One of the main reasons for the Alliance's failure in 1889 was the lack of political education. Syd Alexander, in particular, saw the vital role of education in teaching the farmers how to vote intelligently and not be swayed by false promises. The debacle over the Railroad Commission Bill in the legislature did, however, galvanize Alliancemen into more organization and a determination to pass such legislation in 1891.[14]

In North Carolina, Democrats held political power. However, Republicans were strong—which was unusual for the South at this time. Indeed, throughout the 1870s and 1880s, Democrats faced either strong opposition or internal divisions that threatened their hold on government. Using their hegemonic power, Democrats used the call to white supremacy in order to cement their power over the subordinate groups in society. In addition, the Democratic elites used the County Government Act and Election Law of 1877 to further their hold on power. Democrats had succeeded in holding onto power because they controlled the election system in North Carolina. The Democratic-controlled legislature appointed Democratic justices of the peace and county commissioners who organized the elections and counted the votes. It is not surprising that the election results produced victories for the Democratic parties up to 1894. These activities at the state level served as a tool to keep those below from mounting any serious challenge to the status quo. But an internal split might cost Democrats dearly. Thus, they did not want to jeopardize their position; and, therefore, they employed tax abatements to attract industry to North Carolina. Only in one area did Democrats make concessions to the farmers. In 1877, the state legislature established a Department of Agriculture and appointed Polk the commissioner, clearly a move to appease the farmers. The Bourbon Democrats had the support of a powerful press. These papers played the pivotal function of forming public opinion on events and political situations in North Carolina. Perhaps the most important of these papers was the *Raleigh News and Observer*, edited by Samuel A'Court Ashe. Other leading papers included the *Wilmington Messenger, Statesville Landmarker,* and *Charlotte Observer.* These papers all attempted to discredit the leadership of the North Carolina Farmers' Alliance.[15]

The Alliancemen were mostly Democrats. All the leaders, Polk, Alexander, Carr, and Eugene Beddingfield, supported Democrats. Nevertheless, by 1890, with a membership approaching one hundred thousand, the Alliance hoped to dominate the political agenda, reform the state Democratic Party from within, and force a renegotiation of state policy, so that the Democratic Party once again supported the lot of the farmer, and not the planter, industrialist, and capitalist. This was a pragmatic strategy in 1890. There was little sentiment for breaking with the Democrats at this time. In an age of intense party loyalty, voting Democrat was a way of life for the Alliance membership. To bolt from the party could lead to the end of lifelong friendships, the disintegration of the family, and social ostracism. In addition, many white Alliancemen feared that if they broke with Democrats the state Republicans might benefit and open the way to black Republican office-holding in the Black Belt of eastern North Carolina. However, it was one thing to stay with the Democrats; it was another to do so passively. Bourbon leader and U.S. senator Matt Ransom received several warnings that the Alliance meant business in the politics of North Carolina.[16]

The subtreasury plan became the issue that galvanized the Alliancemen in the West and South and also in North Carolina. The plan proposed building federal warehouses for nonperishable agricultural goods, where farmers could store crops and receive a cash loan of up to 80 percent of the market value, repayable at 1 percent interest rate when the farmer sold his crop. As a result, the farmer would free himself from the situation of cashless debt peonage and sell his crop at a time when the supply was lower and the prices higher. Small cotton farmers particularly favored the plan because it prevented a glut on the market and the price of cotton would increase to a level that enabled farmers to break even or to improve profit margins. With the subtreasury plan Alliancemen realized that real economic change must come at the national level. The St. Louis conference of December 1889 endorsed the subtreasury plan, and the Ocala convention of 1890 reiterated its adherence to the St. Louis conference and to the subtreasury plan.[17]

Polk embraced the subtreasury plan completely. However, in North Carolina it seemed that the plan would badly disrupt Democrats. Senator Zebulon Vance found himself at the center of the controversy over the bill. Vance, under pressure from Polk, had introduced the bill to the U.S. Senate in February 1890, but he did not push it enthusiastically. Polk and the *Progressive Farmer* attacked Vance, calling him an enemy of the people. The senator wanted to fudge the issue, and in an open letter to the state president of the Alliance, Vance argued that he opposed the subtreasury bill as written, but he was in favor of the principles and its purpose to help the farming communities. Vance chose to blame the problems farmers faced on the high tariff and contracted currency policies of the Republican Party. The attempt at a fudge failed, and his letter produced a storm of controversy in North Carolina.[18]

The Vance affair splintered the Alliance leadership in the Old North State. James Ramsey, editor of the *Progressive Farmer*, accused Vance of bad faith, charging that Vance's opposition to the subtreasury plan made him seem an enemy of the people at a time of economic hardship. Ramsey's attack received a mixed response. Elias Carr criticized the *Progressive Farmer* for attacking Vance, while Beddingfield felt Vance deserved the criticism. There was also division among the rank and file. However, the majority supported both the subtreasury plan and Vance. As governor of North Carolina during the Civil War, Vance's popularity was second to none in North Carolina. With this in mind, some Democrats hoped that Polk might find himself isolated from other Democrats by his open denunciations of Vance. The historical sources make it difficult to estimate how many of the rank-and-file Alliancemen supported criticism of

Vance, but there are estimates that about two-thirds of Alliancemen favored the subtreasury plan. Whatever the numbers, it is clear that the North Carolina Alliance muddied the political waters in North Carolina and created problems for the Bourbon Democrats as they tried to continue their unrelenting monopoly of political power in the Old North State.[19]

To make the situation more complex for the Democratic leadership, 1890 was also an election year, and the subtreasury controversy threatened to overwhelm the election campaign and even prevent the reselection of Zebulon Vance as U.S. senator in the 1891 session of the North Carolina state legislature—something that was unthinkable just a year before. Democratic leaders such as Edward Chambers Smith, the new state Democratic executive committee chairman, and Spier Whitaker, the outgoing chairman, advocated appeasement of the Alliance. In private, E. Chambers Smith warned Senator Matt Ransom, "At any moment a conflict may spring up between the Alliance and non-Alliance Democrats, which may result in the defeat of all the Congressional candidates. We must be harmonious and thoroughly organized." The Democrats were responding to the fluctuating political strength of the subordinate classes that were in the ascendancy, hoping to entice the Alliance leadership by offering them high positions in the party.[20]

The Republican Party of North Carolina approached the 1890 elections with renewed vigor. Prior to 1888, Republicans lacked a combination of issues to defeat the Democrats, although they had come close to defeating Democrats on several occasions since Reconstruction—this parity in numbers often meant Democrats papered over division in their own ranks. In addition, Democrats held Republicans accountable for the so-called evils of Reconstruction, labeling the GOP the party of African American social equality and pointing out at every opportunity that 80 percent of the GOP was black. But the discontent within the ranks of the Democratic Party from 1888 onwards seemed to offer Republicans a chance to gain political power in North Carolina. Debates over strategy and policy led to even more factionalism within the GOP. The Republican Party's electoral support split into two distinct and geographically opposite areas of the state. Sixteen counties in eastern North Carolina, where blacks made up the majority of the population, gave Republicans a great deal of political strength, although Democrats tended to remain in control through the use of fraud and bribery and the use of the 1877 election law. The other concentration of Republican strength existed in the western counties. Here, in nearly an all-white region, former Unionists remained allied to the Republican Party. In addition, the GOP garnered strong support in the Piedmont counties, though here the party garnered votes from both blacks and whites.[21]

In 1890, Republicans seemed to be in a good position in North Carolina, despite factional differences within the leadership and African American ambivalence toward the GOP's white leadership. In 1888, the GOP performed well at the polls, and many of the Republican leaders, such as Daniel L. Russell, J. B. Eaves, Jeter C. Pritchard, Thomas Settle, and Dr. J. J. Mott, took heart from the election of Republican president Benjamin Harrison. In addition, the subtreasury debate offered Republicans a chance to capitalize in the upcoming election. However, the introduction of a bill in the U.S. Congress by Henry Cabot Lodge to regulate federal elections dashed these hopes. The details of the bill are complex, but the most controversial clause in the bill provided for military protection at the polls, if necessary, for the federal election supervisors. Opponents of the bill termed the Lodge Election Bill the "Force Bill." Although this bill was designed to afford much needed protection to African American voters, in North Carolina news of the bill posed serious problems for North Carolina's Republicans. Most Republican leaders, such as Dr. J. J. Mott of Statesville, and the *Union Republican* of Winston initially supported it. Mott wrote President Harrison, "I say, use the army rather than let the Elections go on as they have been." African American Republicans in North Carolina seemed cautious in their support of the Lodge Election Bill. Henry Cheatham, the black U.S. congressman from the Second District, refused to comment publicly about the measure.[22]

Other Republicans opposed the Lodge Bill because they knew Democrats would use it in the 1890 election to portray the GOP as favoring a return to the policies of Reconstruction. One such opponent was the Republican congressman from the Ninth District, Hamilton G. Ewart, a member of the Farmers' Alliance, who hoped to build a lily-white Republican Party in the South. In a speech to Congress, Ewart articulated his position clearly. He denied that election frauds occurred in North Carolina, and he did not think that African Americans voted solidly for the GOP. Ewart insisted that the Tar Heel GOP had grown in strength not because it catered to the interests of African Americans but rather because it appealed "to the sober judgment of the white voters of the South on the great issues of protection to the home industries and home labor." Ewart believed that the Farmers' Alliance had divided Democrats and that Republicans must take advantage of this split. The Lodge Bill, Ewart feared, would stymie any chance Republicans had at electoral growth in the South.[23]

Democrats in North Carolina certainly used the Force Bill to good effect in the summer and autumn of 1890. The Democratic state convention condemned the bill, and the Democratic press jumped at the chance to attack the GOP. For Democrats, the Force Bill was a threat to white supremacy; and the press, in particular, incited white men's passions on the issue to keep the Democratic Party intact. For example, Democratic campaigner (and future governor) Robert Glenn attacked the bill, urging that "every white man and every man with straight hair ought to rebuke the party that champions this bill." As the political heat rose over the Lodge Election Bill, some white Republican leaders deserted. Thomas Settle Jr., a prominent Republican in the Fifth Congressional District, opposed the bill. What is clear about the Lodge Election Bill is that it caused a massive split in the Republican leadership at the moment when the GOP seemed poised to take advantage of the divisions in the Democratic Party. However, despite the splits in the GOP, the election campaign was not plain sailing for the Democratic Party. It faced divisions in its own ranks and an Alliance determined to control the political agenda of the campaign despite the presence of the Lodge Election Bill.[24]

Leonidas Lafayette Polk hoped the Alliance would control the North Carolina legislature after the November elections. In addition, the Alliance saw the congressional elections as vital to the success of their national program, in particular, to the subtreasury plan. In each congressional district the Alliance endeavored to nominate Democratic congressional candidates who would actively work for Alliance-sponsored legislation in the U.S. Congress. This caused no end of turmoil in the Democratic ranks in late summer. For example, in the Third Congressional District, several candidates, including local Alliance leaders Cyrus Thompson, Marion Butler, Charles B. Aycock, and Benjamin Grady, entered the ballot for the nomination for U.S. congressman. On the 179th ballot, Benjamin Grady finally secured the nomination. In the Sixth Congressional District a bitter convention saw the fight for the nomination between Democratic incumbent Alfred B. Rowland and prominent Alliance leader Syd Alexander. Eventually, after much infighting and heated argument, Alexander secured the nomination, much to the chagrin of the Bourbon Democrats. As a result, though the Alliance remained in the Democratic Party, it secured the nomination of Alliancemen in the First, Second, Third, Fifth, and Sixth Congressional Districts.[25]

The elections of 1890 produced an Alliance-controlled North Carolina General Assembly for the 1891 session. Of the 170 members of the state legislature about 110 were Alliancemen. Democrats worried over the predominance of Alliancemen members in the state legislature. The assembly included many prominent Alliancemen, such as Marion Butler, John Atwater, Ambrose Hileman, and A. C. Green. Many of these Alliancemen were destined to play key roles in the Populist Party throughout the remainder of the decade. In addition, the notable Greenville lawyer and farmer advocate Harry Skinner also gained election to the 1891 state legislature. Although barred from the Alliance on the grounds of being a lawyer, Skinner would play a pivotal role in the 1891 legislature and later in the Populist Party. The Alliance seemed in control of the legislature. It also seemed that a non-partisan legislature might accomplish significant reforms for the farmers of the Old North State. However, any notions of bipartisanship between Democrats and Republicans ended when Marion Butler excluded all Republicans from the Alliance caucus. In Butler's view an Allianceman had to also support Democrats.[26]

The first task of the general assembly was choosing a U.S. senator. Zebulon Vance had lost some of his support because of his position on the subtreasury plan, and the Alliance was determined that he pledge himself to the Ocala platform before he was reselected. The Ocala platform of December 1890 had adopted a document that reiterated the 1889 St. Louis demands, but at Ocala there was a formal endorsement of the subtreasury plan. The St. Louis demands had included a call for the free coinage of silver, public ownership of transportation and communication, and traveling lecturers to educate the farmers. Most Democratic legislators, including Marion Butler, were in favor of Vance. Indeed, most Democratic legislators received instructions at the Democratic nominating conventions to vote for Vance. Therefore, the question was whether the Alliance could extract a pledge from Vance to support Ocala.[27]

Marion Butler led the Alliance caucus in the legislature. The first resolution the caucus wrote called for "our Senator and Representatives in Congress to vote for and use all honorable means to secure the financial reforms adopted by the Ocala convention of the Farmers' Alliance." Butler presented this resolution to the North Carolina state senate, but the measure was voted down. Alliancemen sympathetic to Vance also attempted to introduce a new watered-down and rather broad resolution motion that instructed Vance to "secure the objects of financial reform as contemplated in the Ocala meeting." The term "objects" was so broad that Vance supporters could easily do this. Not surprisingly, the resolution passed easily in both the senate and lower house, and Zeb Vance easily won another term as U.S. senator. Vance did not have to vote on the subtreasury bill, because in the 1890–1891 session of Congress it was tied up in committee.[28]

The 1891 North Carolina General Assembly did enact some Alliance demands into law. Marion Butler played a key role in the passage of a Railroad Commission Bill. Butler was determined that any bill must be strong enough to enact real public control of the railroads. The chicanery of the committee, Butler's role, and the heated debate in the legislature are complex. What is important to note is that Butler and Alliancemen resolved that they must achieve a notable policy success in the arena of railroad regulation. Finally the bill passed into law. Although the commission did not have complete regulatory power over the railroad companies, the effect of this bill was a reduction in freight and passenger rates. Although the railroad commissioners were reluctant at first to take on the railroad companies, the 1891 legislature's action in forming the Railroad Commission "was important just to have laid the groundwork for the protection of the farmer." The field of education also received attention from the progressive assembly. North Carolina had one of the lowest levels of expenditure on public education in all the states. Alliance legislators secured a marked increase in taxes for schools. In addition, the legislature appropriated ten thousand dollars to the College of Agriculture and Mechanic Arts and created a "Negro A.

and M. College" as well as an institution for the deaf and dumb.[29] Although in reality these successes were modest, this was perhaps the most prudent way for the Alliance to proceed in 1891. Indeed, some of the more radical measures introduced by the Alliance failed to pass into law despite the hard work of key Alliance figures and supporters. For example, a reduction of the legal rate of interest to 6 percent never got to the vote in the legislature, there was no regulation of state elections, and Harry Skinner's attempts to repeal the agricultural lien law died in the Judiciary Committee.[30]

One of the most important programs carried out by the Alliance in 1891 was in popular education and propaganda. Polk saw 1891 as the year for education, teaching farmers the message of the Alliance. Polk was also drifting toward third-party sentiment at the time and as a result drew criticism from more conservative Alliancemen such as Elias Carr. Other Alliancemen, however, believed that their order was superior to the Democratic Party. Although few Alliancemen approved of the Bourbon Democratic response to the Alliance and to the 1891 legislature, few wanted the Alliance to leave the Democratic Party and form a third party, believing instead that the Alliance should control the Democratic Party from within. Despite this internal debate, educational work continued. Alliance leaders in North Carolina, led by Polk, strengthened the educational work of the Alliance by reorganizing the lecture system. Lecturers received clearer instructions from the leadership on issues to elaborate on in the field, and a more coordinated system enabled the lecturers to reach more small towns and farming communities with the message of the Alliance. Polk believed quite rightly that the success of the lecture system would be crucial for the political success of the Alliance, and he also pressed for large mass meetings that would feature speakers from all over the country, in order to break down old sectional conflicts. Throughout the summer and fall of 1891 the Alliance sponsored picnics, camp meetings, and cook-outs to foster social interaction and the discussion of political and economic questions and issues between small farmers. This laid the groundwork for a grassroots political movement.[31]

The press also played a crucial role in the Alliance movement. Although there was no Alliance daily newspaper to combat the Democrat propaganda, an Alliance Press Bureau managed by Hal W. Ayer kept up with all the information of relevance to the Alliance in North Carolina. Pro-Alliance papers included the *Progressive Farmer*, the *Clinton Caucasian*, the *Carolina Watchman*, and the *Farmers' Advocate*. The goal of the education movement was to secure measures for the relief of farmers. By mid-1891 the subtreasury issue was overshadowed by the Western Alliance's call for a third party. At the National Union Conference in Cincinnati in May 1891 a struggle ensued between those who demanded a third party immediately and those who advised waiting until February 1892. Although Polk did not attend the convention, he advised, through an open letter, that more educational work was needed. Although delegates put off the question of a third party until February 1892, the People's Party did form, and it was clear to many Democrats that the new party would soon engage in political action.[32]

In North Carolina most of the Alliance leaders and the rank and file were not in favor of a third party. Elias Carr, Syd Alexander, and Marion Butler all opposed it. At the state Alliance annual session of 1891 at Morehead City, Polk did not call for a third party but rather for unity and immediate farm relief. However, Polk was clearly moving toward insurgency. At the 1891 Alliance session Marion Butler emerged as a new prominent leader in the Alliance when he became the president of the Alliance. As president, Butler played an active role in Polk's push for increased lecturing to the farmers of North Carolina. He crisscrossed the Old North State lecturing to sub-Alliances and also gave words of encouragement to Alliance newspaper editors. The Bourbon Democrats were becoming increasingly worried by the tone of Polk and the rank-and-file Alliancemen. As a result they agreed to offer a compromise to the more conservative leaders in the Alliance, such as Alexander and Carr. But they also continued to criticize Polk. Marion Butler saw through this Democratic tactic. "The trick is too plain and the people will not be fooled by it," stated the *Caucasian*. "They know these papers would not be attacking Polk and the others if they were not leaders of the Alliance." By the end of 1891, the fissures in the Alliance were beginning to open.[33]

One of the main reasons for the ambivalence of many Alliancemen toward third-party sentiment in the state was due, in part, to the delicate nature of politics. A state third party would divide the white Democratic vote and might enable Republicans and African Americans to achieve victory. Although some North Carolinian Alliancemen could support a national third-party ticket, few could support a state ticket. In addition, the Alliance achieved remarkable successes in the 1891 legislature to offset their failures in 1889 and 1890. Coupled with this, several U.S. congressmen were strong pro-active Alliancemen. It seemed as though the policy of enacting reform within democracy worked. Although some Democratic leaders worried over Polk's actions, other Democratic leaders, perhaps sensing the gravity of the situation, attempted to take a conciliatory approach toward the Alliance.

As the election of 1892 drew closer North Carolina Alliancemen and their southern and western counterparts' conversations on specific issues expanded. The organization, however, wanted some kind of order to the discussion and a clear set of policy priorities to enter the 1892 election campaign. The question Alliancemen grappled with was, Should the Alliance focus on a single issue for the 1892 campaign? The *Progressive Farmer* certainly did not think so. It argued that "to select one issue out of such a complications of infamous legislation as the country is suffering under at the present time is a very short-sighted and narrow, if not positively blind and fatuous policy." Thus, not surprisingly, policy priorities focused on a set of issues—the subtreasury, the abolition of national banks, and the free and unlimited coinage of silver—collectively termed "financial reform."[34]

By the end of 1891, Polk drifted closer toward supporting a third party, predicting that the third party would sweep the South in 1892. Thomas B. Long, the state lecturer of the Alliance until August 1891, gave an insight into the mindset of radical Alliancemen in North Carolina who favored the third party and, perhaps, Polk's leanings on the independent political question at this time. Long wrote to Polk, "I am prouder + prouder of you every day of my life—Do you know that I would have the imprudence to place your name before the National Convention. . . . The old political tricksters despise you worse than any man living, and I can point my finger at them, in a speech, and tell them that they are not fit to buckle your shoes. . . . [T]he people love to hear me do it." Long also informed Polk, "The *masses* of both old parties are with *you*. . . . The fight is on and we must carry the country in '92." At the November 1891 meeting of the Supreme Council of the National Farmers' Alliance and Industrial Union in Indianapolis, Polk gained re-election to the Alliance presidency, and he reaffirmed the Ocala demands. Interestingly, only radical North Carolina Alliancemen such as William Worth, S. Otho Wilson, and William R. Lindsey attended the meeting. Elias Carr and Syd Alexander were conspicuous by their absence. Marion Butler, the new president of the North Carolina Alliance attended, but he took a more moderate position than Polk and Wilson. Polk was concerned, however, that the Alliance constitution forbade partisan political action. By the end of 1891, the North Carolina Farmers' Alliance as well as the National Alliance had arrived at a crossroad. The North Carolina Farmers' Alliance also witnessed a change in leadership. Although Leonidas Lafayette Polk still led the movement, newer, younger leaders seemed to take a more pro-active and decisive role in the North Carolina Farmers' Alliance. These younger leaders were more aggressive and more energetic than Elias Carr and Syd Alexander. Marion Butler was one such leader, and although he remained loyal to the Democratic Party, he engaged in an energetic policy to control the Democratic leadership and state policy.[35]

The North Carolina Farmers' Alliance is important to the Populist Party of North Carolina because it gave the opportunity for many people to come to political leadership roles outside the confines of the Democratic Party. A large segment of the North Carolina Populist Party got its start in the Alliance. Marion Butler was perhaps the most famous. Born in Sampson County in 1863 to a farmer who ran the naval store business, Butler entered the University of North Carolina in 1881 and planned to enter the legal profession but had to leave behind his hopes to become a lawyer shortly after graduation in 1885, when his father died. He returned to Sampson County to support his family and run the farm. He also became the superintendent of a local school. It was here that he came into contact with the Farmers' Alliance and quickly became the president of the sub-Alliance. Shortly afterwards he purchased a small local newspaper, the *Clinton Caucasian*, which the county Alliance endorsed as its official organ. Butler jumped at every opportunity to engage in politics. He won election to the state senate from Sampson in 1890, at the age of twenty-seven, and in the 1891 state legislature he played a prominent role in the passage of the Railroad Commission Bill. Later in 1891 at the State Alliance Convention meeting, Butler became the new president of the North Carolina State Farmers' Alliance. By the end of that year, at the age of twenty-eight, he had toured North Carolina extensively and gained a reputation as a strong and forceful speaker.[36]

Other new and younger leaders included Cyrus Thompson, the Alliance state lecturer in 1891 and a noted orator in the eastern section of the state. Colonel Harry Skinner did not belong to the Alliance because he was a lawyer; but as a powerful Democrat in the northeastern portion of the state, he gave the younger generation of Alliance leaders much needed credibility. Butler, Thompson, and Skinner were destined to be the three most influential Populist leaders of North Carolina. Second-tier leaders of the Populist Party included James B. Lloyd, J. F. Click, and James W. Denmark, men who started as newspaper editors for Alliance journals in the state. In addition, William Worth and William A. Graham operated the State Business of the Alliance, and S. Otho Wilson played a key role in the Wake County Alliance.

The St. Louis convention of February 1892 would provide the defining moment in the creation of a third party. As 1892 began Alliance men waited in anticipation for the St. Louis convention. Alliance leader Polk sensed the mood of the reform movement in a letter to James Denmark: "Everything indicates that the great bulk of the delegates will be conservative but very determined. . . . I do not believe that any power on earth can prevent independent action. . . . If the Conference acts prudently and wisely there will be a revolution in this country as has never been witnessed." The St. Louis convention met on February 22, 1892, with a variety of reform groups attending. Agrarian organizations took up about two-thirds of the twelve hundred delegates, and the Southern Alliance had the largest representation at the convention. Polk, Marion Butler, and Eugene Beddingfield attended the conference. By this time Polk clearly favored independent political action, and although he did not openly endorse the People's Party, his speech to the convention seemed to reject the possibility of national reforms through the Democratic or Republican parties:

The time has arrived for the great West, the great South and the great Northwest, to link their hands and hearts together and march to the ballot box and take possession of the government, restore it to the principles of our fathers, and run it in the interest of the people. . . .

Sirs, we are not applying to Congress or elsewhere for sympathy or charity, but in the dignity and power of American manhood, we are demanding justice, and under the favor of God, we intend to have it. We want relief from these unjust oppressions, and as I have said from New York to California, in my speeches, we intend to have it if we have to wipe the two old parties from the face of the earth![37]

This speech received thunderous applause and Polk caught the imagination of the convention. The Ocala platform was changed to include the demand for the government ownership of the railroads. After the meeting adjourned, Charles Macune convened a political mass meeting, which called for a national nominating convention of the People's Party to meet at Omaha on July 4, 1892. The conference heaped symbolism upon symbolism. At the meeting in Omaha, 1,776 delegates would gather to enact the second Revolution. The question for North Carolina Alliancemen after the St. Louis convention was, What they should do? Should the state Alliance support a new party at the national level? Would it nominate an independent state and local ticket? In a state with a strong Republican Party and an earnest African American population that continued to play an active role in the politics of the state these were key concerns. It is not surprising, therefore, that these questions engulfed the Alliance leadership and the rank-and-file membership for several months following the St. Louis convention.[38]

North Carolina furnished ten delegates to the St. Louis convention. Butler was one of these delegates, but he did not play a significant role because he did not favor a third party at this time. He hoped that the Alliance would capture the Democratic Party in the Old North State and thus prevent the organization of a new party. Butler wanted to avoid jeopardizing white rule in the state. Indeed, all the North Carolina delegates, except Polk, opposed a third party. But all the North Carolina delegates supported the St. Louis platform. The *Tarboro Farmers' Advocate* summed up the attitude of the Tar Heel delegates: "[They are] impressed with the solemn conviction that the enactment (of the platform) into law, and the faithful enforcement of law, will bring industrial relief to our distressed people." The St. Louis convention marked a clear turning point in the history of the Alliance. Southern Alliance leaders such as Polk and Charles Macune seemed to approve of the Alliance's new direction. Politics, rather than self-help, became the catchword for the Alliance after February 1892. Events in spring and early summer played a crucial role in the formation of the North Carolina Populist Party, and, indeed, these events influenced the entire life span of the Populist Party of the Old North State.[39]

Chapter Two

"WE HAVE PUT OUR HANDS ON THE PLOW AND WE WILL NOT LOOK BACK"

The People's Party and the Election of 1892

The St. Louis convention deeply divided the North Carolina Alliance. One group of Alliancemen including Polk favored the formation of the third party. Another group including Alexander, Beddingfield, and Butler endorsed the St. Louis platform but declared loyalty to the Democratic Party. Another group led by Elias Carr opposed the St. Louis platform and the formation of the third party. These divisions within the Alliance did not bode well for the elections. Throughout the early part of 1892 these three groups jostled with one another for prominence in the Alliance. In many ways the debates over the St. Louis platform dogged the North Carolina Populist Party throughout the remainder of the decade. A radical group favored independent action, another favored moderate goals and possible cooperation, and a final group, though sympathetic to Populist policy, never left the Democrats.

The schism between Polk and Carr on the issue of an independent state third party was an ominous sign for the North Carolina Alliance. Each leader had a sizable following in North Carolina. However, despite the growing controversy between Polk and Carr, the endorsement of St. Louis demands by subordinate Alliances and county Alliances proceeded. In part, the continued Alliance endorsement of the St. Louis platform was due to the work of Marion Butler. Although Butler and Polk's relationship seemed strained at times, they both realized that they must work with one another to ensure the success of the Alliance. Butler supported the St. Louis platform but was not in favor of political independence at the state or national level. The Democratic press seemed relieved by Butler's moderation. Butler laid plans to remain within the Democratic Party at least at the state level and to control the Democratic Party from within. This approach seemed to worry Polk, who feared that he could not persuade Butler into independent political action if the circumstances warranted. Polk was a leading candidate to head the national ticket of the third party in the November elections. This, coupled with his tremendous popularity and influence in North Carolina, gave hope to those Tar Heels who favored a state third party. It also made Democrats extremely anxious for the national, state, and congressional elections later in the year. Leading Democrats realized that the Alliance had controlled the state legislature in 1891 and in many ways had dominated the political debate over the previous four years in North Carolina. One correspondent warned Senator Zebulon Vance, "The outlook for us seems to be gloomy. . . . The indications here are not favorable. Polk + his crowd have gone boldly into the 3rd party and this time undoubtedly a good many farmers are inclined to go with them."[1]

Marion Butler's state policy was to uphold the non-partisanship of the Alliance at all costs. Butler worried that a third party at the state level would cripple Democrats and only aid Republicans in their quest for political power. Butler also wanted the Alliance to *control* the Democratic Party. Butler worried over the tendency of rank-and-file Alliancemen in late 1891 to turn Alliance meetings into People's Party organizing meetings. This development also worried Polk, and the *Progressive Farmer* did not publish Populist resolutions in the name of Alliance units. Even though Polk was on the brink of arguing for a state Populist Party, he did not want the Alliance to face the wrath of Democrats on the question of political partisanship. However, even though those in Alliance leadership positions in North Carolina may have opposed such activities by the rank and file, they determined that the membership would not totally dominate the nomination of candidates for state and county offices if a state Populist Party did formally organize.[2]

Butler's plan to control the Democratic Party from within revolved around two interlocking strategies. First, the Alliance must nominate Alliance delegates at the district level to attend the Democratic state convention so that at the Democratic state convention the Alliance would direct the state platform. Second, Butler called a meeting of the Alliance caucus to meet in Raleigh the day before the Democratic state convention to formulate strategy and agree on state candidates. This was a bold strategy, indeed, and illustrates both Butler's own political ambitions and his belief that the Alliance might position itself to dictate political and economic policy. Butler's adherence to the St. Louis platform, however, put him in direct opposition to the Democratic leadership in the state.[3]

Events in late spring and summer, however, ruined Butler's ambitious plan to control the Democratic Party. The Alliance itself split on Butler's plan. One faction seemed sympathetic. For example, the *Raleigh Progressive Farmer* changed its mind on third party sentiment, calling for the Alliance to control the Democratic primaries, explaining, "We will get as much reform as through a new party, and not run the risk of losing all chances." Harry Skinner, an important advocate for farmers' rights, also agreed with Butler. At a speech to Clinton Alliancemen in March 1892, Skinner spoke as a Democrat on the subtreasury and other reforms and "favored the advocation of these principles within the pall of the Democratic party." The real issues, Skinner believed, would find their solution in the Democratic primaries.[4]

A second faction of the Alliance, however, opposed the move to dominate the Democrats and instead favored independent political action. In the early spring of 1892 many local People's Party clubs continued to appear throughout North Carolina. Third party political sentiment seemed on the increase at the local level, but there was as yet no formal state organization of the People's Party. Despite the lack of authoritative leadership at the state level, local rank-and-file Alliancemen, no doubt sensing the attitude of their beloved leader Polk, moved toward the new political party. Indeed, while the evidence is sketchy, it seems that the rank and file radicalized more quickly than the leadership. In Wayne County, for example, Abbott Swinson, secretary of the Wayne County Farmers' Alliance and editor of the local Alliance newspaper, the *Goldsboro Agricultural Bee*, criticized Butler's plans. Swinson argued in a letter to Polk that the actions of the Democratic Party executive committee showed there was no hope for the Alliance to control the Democrats. The solution, Swinson claimed, was to form a new political party. "The People's party is the labor party and should be kept so and now is the time to push it to the front," Swinson admonished. Swinson went even further and predicted that Butler's attempt at controlling Democrats was hopeless. He pledged himself to the reform movement and the People's Party and offered the *Agricultural Bee* as the Populist Party organ in eastern North Carolina. In a published call in the *Argus* he went further, "We will organize for this county a People's Party, promising in advance that no Butler be allowed to wine and dine us in perversion of our purpose and principles." Swinson continued, "Every person who favors the formation of a People's Party upon the St. Louis platform and willing to stand by principle, rather than policy and intrigue in obtaining, and repudiates the idea of capturing ANY OTHER PARTY MACHINE as a means to gain their ends, are invited to come."[5]

Another faction of the Alliance, more numerous than the People's Party faction, disagreed with both independent political action and Butler's plan to control the Democratic Party. Elias Carr led this faction, which feared a resurgent Republican Party and a high tariff as more evil than a Democratic Party. It seems that the old guard Alliance leadership opposed any moves to control the Democratic Party. Carr's position on Butler's plan is clear in a letter he wrote Polk, "I am not a candidate for any office and I was unfortunate in expressing myself to have left that impression in your mind." Carr finished his letter to Polk, "I am an Allianceman now and forever but not a Third party man by any means."[6]

Democrats, sensing the gravity of the situation, hoped to placate the Alliance and reinforce the Democratic ranks in time for the November elections. Thomas Jarvis, so often the voice of moderation, hoped that the Alliance and Democrats could put their differences aside for the good of the state. Democratic state chairman Edward Chambers Smith also tried to conciliate the Alliance by calling on all factions to work together in the upcoming elections. James H. Pou advised E. Chambers Smith that an early state convention would help Democrats in North Carolina. Pou argued that an early convention would prevent the formation of a People's Party because the lure of office would keep Alliancemen from bolting. But Pou admitted, "We are to have trouble in this campaign—no doubt of that—and our efforts now should be to prepare to meet and overcome it."[7]

Not all Democrats agreed with the efforts to placate the Alliance. Not surprisingly, conservative Democrats were the most vocal in their condemnation of Butler's strategy to control the state Democratic Party. Thomas Sutton, a member of the Democratic state executive committee, wrote Samuel A'Court Ashe that Democrats must reserve the right to ignore the Alliance in its strategy to control the Democratic state convention. In Sutton's mind the Alliance and the People's Party were one and the same. He warned, "If the Third party men should capture our State Convention, get aside our chosen leaders and incorporate the Sub-treasury rainbow and other political heresies on our platform, it will be certain to result in at least in 25,000 true + trusted Democrats to leave." The *Wilmington Messenger* vocalized hostility and in an editorial it noted, "The question is now no longer—will there be a third party? The simple question is—Will the Democratic party allow itself to be led as sheep to the shambles to be slaughter by the Polk-Butler butchers, and be cooked upon the St. Louis spits."[8]

Marion Butler, sensing the mood of the more radical element of the Alliance, the conservative Democratic response, and the need for Alliance control of the Democratic state convention by the Alliance, called a meeting of the Alliance at Raleigh for May 17, the day before the Democratic state convention was due to meet. It seems that Butler hoped to capture the Democratic convention and send delegates to Omaha in July. At first, it seems that Polk supported Butler in this endeavor. Later, however, Polk seemed more skeptical of Butler's plan.[9] At the Alliance caucus meeting Butler hoped to control the Democratic convention by agreeing on a gubernatorial candidate sympathetic to Alliance demands. Over eighty delegates attended the caucus. Butler presided over the meeting, which Polk also attended. Although the caucus proceedings remained secret, it does appear that the Alliance divided into the same factions that existed after the St. Louis convention. Although historians disagree over the exact procedures of the meeting, it does seem that Elias Carr received the endorsement of the Alliance for governor.[10]

As the Democratic state convention met on May 18, 1892, Alliancemen gathered with some excitement. The question was who would control the convention and dominate the ticket. In the end, however, the convention affected a compromise. On the governorship a four-way fight developed between Durham industrialist Julian S. Carr; George W. Sanderlin, the state auditor; Thomas Holt, the sitting governor of the state; and Elias Carr, past president of the state Alliance. Eventually, on the sixth ballot, Elias Carr emerged as the victor. Carr was a conservative Allianceman who rejected the St. Louis platform. Straight-out Democrats no doubt thought Carr was a good compromise candidate. The state platform also seemed conciliatory toward the Alliance. It demanded the free coinage of silver and the abolition of national banks, but it was less radical than the St. Louis platform on railroad ownership and the money question. And, importantly, the convention gave no instructions to the delegates to the Democratic national convention on whom to support for president.[11]

Throughout June and July of 1892, Butler's ambitious plan to control the Democratic Party from within imploded on itself. Rank-and-file Alliance men, sickened by the continued hostility of the Democratic press to the Alliance and the Democratic opposition to Alliance economic policy, grew increasingly restless. Throughout late 1891 and 1892, Populist clubs organized throughout North Carolina on an ad-hoc basis. Polk also seemed to lean increasingly toward the Populist Party and this encouraged rank-and-file Alliancemen to take the next step in political independence. The moderate policy of State President Butler was alien to them. As soon as the Democratic state convention finished on May 18, about 150 Alliancemen from seventy-five counties met at Raleigh. William R. Lindsey, president of the Rockingham County Alliance, chaired the meeting, and the convention selected delegates for the People's Party Omaha convention in July. This meeting, the *Progressive Farmer* reported, was a preliminary meeting "to arrange an electoral ticket for the State and for proper representation at the Omaha convention." The meeting also decided on chairmen for the People's Party's congressional committees. The news that Harry Skinner was a delegate to Omaha shocked the *News and Observer*. In an editorial the paper lamented, "Mr. Skinner is a brilliant man, a man of decided parts, and his friends within the Democratic Party might well expect for him a useful and conspicuous career as a Democratic leader. But if he shall prove to be so unstable as this development indicates, to say nothing else, the soundness of his judgment will be seriously questioned."[12]

Details on the local Populist leaders are scarce. However, it does appear that most of them gained their start in the Alliance. For example, William Lindsey, S. Otho Wilson, Alonzo Shuford, and William Worth had close ties with the Alliance. These men saw at firsthand the economic problems facing farmers in North Carolina and the continued intransigence of the national and state Democratic Party to the plight of farmers. Lindsey was somewhat older than the other Alliancemen. He was born in 1836 and attended Wake Forest College. Lindsey was a tobacco farmer of some note in Rockingham County and, indeed, had represented his county as a Democrat in the state lower house on four previous occasions. As an active political animal he perhaps discerned that the state Democrats would not carry out meaningful reform of the state's economy and therefore decided to throw his weight behind the new third party. William Worth, a Quaker from the Piedmont and an active member of the Alliance, also viewed the inactivity of Democrats with dismay. In 1892 he too moved toward the People's Party as the only way to alleviate the problems facing the farmers in the Old North State. Once these men and others like them began to organize the People's Party, more moderate Alliancemen like Marion Butler found it increasingly difficult to ignore the growing sentiment among the rank and file for a new political party. The grassroots seemed to push the state leadership toward political insurgency. Once local leaders built on this sentiment, the momentum toward a third party was unstoppable. Militant Alliance leader S. Otho Wilson answered, "No," when asked, "Cannot a man be an Allianceman and a real, old fashioned straight-out Democrat at the same time?" If Wilson spoke for many Alliancemen in the state, Democrats faced a huge problem.[13]

Events now moved at a rapid pace for the Populist Party in North Carolina. On May 23, an organizational meeting of a state Populist Party met in Charlotte. William R. Lindsey again chaired this meeting. The meeting set county organizing conventions for June 11 and congressional nominating conventions for June 16. Lindsey notified the Republican newspaper, the *Union Republican*, that the meeting nominated Polk for president. In addition, the meeting finally agreed upon the formal Populist Party organization. An executive committee of three or more members would organize in each county in the state. The committee had the power to appoint a subcommittee of five or more in each township. The chairman of each committee would constitute the executive committee of the congressional district. The appointed township, county, and district committees remained provisional. Thus, at the first authorized conventions, the people would elect new committees to constitute a permanent organization of the Populist Party. Lindsey again notified the public of the names of the chairmen of the congressional districts and the delegates to the Omaha convention. It is clear that despite the reluctance of the Alliance leadership to take a lead in the organization of the third party in the state, some members of the Alliance's rank and file took matters into their own hands. Eschewing directions from their state president, Marion Butler, these grassroots activists pushed for independent political action. Notwithstanding the possible social ostracism and derision from the Democratic press, these Alliancemen were determined to take matters into their own hands. Marion Butler seemed to lose control of his activists at a key moment. As if this was not bad enough for the state Alliance leader, the national leader of the Farmers' Alliance, L. L. Polk, also moved toward the third party.[14]

As late as the Democratic state convention, Polk supported a Democratic state ticket, even though he pushed for a third party at the national level. But after the state Democratic convention Polk's position altered markedly. On May 24, 1892, the *Progressive Farmer* seemed more of a Populist paper than an Alliance paper to many voters in North Carolina. As a result, the executive committee of the state Alliance disapproved of such sentiment in the official organ of the Alliance and issued a warning to Polk to change his ways. On May 31, 1892, instead of adhering to the Alliance's executive committee's demands, Polk resigned the *Progressive Farmer* as the state Alliance organ. In a handwritten editorial, Polk explained that the only hope for the farmers is with the "People's Party which is to hold its National Convention at the Omaha on the 4th next July. The only consistent, logical, and manly course for the Progressive Farmer is to go with them and stand by them, get relief through the ballot box, that we must vote for such men only as would honestly advocate our principles. We have tried this through both the old parties and have signally failed." Polk continued that the farmers must assert themselves and that independent action was the inevitable result of the education gained through the Alliance. Now freed from the shackles of the Alliance, Polk pursued a policy of total support for the Populist Party at the national and state level. During the spring of 1892, Polk's movement toward gaining the Populist nomination for president at the Omaha convention seemed on the road to success.[15]

One will never know the possible long-term ramifications of Polk's actions. On June 11, 1892, Polk died suddenly in Washington, D.C. A few days earlier in correspondence to Denmark, Polk had disclosed that he was ill. However, the nature of the sickness was a secret to all but a few close family members. The death of Polk came as a sudden devastating blow to the Alliance and the Populist Party in North Carolina and in the country at large because Polk was the leading candidate for the Populist presidential nomination in July.[16]

Local organization of the People's Party continued at a rapid pace throughout North Carolina despite Polk's death because at its core the Populist Party was a rank-and-file movement of disaffected small farmers. By the end of June, the Populist Party was organized in fifty-six counties in the eastern and Piedmont sections of the state. In addition, several congressional districts nominated Populist candidates in the summer of 1892. In mid-June 1892, People's Party conventions met in the Fourth District, the Fifth District, and the Seventh District. For example, at the Fourth Congressional District Convention, 105 delegates met to nominate delegates to the Omaha convention. S. Otho Wilson, the state Alliance lecturer, presided at the convention. The convention put off the nomination for a congressional candidate until July 12, 1892. According to the *Progressive Farmer*, "The meeting was harmonious throughout."[17]

Not surprisingly, perhaps, the *News and Observer* ridiculed the formation of the Populist Party at the state level. In a damning editorial, the paper wrote, "The agitation of the political waters by the Third Party had set free a good deal of light-weight rubbish that has heretofore been held down by its environments. Released from its confinement it has popped up to the surface with a spring, the movement reminding one of the sudden appearance of a jack-in-the-box."

But the paper also issued a warning to Butler, and although it regretted the breaks in the Democratic Party, it concluded, "We prefer to have open enemies rather than treacherous friends." Privately, however, Democrats remained deeply worried about the presence of a Populist Party ticket. For example, Charles B. Aycock warned Matt Ransom that North Carolina "is in danger and that early and vigorous efforts must be taken if we expect to carry it." Thus, despite their public veneer of derision toward Populists and belief in Democracy's strength, some notable Democrats in private seemed resigned to losing in November.[18]

In late June 1892, the Democratic national convention at Chicago nominated former president Grover Cleveland of New York as its standard bearer for the upcoming campaign, a decision that divided the Democratic Party in North Carolina. Zebulon Vance and E. Chambers Smith opposed Cleveland's nomination, while Matt Ransom and Samuel A'Court Ashe supported Cleveland's candidacy. What seems clear is that the nomination of Cleveland, an avowed anti-silverite and opponent of the St. Louis platform, gave renewed vigor to those Alliancemen who favored a third party in North Carolina.[19]

To the chagrin of Democrats, rank-and-file Populists continued to organize throughout North Carolina. In early July, North Carolina sent a delegation to the Omaha convention. The most prominent delegate at Omaha was Harry Skinner. In addition, Thomas B. Long, vice president of the state Alliance, and S. Otho Wilson, the state lecturer, also attended. James B. Weaver of Iowa received the nomination as the presidential candidate for the Populist Party, and James G. Field of Virginia received the vice presidential nomination. In addition, the Omaha convention adopted the St. Louis platform. In North Carolina questions remained for the newly formed Populist Party. Would the party run a state and county ticket? Finally, in mid-July, Chairman Lindsey called for county conventions to meet on August 6 and a state nominating convention to meet in Raleigh on August 16. Most of the militant leaders came from the eastern section of the state, the area of the state controlled by Senator Matt Ransom and the Democratic machines. These Alliancemen chafed at the hands of an undemocratic and unresponsive state government, and it is not surprising therefore that these men led the push toward a third party. Although the sources are sketchy, it does appear that the Populist organization coalesced around the actions of a small cadre of militant Alliance leaders and earnest grassroots activists in 1892.[20]

A potentially crucial player throughout the months of June and July was Marion Butler, but he played no active part in the organization of the Populist Party and, indeed, tried to derail it. In a July 14 editorial, Butler pleaded with his Alliance constituents, "Let our friends of the People's Party banish every idea of nominating a State ticket, but rally to the support of Elias Carr and elect him by 40,000 majority." In another editorial piece on the same day, Butler gave his reasons for opposing a state ticket. He warned that the Populist Party could not win in North

Carolina, but would only succeed in defeating Allianceman Elias Carr and letting in the Republican Party. Butler vainly clung to the notion that his policy of controlling the Democratic Party from within would work in the November elections. Butler went even further in his editorial, arguing that the *Caucasian* does "not believe in machine politics, and whenever a man is nominated who does not represent Democratic principles and who is at heart against the interest of the masses, we think that every voter should have the manhood to condemn him."[21]

Events in North Carolina threatened to leave Butler behind in the political backwaters of Sampson County. Despite all Butler's hard work, his plan had utterly failed, with perhaps the exception of Elias Carr's nomination as the Democratic gubernatorial candidate. Even Carr's nomination was a muted victory because Carr vehemently opposed the St. Louis platform and represented the more conservative wing of the Alliance. In addition, rank-and-file Populists, even those in Butler's home county, did not listen to the warnings of the North Carolina Alliance leader on a third party ticket. As early as July 7, citizens of Sampson County organized a Populist Party. On July 21, M. M. Killett, the new chairman of Sampson County's Populist Party, called a county convention for August 6. Butler retorted to this news, "We regret to see this, for in our opinion it is a mistake. . . . [I]t will divide our people and we fear put the next Legislature in the hands of the enemies of the people. We trust that the delegates to the State Convention will be instructed not to put up a State ticket. There is nothing to be gained from defeating the present State ticket."[22]

The presence of a growing third party in the Old North State, the nomination of goldbug Grover Cleveland by the Democratic national convention, and disagreement among the Alliance leadership on electoral policy created turmoil in the North Carolina Farmers' Alliance. This turmoil reached its height at the Third Congressional District Democratic convention at Fayetteville on July 20, 1892, to nominate a congressional candidate and a presidential elector. Butler and the new Democratic state executive committee chairman, Furnifold Simmons from Craven County, attended. Benjamin Grady, the incumbent congressman, received the congressional nomination. The battle for the presidential elector, however, produced heated debate. Butler could not support Cleveland and the Chicago platform. Eventually, Cyrus Thompson withdrew from the Democratic convention with all the anti-Cleveland men. Those that remained nominated John G. Shaw, who disclosed to Senator Ransom the gravity of the situation in the Third Congressional District. Shaw warned, "Third District is in a bad condition, a great many men favor the election of Weaver and if there is not a great deal of work done the district will be lost."[23]

Those delegates who left the convention chose to set up their own meeting, with Cyrus Thompson as chairman and John Fowler of Sampson County as secretary. Although this meeting supported Benjamin Grady for Congress, it nominated Cyrus Thompson as the Weaver presidential elector and repudiated Cleveland. This breakaway group included Butler, who now moved toward a Populist national ticket. Butler argued that, although he was opposed to Cleveland, he would support Elias Carr for governor. Democratic chairman Simmons, sensing that the Populist Party at the state level was a foregone conclusion, directed the upcoming local conventions to ban opponents of Cleveland from nomination. With this order the Democratic Party of North Carolina committed itself to Cleveland and adopted a policy of zero toleration toward any opposition to Cleveland. Simmons argued that it was vital to turn the tide, and his statement on Cleveland, perhaps, was a way of preventing further hemorrhaging of the Democratic Party by stifling debate. This judgment was a mistake because it forced some more moderate Alliancemen to leave the party.[24]

Rank-and-file Populists refused to follow Butler's ideas and advice throughout June and July. William R. Lindsey was extremely vocal in his condemnation of the Democratic Party. He supported an independent state ticket and went on the offensive in a series of printed articles in local newspapers. One article is worth quoting in detail because it illustrates the sentiments of the Populist rank and file during the initial formation of the party:

> If the people believed Democracy could trust that they could speak through the party to the throne of power not a single Allianceman would desert its banner. What do we see? Not a single Alliance measure has been gained in the Democratic conventions or legislatures except under the smoke of political opposition. They longed for freedom of olden time and they are going to have it. They are not going to be chained to the rock on the side of the sea to be plucked by the vultures at will. There is a mutiny in camp. There is a revolt among the soldiers. There is a pent up wrath in the breast of manhood. The people have taken up their march in the middle of the road, pressing down and trampling under foot all opposition. On the banner is inscribed "death to plutocracy" "Equal rights to all men." . . . [T]he people are going to put the spirit of the self-government to the test. If they cannot pull down disobedient parties, establish one of their own, open the road to moral progress and Christian civilization, they will confess their weakness and bow to the inevitable.[25]

Lindsey saw this fight as a noble battle between the forces of good and evil, and in a veiled threat to Butler and his policy, Lindsey argued that it was better to fight than to acquiesce meekly.

By the end of July, Butler's plans were in ruins. In addition, Butler found himself out on a limb, with no political home. The Populist Party county convention met on August 6 at 11.00 a.m. at the Sampson County courthouse in Clinton. According to Josephus Daniels, on the night before the convention

Butler told him that the farmers were about to "make damn fools of themselves." What caused Butler to change his mind is unclear. According to Daniels, on the morning on the 6th, a delegation of Populists stopped by Butler's newspaper office in Clinton to inform him that the Populist convention would formally organize that afternoon. Butler tried to change their minds, but he failed. According to a friend of Daniels, a spokesman for the group turned to Butler and said, "Marion, the Convention will meet at twelve o'clock in the courthouse upon the ringing of the bell. We invite you to come over and preside over the meeting and lead the movement. If you come there is a great future for you. If you stay out, we are going ahead anyhow and your enemies in Clinton and the towns will destroy you." There is no way of ascertaining the accuracy of this story, but what is clear is that at midday Butler was at the Clinton courthouse and assumed the leadership of the Sampson Populists. The convention nominated Butler for state senator from the Fourteenth District and John E. Fowler and C. H. Johnson to the lower house, and chose delegates for the People Party's state convention on August 16 and the Third Congressional District convention at Fayetteville on August 23. For Butler, the dye was cast.[26]

At the meeting of the Populist convention Butler became the leader of the Sampson Populists. He addressed the convention, and the *Caucasian* printed Butler's address. His address is interesting because it illustrates Butler's departure from his old plan to control the Democratic Party to now aligning himself entirely with the Populist Party. Butler thanked the convention for its respect, confidence, and esteem toward him. He argued that he appreciated this even more because he had advised a different route for reform. In Butler's mind the Populist Party was truly a people's movement because the state leadership of the Alliance had advised a different course. Butler stated that "it was now the duty of every reformer to go with the majority into the People's Party, which was now the only party of and for the people." The exodus of thousands of reformers from the Democratic Party, Butler believed, "sounded the death knell of the Democratic Party and made victory for the People's party a certainty."[27]

Throughout early August the newspapers were full of details on the flurry of Populist Party activism in preparation for the state convention of August 16. The first major political convert to Populism during August was not Butler, but noted Greenville lawyer and farmer advocate Harry Skinner. The *Elizabeth City North Carolinian* reported, "Col. Harry Skinner has left the old rotten Bourbon bulk and taken passage on the new craft 'People's Party.' When the 'silver tongued orator' enters the campaign he may feel disposed to reveal somethings those now abusing him would rather not have exposed." The *Wilmington Messenger* derided Skinner's actions, "We regret to see him perpetuate on himself the dangerous feat of hara-kiri. If he remains in enforced retirement all his life it will be his own fault and misfortune. He is of unsound judgment, however intellectual he may be."

Other newspapers noted more political converts to Populism. The Republican newspaper, the *Raleigh Signal*, noted that William F. Strowd of Chatham and James Mewboorne of Lenoir, "leading and influential Democrats have declared for the People's party." The *News and Observer* reported that at the Wake County Populist convention two hundred delegates gathered. Prominent Alliancemen at the convention included S. Otho Wilson and J. W. Denmark. The Wake County Populists agreed on a full county and state ticket. A. C. Greene gave a short speech to the convention, underlying the formation of the People's Party as a response to Democratic hegemony. Greene, according to the *News and Observer*, argued that "he has been sorry to leave the Democratic Party, but he had found that he had to keep step with the People's Party band. The Democratic Party had ignored every principle that his father had fought for and had taught him, and he could not go with it anymore." The leaders followed the rank and file, and throughout early August scores of Democrats left for the Populist Party, or People's Party. The question was how many, and how would it impact the election in November.[28]

Attention now turned to the Populist state convention on Tuesday, August 16, 1892. There were 357 delegates from seventy-one counties in attendance. The Metropolitan Hall and its galleries overflowed with Populist delegates and inquisitive onlookers. At 12:30 p.m., William R. Lindsey, chairman of the third party state committee, called the meeting to order. Butler and Skinner emerged as the People's Party's leading spokesmen at the convention, which chose Butler as the chairman of the convention, chairman of the platform committee, and presidential elector at large. Butler addressed the convention and received rapturous applause when he stated that their ancestors had fought for reform: "But this was a greater battle with the ballot and not with the bullet." The convention named committees of permanent organization and platform and then adjourned to 3:00 p.m. in order to allow the platform committee to write the planks of the Populist state platform.[29]

At 3:30 p.m. the convention reconvened. The platform committee gave the various planks of the Populist Party in North Carolina. The platform received loud applause, especially the planks demanding a 6 percent interest rate, taxation of the railroads, and the endorsement of the Omaha platform. The convention adopted the platform unanimously. Following this came the nomination for state offices. W. P. Exum of Wayne County nominated Harry Skinner for governor. A succession of delegates gave glowing speeches in favor of Skinner. Democratic papers noted that an African American delegate from Vance County said, "We had a Weaver, a Field; and as we did not want to go bare footed we wanted Skin, and he therefore seconded the nomination of Skinner. The convention shouted wildly at his far-fetched joke" and proceeded to nominate Skinner by acclamation. Everything was going well for Populists until Harry Skinner got up and made a speech following his nomination. According to the *Wilmington Messenger*, the nomination surprised Skinner, and he stated that he merely wanted to fight for principle and did not seek political office. He stated that he had hoped to remain in the Democratic Party but the nomination of Cleveland made this impossible. Skinner then dropped a bombshell on the convention. Worried about a strong Republican Party and the presence of many African American voters in North Carolina, he told the convention that if Republicans nominated a state ticket and as a result hoped to divide the white people of the state, that the convention must be allow him to make his stand for the white people of North Carolina. Therefore, Skinner argued, he must have the liberty to drop out of the race if Republicans threatened the rule of the "white man" in North Carolina. If the convention would not give him this option, Skinner stated he would not accept the nomination. Clearly, Skinner worried that the presence of the Populist Party at the state level would only succeed in dividing the Democratic vote and, therefore, the white vote and let in the Republican Party, or, in Skinner's mind, African Americans. Consternation gripped the delegates.[30]

The delegates demanded to know what Skinner meant by his speech. Butler was furious. According to the *Wilmington Messenger*, "Delegates rose in wrath, and some of them spoke of themselves as clodhoppers and hayseeds, but swore they did not want to sell out. They shouted they wanted a farmer put up. They wanted no uncertain sound. They wanted a People's man." Skinner, responding to delegates' questions, explained that he thought questions of home government for whites were above questions of financial reform. He went further, stating that in a straight race between Republicans and Democrats for governor, he would vote for the Democrat. Shouts from the floor demanded Skinner's name be withdrawn. Dr. Exum moved that the earlier vote that declared Skinner nominated must be reconsidered. Twenty-five men seconded this. Skinner now addressed the convention for the third and final time:

It seems that I create trouble every time I speak. I know it is not my purpose to create trouble.

I had the courage of my convictions and stand for financial reform. I have the courage now to stand and say what may be a possible danger will enter our State matters. I expect to support Weaver and Field; to advocate financial reform; to never swerve in my energy to accomplish the revolution that must come. I will support your ticket as long as it is in the field, but I am not going to allow my name any longer to be an encumbrance or embarrassment to you. I will support the ticket you nominate here.[31]

With this statement Skinner withdrew his name from the gubernatorial nomination. At this point the convention descended into turmoil. Eventually, the convention adjourned until 8:00 p.m. in order to catch its breath and reorganize itself out of the chaos of the afternoon session. This episode suggests just how spontaneous the Populist Party was in North Carolina and also how the race issue would plague the party for its entire political life.[32]

At 8:15 p.m., the convention again reconvened. In an attempt to prevent a repeat of the embarrassing spectacle earlier that day, each candidate for state office was ordered to articulate his position with regard to a state ticket before nominations commenced. For elector at large Butler and Harry Skinner received nominations by acclamation. Thus, despite Skinner's afternoon pronouncements on the gubernatorial question, the convention still recognized his potential benefit to the Populist Party in the upcoming election campaign. Electors at large potentially played a pivotal role in the state. As the state electors at large, Butler and Skinner could address a large number of potential voters. Both men had reputations as excellent speakers and debaters. The convention then turned back to the tricky matter of the nomination for governor. E. N. Hardy of Wayne County placed Wyatt P. Exum of Wayne County and James M. Mewboorne of Lenoir County for nomination. Dr. Exum in his speech said he stood for the people and with the people and was for the Omaha platform and would stay in the race until Election Day. The first ballot produced 263 votes for Exum and 220 votes for Mewboorne, but the delegates quickly made Exum's nomination unanimous. A wealthy farmer from Wayne County in the eastern section of the state, Exum was an unknown political figure.[33]

By the end of the day the Populist Party had a state platform and a full state ticket. But the battle of the governorship foreshadowed the problems the Populist Party would face throughout the 1890s. Many Alliancemen and Populists continually worried that a state Populist Party would merely succeed in dividing the Democratic vote and opening the way for the Republican Party. For most Populists, Republicans were the party of Reconstruction and African American office-holding. The majority of Populists opposed both African American office-holding and a resurgent GOP—it was also a goldbug party. Republicans remained in a powerful political position in the state from the end of Reconstruction, and Harry Skinner clearly grappled with these problems in his speech to the convention. However, in 1892 the Populist Party had radicalized to such an extent that the rank-and-file members of the party could pull down a noted lawyer, in this case Harry Skinner, and place a little-known farmer at the head of a state ticket. For the rank-and-file members the Populist Party must fight for principle and not just for the spoils of office. In 1892, at least, rank-and-file Populists naively believed that they could dominate the convention and nominate a candidate who would sweep the state. However, the ensuing months of campaigning quickly shattered the Populists' dreams and Wyatt P. Exum would prove a terrible nominee.[34]

The Alliance and Populist newspapers greeted the news of the state convention with delight. According to the *Caucasian*, the convention was full of intelligent men, and they "represented the great rank and file of the people, they were a part of the people. There has never been a convention in the State that had the interest of the State more at heart. It was a convention of the people and the most democratic convention we have ever seen." The paper did not mention the debacle over the governorship. The *Salisbury Carolina Watchman* reported, "Those who know them say the ticket nominated by the People's Party are gentlemen of ability and character. The ticket ought to be satisfactory to all parties, for it is made up of all. We believe five of them have been democrats, four republicans, and two prohibitionists."[35]

Following the state convention, Marion Butler assumed control of the state organization. As the state Alliance president, Butler was one of the few Populists who possessed the organizational skill and experience to mount a statewide election campaign. The Populist campaign of 1892 consisted primarily of passionate stump speeches and the editorial reporting of a small but committed Populist press. Although many Populists were inexperienced in organizing a political campaign, the leadership of the new party had played an active role in either the Alliance organization or the Democratic Party, and even, in a few instances, the Republican Party. Therefore, individuals such as Butler, Harry Skinner, William H. Worth, S. Otho Wilson, Cyrus Thompson, Thomas B. Long, and William R. Lindsey knew the various tactics to garner votes, and perhaps equally as important, the tactics Democrats would use to prevent a mass exodus of from their party to the Populists. Butler, in particular, played a pivotal role in organizing the campaign; and, as one of the presidential electors at large, he could travel across the entire state endeavoring to persuade Alliancemen to join the new party.[36]

While it is true, however, that the party possessed experienced leaders, there is no denying that Populists faced overwhelming odds as they entered the political campaign. First, the Populist's natural leader, Leonidas Lafayette Polk, was dead. Despite the organizational skills of Butler, no one could replace the charismatic, hardworking, and ideologically sound Polk. His death, so close to the election campaign, robbed Populists of any real chance to carry the state. Second, Populists lacked the considerable funds necessary for electioneering that the two major parties could draw on at will. Third, Democrats possessed all the benefits of an entrenched party. The Democratic Party had skillfully distributed patronage to enough key figures to prevent a mass exodus of diehard Democrats to the Populists and kept local Democratic leaders on board, and Democrats were skillful campaigners themselves—they knew the various "means" to get voters to the polls. The Payne election law also reinforced Democratic hegemony. Unelected Democratic registrars and justices of the peace could throw out votes on the slightest technicality. Republicans had complained about these practices for years, and Populists knew full well that Democrats would engage in such activities in 1892. Fourth, Populists in mid-August had no idea what the North Carolina Republicans would do in the state election. If Republicans entered the state campaign, it could decimate the Populists and prevent wavering Democrats from leaving their party. Fifth, many of the Populist's state candidates proved an embarrassment to the party, and the Democratic press seized on any half-truth or outrageous story to discredit Populists. The Populist gubernatorial candidate, Wyatt P. Exum, would prove especially vulnerable and would receive the most attention from the Democratic press. Sixth, the People's Party nominated an ex-northern Union general, James B. Weaver, for president. This was a hindrance for Populists in North Carolina because Democrats never eased up on the allegations that Weaver was a war criminal.

If all this did not make the odds high enough, Populists had no daily newspaper to counteract the Democratic daily press and its high circulation figures throughout the state. Even so the *Progressive Farmer*, the *Caucasian*, the *Goldsboro Agricultural Bee*, the *Henderson Vance Farmer*, the *Marshville Our Home*, the Moncure *Alliance Echo*, the *Pinnacles Workingman's Helper*, the *Tarboro Farmers' Advocate*, the *Trinity College Country Life*, and the *Whitakers Rattler* carried the Populist banner throughout the summer and fall of 1892. Nevertheless, most of these Populist weeklies had a circulation of less than two thousand copies. Although getting the message out by print was difficult, these local newspapers relished the opportunity to push Populist ideology and campaign strategy. For example, the *Whitakers Rattler*, the official organ of the Edgecombe, Halifax, and Nash Populists, denounced Democrats for focusing on the Force Bill and the issue of "Negro Supremacy." The paper chose to emphasize the government ownership of the railroads and printed the Omaha platform. The paper also argued that only Populists could revive the days of Jacksonian Democracy. For the *Whittakers Rattler*, the issue of honesty in government and the notion of traditional republican government figured as highly as economic reforms.[37]

Populist leaders put their greatest hope in converting doubtful Democrats and Republicans to the Populist cause through campaign stump debates. At this time debates between opposing candidates had a carnival-like nature to them. Speeches often lasted over two hours, and debates even longer; and these were community events for all the family. A political candidate's career was either made or ruined on the stump. Audiences demanded exciting and informed speeches, and those speakers who did not live up to these expectations faced hisses and general derision. Political debates were partisan affairs, and politics mattered to local people. Hecklers and noisy crowds were common. Campaign debates took place in high summer and no doubt the heat and emotion took its toll on the speakers and stirred up the audience. One can imagine that the local population gossiped about speeches and argued incessantly on who performed better. In addition, local newspapers covered political speeches in some detail, and how these papers reported a speech or a debate and the crowd's response could potentially sway doubtful voters who could not make it to hear the speech. More importantly, however, the partisan nature of journalism meant that the purpose was probably to fire up the core voters and activists in the party as much as to seek new converts. As a result, each party put its own spin on a debate. Populist newspapers praised Populist speakers and ridiculed Democratic speakers. The Democratic dailies and weeklies likewise praised their speakers and discredited their opponents. Thus, in a campaign of a decidedly local and rural nature, the press played a pivotal role. Firing up grassroots party activists made it more likely that a party could engage in a house-to-house canvass. If the People's Party hoped to defeat the Democrats in 1892, it needed hardworking and committed local activists campaigning door-to-door in the rural districts of the Old North State.

From the middle of August into November, Populists in North Carolina made scores of speeches in the state and participated in numerous debates with Democrats and even Republicans. Marion Butler, in particular, crossed the entire state delivering speeches to voters. For example, in September, he spoke in twenty-seven cities in just twenty-seven days, traveling from the eastern portion of the state to the western areas, drumming up support for the new political party. In October he continued his tour but spent the majority of his time in the eastern section, where he hoped to make inroads into the heart of the Democrats' political powerbase. According to Butler's biographer, he spoke in thirty cites from October 5 to November 4, 1892. During this time he often spoke with the Populist gubernatorial candidate, Wyatt P. Exum, and the Populists' other elector at large, Harry Skinner. In addition, Butler debated Charles B. Aycock and Robert B. Glenn, notable Democrats of the eastern section.[38]

Cyrus Thompson used all the emotions and humor of the debate to sway local voters in the Third Congressional District to join the Populist Party. For example, on September 15, 1892, a crowd of one thousand people gathered at Warsaw, a small railroad town in Duplin County, to hear a six-hour debate between Populist Cyrus Thompson and Democrat John G. Shaw. The *Caucasian* reported that Thompson "is an active and quick thinker to say the least, he is an orator. It was an easy matter for him to hold the individual attention of the entire audience. He made a powerful speech throwing the occasional bomb into the camp of his adversaries. The Doctor's speech was to say the least highly entertaining." The paper then proceeded to discredit John G. Shaw's speech. The paper noted that Shaw only dealt in abuse and ridicule. Cyrus Thompson's reputation as a superior orator swept the Third Congressional District.[39]

Marion Butler, Harry Skinner, Cyrus Thompson, and other Populists found that they had to take up the bulk of the state campaigning after they realized the Populist gubernatorial candidate, Wyatt P. Exum, was not only a poor speaker and debater, but also prone to losing his temper and attacking his opponents.

Democrats ridiculed Exum at each opportunity. Just two weeks after receiving the gubernatorial nomination, the mayor's court at Goldsboro, Wayne County, found Exum guilty of using loud and obscene language in front of ladies in the local post office. According to the *News and Observer*, Exum was fined $7.50 by the mayor. It then came to light that Exum had previously been indicted for carrying a concealed weapon and threatening a man's life. The *Wilmington Messenger* took great delight in this story, stating, "How such an ill-tempered man who takes the law into his own hands would do to occupy the gubernatorial chair of the good old North State is a question our citizens are asking themselves just now." Throughout the campaign, reports circulated that Exum would withdraw from the ticket or the Populist would replace him. During the campaign Exum's worst mistake came after a debate with Charles B. Aycock at Snow Hill in the closing days of the campaign. During the debate Exum called Aycock a liar and then refused to apologize. Following the confrontation, Aycock, Butler, and Exum left for Goldsboro. On the way they stopped at Exum's home. After arriving at Exum's house, Aycock again asked Exum to retract his statement. Butler also asked Exum to apologize. Exum refused and tempers quickened. Aycock called Exum a liar and a scoundrel. Exum responded by pulling out a big knife. Aycock took a stick from Butler and struck Exum. Exum then jumped on Aycock, cutting his arm and head. Butler managed to separate the two. Apparently, Exum cursed Butler and told him if he did not stand back he would kill him. At that point Mrs. Exum ran out of the house and begged both her husband and Aycock to yield in their fight. Not surprisingly, the Democratic press jumped at the chance to ridicule Exum and carried the story in many newspapers, gleefully adding that Exum was unfit for high office. Exum was by this stage a total embarrassment to the Populist Party in North Carolina.[40]

These news stories indicate the degree to which Democrats feared the state campaign of the People's Party. Instead of focusing on the issues, Democrats attempted to discredit their opponents by arguing that the Populist leadership was a bunch of "hayseeders" who threatened the peace and tranquility of the Old North State. The Populist papers response to the Democrats and their reports of the campaign illustrate the degree to which the People's Party focused on the economic issues facing farmers and laborers in the state and the proactive position of Populists in solving these problems. Because the newspapers fired up the rank and file of the party, the Populist newspapers played a crucial role in keeping up morale and confidence among the party activists in the face of the Democrat's political slander and mudslinging.

The Democratic Party entered the campaign much earlier than Populists. Furnifold Simmons, a thirty-eight-year-old lawyer and former U.S. congressman from New Berne, Craven County, coordinated the campaign and busied himself distributing Democratic literature to Democratic diehards and to wavering voters. Through careful organization Democrats pushed three inter-locking themes throughout their campaign: the radicalism of the Populist Party, the bad personal characters of the Populist leadership, and the threat of black Republican rule if the white vote divided in the state. In October, Simmons issued an "address to the people of North Carolina." He argued that the third party strength throughout the United States was weak and claimed that this was a Democratic year. According to Simmons, Populists were merely annexes of the GOP: "Between the leaders of the Third party and those of the Republican party there is undoubtedly perfect understanding and entire harmony and concert, although erstwhile from motives of shrew policy, they fain would conceal this fact from their followers." Simmons implored the Populist follow-ers to return to the Democratic Party because the only possible outcome for a third party was the victory of Benjamin Harrison. Utilizing the race issue, Simmons claimed the GOP would pass the "Force Bill" and this would threaten the liberty of Tar Heels. Although Simmons admitted that grievances existed, he placed the responsibility solely at the door of the national GOP. Simmons ignored Populist anger at Democratic state policy.[41]

The Democratic Party press adopted several approaches to the campaign in the face of the new political party. The papers endeavored to ridicule Populists by refusing to call the new party the Populist or People's Party. Rather, the Democratic press constantly used the term "the third party" in their editori-als and news stories, to delegitimize the Populist's campaign. In addition, the papers mocked the Populist leadership and stirred up memories of the Civil War by constantly referring to Populist presidential candidate James B. Weaver, a Union general, as a war criminal. The papers also tried to persuade Populist voters to return to the Democratic Party. This approach took discreet strands. First, Democrats ridiculed Populists' claim that they could carry the state. For example, the *Red Springs Comet* reported, "The news from everywhere is that the Third party is going to pieces with the greatest rapidity ever known in the records of any political party." It then chided, "What else could be expected from a party born and nursed by such political shysters and political mounter-banks as Polk, Macune and Mary Ann Butler."[42]

Second, the papers argued that the Populist leaders were disappointed office seekers when they were in the Democratic Party and now they merely wanted the trappings of office, and as a result Democrats only opposed the leadership of the third party and not the rank-and-file membership. News story after news story attempted to strip the Populist leaders of their integrity. Marion Butler received perhaps the most attention from the Democratic press because he was recognized as the strongest Populist leader in North Carolina. The press and Democratic politicians accused Butler of many evils and wrongdoings. For example, the Democratic press accused Butler of accepting campaign funds from Republicans and of being a gambler and a drunkard. The *Red Springs Comet* sarcastically urged a Lumberton crowd to treat Butler with disrespect, "We hope (he) will not be rotten-egged, as he is a bad egg himself, and it would be a waste of materials to throw them at him." In addition, the newspapers ridiculed Butler and stripped away his manhood by calling him "Mary Ann" Butler.[43]

Third, the papers warned voters that the Populist Party would only succeed in dividing the white vote and, consequently, allow the Republican Party and African Americans back in to run the state. The newspapers stirred up racial prejudice and the threat of a Force Bill. The *News and Observer* led the press in this approach. Democrats accused Populists of advocating social equality between the races and supporting desegregated schools. According to the *News and Observer*, Populist A. C. Green would vote for Populists even if the result should be that "his children would have to go to school with negro children!" Time and again, the Democratic papers dwelt on African American participation at Populist conventions or meetings. For example, the *News and Observer* noted that at a speech by Marion Butler in Raleigh, "There was a sprinkling of negroes all over the hall and the gallery was filled with them and they made themselves at home."[44]

In public, Democrats seemed in a strong, if not unassailable, position in their campaign against Populists and Republicans. The newspapers and public speakers appeared to relish the opportunity to lambaste the Populist Party and its candidates. However, this public facade belied a deep anxiety over the prospect of losing the state for the first time in two decades. Democrats worried that Populists might pull enough support to throw the state to Republicans or that Populists might hold the balance of power in the North Carolina state legislature. A. A. Sherrill of Catawba County warned Senator Matt Ransom that the situation in the county was in danger. "A large portion of her people have become dissatisfied with both the old parties, and are determined to support the so call Third party." Sherrill urged Ransom to send Democratic campaign literature to get them back in the Democratic Party.[45]

Throughout the summer and fall of 1892, Populists looked anxiously toward the North Carolina Republican Party and the electoral strategy the GOP would pursue for the November elections. The rise of the Populist Party in 1892 no doubt cheered the Republican state leadership because it saw a divided Democratic Party. However, within the leadership strong disagreement existed over how best to respond to such an opportunity. By 1890, the state GOP was riddled with factions who quarreled over the issues of the role of African Americans in the party, party policy, and patronage. Republicans in the western section or majority-white areas hoped to promote issues such as the tariff that might override the race issue. White Republicans in the majority-black areas of the eastern section of the state tried to eliminate the race issue in the state while at the same time relying on black votes for office. Daniel L. Russell led this faction. At the same time, the black leadership in the state grew more assertive and demanded recognition for its powerful role in the party. The most important question facing Republicans after the Populist state convention was whether to put out a full GOP state ticket or support Populists. As early as March, the GOP split into two factions over this question. One faction, led by J. B. Eaves, the chairman of the Republican executive committee, favored a full state ticket, while the second faction, led by J.C.L. Harris of Raleigh and Dr. J. J. Mott of Statesville, advocated no state ticket and backed the Populists. J.C.L. Harris in an editorial delineated the position of the cooperationists: "With no Republican ticket in the field I believe the People's Party will win and with the defeat of the regular Democracy would follow a new realignment of parties in which the color of the skin would not denote the politics of the voter."[46]

Arguments for and against a Republican state ticket climaxed in July and August. The *Union Republican* wanted a full state ticket and attacked Dr. J. J. Mott for criticizing the position of Chairman James B. Eaves. J.C.L. Harris's *Raleigh Signal* opposed state nominations. Harris claimed that if the anti-Democratic forces unified on the state ticket, Republicans stood more chance of succeeding in the national campaign. He also argued that African Americans and a small number of white federal office holders who cared little for the state party but rather their own gain unfairly controlled the Republican Party in North Carolina. Harris, Mott, and many of their supporters also agreed with much of the Populists' national and state platform, such as the free coinage of silver at a ratio of 16 to 1, income tax regulation, regulation of the railroads, and less emphasis on the race issue. In addition, Harris and Mott saw the People's Party as the only way to ensure fair elections in the future.[47]

J. B. Eaves believed that the opportunity for a GOP victory in the state election was its best in twenty years, and he incorrectly believed that all the Populist support came from the Democratic Party. The *Union-Republican* echoed Eaves sentiments. It argued, "The People's Party strength comes mainly from the Democratic Party and is largely the result of the efforts of one wing of the party to force the other to accept Cleveland." J. J. Mott in a public letter disagreed with Eaves's sentiments. Realizing that Democrats would surely use the race issue in the upcoming campaign, Mott asked, "Shall we by running a State ticket, enable the Democratic party to again hold us as traitors to our race, aliens, an infamous, degraded set trying to put the State under Negro rule?"[48]

Populists looked on at the debate within the Republican Party. The turmoil at the Populist state convention had revolved around the question of running a gubernatorial candidate. Many Populists feared turning the state over to Republicans and African Americans, or that the Democratic press would use the race issue to dissuade many disenchanted Democrats from joining the ranks of the Populist Party. However, the anticipation that the GOP would not nominate a state ticket proved a false hope. On September 7, 1892, the Republican state convention, controlled by state executive committee chairman J. B. Eaves, put out a full state ticket with David M. Furches as the GOP gubernatorial candidate. Not surprisingly, Harris and Mott derided the state ticket and referred to it as the "Dominicker ticket."[49]

The Populists, Republicans, and Democrats now began a three-cornered fight for the national, state, and local offices. The Populists' chances for success in light of the Republican state convention diminished considerably. James B. Eaves was a skilled party chairman, and he sensibly argued to the GOP rank and file that not running a state ticket threatened to permanently disorganize the GOP in North Carolina. In a closely fought national election, Eaves no doubt saw the strategy of the cooperationists as suicidal, and the 1892 campaign seemed to offer the opportunity to take advantage of the split in the Democratic Party and finally defeat the entrenched Bourbon Democrats. But Eaves fatally overestimated the GOP's strength. It too had lost supporters to the Populist Party. The Republican cooperationists, a largely white group of leaders in the party from the eastern and the Piedmont counties, articulated the concerns of many white Republicans in North Carolina who saw their party stymied in state elections by the Democrats' successful use of the race issue. Indeed, a few isolated counties and districts witnessed cooperation between Populists and Republicans. In the First Congressional District, Populists and Republicans rallied together, and in the Third District some cooperation occurred. But this cooperation was not extensive (but this group laid the foundation for cooperation in 1894 with the Populists) and Republicans belatedly entered the state campaign determined to oust the Democrats.[50]

The highlight for the Populist Party campaign came with the visit of Populist presidential candidate James B. Weaver and Kansas orator Mary E. Lease in October. They appeared before large audiences at Raleigh, Rocky Mount, Greensboro, and Fayetteville. For example, all night long before the Raleigh meeting, Populists arrived by train, wagon, buggies, and on horseback to witness these notable Populists speak. The Raleigh speeches marked the height of Populist strength during the campaign. Three hundred and fifty mounted Populists met Weaver and Lease on their arrival and escorted them through the city. According to the *Progressive Farmer*, A. C. Green was the chief marshal and rode in the front of the procession with a sash of red, white, and blue; Capt. John Smith joined him, carrying an immense flag. Cheers from thousands filled the streets. Populist officials and horseback riders symbolically wore sashes of white cotton bagging. The rank and file wore blue badges, and some wore white medals bearing Weaver's portrait. A crowd of three thousand people witnessed the speeches of Weaver and Lease at Brookside Park.[51]

The sight must have gladdened the hearts of devout Populists at a time of stress and strain in a divisive and heated campaign. The speech by Mary Lease in particular captivated the audience. Southern tradition, on the whole, prevented southern women from engaging in such political activity, and this was not lost on Populists. But the *Progressive Farmer* noted that the crowd "stood spell bound by her magic oratory. . . . She declared that this movement would not stop until the reins of government should be in the hands of the people; and equal rights should be the motto of those in power." At their speech in Fayetteville on September 27, 1892, a crowd of over two thousand met Weaver and Lease. Weaver spoke for one hour, according to the *Caucasian*, with eloquence and strong reasoning. Mary Lease also spoke for one hour, and "her appeal for 'the homes of America' was, to say the least, very touching, and caused tears to glisten in the eyes of her hearers. It is impossible for those who have not heard her to appreciate her course. Her motives are pure, and her eloquence knows no bounds. Words fail us when we further attempt to describe this wonderful woman." The presence of a woman on the campaign stump no doubt evoked strong emotions from the Populist audience, who were not used to such public speeches by women.[52]

Despite the insurmountable odds, Populists continued to campaign feverishly throughout late September and October. Populist editorials and reports responded to Democratic lies and half-truths as best they could. Butler's *Caucasian* led the way. The paper thought it was ironic that Democrats claimed the Populist Party was dead but still kept over forty speakers in the field. The paper asked how Democrats could fight a party that did not exist. The paper also reported the "great speeches" given by Butler throughout the eastern portion of the state. The *Caucasian* chastised those who tried to disrupt Butler's speaking engagements and those that rotten-egged him at Wilson. The paper warned that Butler would stay in the fight until the last "ditch," and it rhetorically asked, "Was this done because Mr. Butler in his speech severely and boldly denounced certain election methods? Did he strike home in a tender spot?"[53]

The *Caucasian* also expressed the Populist ideology that the People's Party was now the true party of Jefferson and Jackson. Throughout the campaign Butler argued that reform under the Bourbon Democrats was impossible once Grover Cleveland received the presidential nomination. Butler argued that the Democrats no longer represented the traditional American values of democratic republicanism. Democrats were no longer the party of Jefferson and the people but rather the party of plutocracy. Only by voting the Populist ticket, Butler argued, could the tradition of Jefferson and Jackson remain alive in America. A Populist in Richmond County echoed these sentiments in a letter to the *Progressive Farmer*, "Our servants in Congress have bowed to the bidding of Wall Street. The whole machinery of our government is tainted and besmirched by the vile and filthy touch of the worshippers of mammon." The Populist continued that the fight is now on and "we are compelled to come out for the machine rule or bossism or strike for the rule of the people, by the people and for the people. We have put our hands on the plow and we will not look back."[54]

Populist papers also attacked the Democrats' use of the race issue. As early as August, Butler understood the Democratic game. Butler argued in a lengthy editorial that Democrats used the race issue as a smoke-and-mirrors ploy to distract voters from the real issues involved in the election. Butler asked, if Democrats worried so much about the race issue, why had they done nothing about it for twenty years:

> How amusing it must be to the money devil and the politician to see a brave man with convictions thus turned into a contemptible puppet by the cry of "negro in the wood pile." Dear voter they are working you this way now. They will work you this way at the next election, they will work you this way till you die, for as long as you live the negro will be here. Yes, the negro is here, and here to stay. The politician has killed every reform by crying negro. Will you allow him to kill this reform and every hope of just laws in the future by crying negro again? Stop and think! There are not more than 100,000 negro voters in the State to-day. There are over 200,000 white voters. Can the negro with less than half the intelligence, and with less than half the votes ever dominate the State? It is absurd. Let us think for ourselves, let us use common sense, let us have the courage to vote for an issue, let us vote for living issues and principles. The negro question and the demagogues who use it and live by it must be crushed before there is any hope for the people. Let us do it now. It will take courage, have you got it?[55]

This editorial illuminates the North Carolina Populist Party's position on race. Populists were racist and believed in the inferiority of African Americans. In this regard they did not differ from either Democrats or white Republicans. But, unlike Democrats, Populists could see beyond the race issue. Populists believed that real reform was only possible through a focus on *real* economic issues. Time and again, Populists argued, with some merit, that Democrats used the African American "scarecrow" to prevent meaningful debate and much-needed reform for the toiling masses of the United States, white and black. For Populists, the race issue prevented both economic and political reform. But the presence of the Populist Party, Butler hoped, would facilitate a revolution in state government by white reformers. The *Progressive Farmer* concurred with Butler's sentiments. It also added that if African Americans joined the Populist Party, Populists should welcome this. The *Progressive Farmer* also reminded black and white voters that Democrats would always steal the election. It attacked Democratic state chairman Furnifold Simmons for saying, "There are three ways to carry North Carolina Democratic this year. One is to assess the railroads and banks $100,000.

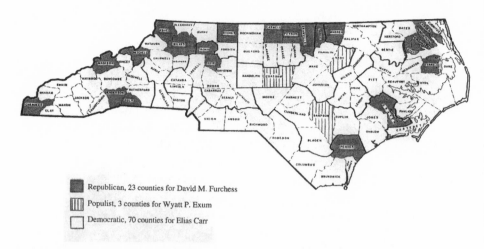

Republican, 23 counties for David M. Furchess

Populist, 3 counties for Wyatt P. Exum

Democratic, 70 counties for Elias Carr

Gubernatorial election, 1892. R.D.W. Connor, comp. and ed., *North Carolina Manual*, issued by the North Carolina Historical Commission (Raleigh: E. M. Uzzell and Company, State Printers, 1913), 1005–1006.

Another is to put 500 barrels of whiskey east of the Wilmington and Weldon Railroad. Failing this, I guess, I know how to count."[56]

As the campaign drew to a close each party attempted to shore up its vote and persuade wavering voters of the merits of supporting its platform or not supporting the other party's platform. Democrats, in particular, chose the latter way to persuade voters. Throughout the campaign the Democratic press tried to scare doubting voters. At the close of the campaign this tactic focused on the alleged existence of a secret society called the "Gideon Band." According to Democratic newspapers, this group threatened assassination and even revolution to achieve its ends. The Democratic press identified the Populist leader of Wake County, S. Otho Wilson, as the leader of the North Carolina Gideonites. The Democratic press seized on the rumors. Simmons turned the ideology of the Populist Party around and argued that the Gideonites attempted to "transplant and introduce here an institution so obnoxious to our most cherished conceptions and ideas of free, open and honorable political action." In Simmons's mind, it was up to S. Otho Wilson to refute the claims.[57]

On Election Day, November 8, 1892, Democrats achieved a sweeping victory. They won the state's presidential votes, all the state executive offices, eight of the nine congressional seats, and 139 of the 170 state representatives and senators. The Populist Party performed poorly, electing just three state senators and eleven members of the lower house. At the state level, Populists achieved just 17 percent of the total vote. For governor, Elias Carr won the governorship with 135,000 votes, while Republican candidate David M. Furches received 94,684 votes and Populist Wyatt P. Exum won just 47,840 votes. Importantly, although Elias Carr won the

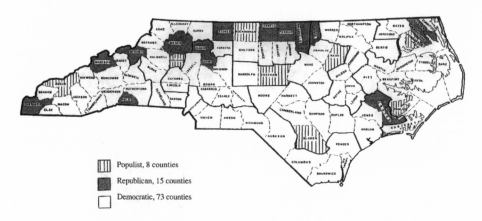

Populist, 8 counties

Republican, 15 counties

Democratic, 73 counties

State election to the North Carolina House of Representatives, 1892. W. F. Tomlinson, *Biography of the State Officers and Members of the General Assembly of North Carolina, 1893* (Raleigh: n.p., 1893).

election, he only received about 47 percent of the vote (see figs. 2.1–2.3). Only three counties, Chatham, Nash, and Sampson, produced a Populist plurality.[58]

The low Populist vote is difficult to explain. The party certainly failed to win in many counties on account of the Democratic use of fraud, bribery, and the election law. Evidence exists that Democrats tampered with ballot papers, bought black votes, and employed ignorant or illiterate whites and blacks as poll holders and judges in order to tamper with ballots and ballot boxes. Populists performed better in the eastern portion of the state, where they received over 20 percent of the vote, than in the white counties of the western section of the state. The Populist strength varied from congressional district to district. In the Third District, for example, Populist candidate Frank Koonce received 9,869 votes out of a total of 27,597, or 35 percent of the vote. In the Fourth District, Populist candidate William Strowd received 12,916 votes out of a total of 29,662, or 44 percent of the vote. Strowd's vote varied throughout the district. In Chatham County, a hotbed of Populism, he received even more votes than Exum. Strowd received 2,511 votes or a staggering 62 percent of the vote. From the voting records that survive, the Populist Party seemed to attract more votes in the coastal plain and Piedmont sections of North Carolina. Populists garnered few votes in the western mountain section, where the white faction of the GOP remained strong, or in the eastern Black Belt, where Democrats secured huge victories in the vast majority of the counties.[59]

It does appear that in some counties African Americans did vote for the People's Party. The hostile attitude of the GOP white leadership in the eastern section of the state toward blacks and the qualified overtures from Populists may

North Carolina congressional districts, 1891–1901.

have attracted some African Americans to desert the party of Lincoln. According to J. Morgan Kousser, the People's Party did best in counties that were about one-third black, where whites would not vote Republican, but would vote for Populists. This seems the case for Sampson, Chatham, and Pamlico counties. But the People's Party also captured counties with significantly large numbers of African Americans. Populists captured Rockingham, which had a 40 percent black population, Nash with 41 percent, Bladen with 48 percent, and Perquimans with a 49 percent black population.[60] Indeed, it appears that in five counties (Franklin, Pitt, Vance, Wake, and Warren) where African Americans made up to 43 percent or more of the eligible voters, Populists polled a larger number than their statewide average. These included Vance and Warren counties, where Populists put up African American candidates and drew 27 and 31 percent of the vote, respectively. The Populist Party's courting of the black vote, while limited to a few counties and initiated by local leadership, was a significant departure from the norms of southern politics in the post-Reconstruction period.[61]

It is worth noting that Populists attracted only half the votes of the number of Alliancemen in the state. Lala Carr Steelman argues that stronger Populist counties tended to be those with lower land values, and notes that Republicans seemed to lose out to Populists more than Democrats. According to Steelman's comparison of the 1888 and 1892 vote for governor, Republicans witnessed a decline of 13 percent, while Democrats only lost 5 percent. Such figures no doubt underscored the success of the cooperationists, who advocated supporting the Populist state ticket, and came as a severe rebuttal to chairman Eaves's support for a straight ticket. At the same time, however, it is worth remembering that Democrats counted out thousands of Republican votes in the eastern section of the state, and in a three-way fight for the governorship it is reasonable

Leonidas Lafayette Polk. Courtesy of the North
Carolina Division of Archives and History,
Raleigh, NC.

to assume that Democrats made doubly certain that they would count out both
Republicans and Populists in marginal counties. Alan Bromberg argues that
Populists received their best support in counties with high cotton production. He
argues that Populists consistently performed well in the eastern cotton counties
and the few cotton counties in the southeastern part of the state that bordered
South Carolina. However, if one compares the Populist counties in 1892 with
the top twenty cotton-producing counties of 1890 in North Carolina, Populists
only carried one of these twenty counties, Nash, in the eastern section of the
state. Indeed, Democrats carried the other nineteen counties. Of the eight counties Populists captured in 1892, only two, Rockingham and Nash, had tenancy
and sharecroppers at the level of 40 to 50 percent of the distribution of total farm
operators in 1890. J. Morgan Kousser, on the other hand, argues that Populists
drew support overwhelmingly from Democrats. However, Democrats counted
out so many Populist votes under the Payne election law that it is impossible to
calculate how many votes Democrats lost in 1892 to the Populists.[62]

The new party's success relied as much on the activism of local leaders and
the action of grassroots supporters as on larger socioeconomic forces. For example, in Rockingham County, the Populist Party produced one of its more radical leaders, William R. Lindsey, who championed the organization of the party

Marion Butler. Courtesy of
the North Carolina Division
of Archives and History,
Raleigh, NC.

before the majority of the Alliance leadership favored such a strategy, using his considerable local political knowledge (he had represented his county in the general assembly four times) to build an effective organization. Once he decided on such a policy, Lindsey worked earnestly for the Populists. This early organization of a local Populist Party in Rockingham County no doubt aided the People's Party in undermining the Democratic Party in that county. Populist strength in Sampson County was due to the strong leadership of local hero Marion Butler. With a well-written weekly newspaper with biting editorials supporting the cause, Populists became a dominant force in that county. Local factors and politics seem to have played a key role in the state elections. However, in Sampson County Populists only managed to carry the county for Exum but they failed to elect their candidates to the state legislature. Indeed, it is worth noting that in a three-way fight in Sampson, Exum garnered 1,585 votes and carried the county, while in the election for the lower house, John E. Fowler garnered 1,824 votes but lost to a Democrat by 8 votes. In Brunswick County, the home of Daniel L. Russell, the Republican vote fell from about 50 percent in 1888 to almost 9 percent, as the former congressman urged Republicans to vote for Populists. Populists garnered 45 percent of the vote but again failed to carry the county by 22 votes. In Wake County, the home of S. Otho Wilson,

Harry Skinner. Courtesy of the North
Carolina Division of Archives and History,
Raleigh, NC.

the *Progressive Farmer*, and the sympathetic Republican J.C.L. Harris, the
Republican vote for governor plummeted from 51 percent in 1888 to just 20 percent in 1892 because the local GOP leadership urged Republicans to vote for
Populists, and thus Populists received 35 percent of the vote. However, Democrats
still carried the county with just a 44 percent share of the vote.[63]

The reaction to the election results in North Carolina was emotional. The
campaign had drained the strength of many of the leading politicians in all
three parties. The rank and file perhaps felt this even more. Democrats boasted
that the election signaled the death of the Populists. The *News and Observer*
wrote the day after the election, "We rejoice that the Third party has been
wiped off the face of the earth in this State. Well done for our people! Well
done that our people have repudiated in such thunder tones the fellows who
have sought to lead them astray to false doctrine and appeals to their cupidity."
Josephus Daniels recalled that Democrats thought Butler was now a lame duck;
and in Clinton, Democrats carried out a mock funeral for Butler and wrote on
his grave, "to the memory of Mary Ann Butler. He died young."[64]

Populists and Republicans dismissed the election as fraudulent. They accused
Democrats of engaging in bribery, intimidation, refusing ballots, and false
counts to prevent Populists and Republicans from achieving victory in some

Cyrus Thompson. Courtesy of the
North Carolina Division of Archives
and History, Raleigh, NC.

counties. Few letters from this time survive in the collections of Populist Party
leaders. But Cyrus Thompson received a letter from William E. Clarke of New
Berne, Craven County, claiming extensive fraud in the county. In James City,
according to Clarke a vote was thrown out because "one man voted whom
Registrar thought had too little sense." Clarke continued with his accusations:
"Everything was done that the ingenuity of unscrupulous rascals could devise
to prevent a full vote getting into the vote." Clarke hoped Thompson would
contest the election to expose the election frauds and expressed a common
complaint from Populists that Democrats ignored traditional democratic
republicanism. He urged Thompson, "Don't let political liberty in NC be kept
down by Simmons. He has the proud satisfaction of knowing he has organized
a systematic fraudulent system all over the State."[65]

Marion Butler argued that Democrats used money and corruption to
carry the election. According to Butler, up to a few weeks before the election
the Democratic machine "was howling about negro domination and begging
Populists to go back in the old party. They found this racket would not work."
So, according to Butler, "about ten days ago the machine politicians" decided to
"buy the negro vote." However, Butler did not push these charges too far. He
may have hoped to form some kind of reconciliation with the Democratic Party

in the future. Late in December 1892, Butler disclosed that he never wanted to put out a state ticket but that he was overruled. But as his editorial continued, he issued a warning to Democrats as they gloated over their victory. Butler wrote, "The People's party is stronger to-day then it was on the morning of the 8th day of November and we are wiser than we were before the campaign begun. So if the protection of the People's party, we have now been better prepared to work."[66]

As the tumultuous year of 1892 came to a close many in North Carolina reflected over the past year. It was certainly a year to remember. Democrats had split for the first time in a generation and opened the possibility of genuine political contest. The year had also witnessed a worsening economic climate as cotton prices continued to spiral downwards with no sign of bottoming out; the emergence of a Populist Party gave many farmers hope and an opportunity to play an active role in economic and political affairs. The political campaign was the most heated one in many years, and the Democrats used every trick to win the election in the face of a new political party and a hopeful GOP. They succeeded with a Democrat, Grover Cleveland, triumphantly returning to the White House and eight of the nine U.S. Congressmen from North Carolina representing the Democratic Party as well as an overwhelming majority in the state legislature, and this time there were few of the Alliance-styled reformers indicative of the 1891 legislature. Democrats were elated, but national and state events in 1893 quickly smashed the Democratic optimism.

Chapter Three

THE PEOPLE'S PARTY TRIUMPHANT

The Politics of Cooperation in 1894

The 1892 election campaign was bitter, and the 1893 Democratic-controlled state legislature was a conservative body and extremely hostile toward the Populists. Democrats swept the state in 1892, but the Populist campaign outraged Democrats, who worried that Populists would only succeed in throwing the state to Republicans and black rule. The majority of the Democratic leaders viewed Populists and Alliancemen as one and the same, and they determined to smash the North Carolina Farmers' Alliance. The reactionary nature of the Democratic-controlled state legislature, however, did not smash the Farmers' Alliance or the People's Party. Rather, during the remainder of the year Populists reorganized their party in readiness for the 1894 elections. Democrats faced insurmountable problems as the national economy entered a deep depression and the leadership of the Democratic state leadership began a crippling internal war that depressed its activists. At the same time, Marion Butler began to negotiate with the North Carolina GOP to cooperate in the 1894 state elections in order to topple Democrats. The Populists and GOP came together around the issue of reforming the state's election laws that unfairly benefited the Democrats in the eastern section of the state. As Democrats continued their bellicose stance toward the People's Party, rank-and-file Populists as well as their leaders began to enact cooperative arrangements throughout the state. As a result, the 1894 elections were destined to be the most exciting in a generation.

As the state legislature opened, Democrats decided that they would crush the Farmers' Alliance and also the People's Party. As a result Democrats passed a bill that effectively repealed the corporate charter of the state Alliance, charging the Alliance with funding the Populist campaign. Leading Populists and Alliancemen fought the passage of the bill and demanded a hearing before the senate agricultural committee. However, despite Alliance and Populist opposition to the bill, and their attempts to offer amendments, the state legislature passed the bill into law. The law limited officers' salaries, allowed Alliancemen to withdraw their funds from the agency funds, and put other strictures on the Alliance's business operations. Butler argued that Democrats were being coercive and vindictive toward the Alliance and that they sought to destroy any opposition to Bourbon state policy. The *Progressive Farmer* considered the law "the blackest conspiracy in North Carolina."[1]

The actions of the Democratic-dominated state legislature and the Democratic press throughout 1893 did not offer an olive branch to the Populists or attempt to persuade activists to turn back to the Democrats. Rather, Democrats took every opportunity to attack Populists. This attitude, in part, ensured that Populists had a political enemy to target throughout the year and prevented wavering Populists from returning to the Democrats. One event in particular outraged the Populists: the trial of S. Otho Wilson on the grounds that he was the leader of the secret and illegal Gideon's Band during the 1892 election. The Democratic press made a great deal of Wilson's trial. Even before the case came to trial, the *Wilmington Messenger* in an editorial in early 1893 called Wilson a "Communist." The paper argued that Wilson was guilty and he and his conspirators must be "ferreted out, prosecuted and punished to the extent of the law." The paper also advocated, "If Wilson and his gang can be reached it should be done at every hazard" because, the paper argued, "it is a great disgrace to any free commonwealth to allow a band of midnight conspirators, bound together by a most horrible oath to live among peaceful and honorable citizens, much less to pass over their attempts to sow the seeds of anarchy and bring trouble, perhaps ruin upon the unsuspecting." The paper clearly had passed judgment on the case before it had even reached the courtroom. It was also an indication that the trial was a political stunt by Democrats to discredit Populists and convince rank-and-file Populists to return to the Democratic Party.[2]

On the morning of March 31, 1893, the trial of S. Otho Wilson began in Raleigh. By this time the case was a cause celebre. Not surprisingly, inquisitive spectators and newspapermen packed the courtroom to catch a glimpse of Wilson and witness the court proceedings. Wilson gathered an excellent defense team around him, illustrating the degree to which Populists saw this case as a referendum on the party's legitimacy in North Carolina. Four well-known lawyers, all either Republican or Populist sympathizers, represented Wilson: J.C.L. Harris, the editor of the *Raleigh Signal*, Walter L. Montgomery, R. H. Battle, and W. J. Peele. The prosecutor, Democrat James Pou, faced this illustrious defense team.

At the beginning of the trial Battle rose and addressed Judge Brown: "While the defendant protests his innocence he is willing to enter the plea of *nolo contendere* and pay the costs of the prosecution, if this be agreeable to the State." Solicitor Pou responded with what amounted to a political statement. He argued that the secret organization known as the Gideon's Band was a danger to the

people of North Carolina; and, by bringing the case to trial, the state had succeeded in drawing attention to the issue. According to Pou, it was never the
intention of the state to punish the defendant severely. Pou's claim went against
the arguments in the Democratic editorials. Pou's speech infuriated the defense
counsel. Walter Montgomery addressed the judge and argued that the prosecution's speech was very surprising to the defense and that such a political statement was not part of normal court proceedings. Judge Brown accepted Wilson's
plea of *nolo contendere* and ordered Wilson to pay costs. The proceedings only
lasted thirty minutes. Wilson entered this plea, perhaps, because he realized
Democrats would use the spectacle of the trial to discredit the Populists. Thus,
in order to end the trial as quickly as possible, Wilson pleaded nolo contendere.
Interestingly, the following day Wilson and his four lawyers attempted to get the
judge to strike the plea of nolo contendere from the record and enter the plea
of not guilty and set a day for a trial by jury. However, the prosecution resisted
this request and Judge Brown denied the defense team's efforts to change the plea.
Democratic newspapers quickly pounced on this move by Wilson. According to
the *Wilmington Messenger*, Wilson's actions on the second day were entirely political. Wilson knew the court would not change the ruling, but in the future he
could claim to Populist followers that he was innocent of all charges all along
and that Democrats had pushed for the trial, not for the welfare of the state, but
as a means to politically discredit him and the Populists. The trial is significant
because it illustrates that Democrats attempted to smash the Populists and humil-
iate its leaders. However, this approach rebounded on Democrats. The leadership
of the People's Party circled the political wagons and used the trial of Wilson to
argue that Democrats merely engaged in character assassination to stay in power.
The trial convinced wavering Populists that they could not hope to enact state
reforms through the Democratic Party and the People's Party must take power in
the upcoming elections.[3]

The ramifications of the case, however, were significant. First, Democrats
were determined to discredit the Populists and therefore milked the trial for
every possible political benefit. The trial gave Democrats more opportunities to argue that Populists were anarchists and communists who threatened
the livelihood of the state. Second, Democrats believed that they had a strong
case and hoped to discredit Wilson, an important Populist leader. Third,
Populists saw the trial as a further example of political persecution from the
Democratic Party. Populists no doubt saw it as rather ironical that Democrats
worried over abuses in the election campaign when, according to Populists,
the Bourbon machine engaged in blatant fraudulent election practices
that made a mockery of democracy. Fourth, Wilson never admitted to the charge
of leading the Gideon's Band and, instead, gathered a high-powered defense team
in the case. This illustrates that to many North Carolinians, Populists were a

respectable political organization that attracted notablelawyers to aid the party at a difficult time. Wilson's trial succeeded in galvanizing the Populist Party in North Carolina at a time when it could easily have fallen to pieces after the poor election showing of 1892.

The Populist Party kept its political organization intact during 1893 and in some instances expanded. The party itself took a pro-active route to expansion, with Populist newspapers leading the way. For example, R. A. Cobb established the *People's Party Advocate* in Morganton, Burke County. According to a published card in the *Caucasian*, Cobb announced that the paper's aim was "to look after the interests of the wage earners and the toiling masses, and keep them posted on all the matters which are of vital importance to them, and we expect the hearty cooperation of friends who have the best interests of the named class at heart." New Populist papers played a pivotal role in reaching potential political converts and keeping the party faithful abreast of Populist ideology and party policy. The Populist state leader, Marion Butler, expanded the circulation of his weekly newspaper. He moved the *Caucasian* from Clinton to the city of Goldsboro in Wayne County. On February 2, 1893, the first edition from the new press hit the streets, and by March 1893 the paper had over ten thousand subscribers and a full-time professional staff. Such a move and expansion helped Butler to consolidate his position as leader of the Populists in North Carolina and to broaden the appeal of Populist Party doctrine. On the whole, despite the expansion of the *Caucasian* and the continued work of the *Progressive Farmer*, the Populist Party suffered from having no daily newspaper and a limited number of papers.[4]

The Populist Party remained a vocal opponent of Democrats. The Populist papers mocked Democratic attempts to argue that the People's Party was dead in North Carolina. According to the *Caucasian*, Populist legislators in Raleigh mistaken for Democrats received advice from a notable Democrat who warned them not to do anything in the session that might give the People's Party some hold on them in the future. According to the article, the Democrat said, "'Our papers say the People's party is dead, but we know better. They are wide awake and will watch everything you do.'" The purpose of this article was twofold. First, the *Caucasian* argued the Populist Party was not dead and Democrats, despite all their public statements, were well aware of this and were, in fact, afraid of the People's Party. Second, the *Caucasian* implicitly stated that Democrats must be careful in the state legislature because many wavering Democrats would leave their party if they acted in a hostile manner toward the Alliance.[5]

The Populists also kept their party organization intact by charging Democrats with election fraud. According to prominent Populists, Democrats counted out Populist candidates in key races in the state. The *Caucasian* quoted an anonymous Democratic source from Wake County who admitted that Democrats bought seven hundred votes in the Fourth Ward of Raleigh, and contended that if they had not done this Populists would have carried the county. Later in the year, the paper printed a series of scathing attacks against Democrats and their alleged fraudulent practices on Election Day. The paper accused Democrats of throwing out more townships in November than ever before in the history of the state. Populist J. E. Spence of Haywood, Chatham County, wrote the *Caucasian* that the "Democratic machine had undoubtedly maintained its power by its control of the county and State offices. This control has not been secured by the voice of the people, but by force and fraud sometimes, and often contrary to the wishes of the majority at the ballot box." Spence noted that in Chatham County, despite the sweeping Populist victory in the county, all the county commissioners were Democrats; and as a result the machine controlled the elections and levied taxes on the people. These stories and editorials resonated with rank-and-file Populists.[6]

Butler and the *Caucasian* did not end with mere accusations against the Democratic machine. Rather, the paper took a pro-active stance and promised sweeping reforms of the election law and the machinery of local elections once the Populist Party gained power. Butler argued that once in power Populists would not try to benefit from the existing unfair practices of the political machine, even though they could do so. If Populists did not change the election law and county government they too would lose power because, in the words of the paper, the people "would rise up in their boldest indignation and drive" them from power. Butler ended with a plea to the voters of North Carolina and a pledge that Populists would end machine and ring-rule: "The people are law abiding and conservative, but they are not slaves or children and will not be trifled with when they know all the facts. But the People's party is pledged to correct this system and if put in power it will do it. The old parties do not even promise to correct these evils. They know they can never again get a majority of the votes of the people and the only hope of the bosses to get in power and get the offices is to pervert the will of the people. But the people will not suffer it again. Mark the prediction!"[7] Butler had finally seized on an issue that he thought would galvanize the masses to support the Populist Party. J. E. Spence concurred, arguing, "It is time for patriots to arouse. Men who love our free institutions and place patriotism above the love of office are needed. He who would restore the control of our government to the voice of the free men will richly deserve the gratitude of all good citizens." The *Caucasian* and Populists would constantly advocate changes in the election law and county government.[8]

Butler's position on the election law and the issue of home rule may have influenced his secret meetings with the GOP in 1893, or his meetings with Republicans may have helped him decide to push these issues in the *Caucasian*. Republicans felt very strongly about the same issues, and therefore such a position acted as a perfect match between the two parties. Throughout 1893 Butler and several key Republican leaders engaged in clandestine discussions over the upcoming 1894 election campaign and how best the two parties could cooperate to ensure the defeat of the Bourbon Democrats. On the one hand, perhaps, Butler realized that Populists now held the balance of power in North Carolina, and he hoped to maximize this position for benefit of the Populist Party. On the other hand, however, Butler may have determined that the Populists would eventually take the place of the Democrats in the state and any short-term allegiance with the GOP would merely help in the reconfiguring of state politics. As a result, in Butler's mind, cooperation with Republicans was a sensible and pragmatic solution in a complex political world. In addition, Butler could legitimately argue that a sizable portion of the GOP leadership in North Carolina agreed with the Populist state and monetary policy of the 1892 campaign. Republican heavyweights such as Daniel L. Russell, Oliver Dockery, J. J. Mott, J.C.L. Harris, William Guthrie, Richmond Pearson, and others seemed more Populist in their ideological arguments than Republican. Although little direct evidence exists for negotiations in 1893 between the leadership of Populists and the Republicans, it does seem that Butler, without his party being aware of such maneuverings or approving of such a policy, held several meetings with Republicans Richmond Pearson and Thomas Settle, and perhaps others, in order to formulate an electoral strategy that all participants hoped would end Bourbon rule in North Carolina.[9]

Butler was in close contact with Richmond Pearson. He wrote Pearson, "We already agreed upon the general lines of policy and action." Butler advised Pearson that the details needed working out at their next meeting to ensure victory. According to Butler, "The thing we all desire, is not only to combine those who have interest in common outside of the Democratic Party, but to draw practically every man from the organization who is now disgusted with Democracy as it is run." Butler did not limit his discussions with Pearson. He also desired a meeting with Republican congressman Thomas Settle to get a fair and just election law for North Carolina. It is safe to assume that the two met at some juncture during 1893.[10]

At the state Alliance annual meeting in Greensboro in early August, the Populist Party dominated the Alliance leadership positions. Populists Marion Butler, Thomas B. Long, W. S. Barnes, Cyrus Thompson, H. E. King, William H. Worth, William A. Graham, and James M. Mewboorne all held prominent positions in the Alliance throughout 1893. At the August meeting, outgoing President Marion Butler gave the annual address to the activists. He advocated the continued organization of the Alliance in the face of a strong opposition. Organization was crucial, Butler argued, because in a republican democracy it is vital that the people through the ballot box prevent hostile legislation. In an obvious attack on the Democrats, Butler further declared, "They use their power to inaugurate and execute hostile legislation against other classes not organized or poorly organized and weak. The latter exercise of this power in defiance of the right, but too often under the cover of unjust laws, is the snake in our body politic, and the curse of our civilization."[11]

Cyrus Thompson, the state lecturer of the Alliance, echoed Butler's sentiments. He argued that the mission of the Alliance was to educate all individuals on the evils facing the people. Because the evils were political, Thompson postulated that the only way to rid the country of such evils was through politics and political wisdom through education. He further argued that the Alliance did not serve the purpose of any political party, including the People's Party; rather the Alliance aimed to make "every political party serve the interests of every legitimate industry; and this can be done only as we educate men to be wise and patriotic rather than partisan." Although the Alliance leadership argued that the Alliance was non-partisan, it was noticeable to all that the Populist Party seemed to furnish the vast majority of the Alliance state leadership. The new president of the Alliance was Populist James M. Mewboorne, while Cyrus Thompson remained the state lecturer and William Worth stayed on as the business agent. Although Marion Butler stepped down as the state president, the meeting elected the Populist leader to the North Carolina Alliance executive committee. In addition, the delegates demanded a new election law. If Populists remained united throughout 1893, they also received indirect help from the actions of the national Democratic Party and the presidency of Grover Cleveland.[12]

At the beginning of 1893, the Democratic Party looked forward to the inauguration of Grover Cleveland as president of the United States. However, Democratic delight proved short-lived. During 1893, the U.S. economy suffered a depression caused by the third banking panic of the post-Civil War period. The causes of the banking crisis are complex. Goldbugs argued that the provisions of the silver purchasing legislation debased the currency and created concern over America's money supply. A crisis of confidence, the gold advocates argued, caused investors to hoard gold. Bimetallists disagreed with the goldbugs' reading of the financial crisis. They argued instead that the international monetary depression and the power of Great Britain to control the world gold market caused the banking crisis in the United States and the subsequent economic depression. Whatever the causes, President Cleveland blamed silver for the economic downturn and sought to protect the gold standard.[13]

During the summer of 1893, national issues took center stage in North Carolina and in the life of the Populist Party. Congressional debate over John Sherman's Silver Purchase Act threatened the Democratic Party on both the national and state scenes. Cleveland wanted to keep the gold standard and end the coinage of silver. In July 1893, Cleveland called a special session of Congress to repeal the Sherman Silver Purchase Act of 1890. Cleveland's action caused outrage among the farmers of the South and West, especially those who supported the Populist Party. Populists argued that Cleveland's actions illustrated his allegiance to northeastern financial interests and his total disregard for the average American. These farmers, facing a worsening economy and organized into an Alliance that advocated free silver, opposed Cleveland's monetary policy. Despite the opposition of farmers and silver Democrats throughout the country, Cleveland managed to get his bill through Congress. Whatever the merits of Cleveland's position, the repeal of the Sherman Silver Purchase Act succeeded in alienating pro-silver Democrats and uniting pro-silver groups against Democrats.

In North Carolina, the Populists hoped the actions of the national Democratic Party would attract pro-silver Democrats to the Populist Party. Butler described Cleveland as a plutocratic tyrant. However, it seems that Butler's advocacy of free silver was more of a political tactic to garner support for the People's Party in North Carolina than an expression of deeply held support for Populist monetary reform. Butler saw the silver issue as politically effective for the Populists, particularly at the national level. At the state level, Butler and the Populists continued to stress the urgent need for fair election laws, home rule for the counties, and increased spending on education.[14]

Cleveland's position on the silver question threatened the North Carolina state Democratic Party. However, the party could expect to ride out the storm as long as it remained relatively united on other issues. One silverite Democrat, A. R. Kindill, wrote Senator Vance, "I sincerely hope that you and your noble fight for the restoration of silver, will come out victorious. Yours is a fight for the great mass of American people against the bankers, shylocks, and money kings." However, Democrats were far from united. Toward the end of 1893 and into 1894 a quarrel erupted between the two U.S. senators, Zebulon Vance and Matt Ransom, over the issue of patronage; and as a consequence the Democratic state leadership divided into two factions. This division offered Populists and Republicans the opportunity to drive a wedge between the two factions and siphon off a crucial number of disgruntled voters for the 1894 election. In normal circumstances an intra-party fight in the Democratic Party would not have significant ramifications for North Carolina. However, these were not normal times. The 1892 campaign was a bitter memory and the presence of a new political party, holding the balance of power, potentially, made the situation worse for Democrats. Any political or personal spats between the two Democratic U.S. senators threatened to rupture the fragile coalition of Democratic forces in North Carolina and let either the Populists or the GOP into power.[15]

The causes of the fight between Vance and Ransom are complicated. Essentially, each wanted to control federal patronage in the state and neither liked or trusted the other. During 1893, Vance suffered from recurring illnesses, and Ransom took charge of patronage in the state. He proceeded to nominate

Kope Elias and Furnifold Simmons as the state's Internal Revenue collectors. In September of 1893, Senator Vance voiced his opposition to the confirmation of both men. Vance in particular opposed the nomination of Kope Elias because Elias, like Senator Vance, was from the west and in Vance's mind only he could nominate candidates from the western section of North Carolina to federal positions. Vance saw Ransom's moves as an attempt to control the party in the state and a slap in the face to his senatorial prerogatives, and therefore he opposed the confirmation of both Elias and Simmons. The Populists despised Simmons for what they saw as fraudulent election activities in 1892, and, not surprisingly, they threw their support behind Senator Vance in his opposition to Simmons.[16]

The state Democratic Party, shell-shocked by the actions of Grover Cleveland on the silver question and the worsening economic conditions, now proceeded to subject itself to a long drawn out and bitter internecine war. Although Vance received numerous warnings about the political implications for the state Democratic Party due to his continued opposition to Elias and Simmons, he refused to back down. He received strong support for his actions from key Populists. For example, Harry Skinner wrote that the people of North Carolina supported Vance's actions: "You never held such a place as you now command in the affection of the plain masses, they feel that they have a champion in you of their rights and they are with you entirely except such men as been the color of Cleveland + Ransom, they are of course criticizing you." For Populists, Vance's position was a heroic stand against the Democratic machine and the power of Bourbon leader Ransom and his despised second in command, Furnifold Simmons. Many Populists admired Vance and seized on the opportunity to support him in his "noble crusade" against the power of Ransom, whom Populists singled out for their political wrath. The political spat between Vance and Ransom continued through to April 1894, and it continued to disrupt and demoralize the state Democratic Party.[17]

As the new year opened, Populists geared themselves up for the midterm elections. Without the distraction of a national campaign, the North Carolina Populists could focus on local and state issues. The new year seemed to promise success for the People's Party. The question now was whether the Populists could turn that promise into a political reality, and what was the pragmatic way to achieve this goal. As the leader of the Populist Party in North Carolina, Marion Butler led the way in organizing the party for the upcoming elections. In the first issue of 1894, the *Caucasian* reminded Populists that all patriots must ready themselves for the election. Butler carefully tied national and state issues together. In an editorial on January 4, Butler wrote, "The CAUCASIAN wants to see North Carolina condemn the goldbug policy of Grover Cleveland, it wants to see the Old North State condemn the traitors to Democracy, and first and above all it wants to see the ballot box stuffers, the vote thieves and election perjuries condemned, crushed and forever buried in political disgrace."[18]

The Populist Party did not want to repeat their failure of the last election campaign. On January 11, 1894, Butler issued an address to the people of North Carolina in his capacity as chairman of the Populist Party executive committee. He accused Democrats of hypocrisy and fraud at the election place in 1892. According to Butler, "These frauds were so glaring and outrageous that they are condemned by thousands who voted the Democratic ticket." Butler continued, "A Party led by such men cannot be true to the masses of even its own parties." Lacing his address with an appeal to traditional republican values, Butler admonished the voters of North Carolina to join the Populist Party because "in short the party is the party of the people. It stands for the interests of the masses against the classes. Patriots from every where are invited to enlist under its standard and cast their votes solidly for good government." Butler also hoped to broaden the base of Populist support. He urged merchants and lawyers to join the party. Butler focused on state issues in his address. He argued that one issue and one issue alone would take precedence in the upcoming election. This issue was honest and fair elections. In a direct attack on the Democratic Party and an implicit overture to the GOP, Butler wrote that the foundation of free government was honest elections and "any man who will deprive another of his ballot is a dangerous citizen, he is worse than an anarchist. Any party that will use dishonest methods to defraud the voters is unfit to legislate for the people and unworthy to be trusted." Although the majority of the people might be with the cause of reform, Butler warned Populists that they faced a strong and resourceful enemy in the guise of the Democratic Party. Each county, Butler urged, must organize itself, and each district and township must have a strong and determined Populist executive committee led by an earnest chairman.[19]

The organization of the Populist Party did not end at the township level. In order to achieve a strong political base for the upcoming campaign, Butler urged the organization of People's Party clubs throughout North Carolina. The clubs could organize in any locality with five or more members. In order to avoid charges of secrecy and illegality from the Democratic press, Butler announced that all meetings must be public and the club must not use or impose fees, dues, grips, passwords, or obligations on its members. Each club had a president, vice president, secretary, and treasurer. As soon as a club organized in a locality Butler mandated the secretary to inform him (as the state chairman of the Populist executive committee) of the club's existence and the number of members. In that way, Butler hoped to keep a relatively accurate ledger of Populist Party strength throughout North Carolina as well as the names of Populists to send his newspaper and campaign literature. The conditions for membership illustrate the nature of the Populist insurgency in North Carolina. The condition for membership, according to Butler, "shall be opposition to the financial policy of Grover Cleveland and the Democratic Party and a promise to vote with the People's

Party to secure a legislature next fall that will give the people a free ballot and fair count." In Butler's mind the Populist Party was as much a political manifestation against Bourbon hegemony as it was an economic response to the depression and the policies of Grover Cleveland.[20]

The People's Party clubs no doubt served an important function at the grass-roots level in much the same way the Alliance had done so before. However, this time members met to discuss political doctrine and party policy. Undoubtedly, the clubs received Populist literature and newspapers and served as an important hub to disseminate Populist propaganda. The clubs also served an important social function during a time of economic dislocation and heightened anxiety. Thus, the formation of People's Party clubs in part enabled the Populist Party to flourish throughout the winter and spring of 1894. The *Hertford Perquimans Record* argued there was no better way of bringing the whole force of the People's Party "to bear effectually upon the coming election than by forming People Party clubs in every community and giving a hearty, liberal support to your local newspaper." The importance of the clubs for local Populist activism is clear in the letters to Populist orator Cyrus Thompson. Thompson, a leading Populist and the Alliance state lecturer, received several invitations to speak at People's Party clubs during the spring of 1894. For example, R. H. Lane, chairman of the Populist Party executive committee at Aurora, asked Thompson to give a speech at Aurora on April 28 because Lane hoped to organize a club on that day. Lane, no doubt, hoped the presence of the charismatic Thompson would aid his efforts to form such a club.[21]

Throughout the winter of 1894, the *Caucasian* constantly pushed the theme that only the Populists were the voice of the people. Butler printed stinging editorials against the Democratic Party. He argued that the *Caucasian* had always stood by the people "and advocated and defended pure Jeffersonian Democracy." The paper deserted the Democratic Party, Butler claimed, when it became clear that the Democrats were dominated by a political machine that hated the principles of democracy. As a result the paper "took up the march under the People's banner, down the road that leads to the station of equal rights to all, and special privileges to none." Now that a new campaign approached, Butler urged all those who believed in good government and the rule of the people to join the People's Party in order to "dethrone the machine and the plutocracy that now control the Democratic and Republican parties." Butler also urged his readers, "Let us redeem the country with ballots and leave to the next generation a government under which every man who will work can earn an honest and decent living."[22]

Throughout the spring of 1894, the *Caucasian* published news of local Populist Party activism. C. J. Braswell of Unionville informed the paper that Populist sentiment was on the increase in his township because the conduct in Washington had disgusted many honest Democrats. In addition, Braswell noted that the Democratic attempts to break up a Populist rally in Monroe in late 1893, "by sprinkling pepper in the court house, was an example of the methods used by the machine to carry its point" and had only succeeded in attracting more voters to the Populists. Braswell also reported that the Populists were in good shape with several People's Party clubs at work in every township. Another letter from Warsaw, Duplin County, concurred with Braswell's letter. The anonymous writer informed the *Caucasian* that the "People's party is steadily growing in this section."[23]

The Populist press received a welcome pick-me-up when the *Hertford Perquimans Record* returned to the Populist fold in 1894. In an editorial in late March the paper echoed the sentiments of Marion Butler, arguing that the Populists were right to warn the people of the danger of the hour because through "the disfranchisement of the masses by fraud in election" the door is open door to "despotism and ruin." The Populist Party, the paper claimed "is laboring" for a great revolution "through organization and proposes to make it hot for the goldbugs and their allies. Its motto is equal rights to all and special privileges to none, its rallying cry is a free ballot and a fair count." Other Populist newspapers formed in the spring of 1894. J. Z. Green and J. P. Sossaman founded the *People's Paper* at Charlotte. These two editors already had two other Populist papers, the *Lumberton Populist* and the *Beaver Dam Our Home*.[24]

Although Butler charged both Democrats and the GOP with representing the moneyed interests of the United States, he kept in close contact with sympathetic Republicans. On January 22, 1894, Butler wrote Richmond Pearson, "If those who are opposed to the election methods of the Democratic Party in North Carolina and disgusted with the Democratic hypocrisy and incompetency at Washington do not concentrate their thought to redeem North Carolina to the people this year they will be guilty of folly that will be little less than a crime." According to Butler, cooperation was mutually beneficial to both parties because without it there was no chance for ballot reform, and without ballot reform no other active reform was possible.[25]

The clandestine meetings and correspondences between Butler, Settle, and Pearson eventually leaked out to the general public in the early months of 1894. Replying to these rumors, the *Caucasian* stated that cooperation would not occur for office but *only* for principle. The *Winston Union Republican* responded to the rumors of cooperation. It argued that there would be no cooperation if principles were sacrificed, but the paper acknowledged the growing sentiment among the rank and file of the Populist Party and the GOP that the great power of the Democratic machine prevented fair elections; and, therefore, the paper argued, "Republicans and Populists ought to come to an agreement in the matter of honest elections and make a common or coalition fight against for county officers and the control of the legislature."[26]

The rank and file of the Populist and Republican parties seemed to engage in local cooperation without the sanction of their respective executive committees.

The rank and file of the parties in many ways drove the deliberations of the state leadership. Party activists reasoned that only a well-organized cooperative movement between the GOP and People's Party had any chance of defeating the machine rule of the Democratic Party, especially in counties where Democrats controlled the election machinery. In April 1894, Thomas Settle sent a letter to Republicans throughout North Carolina about the nature of relations between Republicans and Populists and asked if the two parties should cooperate in the election of members of Congress, the state senate, and the lower house. Finally, Settle wanted to know if such cooperation was desirable from a Republican standpoint. Settle received scores of replies to these questions. R. P. Hughes wrote Settle that the rank-and-file Populists in his county favored cooperation with Republicans and therefore "the ball should be put in motion or can early a date as possible." James A. Bullock of Granville County concurred with Hughes. He informed Settle, "The Populists and Republicans in our county are working together to defeat the Demos." A prominent African American politician and editor of the *Raleigh Gazette*, James H. Young, wrote Settle that the political situation now looked favorable. He also informed Settle, "The feeling between the Republicans and Populists is good and friendly and in fact they are both inclined to fusion." Young expressed his opinion, "I favor this fusion heartily hoping thereby to defeat the Democrats."[27] Each of the letters suggested that cooperation, even cooperation between Populists and Republicans, was occurring without any direct orders from the state leadership. The rank-and-file activists and voters took matters into their own hand and saw cooperation as the only way to defeat the machine rule and fraudulent election practices of the Democrats. It appears that cooperation sentiment was strongest in the eastern section of the state because in many counties Democrats remained in power through outright fraud. Rank-and-file Populists and Republicans discerned that a well-coordinated cooperative movement offered the best opportunity to overturn the Democratic hold on the eastern section of the state.[28]

The Populist Party held numerous rallies during the early summer months. At a "great rally" in Edgecombe County two thousand people attended a day of speeches by newly converted Populist William Buck Kitchin and Populist stalwart Harry Skinner. According to James B. Lloyd, Edgecombe County was thoroughly organized with five clubs "and their influence will surely be effective." Lloyd informed Thompson, "We mean business this year and we are determined to have our rights." On June 6, Harry Skinner gave a lengthy speech at Pittsboro, attacking the gold standard. According to a letter from a Pittsboro Populist, Skinner "denounced in severe terms the ballot box stuffers and election frauds." Skinner finished his speech by urging "all those of the two old parties who were in accord with us on the financial question to join the People's Party, and showed the utter folly of ever hoping to get relief through either the democratic or republican legislature as both were in the clutches of Wall Street and England." The Populists could also put on a highly organized political event. For example, John McDuffie wrote Thompson that a parade of five thousand men wearing regalia, one thousand horsemen, and four bands "will sign a petition asking the County Commissioners to appoint who we elect as judges."[29]

From January through July 1894, each party jostled with the other parties for political prominence. If Populists appeared in the ascendancy during the summer, Democrats remained badly split throughout the early months of 1894. Senator Ransom received scores of letters from anxious North Carolinian Democrats. For example, Julian S. Carr wrote Ransom that the voters of North Carolina grew increasingly disappointed with Cleveland's administration and "the disposition to 'cuss' the administration grows daily." Carr implored Ransom to fight for silver in order "to draw the hearts of the people to you." He warned the senator, "Don't be misled by the wishes of the capitalists and money leaders, but stand up as the champion of the people's rights."[30]

The political decline of the state Democratic Party continued throughout 1894 as political in-fighting between Democrats heightened throughout February and March. The death of Senator Zeb Vance in April seemed to offer some respite for the besieged Democratic Party in North Carolina and the future of Matt Ransom, whose term as U.S. senator expired in 1895. However, Ransom suffered a significant blow when Governor Carr appointed his political confidant, ex-governor Thomas Jarvis, as Vance's replacement in the Senate. This appointment was clearly a snub to Ransom. Not only was Jarvis a respected Democrat, he was also pro-silver. In addition, Jarvis, like Ransom, was from the eastern section of North Carolina. Political tradition in North Carolina mandated that one U.S. senator in North Carolina came from west while the other came from the east. Two senators from the east would only last until the state legislature chose a replacement for Jarvis and a senator for a new six-year term. In Ransom's mind those who had supported Vance would now support Jarvis in order to defeat him at all costs.[31]

By July, the Democratic Party was completely at sea. Nothing seemed to solve their problems. Some Democrats hoped a strong campaign effort might stem the hemorrhaging of the party. For example, Dewill C. Pessy of Trenton urged Senator Ransom to send Democratic newspapers to Jones County to "hold in check scores that are upon halfway ground." If the papers were slow to materialize, Pessy warned that the "third party will surely win." G. W. Blackwall of Goldsboro traveled the counties of Alamance, Orange, Halifax, Wayne, Pamlico, and Craven and found the people "wild and crazy." Only a rousing Democratic rally and a big barbecue, Blackwall advised, might stem the exodus from the party. Clearly, the threat of cooperation deeply worried Democrats.[32]

Democratic fears of a possible cooperation between the GOP and Populists seemed well founded. Before the Populist state convention formally gathered in

Raleigh, a Populist caucus of two hundred people gathered in the state capitol on July 31 to agree on a state platform. Although the caucus's discussions were secret, the Democratic *Wilmington Messenger* noted that the GOP appointed a committee to confer with Populists on the issue of cooperation. According to the paper, this Republican committee met with the Populists for several hours to agree on a cooperation package. The Republican committee suggested to the Populists that they nominate Judges William Faircloth and David Furches for the state supreme court ticket.[33]

The Populist state convention met on August 1, 1894, at the Metropolitan Hall in Raleigh. Marion Butler controlled the convention. The last Populist convention in 1892 had been a fiasco, and Populists determined that such a fate would not befall this convention, especially now that the Democratic Party was at sea and the GOP seemed more favorable to cooperate with Populists to defeat the Democratic machine and ring-rule. Over four hundred delegates and about three hundred spectators in the galleries packed the Metropolitan Hall for the Populist convention. Notable Populists attending included S. Otho Wilson, Harry Skinner, Cyrus Thompson, W. S. Barnes, J. W. Denmark, and William Kitchin. The temperature in the hall was so warm that fans and hats waved constantly. The convention opened with a prayer from the Rev. O. S. Norris, who prayed for Populist Party and its success. Marion Butler addressed the convention with a few brief remarks, noting that since 1892 the party had doubled its membership, and predicted that the cause of reform would be successful. He announced that the convention would issue a state platform and decide on nominations for state treasurer and candidates for the state supreme court bench.[34]

Following this the convention called for Harry Skinner to address the delegates. Skinner gave a rousing speech to the convention that, according to the *Caucasian*, was "one of the most powerful and eloquent of his life." This time Skinner did not dwell on the race issue or cause consternation in the delegates. He chose to argue that only the People's Party could save the country. He urged the convention to put up the ablest candidates for state treasurer and the state supreme court. After he finished his speech, the convention gave him a thunderous ovation. The platform committee outlined the various planks of the People's Party platform and endorsed the principles of the national Populist Party. The platform included the following planks: the coinage of silver at the ratio of 16 to 1, the abolition of a national bank, an increase in the money supply, a denunciation of the McKinley tariff bill and combines that oppress the people, a graduated income tax, and the direct election of senators. At the state level the platform demanded public schooling for four months to all races and the reformation of state institutions. In addition, the platform demanded an honest government and condemned the election methods resorted to by Democrats in certain counties in the eastern and southeastern sections of the state. The state platform received overwhelming support from the delegates. The platform committee then announced the names of the four candidates for the North Carolina Supreme Court, putting forward a non-partisan slate of candidates: W. T. Faircloth for chief justice and Walter Clark, D. M. Furches, and H. G. Connor for associate justices. The convention nominated these candidates by acclamation and gave the Populist executive committee the power to fill any vacancies if any of these candidates declined the nomination. The convention proceeded to elect six members of the state executive committee at large. These members were Harry Skinner, Cyrus Thompson, Captain A. S. Peace, Marion Butler, and recent converts W. H. Kitchin (from the Democratic Party) and William A. Guthrie (from the GOP). These men were prominent Populist leaders and reflected the growing number of converts to the People's Party. Finally, the convention nominated William H. Worth for state treasurer and then adjourned at 6:30 p.m.[35]

News and editorials concerning the Populist convention followed predictable party lines. The Populist press praised the convention. The *Caucasian* announced, "It was the best days work ever done for the people and the Populist Party. No other political convention that has ever assembled in North Carolina has made by its actions more votes for its party than the People's party has today." The *Progressive Farmer* noted that "there were but few rich men, no dudes and no free pass delegates, such as usually attend conventions. But a more intelligent, better behaved or more earnest body of citizens never met for a similar purpose in the State."[36]

The Democratic press ridiculed the convention. For example, the *News and Observer* wondered where the subtreasury had gone. The paper thought this omission was strange. But the paper argued Populists would "get whipped on election day." The paper also reported the Populist convention ended the possibility for cooperation because Populists "wanted the earth or such a portion of it that the Republicans couldn't see much in it for them, so they drew in their horns and both parties concluded to play it alone." The *Charlotte Observer* thought the efforts to secure the cooperation between the GOP and Populists were "the funniest spectacle ever witnessed in North Carolina." The paper echoed the sentiments of the *News and Observer* that cooperation was unlikely because there "is about as much natural affinity between oil and water as there is between these two elements."[37]

One week after the Populist convention Democrats met in Raleigh for their state convention. The Democratic Party remained badly divided and its state platform lacked coherency and purpose. The convention did, however, choose to attack the Populist Party. A Democratic speaker associated Populists with "Coxeyism," as radicals that threatened the stability of the nation. The speaker argued that Populists were paternalists and semi-socialistic. The state convention made no attempt to offer an olive branch to the Populist Party and thereby prevent the move toward cooperation between the People's Party and the GOP. Democrats offered a rather vague state platform that, while it demanded free silver, also praised the actions of President Cleveland. They offered nothing on new voting laws, anti-trust legislation, railroad taxation, or increased spending on public education. Democrats elected a new state chairman, the young and inexperienced Solicitor James H. Pou, a choice that would return to haunt them throughout a difficult election campaign. Democrats, badly disorganized, ridden with internal factions, and discredited in Washington, needed a strong, capable, and experienced campaign manager—Pou certainly did not meet any of these criteria.[38]

The Populist Party did not rest on the laurels of an excellent state convention. Sensing the Democrats' weakening position and the willingness of the rank and file to organize in cooperation with the local GOP, the People's Party busied itself with congressional and county conventions as well as political rallies and campaign speeches. In 1892 Populists had entered the field last. This time they learned from their mistakes and entered the field first, even though there was no formal agreement on cooperation with the GOP. Immediately after the Populist convention, William Strowd received the nomination for Congress in the Fourth District. On August 29, Cyrus Thompson received the nomination for Congress by the Populist Party for the Third Congressional District at Jacksonville. The next day, Charles H. Martin received the nomination for Congress in the Sixth District at a Populist convention in Rockingham. These conventions were organized by the People's Party leaders and were a sign of the growing organizational sophistication of the party in 1894.[39]

On August 17, Marion Butler signaled the beginning of the Populist campaign with an address to the Populist Party of North Carolina. In the address he dwelt on the desire to wrest political power from the Democratic machine and place it in the hands of the people. This could only come through fair and honest elections. Butler declared, "Let us as good citizens of the State rise to the patriotic duty and on our part discard forever and root out of our political system all fraudulent methods and practices, which tend to impair the ballot and suppress the voice of the people fairly expressed at the ballot box." Cheating at elections, Butler wrote, only succeeded in undermining the foundations of government, destroying the stability of institutions and capital, and breeding anarchy, lawlessness, and immorality. Although Butler sincerely believed in the cause of honest elections, he no doubt hoped that such an address would attract wavering Democrats to the Populist Party and ensure the success of the cooperationists in the GOP at their state convention at the end of August.[40]

Attention now turned toward the Republican state convention scheduled for August 30, 1894. Throughout the preceding eight months several key Republicans corresponded with Butler on the question of cooperation, and in many localities the rank and file of the two parties engaged in cooperation. But these maneuvers might come to naught if state chairman J. B. Eaves remained in control of the GOP and dominated the convention in the same way as in 1892. At a stormy Republican state convention the forces of cooperation out-played the straight-out wing of the party. The convention replaced J. B. Eaves with cooperationist Alfred E. Holton as the chairman of the state executive committee, and the convention adopted cooperation and endorsed the entire Populist state ticket. Although the convention endorsed a protective tariff, it favored the free coinage of silver. Most importantly, the platform favored the abolition of the county government system and major reforms to the state's election law.[41]

News of the cooperation agreement between Populists and Republicans shocked the Democrats. The *Charlotte Observer* could not believe the news. Its editorial blasted, "A more unnatural alliance was never formed. They think alike about nothing, they agree about nothing, except their desire to 'get there.'" The *News and Observer* took a slightly different approach. It argued that the fusion of the two parties spelled the end of the Populists in North Carolina. But it also noted, "Their absorption by the Republicans was inevitable. Like all other crank parties, the Populists had no convictions, no beliefs, no principles as a party," and therefore the People's Party had gone the way of the Know-Nothings, the Greenbackers, the Knights of Labor, and other "ephemeral crank parties of the past."[42]

The cooperation agreement between Populists and Republicans was not fusion. Each party kept its organization intact and separate. Cooperation occurred in different ways throughout North Carolina. In some cases the two parties jointly selected local and county candidates, while in other areas one party nominated a partial ticket and waited for the other party to fill out the remainder of the ticket. In some places one party merely ratified the choices of the other party; and in others, where the two parties could not reach an agreement, each party ran its own candidate. Finally, in certain areas where cooperation between Populists and Republicans was unlikely, Populists nominated a "buffer candidate" to hold its members in line and even to draw some Republican votes. Such agreements rested on several factors. First and foremost, the main issue was to defeat the Democrats, and therefore the parties put great efforts into maximizing the potential vote for the anti-Democrat candidates. Second, the cooperation agreements depended on the relative strength of the Populists in a county or congressional district. For example, in the Seventh District, where the Populist Party had a strong presence, it gained the congressional nomination. Third, the agreement depended on local factors and personalities. In the Sixth District, for example, Republicans had struggled to capture the district from Democrats for years. As a result, the GOP threw its weight behind the Populist candidate, Charles H. Martin, who seemed to offer the best chance in a generation to beat the Democrats. Fourth, race issues played a significant role in the eastern section of North Carolina. Many white Populists refused to back the African American congressional candidate Henry Cheatham in the majority-black Second District and, instead, nominated their own "buffer" candidate. Personalities also played a strong part in determining cooperation procedures. In the First District the Populist nomination of Populist Harry Skinner for congressman meant that many Republicans supported him even though the GOP had a strong presence in that district.[43]

However, cooperation did not always run smoothly. In the Third Congressional District Cyrus Thompson gained the Populist nomination, while Republican Oscar J. Spears gained the GOP nomination before an agreement on cooperation was reached by the GOP and Populists at their respective state conventions. In the ensuing months, Spears refused to back down even when the Third Congressional District executive committee under the leadership of African American A. R. Middleton, and later the state executive committee, demanded his withdrawal. Clearly, in some cases, logical argument could not convince a strong personality to back down even when, as in the case of Spears; he had no chance to win the seat. In addition, cooperation was a new political movement in North Carolina, and individuals in certain locales might not understand the larger picture of state politics and thus refuse to come off their respective tickets. Problems seemed to arise in the Fourth Congressional District over the presence of an African American, James H. Young, on the Wake County ticket. Populists threatened not to vote for Young and thereby throw the entire cooperation ticket in the Fourth District into jeopardy. As a result, the cooperationists met in Raleigh on October 19 to straighten out tensions between the GOP and Populists. According to the *News and Observer*, prominent Populists and Republicans tried to iron out their difficulties. J.C.L. Harris reminded the GOP activists that Populists had decided to support Young for the North Carolina lower house and "they have no prejudice against him on account of race." Populist William Strowd then took the stage and stated that he was for "co-operation from start to finish." Strowd also told the audience he would vote for Young and, indeed, for any African American "whenever it is necessary to do it to save both the white and colored people from the condition of the free negro before the war." Through this speech Strowd allayed the Populists' fear of voting for such an outspoken African American politician and newspaperman and the Populists fell into line behind their leaders.[44]

Marion Butler and the Populist executive committee realized that Democrats might try to prevent an honest election and, therefore, the People's Party determined to prevent fraud at the election place. On August 18, Butler issued a circular to the Populist county chairmen urging the party to apply to the board of county commissioners on the first Monday in September for representation among poll holders at the November elections. Butler warned the Populist chairmen that the Republicans might also move to get their men appointed as poll holders, but advised that to prevent confusion the two parties should confer with one another. Butler followed up with another circular on August 20. He wrote to the Populist township chairmen that if Democrats refused to appoint a Populist poll holder in September then the party must try to get an appointment in October. Butler warned the precinct chairmen, "Don't fail to attend to this at once. It is the first and most important step in guarding the sufferages [*sic*] of the people."[45]

The 1894 campaign was very different from that of 1892. In 1892 Populists continually campaigned on the defensive, but this time the People's Party went on the offensive and put Democrats on the defensive for the entire state campaign. For example, the recent Populist convert William H. Kitchin canvassed the state denouncing President Cleveland on the silver question and the worsening economic conditions in America. The texts of Populist speeches from the 1894 election are scarce, but those that survive suggest that the majority of the speakers focused on state issues and pushed the cause of honest elections and a responsive state government. Each speaker used the opportunity to lambaste the Democrats' use of the machine and ring-rule to remain in power. Populist congressional candidates, such as Harry Skinner, Cyrus Thompson, William F. Strowd, Alonzo Shuford, and Charles H. Martin, and other leading Populists, such as S. Otho Wilson and William Guthrie, toured their respective localities whipping up their audiences into a political frenzy. Each of the speakers promised that 1894 was the year of Populists and pledged that the party would enact broad sweeping reforms to place the government back into the hands of the people. Populists mounted a door-to-door canvass as party activists, fired up by the Populist press, Populist speakers, and the continual intransigence of Democrats toward reformist legislation and their use of an undemocratic election law to maintain power, worked to persuade voters to join the Populists.[46]

Some cooperationists worried that the Democratic machine would once again "steal" the election. Republican Daniel L. Russell warned Populists and Republicans that Democrats would steal the election regardless of the policy of cooperation. In an interview with the Democratic *Wilmington Messenger* that, amazingly, the paper published, Russell accused Democrats of out-right fraud. He stated, "The fact is the Democracy will carry everything. They couldn't though if they would have elections. They don't do that. They just name their man and put him in office. They won't count the votes. If they did, they wouldn't possibly carry twenty counties. No, not even twenty."[47]

In contrast the Democratic campaign was weak and disjointed. Democrats were in a terrible position. The majority of voters in North Carolina disliked the political actions of Grover Cleveland and blamed his policies for the worsening economic condition of the nation. The state Democratic Party was riven with factions, and the silver issue threatened to permanently destroy the party. The inexperienced state chairman, James Pou, ignored the silver issue and instead wasted his time and his party's efforts on his claim that the cooperationists intimidated the voters. He tried to split Populists and Republicans. In the face of Populist organization and resurgence, Pou tried to claim that the Populists were dying in the state. The fight between Senators Ransom and Jarvis also hindered Democrats. The party spent a great deal of time making certain that the two senators would not meet, and the senators agreed not to attack one another on the campaign trail.[48]

Despite the party's problems, the Democratic press tried to fire up the party faithful. The papers tried to show that cooperation was coming apart. The papers also tried to tempt Populists back into the Democratic Party. The *Charlotte Observer* accused Populist leader Marion Butler of political bossism and urged Populist supporters to leave for the Democrats. The *Southport Leader* gleefully noted what it saw as a weakening of Populists in Brunswick County. According to an editorial in late October, "as the election draws near, it must be acknowledged that Populists of Brunswick County are losing confidence in their position and from the highly exaggerated estimated majority of four hundred or more . . . to a simple claim of feeling certain that they, the Populists will elect their ticket." The paper also claimed that Populists refused to debate the Democratic speakers, and when they did speak, they only dealt in abuse.[49]

The Democratic press was not afraid to invoke the tried and trusted theme of race and the evils of Reconstruction to hold the Democratic faithful in line and persuade Populists to return to their "natural home." An editorial in the *Wilmington Messenger* admonished voters not to vote for Populists and "Radicals" because it would amount to a revolution in the state, a situation full of "disorder, of discontent, of extravagance, waste and incompetency." The paper, however, still showed Democrats in a poor position. It admitted that the voters "might find names on the tickets this year that are offensive to you and your judgements." But the paper urged, "Do not throw them aside. Vote the ticket. This is necessary now almost beyond any other year because of the truly infamous conspiracy afoot to ruin and blast North Carolina." The *Lenoir Topic* attempted to portray Populists in a worse light than Republicans. According to the paper, "Populist rule means war, bloodshed, strife and turmoil." The *Wilmington Messenger* also chimed in on the evils of Populism. The paper chose to focus on "Butler bossism" instead of the rank-and-file Populists. The paper likened Butlerism to the "Reign of Terror in France" and noted "what a horror it would be—what an absolute curse if Butlerism was to become a fixed, a permanent factor in North Carolina."[50]

The race issue did not figure as prominently in the election of 1894 as many Populists feared. This was, in part, because Democrats sought the black vote in marginal counties. However, the Democratic press could not resist attacking Populists on the race issue toward the end of the campaign in a desperate attempt to stem the exodus of voters to the cooperationists' ranks. But even on this issue the Democratic papers sent mixed signals. True to form, the *News and Observer* called attention to the Populists' attempt to "capture and organize the colored vote in North Carolina." The African American voters would gain nothing because "the Populists propose to make him only a cat's-paw, a stepping stone to power, and have not real interest in his welfare and prosperity." However, the paper then went onto argue that only the Democratic Party looked after the rights of African Americans. The paper claimed that only Democrats have "given him his full political rights and contributed millions of dollars to his schools and charitable institutions." Such claims were in marked contrast to racist editorials and news stories in the 1892 campaign.[51]

The Populist press reported the campaign in a completely different light. The papers noted the excellent content of Populist speeches and the large and enthusiastic crowds that attended the political debates. For example, the *Caucasian* reported a joint debate between Populist Cyrus Thompson and Democrat John G. Shaw at Wallace on September 8. According to the paper, Thompson's speech of seventy-five minutes totally outshone Shaw's speech. The audience, according to the paper, sided with Thompson, who used sarcasm and skill as well as documents of fact to discredit his Democratic opponent. The Populist press also noted that Democrats tried to use the same election tactics in 1894 as they had two years earlier. According to the *Caucasian*, this meant "misrepresentation, and deception then. It is a campaign of lying, cowardice, and abuse now." The Populist press implored its supporters to ignore these tactics and instead vote for honest elections and government and reform of the state. In addition, the papers disagreed with the Democratic Party's claims that Populists were returning to the Democratic Party. The *Perquimans Record*, for example, said such claims were mere "chirpings" and the Populist Party was never in better shape in the state. The paper also warned Populists that Democrats aimed to steal the election in the same way as in 1892. In an editorial on the eve of the election, the paper reminded its readers of Democratic tactics in the election, in the process illustrating what Populists in North Carolina were fighting to correct:

We would be dull indeed, who would not realize that in the Democratic party we have an enemy skillful, organized and determined, whose strength lies in the use of money to corrupt the voter and fraud at the ballot box, which through the means of unfair appointments of judges of election, they in great measure control. This then is now enemies strength: money with which to buy votes and corrupt the voter, and in unfair election laws when their corruption fund should fail. Without cause and without the support of the masses, they are desperate, and we must expect them to stop at nothing however dishonorable that promises a continuation of that lease of power which the people of their right have determined to withdraw. Upon the other hand, we enter the field with a clean record: we have a cause, and it is the cause of the people, and it is supported by the great masses of the people, both black and white.

The laboring millions of the land are with us and we join battle with the enemy, relying not upon victory set upon the use of money or fraudulent election, but upon the will of the people honestly expressed through the means of the ballot. A free ballot and a fair count is all we ask, and we send the drumbeat of victory rolling through the land.[52]

This quote encapsulates all the tenets of North Carolina Populism. The People's Party, disgusted with the actions of the Democratic machine and ring-rule and the Democrats' disregard of republican government, resolved to join with all those, black and white, who supported real democracy and a change in the election laws of North Carolina. To Populists this was a noble calling of the highest order; and, despite a spirited and resourceful opposition, they believed destiny was on the side of the righteous.

On Election Day, November 6, 1894, Populists in cooperation with Republicans swept the state. Figures for the number of Populist representatives in the state legislature vary, due in part to the convoluted nature of local politics and cooperative arrangements in the counties as well as the contested elections in the lower house. In a general assembly of 170 members, and utilizing all the available sources from the time, it seems that Populists won 42 seats in the lower house and 24 seats in the senate, making a total of 66 representatives in the legislature for the 1895 session. Republicans captured 35 seats in the lower house and 18 in the senate. The Prohibitionist Party shared Buncombe County with Republicans. Democrats suffered a humiliating defeat, losing control of the state legislature for the first time since 1868. In the state legislature Democrats retained 46 seats in the house (they subsequently lost 4 seats in contest, taking their number down to 42) and just 8 seats in the senate. The cooperationists elected their entire state supreme court ticket and the Populist state treasurer, William H. Worth.[53]

In the House of Representatives Populists captured the following counties: Alexander, Bladen, Brunswick, Burke, Cabarrus, Catawba, Chatham (2 seats), Chowan, Clay, Cleveland, Cumberland (2 seats), Duplin, Durham, Franklin, Gaston, Greene, Harnett, Hyde, Jones, Montgomery, Nash, Person, Richmond (2 seats), Robeson (2 seats), Rockingham (2 seats), Rutherford, Sampson (2 seats), Surry, Vance, Warren, and Washington. They also captured the following counties, with the Republican Party capturing the other seat: Forsyth, Iredell, Pitt, and Wake (Republicans gained 2 of the 3 seats). Populists certainly increased their representation from 1892. The Populist strength seemed particularly strong in the southeastern section of the state. In particular, Populists fared well in the counties

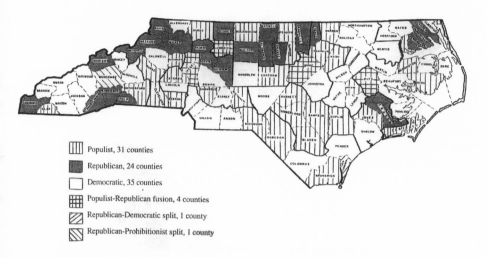

Populist, 31 counties

Republican, 24 counties

Democratic, 35 counties

Populist-Republican fusion, 4 counties

Republican-Democratic split, 1 county

Republican-Prohibitionist split, 1 county

State election to the North Carolina House of Representatives, 1894. Collins and Goodwin, *Biographical Sketches of the Members of the General Assembly of North Carolina, 1895* (Raleigh: Edwards and Broughton, 1895).

in the Third Congressional District. However, Populists performed poorly in the mountain section, losing Swain County to the Democrats. Interestingly, Populists won seats in four majority-black counties: Chowan, Richmond, Warren, and Washington. Given the number of black voters in these counties, a sizable portion of African Americans cast their votes for the Populist Party. These facts indicate that the Populist Party increased its vote from 1892 and that cooperation with Republicans directly benefited the Populists' quest for political power in the state in order to change North Carolina's election law and county government law. Cooperation made the biggest difference in the eastern section of the state, where Democrats had traditionally used fraud, bribery, violence, and the election law to remain in power. Populists gained the most seats from Democrats in the eastern section of the state because the party put up white candidates in heavily black counties. Populists carried twelve counties east of Raleigh, while Republicans managed to carry just four and one other with Democrats. In addition, the People's Party and the GOP also cooperated in the Piedmont section of the state because neither party could hope to garner enough votes on its own to defeat the Democrats. Thus, a sophisticated cooperative movement, based partly on electoral necessity and a hope for state reform, fueled the cooperation of Populists and Republicans.[54]

Explanations for the increased Populist vote are difficult to pinpoint. In part the increase in the Populist vote and the number of Populist representatives was a product of cooperation with the Republican Party. It is impossible to discern the degree to which the cooperative movement gave votes to Populists, but in some counties in the east and Piedmont, Populists did gain votes from the GOP.

In many counties Republicans did not run a candidate and instead threw their support behind the Populists. Cumberland County bordered Sampson, and perhaps Butler's influence was felt quite strongly in that county. Chatham County was a center of People's Party strength in 1892, producing notable Populists such as William F. Strowd and John Atwater, and the Populist Party remained well organized there in 1894. Rockingham County provided the first Populist leader, W. R. Lindsey, in 1892 and again returned two Populists to the state lower house and W. R. Lindsey to the state senate. In Sampson County, however, Republicans ran their own ticket, but Populists still managed to win a three-cornered race. This success was due in part to the presence of the Populist weekly, the *Caucasian*, and because Sampson was Butler's home county. The Populist increase was due to the decline and disintegration of the Democrats, the worsening economic conditions of the majority of small farmers, the cooperation movement with Republicans, the simultaneous re-organization of the Populist Party in 1893 and 1894, and its excellent pro-active and well-coordinated election campaign in 1894.

In the congressional races Populists and Republicans also did very well. The Populists won the First, Fourth, and Seventh Districts, with their respective candidates, Harry Skinner, William Strowd, and Alonzo Shuford, garnering a sizable portion of the vote. The Republicans carried the Fifth, Eighth, and Ninth Districts. Democrats captured the Second District, the majority-black district, probably through fraud and the use of the election law. The Third and Sixth District also appeared to produce a narrow victory for the Democratic Party, but rumors of Democratic fraud in these races circulated throughout the state, and in December Populists issued a notice of contest for these two districts. After protracted hearings, Populists eventually succeeded in gaining the Sixth District.

The reactions to the election results in North Carolina were emotional. The level of vitriol for an off-year election was unseasonably high. The Populist press gleefully reported that the cooperation forces had swept the state due to Democrats' support for "bad government." Butler wrote a scathing editorial against the Democratic Party, noting that for the past twenty years Democrats had used the race issue to scare the voters and prevent any meaningful reform of the state's ills. He urged the next legislature to "legislate as to completely destroy the last vestige of power of the old oligarchy to appeal to the prejudices of good men." Butler noted the contradictory nature of Democrats, whom he accused of seeking the African American vote. Butler realized the importance of the upcoming state legislative session and hoped that a political sea change would wash over North Carolina. He took the opportunity of victory to remind Populists that they must not falter in the drive to return North Carolina to honest government and real democracy.[55]

The Populist movement had achieved a notable success in the 1894 elections and the party could afford to look back with satisfaction on the turn of events from December 1892. The party had resisted the threats to disintegration and instead re-organized itself into a well-oiled political movement to oust the Democratic Party. No Populist disagreed openly with the policy of cooperation with the Republican Party. Such a policy was the only way to achieve the reforms the People's Party desired in North Carolina. Cooperation did not mean a sacrifice of party principle or identity during the 1894 campaign. Indeed, the cooperation movement seemed to give Populists renewed vigor to articulate their ideology and reform program to the voters of the Old North State. The question now was how would Populism, in cooperation with Republicans, transform itself from a political movement into a party of government in the state legislature, and how would the party attempt to attract more supporters to its ranks in the face of a resurgent GOP and a threatened Democratic Party that historically would pull out every stop to prevent its opponents from retaining political power in the Tar Heel State? These questions would vex the Populist Party throughout the next two years, and their response signifies the degree to which Marion Butler, Harry Skinner, Cyrus Thompson, and other Populists could not rest on the laurels of a magnificent victory in November 1894.

CHAPTER FOUR

"EQUAL RIGHTS TO ALL AND SPECIAL PRIVILEGES TO NONE"

Grassroots Populism in North Carolina

Grassroots Populism in North Carolina was strong and enabled the state leadership to achieve significant success in the 1894 elections. However, elucidating reasons why voters joined the Populists is fraught with methodological difficulties, and North Carolina is certainly not unique here. First, there are few sources pertaining to the rank-and-file Populists; indeed, many were illiterate. Instead, historians have traditionally relied on letters from district Populist leaders to the Populist state leadership to unearth the political culture of the People's Party. Statistical analyses of Populism, though growing in sophistication, provide only rather vague and generalized characteristics of the rank-and-file Populists. Other sources, such as newspaper columns, political broadsides, and campaign speeches, give some sense of the type of political campaigns in which Populists engaged. However, at the same time, the voice of the rank-and-file Populist still remains absent from the historical record.[1]

Contested election cases of U.S. congressional races provide a unique insight into the political culture of the 1890s and the Populist Party in North Carolina, the politics of cooperation between Populists and Republicans, and a greater understanding of the Populist rank-and-file. During the tumultuous political, social, and economic decade of the 1890s, North Carolina witnessed several contested election cases, two of which directly involved the Populist Party at the height of its electoral success. The two cases, both brought in 1894, *Charles H. Martin (Populist) vs. James A. Lockhart (Democrat)* of the Sixth Congressional District and *Cyrus Thompson (Populist) vs. John G. Shaw (Democrat)* of the Third Congressional District, offer a wonderful opportunity to explicate the political maneuverings and culture of local party politics. In the campaign of 1894, the Sixth Congressional District witnessed a straight-out fight between

Democrat James A. Lockhart and Populist Charles H. Martin, who received the Republicans' endorsement. In the Third Congressional District the election was more complex. Democrat John G. Shaw squared off against Populist Cyrus Thompson and Republican Oscar J. Spears in a three-cornered race.[2]

In the autumn of 1894, Lewis N. Jones, a forty-two-year old farmer from Anson County in North Carolina and an active member in the People's Party and a member of the Populist executive committee of Anson, found himself to be a "marked man." Three Saturdays before the November election, while Jones was grinding corn on his farm, a Mr. George Wilson came to his mill and the two men began to discuss politics. Jones informed Wilson that he was going to the town of Lilesville to register to vote. Wilson advised Jones to keep away and warned the Populist that some fellows at Lilesville would mob him. Jones ignored this advice and proceeded to Lilesville to register, whereupon he got into an argument with the registrar over some changes that Jones demanded to his registration details. A few weeks later, Jones attended a Populist Party executive committee meeting in Wadesboro, and on his return to Lilesville he stopped at the post office to collect his mail. Mr. T. A. Thorne, a well-known Democrat in the town and the owner of the store, inquired if Jones had any political news and, much to the chagrin of Thorne, Jones replied, "I told them it was just as good as I wanted, for we (the Populists) would sweep the State to-morrow by 15,000 to 20,000 majority." Dr. Gaither took Jones to one side and warned him he would meet his God, to which Jones replied that he intended "to stand up for [his] rights and [his] people." Thorne then informed Jones that he would challenge his right to vote. Jones was clearly a marked man and disliked because of his strong Populist convictions.[3]

On the day of election, Lewis Jones proceeded to Lilesville to cast his ballot. At 9.00 a.m., Jones tried to vote, only to face a challenge from Democrats. The registrar, Mr. Henry, challenged Jones on grounds of residency and prevented the Populist from voting. Jones, no doubt furious at his rejection, left the voting place and entered Thorne's store and asked him why he had challenged his right to vote. Thorne, perhaps sensing the mood of Jones, denied the charge and stated that he had not even gotten over to the voting place that morning. Jones retorted that early in the morning the registration books were in Thorne's store, and, therefore, Thorne could have challenged Jones at that time. An argument then ensued between Thorne and Jones in the middle of the store. At this point, Jones's testimony makes compelling reading: "I said, 'Look here, old fellow, I owe you a little account and you have challenged me, and now let's balance off.' He says to me, 'I will indict you.' I says, 'What good will that do?' He says, 'I will sue you and get a judgement.' I says, 'What good would a judgment be against me?' He says, 'You are a damn rascal' That was the first time I got mad, I says, 'You are an informal scoundrel.' He struck me with his left hand,

and as I went to strike him with my right hand, he drew his pistol and shot me through the left leg and went into the right heel."[4] The indefatigable attitude of Lewis Jones made him, literally, a marked man. Democrats at Lilesville, determined to keep a local Populist leader from the polls, denied Jones the right to vote in a crucial election. Jones, and other Populists like him, refused to bow to such pressure and intimidation. Although the example of Jones may seem an extreme and an unusual case, it is a clear example of the heated nature of local politics and the loyalty of the rank-and-file Populists to the cause of reform.

Why did white farmers in the South risk social ostracism and economic and personal reprisals to join the Populists? What motivated these voters, and why did many of them volunteer their valuable time to play a pro-active role in the People's Party? Analysis of Populism at the local level might offer a reliable way to grapple with the Populist movement. Were the ordinary Populists radically disenchanted with America's political system and capitalistic economy? Or, did more local issues play a primary role in motivating voters to switch political party? What was the political consciousness of the small township leader or the poll book writer, who spent an entire election day meticulously recording the names of Populist voters? Why would some voters risk social ostracism, intimidation, and even violence to vote for a new political party? Perhaps the Populist Party contained merely disappointed and disgruntled Democrats, sick and tired of machine and ring-rule and an unresponsive state government. Perhaps a combination of causes or other issues motivated the rank and file into a political repudiation of the Bourbons Democrats. How did Populists organize themselves into a powerful electoral organization that sent shock waves throughout North Carolina in the mid-1890s?

From the contested election testimony in both cases it is clear that four key issues propelled rank-and-file voters to switch to the Populists and, in many cases, to play a pro-active organizing role in the party during the election campaign and also on the day of election. First, Populists believed in the party's political agenda and its commitment to reform, and thus volunteered to help the party on Election Day. In other words, Populists were not merely disgruntled Democrats who desired office, but principled opponents of Democrats, and they viewed party organization as the key to success. Second, the Populist Party's promise to reform the state and county government, to return the counties to home rule, and, more importantly, to reform the North Carolina election law resonated with many voters. The Populists positioned themselves as the *real* descendants of the Jeffersonian and Jacksonian tradition of republican government, and this struck a responsive chord with the voters. Third, the economic policies of the party, such as free silver, the subtreasury, government ownership of the railroads and banks, and a more sympathetic government, drew significant support from the small farmers suffering at a time of economic depression. Fourth, Populists engaged in a cooperation movement with Republicans.

The Sixth Congressional District, commonly called "the shoe string district," straddled the South Carolina border and was the jewel in the crown of Democratic hegemony. The contestant in the disputed congressional election, Populist Rev. Charles H. Martin, and his leading attorney, the prominent Republican judge Daniel L. Russell, endeavored to prove that Democrats had stolen the congressional election. Many of the questions put to the witnesses for the contestant elaborate on the charges of unfair registration challenges, miscast ballots, ballot-box stuffing, missing tickets, faulty election returns, intimidation, violence, and general Democratic contempt for the democratic process on Election Day. Contestee James A. Lockhart and his counsel spent the majority of their time trying to disprove such allegations, while also taking every opportunity to discredit Martin's witnesses, particularly on the issue of cooperation.[5]

Charles H. Martin, the Populist candidate in the Sixth Congressional District, was born into a farming family in Franklin County on August 28, 1848. Martin attended Wake Forest College and graduated with first honors in 1872. After graduation, he stayed on to teach at Wake Forest College for eighteen months and then entered the University of Virginia, where he spent two years. Following this, Martin gained a professorship in Latin at the Baptist Female Institute at Murfreesboro, North Carolina. He then practiced law at Louisburg and at Raleigh. As if this was not enough, he decided to enter seminary at the Technological Seminary in Louisville, Kentucky, and, according to the *Progressive Farmer*, "has since been following the grand and noble calling with a degree of devotion and interest seldom surpassed by any. His manner is of high and lofty character, his language well nigh perfect, and his preaching carries with it a power that thrills the hearts and souls of men." Martin joined the Populists in 1892. At the Populist Party convention of August 1894 at Rockingham he received the party's nomination. The election of 1894 seemed to produce, at first glance, a slim majority of 384 votes for James A. Lockhart.[6]

The Third Congressional District lay adjacent to the Sixth Congressional District. In this contested election case, Populist Cyrus Thompson and his attorney Thomas Sutton endeavored, in the same way Martin and Russell attempted in the Sixth Congressional District contested election case, to prove that Democrats had stolen the election. The majority of the questions put to the witnesses for the contestant center on similar charges made in the Sixth District, that unfair registration challenges, miscast ballots, ballot-box stuffing, missing tickets, faulty election returns, intimidation, violence, and general Democratic chicanery prevented a fair and just election of a U.S. representative. Contestee John G. Shaw and his counsel spent the majority of their time endeavoring to disprove such allegations and to discredit Thompson's witnesses. What made the contested election case in the Third District very different from that in the Sixth District was the presence of a Republican candidate, Oscar J. Spears, who refused to come off the ticket, even though both the Republican Third District congressional executive committee and the Republican state executive committee demanded that Spears withdraw.

Cyrus Thompson, the Populist Party candidate in the Third Congressional District, was born in 1853 into an antebellum Whig family of Richlands, Onslow County. After receiving a private schooling in the 1870s, he entered into a four-year course at Randolph Macon College in Virginia in 1872. Following this, Thompson studied medicine for two sessions at the University of Virginia and then at the University of Louisiana and graduated with distinction in medicine in 1878. He practiced medicine in his home county of Onslow from 1878 to 1883 and then switched to farming. He represented his county in the state house of representatives in 1883 and in the state senate in 1885. With the formation of the Farmers' Alliance in North Carolina in 1887, Thompson became one of its principal spokesmen, spending much time traveling across North Carolina as state lecturer. Through his work as the North Carolina State Farmers' Alliance state lecturer, Thompson became a well-known public figure. By 1892, when Thompson entered the Populist Party, he was a well-known and well-respected political player in eastern North Carolina. In the campaign of 1894, Cyrus Thompson seemed the natural Populist candidate for the Third Congressional District. The election of 1894 seemed to produce a slim majority of 994 votes for Democrat John G. Shaw. In the official election returns Shaw received 10,699 votes; Thompson, 9,705, and Oscar J. Spears garnered 6,966 votes.[7]

From the evidence that emerged in the testimony before the House Committee on Elections, Number 2, one can identify a number of issues pertaining to grassroots activism and the Populist Party. Farmers seemed to join the Populists for a variety of reasons. For some farmers, the Populists promised economic improvements and financial reform. For others, the Farmers' Alliance provided education and a raising of political consciousness to farmers who yearned for economic and social improvement in their lives. Other voters saw in Populism a chance to break the machine and ring-rule of the Democrats. Still others decided cooperation was a safer alternative than a straight-out Populist ticket. However, Thomas B. Russell of Blue Springs Township joined the Populists out of principle. "I am a member of the Alliance," Russell argued, and "I went with them" to the Populist Party. To some farmers, Populism seemed to offer something new and exciting. Nathan Andrews had a clear motive for joining the Populist Party and voting for Martin for Congress. When asked to explain the difference between Populists and Republicans as they existed in Robeson County, Andrews responded, "Well, I don't know more than the platforms of the two parties. There is a clause in the Populist party platform that I have never seen in any other party—equal rights to all and special privileges to none." The party slogan of "special privileges to none" resonated with many poor farmers and workers in North Carolina at the height of the depression of the 1890s. While they suffered economic hardships, these rank-and-file Populists witnessed the increasing wealth of the railroad barons, the industrialists, and the affluence of the upper class in the Northeast. Populists, on the other hand, promised an end to the depression and a government more responsive to the needs of the "producing classes." Isaac T. McLean of Alfordsville Township, Robeson County, gave perhaps the clearest reason for joining the Populists rather than the Republicans. "So far as the election law is concerned and the county government, I suppose that they are about the same," McLean stated. He continued, "The Populists are in favor of the free and unlimited coinage of silver at the ratio of 16 to 1. I don't think that is Republican doctrine. The Populists are in favor of the Government ownership of the railroads, and I don't think the Republicans are"; and lastly McLean argued, "The Populists are opposed to National banks." This testimony underscores the fact that rank-and-file Populists could, and often did, understand what it meant to be a Populist; and even though there may be differences between individuals on Populist doctrine, these differences were put aside for electoral success.[8]

The testimony of the rank-and-file Populists in the contested election case of the Third District indicates that the voters seemed to join the Populist Party for reasons similar to those in the Sixth District. For some farmers Populism offered a chance for economic and social improvements. George Robert Ventus decided to switch his allegiance to the Populist Party and rejected claims that perhaps the People's Party induced him to vote the Populist ticket. According to Ventus, he sometimes voted the Democratic ticket and sometimes the Republican ticket. Not all Populist voters came from the Democratic Party. Henry Murrell, for example, changed from the GOP to the Populists in 1894.[9]

Local Populist leader Thomas L. McLean, chairman of the Populist Party executive committee of Cumberland County, had definite reasons for leaving the Democrats and joining the Populists. From the age of twenty-one, McLean testified, he had always voted Democrat. But he could not bring himself to vote for Grover Cleveland in 1892. Asked in cross-examination what his objections were to Cleveland, McLean replied, "I thought the name of Democrat was a misnomer applied to him. . . . I believe he was a traitor to his party and his country"; and, therefore, McLean argued, his objections to Cleveland were personal and political. Counsel for the contestee asked McLean how long he had personally known Cleveland. McLean responded, "Never; and please God I never may." For McLean, as with many other Populists, the dislike of Grover Cleveland was deep, with little possibility for a return to the Democratic fold while Cleveland remained in charge. Cleveland's monetary policy and coddling of big business infuriated Populists. In the same way Populists of North Carolina despised President Cleveland, they also loathed North Carolina senator Matt Ransom. McLean singled out Ransom for personal scorn, noting that he was sorry that Ransom was one of his personal acquaintances.[10]

Rank-and-file Populists played a key role in the elections in the Third District. T. B. Newberry, an ordained Baptist minister, had sympathies with the Populists; and although he did not consider himself to be a strong partisan, he "heartily" contributed politically to local newspapers. Clearly, for Newberry, religious convictions did not prevent him from engaging in political campaigns. It seems that not all Populists were farmers. Arthur Dixon of Cross Creek, for example, was a locomotive driver. The counsel for the contestee inquired about Dixon's political convictions. Dixon responded, "I have different views; but I identify with the laboring interests of the country." Dixon had once played an active role in the Knights of Labor. He considered the Republicans opposed to laboring interests and, therefore, supported the Populists. Clearly, for Dixon and other Populist voters like him, the People's Party doctrine of equal rights to all and special privileges to none resonated to such an extent that they risked social ostracism, intimidation, and violence to vote the Populist ticket. However, Dixon's testimony further underlies the tensions the Populists brought to bear on local communities. As pro-labor as Dixon claimed, he still voted for the Democratic county officers because "they are my personal friends; but I did not agree with their politics."[11]

Other rank-and-file members joined the Populist Party for different reasons. John G. Brown, a fifty-year-old cooperationist supporter, argued that cooperation would lead to a change "in regard to our election laws and county governments" and that cooperation was a pragmatic solution to gain office. Brown and other cooperationists chafed under the rule of the Democratic machine and looked to the cooperation movement to democratize local government and end fraudulent elections. Other voters joined the Populists from the Republicans. Harry Sampson was one such political convert. A lifelong Republican, he decided to switch to the Populist Party.[12]

In the Sixth Congressional District many witnesses for the contestant advocated cooperation between Republicans and Populists in order to defeat Democrats. Edward Cole, a twenty-three-year-old farmer from Rockingham Township in Richmond County, was one such witness who voted for Martin and the Populist and Republican ticket. Asked whether he was Populist or a Republican, Cole answered, "I am both." Harry Covington, also of Rockingham Township, expressed similar sentiments, and when pushed in cross-examination by the contestee's attorney as to why he could not remember other cooperation candidates, Covington retorted, "They are all . . . I remember, and the only reason I do remember them is what I heard in here yesterday. I had so many hogs to cut open I can't remember all these things." Republicans and Populists worked together in order to defeat Democrats. Henry Terry of Rockingham echoed these sentiments under cross-examination. During the hearings, the counsel for defense tried in vain to trap witnesses into admitting that cooperation confused them and they did not know who was running for office, or that the Populist Party managers tricked them into voting for Martin. Henry Terry would have none of this. In direct response to a question on confusion that may have resulted from voting a cooperation ticket, Terry stated, "I was going to vote for him (Martin) because the Third party and the Republican party had united themselves together to run him." Elijah Leak argued that he believed in the principles of both the Republican and Populist parties and that it would hold the side together.[13]

Not all voters in the Sixth Congressional District had a clear sense of cooperation politics; rather, some voters did seem confused over whom they were voting for and why. This was the result, in part, of illiteracy on the part of many voters and the new phenomenon of cooperation politics. The state leadership of the Populist and Republican parties themselves fumbled through cooperation politics. It is hardly surprising, therefore, that Populist the rank-and-file members had trouble understanding the complexity of the cooperation or cooperation movement. The Sixth District was no different in this regard. For example, Dock Covington, a thirty-nine-year-old farmer, stated, "I am a Republican and a Third Party man; it is all about the same I reckon; I don't know."[14]

The relationship between African Americans and the Populist Party is complex. Populist attitudes toward African Americans in North Carolina varied from place to place and over time. In the Sixth Congressional District, one county, Richmond, had a majority black population. With cooperation in 1894, Populists sought African American votes. From the contested election testimony, it seems as though Populists were partly successful, the mere fact that African Americans would vote for a Populist shows three things. First, African Americans were a sophisticated electorate, and they understood, at least to the same degree as poor whites, that cooperation made political sense to defeat the machine and ring-rule of the Democrats. Second, African Americans could differentiate between Democrats and Populists. Third, African Americans realized that they were a powerful voting block in the 1894 election, and they used their votes strategically. Many African Americans remained Republican but voted for the Populist, Martin. For example, Lemuel Simmons of Rockingham Township voted for Martin, but stated that he was not a Populist and that "no negro is a Populist or Democrat, either. I am a right smart colored." Other African Americans, however, embraced cooperation fully. H. W. Pope, an African American schoolteacher from Maxton, Robeson County, voted for Martin and did so voluntarily, explaining under oath that the sentiment among Republicans in his community was to support Martin and to endorse cooperation. Elias M. Thompson, a forty-six-year-old African American preacher and farmer of Black Swamp in Robeson County, also voted for Martin, and he stated that within his community all African Americans favored cooperation with Populists. Throughout the testimony in the Sixth District, brief testimony from African Americans indicates strong support for Martin.[15]

The evidence in *Cyrus Thompson vs. John G. Shaw* does not describe in as great detail as the evidence in the Sixth Congressional District case why voters became Populists, or why they voted the Populist ticket, in part because the counsel for the contestee did not ask such questions in cross-examination. The main reason, it would seem, for such an approach was the presence of another candidate, Oscar J. Spears. As a result the counsel for the contestee spent most of his time attempting to prove that most voters preferred Spears to Thompson.

Nowhere is this strategy more clear than in the testimony from African American voters. The overwhelming majority of African American witnesses from the Third District voted for Spears. However, not all blacks voted the Republican ticket. Evander Smith and William Smith testified that they voted for Thompson. L. L. Hoyt, a forty-six-year-old engrossing clerk in the North Carolina senate (a position he gained after the 1894 election) who distributed tickets at the election at the Jacksonville precinct in Onslow County, testified that African American voters asked "for a straight ticket; some for a Third Party ticket, and Thompson for Congress; that was known as the straight ticket." The counsel for the contestee seemed surprised at this testimony, and inquired if, indeed, such voting was unusual for African Americans. Hoyt answered that it was unusual for African Americans to switch parties; but, Hoyt noted, sometimes blacks did switch their voting. Hoyt offered an explanation for this change, arguing that he did not consider Spears to be the straight Republican candidate for Congress in the Third Congressional District. Hoyt explained, "He (Spears) was asked to withdraw in favor of Thompson by the district Congressional Committee, and their action was endorsed by the state executive committee." Spears ran as a candidate, Hoyt believed, because the Republican congressional convention nominated him a week before the Republican state convention and the Populist state convention adopted the cooperation movement. According to Hoyt, "If it had not been held prior to that, the Republican Party in the Third District would not have put out any ticket; therefore we Republicans supported Thompson for Congress." Hoyt concluded that on the day of the election, many African American voters demanded Thompson tickets and voted for Thompson.[16]

Whatever the reasons for the continued candidacy of Spears, it is clear that a Republican candidate in the Third District muddied the electoral waters. African Americans in the Third Congressional District, with some notable exceptions, did not embrace Thompson's candidacy. Several factors seem at work. First, a Republican candidate stayed in the campaign in the Third District. Historically, since the Civil War in North Carolina, African Americans had supported the Republicans; and in the eastern section of North Carolina that encompassed the Third Congressional district, African Americans remained loyal to the Republicans. This was certainly the case in 1894. Although the state executive committee of the Republican Party advised voters to switch their vote and line up behind Thompson, the presence of a Republican candidate either confused Republican voters, or many found it impossible to abandon their candidate for a Populist. Second, Populists, it seems, did not make as strong an effort to garner the black vote as they did in the Sixth Congressional District. This was due, in part, to the presence of a Republican candidate, and because Thompson, before joining the Populists, was a prominent Democratic politician and member of the state legislature in the 1880s. Third, Populist doctrine and economic policy did not offer, it seems, enough of an incentive for African Americans to leave the party of Lincoln. Finally, the politics of local cooperation for county and state representatives enabled African Americans to continue to vote for GOP candidates at the local and state level, and no doubt many black voters decided not to switch their party at the congressional elections.[17]

The vast majority of the Populist and cooperationist testimony in the Sixth and Third Congressional Districts does not specifically concern issues as to why an individual became a Populist or would vote for the cooperation ticket. Rather, the testimony gives a unique insight into the political culture of the Populist Party and the Election Day practices at the local polling booth. From the testimony of scores of rank-and-file Populists, it is clear that their commitment to the new party was total. Many Populists volunteered their entire day to aid the People's Party in its quest for honest elections. It is noticeable that in the face of fraud, intimidation, and in some cases violence, the Populist activists remained at the polls to record the names of voters and the practices of the election officials.

The testimony in the Sixth Congressional District focused on the rural counties of Anson, Richmond, and Robeson, where Martin and Russell attempted to prove that Democrats had stolen the election and that Martin must take his rightful place as the U.S. representative for the Sixth District. The Populist Party strength was in the rural districts, and it made sense for the counsel to focus on these areas. In addition, Richmond and Robeson counties had a reputation for fraudulent elections, particularly against African Americans. This time, however, Populists could challenge these illegal election practices. As a result, the testimony of the Populists and Republicans gives a wonderful insight into local politics in rural areas.

In the Sixth District party activism is clear. For example, at Stewartsville Township, Richmond County, John McKinnon, a fifty-six-year-old farmer, kept the poll books for the Populist Party. The book was a simple common blank book, ruled, with no index to it. For the entire Election Day, McKinnon sat at a table outside the voting booth and distributed tickets to Populist voters and recorded the name of each voter in the poll book. McKinnon noted in his book the name of challenged voters and the reason given by the Democratic registrar for the challenges. McKinnon testified that the basis of most challenges revolved around people being "too old, some were too young, and some were not registered right. In a few cases they said they had too many wives to vote, and a great many foolish things; I do not remember them all. The most of them stated they had no hearing whatever; that they were told to get out of the door." McKinnon also testified that of the 380 tickets distributed by Populists on that day only 140 voted. Thus, 240 voters faced a challenge and subsequent rejection. McKinnon had a formula for keeping the book: "If he (Patterson) gave him (the voter) a full Populist ticket we entered the letter S opposite his name, which stood for straight; if it was a county ticket, we entered the letter C, if it was a legislative ticket we entered the letter L; if he was rejected and not allowed to vote we entered the letter R." McKinnon and his Populist companions' belief in the cause of Populism and the hypocrisy of Democrats sustained their campaign work. Like many other Populists in Richmond County, McKinnon had deserted the Democratic Party.[18]

In Blue Springs Township, Robeson County, Populists and Republicans refused to vote for Charles H. Martin because they feared that their vote would end up in the Democratic column. Rather than greatly add to the number of Democratic votes and thus, perhaps, throw the election to Lockhart, cooperationists determined to stay away from the polls. Thomas B. Russell, a Populist of Blue Springs Township and brother of Daniel L. Russell, the leading attorney for Charles H. Martin, stated that reports had circulated before the election that Democrats "were to carry up a majority, all the way up from 250 to 500. Believing that they couldn't poll such a vote, we refused to vote." T. B. Russell estimated that there were about 150 Democrats in his township and about 200 cooperationist voters, including African Americans. The number of Populists was unclear to him, but he estimated from Duncan McBryde's Populist club book about 42. T. B. Russell was happy that Democrats experienced defeat at the state elections of 1894 "and said so a thousand times." McBryde was at the Blue Springs polls from sunup to sunset, but he too did not try to vote. He also heard the report that Democrats intended to carry the township by 500 majority, and "not believing there was that many Democratic voters in the township, I came to the conclusion that their purpose was to count all of the votes for the Democratic Party; therefore, I didn't think it was worth while to vote." McBryde kept a list of all Democrats who voted there that day and witnessed several Democrats pass through the voting place more than once. Robeson County's reputation as a place of fraudulent elections was well known throughout North Carolina. For example, the *Progressive Farmer* noted, "The most damnable and outrageous frauds ever perpetuated against the rights and liberties of a free people were perpetuated by the Democratic machine of Robeson County in the late election. All honest men blush at the shameful, dishonest methods resorted to." Despite this, Populists built a strong cadre of party workers to defeat the Bourbon Democrats ring-rule.[19]

The majority of the testimony in the *Thompson vs. Shaw* election case concerns voting at the Cross Creek Township. In the official returns for Cross Creek, Shaw received 1,120 votes; Spears received 174 votes; and Thompson garnered just 15 votes. Therefore, Thomas Sutton, Thompson's counsel, attempted to show that the Republican and Populist vote was heavier at Cross Creek and that Democrats had expanded Shaw's vote in order to steal the election. In the 1892 congressional election the Democratic candidate had received 826 votes at the official count, and the Republican, 417 votes. At Cross Creek the Populists had a strong local organization. Mr. J. K. Kinlaw was the poll book holder for the Populists at Cross Creek. According to Kinlaw, he saw 400 tickets distributed to Republican voters and 75 to 100 tickets distributed to the Populist voters. The Democrats disliked Kinlaw, due to his deep commitment to the Populist Party, and the counsel for the contestee attempted under cross-examination to discredit both Kinlaw and the Populist Party. Indeed, the counsel went to such lengths to do this that Kinlaw's testimony takes up over ten pages in the printed testimony. Kinlaw was undoubtedly a key witness in the case. To begin with, the counsel for the contestee tried to prove that Kinlaw was drunk on the day of election, and to make matters worse the counsel charged that Kinlaw had been drinking with an African American man named Alex Ray, a charge Kinlaw denied. Next, the counsel for the contestee focused on Kinlaw's ties with the Farmers' Alliance. To the counsel, the Farmers' Alliance and the Populists were one and the same. Kinlaw, however, saw things quite differently. Just because someone belonged to the Farmers' Alliance, it did not mean, Kinlaw argued, that they belonged to the People's Party. The counsel for the contestee attempted to spin a conspiratorial web around the Populist witnesses. The counsel for the contestee implied that it was strange that Kinlaw, Andrew J. Deal (Populist poll holder at Cross Creek Township), Thomas McLean (chairman of the Populist Party executive committee of Cumberland), and Thompson were all prominent members of the Farmers' Alliance, a secret organization, as well as members of the Populist Party. Perhaps the Populist Party was a secret organization also? Perhaps only certain leaders of the Populist Party could meet at Kinlaw's house?[20]

Clearly, such questions aimed to discredit Kinlaw and the People's Party of Cumberland County. What the testimony also showed was the sophisticated organization of the Populists in Cumberland. Kinlaw's house hosted regular "open meetings," where leaders discussed election strategy and engaged in discussion of Populist doctrine. Thomas McLean, who attended these open meetings, made it clear that Alliance meetings did not occur on the same day as Populist meetings. The meetings remained open to one and all, according to Kinlaw, perhaps in an endeavor to garner new supporters. The only time guards were present was when the Alliance had meetings in the same building. Clearly, members of the Alliance joined the Populists, but the Populists and the Alliance remained distinct organizations with distinct social practices and policies.[21]

J. K. Kinlaw refused to acknowledge that the Populists and the Alliance were one and the same. He denied that Populists used signs, grips, or passwords.

Kinlaw did admit that the usual place for political meetings in Cross Creek Township was the market house in the town hall, and that Democrats and Republicans used these rooms regularly. Kinlaw also testified that he put in a great deal of work looking for witnesses for Thompson in this case and did not expect to receive any payment for such services. However, one must temper a judgment of what may at first seem a deep devotion to the cause of justice, the Populist Party, and the reform movement with Kinlaw's testimony: "I expected the sheriff to take care of me. When I worked for the sheriff he always pays for it." Although Kinlaw did want to see justice carried out, he did hope to gain from such work. This also indicates that the Populists looked after their own, in the same way Democrats and Republicans looked after their voters and supporters through patronage and political factors. The sheriff was a Populist, and it made perfect sense to those Populists in Cumberland County that Populists would benefit from such a state of affairs. Patronage at the local level was the political glue that held the Populist Party together. At a time of economic dislocation, patronage took on an even greater significance for the party faithful.[22]

Thomas H. McLean played a prominent role in Populist Party organization at the local level. As chairman of Cumberland's Populist executive committee, McLean played a pivotal role as a conduit between the Populist state leadership and the rank-and-file members of Cumberland County. McLean realized the importance of his work and it seems he carried out his duties very well. He knew the Populist state leader, Marion Butler, and he had guided Populist orator Mrs. Mary Lease around Fayetteville during the election campaign of 1892, when she and Populist presidential candidate James B. Weaver campaigned in North Carolina before large audiences. The counsel for the contestee, aware of McLean's hard and successful labors for the Populist Party, sought to discredit McLean. The testimony here makes fascinating reading and is worth quoting in full:

"Q. How about Mrs. Lease?" . . . "A. My arm feels good ever since she had a hold of it." "Q. So then, you were escorting Mrs. Lease around when she visited this county, were you?" "A. I escorted her from the hotel to the stand where she spoke, with Gen. Jas. B. Weaver." "Q. When was Mrs. Lease in this county?" "A. I forget the exact date. It was some time shortly before the election of 1892." "Q. Was she a stump orator of the time?" "A. She made an able speech here; that is all I know." "Q. You say your arm feels good since Mrs. Lease had hold of it. Will you please describe the peculiar sensation or thrilling feeling which that arm has enjoyed ever since that time?" "A. True Democracy—Equal rights to all; special privileges to none." "Q. Please explain what sensation true Democracy—Equal rights to all and special privilege to none—produces in your arm." "A. As my arm is near my heart, I felt when that came to pass it would be the deathblow to the fraudulent

Democratic machine." "Q. Then do you mean to say that Mrs. Lease's hold of your arm produced that pleasing sensation?" "A. I do." "Q. Which arm did Mrs. Lease have hold of?" "A. The one next to my heart—the left." "Q. So Mrs. Lease affected your heart considerably, the effects of which has not yet passed away?" "A. The political principles that she advocated will never pass away." "Q. You have not answered the question. Please answer it." "A. I consider the question answered, as the feelings were entirely political." "Q. Are you a bachelor or a married man?" "A. I am a bachelor."²³

It is clear from this exchange that the counsel for the contestee hoped to discredit Thomas McLean, a prominent local Populist leader, and, by inference, discredit the Populist Party as a whole. Playing on issues of gender and sex, the counsel attempted to show that Populism was like a young man who had recklessly lost his head in love, in the same way McLean had lost his heart to Mrs. Mary Lease. McLean's exchange with the counsel for the contestee serves as a telling metaphor for the Democratic attitude toward Populism. Once Populists grew up or settled down they would see the error of their ways and, like all mature adults, rejoin the Democratic Party. McLean's response to such questions tells us much about Populist doctrine and rhetoric. Mrs. Lease had such an impact on McLean, perhaps because she articulated all the hopes and dreams of the Populist reform movement.

From the testimony of the rank-and-file Populists in both the Sixth and Third Districts, the party activists were determined to prevent Democrats from engaging in fraudulent election-day activities. Rather, Populists saw themselves as the heirs to the Jeffersonian and Jacksonian tradition of a representative republican government. In the mind of the People's Party the Democratic Party no longer represented the people and, in fact, seemed intent on thwarting their will. This explains in large measure the unswerving commitment of the rank-and-file Populists on Election Day.

Apart from the contested election cases material, little evidence exists concerning the activities of the rank-and-file Populists in the Sixth and Third Congressional Districts. But what evidence remains suggests a high degree of Populist organization at the local level and the determination of grassroots activists to play a pro-active role in persuading wavering voters to switch to the People's Party through the use of People's Party clubs and newspapers. In the Sixth District, in 1894, Populists J. Z. Green and J. P. Sossaman established the *Charlotte People's Paper* as a weekly. Although the *People's Paper* began its lengthy run in 1894, no copies exist for that year. However, the paper was a vocal leader in local politics and the organization of the People's Party, not only in Mecklenburg County, but in the Sixth Congressional District as a whole. J. Z. Green wrote letters to Marion Butler detailing the political culture of the

Sixth District, the mood of the rank-and-file Populists, as well as the actions of the Democratic Party. Green and Sossaman also busied themselves in setting up local newspapers. For example, in 1895 they founded the *Wadesboro Plow Boy* in Anson County. This Populist Party newspaper offered local Populists both information and news on the Populist Party in the locale, state, and nation and stinging editorials against the Democratic Party. Unlike the Democratic press, the *Plow Boy* paid close attention to the *Martin vs. Lockhart* contested election case, clearly viewing it as a fight between good and evil. Martin was the knight in shining armor in a battle against the dragon of plutocracy, monopoly, and hegemony in the shape of the Democrats. J. Z. Green and J. P. Sossaman echoed the testimony of the rank-and-file members of the Populist Party in the district, who charged Democrats with stealing the election and policies that injured the toiling masses. As early as February 1895, the paper commented that Martin's case "grows brighter and brighter, and we hope that Mr. Martin will be accorded an impartial hearing in the congress and we predict that the seat in the 54th congress will be filled with a man that will fight for the emancipation of the industrial masses and not by a man who votes with the party that demonstrates by their acts, that rotten eggs, chemical mixtures and bonds are only necessary to save this once proud republic of ours."[24]

The *Progressive Farmer* noted that during the election campaign the Democratic papers ridiculed Charles Martin's candidacy. In addition, James A. Lockhart, the paper alleged, made a campaign of ridicule and personal abuse against Martin. In the face of such abuse, Martin "bore it all patiently without resenting the attacks, but confined himself strictly to the vital issues that were effecting humanity."[25]

In the Third Congressional District contested election case, Cyrus Thompson and his attorney, Thomas H. Sutton, were unsuccessful in their endeavor to prove that Democrats had stolen the election. Warren Miller of West Virginia, from the Committee on Elections, Number 2, issued a brief two-page report to the U.S. Congress on May 6, 1896, explaining the judgment of the committee. Although the committee noted some irregularities, the report stated that this would only have cut the contestee's majority down to 877 votes (from 994). Therefore, the committee concluded, Thompson was not entitled to the take the seat in U.S. House of Representatives, and John G. Shaw was the duly elected U.S. congressman from the Third Congressional District.[26]

At first glance the report no doubt dismayed Populists in the Third Congressional District and delighted the Democrats. Cyrus Thompson and his attorney, Thomas Sutton, had failed to unseat Shaw, and this was obviously disheartening to them. However, beyond the initial dismay of losing the contested election, it was obvious to the Populists that the presence of independent Republican candidate Spears had badly hindered the Populist Party's chances in the Third District. Spears had refused to withdraw from the field, despite the fact that both the Republican executive committee for the Third Congressional District and the Republican state executive committee had ordered him to withdraw. Next time around, Populists and Republicans would not make the same mistake. Cyrus Thompson's loss in the Third District made him a Populist martyr to the machine rule of the Democratic Party, and in just six months he swept into the office of secretary of state for North Carolina on the back of a huge majority.

In the Sixth Congressional District contested election case, the Rev. Charles H. Martin succeeded in proving that Democrats had stolen the election. Jesse Strode of the House Committee on Elections, Number 2, issued a lengthy report to the U.S. Congress on May 26, 1896. Representative Strode gave a forty-page summary of the testimony in the case and concluded that the majority of the committee instructed that 290 votes be added to Charles H. Martin's total. At the same time, the committee deducted 73 votes from Martin's total. This left Martin with a net gain of 219 votes and a total vote of 13,771. The committee then proceeded to deduct 555 votes from James A. Lockhart. This left Lockhart's vote at 13,441 votes and gave Martin a majority of 330 votes, and he took his place as the U.S. representative for the Sixth Congressional District of North Carolina.[27]

The judgment of the House Committee on Elections overjoyed both Populists and Republicans in the Sixth Congressional District. The contested election was a draining experience and no doubt tried the patience of the rank-and-file Populists. Many Populists put their reputations on the line in the case by testifying in open court at the small county courthouses of rural North Carolina, and many faced the prospect of social ostracism for their public display of Populism and their anti-Democratic attitudes. The result vindicated the Populist Party and its organization. In addition, the result vindicated the policy of cooperation at the congressional level. By mid-June 1896, the policy of cooperation between Republicans and Populists in the November elections was not clear. A victory as complete as the one gained in the Sixth District no doubt added fuel to the fire of those Populists and Republicans advocating cooperation on the congressional, state, and local level. In addition, Republican judge Daniel L. Russell, as the leading attorney for the contestant, played a key role in securing the success of Populist Charles H. Martin. One could argue that the contested election case of the Sixth District offered a trial run for the cooperation campaign of 1896. Russell, no doubt, made many Populist friends in the Sixth Congressional District by his excellent counsel in the case and hoped they would support his gubernatorial candidacy in 1896, as a Republican who could work with the Populist Party for each party's mutual benefit and to defeat the Democratic Party.

The Democrats were distraught over the result of the contested election result in the Sixth Congressional District. The *Maxton Scottish Chief* newspaper alleged that the decision was politically motivated and all Democrats must unite with one another to repudiate the judgment. The election reinforced the notion that cooperation was vital for electoral success. Without electoral success neither Populists nor Republicans could hope to enact reform at the local, state, and congressional level. The rank-and-file members of the Populist Party in the Sixth Congressional District clearly understood this and were not merely dupes who followed the will of the party leadership. Rather, they played an active role in constructing party policy and election strategy.[28]

There are a great many similarities in the testimony of rank-and-file members of the Populist Party in both the Third and Sixth Congressional Districts' contested election cases. First, in each district the Populist Party had a strong and coherent party organization from the local leaders down to the rank-and-file members and voters. Second, many rank-and-file members gave up an entire day of work to the party in order to ensure a fair and just election. Although they may have failed in many precincts and townships due to the fraudulent activities of Democrats, the rank-and-file membership obviously believed passionately in the cause of the Populist Party. They not only helped out at the election, instructed illiterate voters how to cast their ballots, and meticulously record such votes, but also risked social ostracism, intimidation, and even violence for their actions and political beliefs, on both the day of the election and in the witness box. Politics mattered to these voters, and they would loiter around the polling booths all day long in an atmosphere of excitement and tension, waiting for the result. Local politics mattered.

Third, Populists gave varied reasons why they joined the People's Party. What this indicates, at the local level, is that the rank-and-file members of the Populist Party do not easily fit into one historiographical category or the other, as some historians would like to think. Political choices are far more complex than that, with a variety of reasons playing on the minds of rank-and-file voters. For some, the Farmers' Alliance provided the entry into the Populist Party. For others, the machine and ring-rule of the local and state Democratic Party was what moved them to join the party. Sick and tired of unelected officials running local government, many voters left the Democrats in disgust. The Populists offered a better alternative to these disgusted voters. For others, the monetary policy of Democratic president Grover Cleveland and U.S. senator Matt Ransom led them to exit the Democratic Party. Others joined the Populists to enact a new county government and election law in the state. Others found the Populist banner of "equal rights to all and special privileges to none" compelling. In a time of economic dislocation and an unresponsive political monopoly on the part of the Bourbon Democrats, the Populists offered a new and exciting alternative. Not all Populists came from the Democrats. For over twenty years the GOP had failed to dislodge the Bourbon Democrats from power. For some Republicans it seemed time to leave the GOP and join a new, vibrant, and politically engaging party. Some African Americans switched to the Populist Party in 1894, perhaps to ensure a Democratic electoral loss, or perhaps because they supported Populist policies or the policy of cooperation.

What seems clear from the contested election testimony in both the Sixth and Third Districts is that Populism was as much a political and social movement as it was an economic reform movement. Throughout the testimony of the rank-and-file Populists in both districts, political motivations, such as fair elections and home rule, seem prevalent in the minds of many for joining the Populists. The People's Party in North Carolina was far more than the revolt of economically disadvantaged farmers in a severe economic downturn. The Populist movement in the Old North State was also a political manifestation of a rebellion of the lower classes against the disdainful and dismissive Bourbon Democrats. For the vast majority, the machine and ring-rule of the local and state Democratic Party angered the voters. Time and again, the rank-and-file members expressed the notion that the Democratic Party eschewed the values of traditional republicanism and Jacksonian democracy. Thus, while some joined the Populists to enact a new county government and election law in the state and others found the Populist banner of "equal rights to all and special privileges to none" compelling, all of these voters shared a strong respect for traditional republican governmental values and participatory democracy.

Chapter Five

"EVER TRUE TO THE PEOPLE'S CAUSE, TRUE TO COUNTRY, TRUE TO HOME"

The Cooperationist Legislature of 1895

The Populists, in cooperation with the GOP, achieved a resounding electoral success in 1894. As the new state legislature convened the *Wadesboro Plow Boy* stated, "No purer, no nobler, no more patriotic body of men ever met in Raleigh than the one now assembled there." It exclaimed to its readership, "There we will see in all their majesty the men who stood the brunt of battle in the last campaign, standing like heroes before the abuse and insults of their enemies, ever true to the people's cause, true to country, true to home." The question facing the Populists in 1895 was how to turn their mass movement into a party of government. Further, how would the policy of cooperation with Republicans play out in the state legislature? Such a three-way split in the legislature was a new phenomenon to North Carolina voters and politicians. How the Populists handled the first three months of cooperative government could affect the longevity of the People's Party at the state level and the success of the reform movement. Populist state leader Marion Butler also hoped that a successful state legislative session might also speed up what he saw as the inevitable reconfiguring of political parties in the South. Other southern states, Butler hoped, would follow the lead of North Carolina and fuel the disintegration of the Democrats in the South.[1]

Determining the Populist legislators' characteristics is important for the study of the nature of the party. The Populist legislators who gathered in the state capitol reflected the cross section of the Populist rank-and-file members and Populist voters. Of the twenty-seven Populists in the House who received short entries in the *Biographical Sketches of the Members of the General Assembly of North Carolina*, twenty-three representatives, or 85 percent, were farmers. Two were teachers, and one was a blacksmith and watchmaker. Seven Populists had seen service in the Civil War. All the Populists were ex-Democrats, and the vast majority had joined the People's Party in 1892. The age range for Populists in the lower house was from twenty-nine to sixty-seven years of age, with an average age of forty-six. Although none of the legislators had previously sat in the assembly, several members had past experience in local or county government. For example, nine representatives were former county commissioners, justices of the peace, or constables. One Populist, L. R. Whitener, was the ex-mayor of the town of Hickory.[2]

If one examines carefully the background of all the twenty-four Populists in the North Carolina senate identified in the *Biographical Sketches of the General Assembly of North Carolina*, 1895, it appears that unlike in the lower house, Populists in the senate came from a slightly higher social class. Only ten Populists were farmers (or 41 percent), while the handbook termed an additional five Populists "prominent farmers." This gave 63 percent of Populist state senators as farmers. Three Populists in the senate were ministers of the gospel. In addition, the remaining Populists listed the following as their profession or occupation: engineer, lawyer, school superintendent, newspaperman, and manufacturer. Clearly, the Populist senators' occupations were more varied and of a slightly higher social status than those in the lower house. This class status is also evident in the education of the state senators. Six senators had received a college education at either the University of North Carolina at Chapel Hill, Wake Forest College, Trinity College, or, in the case of one Populist, at the University of Pennsylvania. The age span of the senators almost mirrored that for the lower house. The senators' ages ranged from twenty-eight to sixty-three, with the average age of a Populist senator at forty-six. The Populist senators also had a smattering of confederate veterans, with nine serving in the Civil War.[3]

Populist senators also had far greater legislative experience than their colleagues in the lower house. Seven senators had represented their counties as Democrats. The senate also housed several noteworthy Populists. For example, William R. Lindsey represented the Twentieth District. James Mewboorne, a prominent Populist and the current president of the North Carolina State Alliance, represented the Eighth District. John E. Fowler was the only lawyer in the Populist ranks, a close associate of Marion Butler, and, at twenty-eight, the youngest Populist in the North Carolina legislature. J. Y. Hamrick was another prominent Populist who had served a term as an Alliance-Democrat in the 1891 state house of representatives. Other notable Populists included J. J. Long, Theo White, H. E. McCaskey, A. H. Paddison, and A. J. Dalby. Although a great many Populists in the house and senate had little legislative experience, each one brought with them a zest for reform, a determination to improve the lot of their constituents, and a desire to break the machine rule of the Democrats. Thus, if one takes all the Populist legislators as a whole, the vast majority, or 65 percent, were small farmers.[4]

If one compares the Populist legislators with their Republican counterparts, it seems clear that Populists were less experienced than the GOP legislators. The professions of the Republican senators suggest that they were of a higher social class than their Populist counterparts. There were more lawyers, teachers, merchants, and businessmen among Republican legislators than among the Populist legislators. Thus, compared to the GOP, the Populist Party representatives were of a lower social class. The Republicans also produced the five African American state legislators. James H. Young, a prominent African American from Wake County, was the proprietor of the *Raleigh Gazette* and a well-known advocate of cooperation with Populists. W. H. Crew, an African American representative from Granville County, was an experienced state legislator, having represented his county in the lower house on five previous occasions. He also had a wide range of experience in county affairs, serving as deputy sheriff, a justice of the peace, and a member of the Oxford school committee. Samuel J. H. Mays, just twenty-four-years old, also represented Granville County. Although he had little political experience, he was a schoolteacher and a "known orator." The fourth African American representative, Calvin L. Smith of Caswell County, did not have an entry in the *Biographical Sketch* book. Moses M. Peace, the fifth African American representative in the lower house, represented Vance County. Peace was raised on a farm, but managed to attend Shaw University in Raleigh for two years. After returning to Henderson, he opened a restaurant and kept a grocery business. In 1892, at the age of thirty-one, he was elected chairman of the Vance County Republican committee and gained election as county coroner in the same year. Although Peace had less governmental experience than Crew and Young, as a young, well-educated African American, his presence in the general assembly was no doubt a welcome sign for the African American community of North Carolina.[5]

As the new state legislators gathered in Raleigh in 1895, Democrats for the first time since Reconstruction would not write the state laws. Populists and Republicans determined to pass a wide range of legislation that would end the dominance of Democrats and lead to urgent reforms that benefited farmers and laborers of North Carolina. The agenda of the new legislature reflected the Populist state platform. The Populists demanded a new state election law, the restoration of local county government or home rule, a reduction of the legal rate of interest to 6 percent, and increased expenditures for public education and state institutions. The other major piece of business was the selection of two U.S. senators, which came first.[6]

Marion Butler moved his newspaper to Raleigh and actively played a role in the legislature's deliberations. The majority of the cooperationists' arguments occurred behind closed doors at a joint caucus. As a result there is little direct evidence of the varying ideological and political differences among the Populist legislators and between Populists and Republicans. Butler led the joint caucus, and it appears he played the most significant role in the 1895 state legislature in keeping bolting Populists in place and effecting cooperation with Republicans on legislative matters. It was an open secret that Butler desired to succeed Matt Ransom for the full six-year term to the U.S. Senate, and as the leader of the Populists, Butler could reasonably assume he would gain the position. Butler could offset any potential difficulties in gaining election because of the opportunity for a Republican to serve the two remaining years of Zebulon Vance's position. This prevented any squabbling over office between Republicans and Populists at a time when concerted action was crucial to pass much-needed reform legislation for the respective parties' constituents. Butler easily gained approval from the Populist caucus for the six-year position.[7]

There was competition for the shorter post, however, in the Republican Party. The U.S. senatorship was the prized possession for a Republican leader. Whoever gained election could look forward to enormous political power in the state GOP and in national affairs. With a subtle use of federal patronage, the new senator could cement his selection in 1897, if the elections transpired as Republicans hoped. Butler played a pivotal role in the deliberations of the joint caucus, pushing for a silverite Republican. After a lengthy debate, Republicans selected Jeter Pritchard over Alfred E. Holton. Why Butler favored Pritchard is difficult to ascertain. Perhaps it was because Pritchard had fewer political enemies within the GOP than J. J. Mott and Oliver Dockery, or because Pritchard was from the west and political tradition in North Carolina required that one U.S. senator must come from the eastern part of the state and the other from the western part. In addition, Pritchard was of a younger generation of Republicans.[8] Jeter Pritchard departed for the Senate in Washington, D.C., but Butler remained behind in Raleigh to play a decisive role in the state legislature. Butler reasoned that the Populist Party's long-term success depended on a smooth session and the enactment of all the planks in the 1894 Populist state platform. The political stakes were high, and Butler was determined that through his careful organization of the Populist caucus and successful passage of a series of impressive reforms, the party could go before the voters in 1896 with a strong record in the 1895 session.[9]

Butler not only played a key role in the legislative session at Raleigh, but also desired to expand the reach and scope of his paper, the *Caucasian*. He hoped to make the paper the first Populist daily in the Old North State in the hope, no doubt, of offsetting the influence of the Democratic *News and Observer*. Such an expansion of his paper seemed to fit Butler's goal for reconfiguring state politics. With an increased circulation, Butler hoped to entice more Democrats to leave their party and join the Populists. A Populist newspaper reporting the state legislature's deliberations and including editorials on the significance of the legislation adopted, Butler reasoned, would aid in the expansion of the Populist Party.[10]

Expanding the *Caucasian*, however, proved financially expensive. To offset such costs, Butler looked to wealthy businessmen to fund the expansion of his paper. He also hoped to legitimize the People's Party in the mind of business interests in North Carolina. At this juncture Butler and the powerful business magnate Benjamin Duke, the owner of the Duke Tobacco, became associates. Simply put, Butler needed money for his paper and Duke, a known Republican supporter, hoped he could use his money to influence Populists in the state legislature. Populist rhetoric in the 1894 campaign promised to end the power of the industrialists in the United States, and Duke no doubt hoped that by closely aligning himself with the Populist leader in the state, Populists would spare his business from any reform legislation. From mid-January onwards, installments of the one-thousand-dollar Duke investment in the newspaper stock of the *Caucasian* went to the North Carolina state treasurer, Populist William H. Worth, who was also the bookkeeper for the Caucasian Publishing Company. Both sides kept this investment secret from the general public. Duke did not want his Republican friends to find out that he supported the leading Populist paper, and Butler and his close group of leading Populists would no do doubt find it difficult to explain to rank-and-file Populists why the paper was supported by the kind of business interests the Populist Party opposed in its platform and campaign. Butler realized the difficulty of his position, but he hoped that the aid from Duke would provide the important first step in expanding the Populist influence in the state and smashing the Democrats. Long-term gains, Butler reasoned, offset short-term contradictions.[11]

From January 9 to March 13, the assembly passed a series of laws that addressed many of the concerns of the Populist state platform. The sympathetic legislature restored the Alliance charter and even liberalized its provisions. To help farmers fight against exploitation, the legislature tackled head-on the issue of high credit and interest rates. Populist state senator John Fowler introduced a bill to reduce the legal rate of interest to 6 percent. Despite the opposition of Democrats and their stalling tactics, it eventually passed into law. The law was not merely symbolic. Farmers who needed credit in North Carolina faced high interest rates on loans. With a new 6 percent interest rate, Populists prevented unscrupulous moneylenders from exploiting small to middling farmers all over the state. At a time of economic dislocation, small farmers and laborers, the grassroots base of the Populist Party, urgently needed such a law. In marked contrast to Democrats, the cooperationists raised taxes on railroads and business. The legislature extended the powers of the Railroad Commission. S. Otho Wilson, a leading Populist, gained one of the railroad commissioners' spots. This appointment no doubt stuck in the throats of the Democratic leadership. In addition, the cooperationists reversed the appalling post-Reconstruction Democratic practice of under-spending on public institutions. The legislature increased spending on schools at all levels and on training for teachers with a school tax levied at twenty cents per one hundred dollars of property as well as a sixty-cent poll tax to supplement the public school fund. The cooperationists also allocated twenty-five thousand dollars, which had been refunded to the state from Congress, to the school fund. The legislature also spent more money on charitable and penal institutions.[12]

Appropriations for higher education in North Carolina threatened the unity of purpose between Republicans and Populists and within the Populist Party itself. Several Methodists, Baptists, and Populists wanted to eliminate the funding for the university at Chapel Hill. Many Populists no doubt disliked what they reasoned was the symbol of class privilege the university represented. Many professors at the university worried that the university might close. For example, Edwin Alderman, professor of pedagogy, wrote to Cornelia Spencer, "The *leaders* of all parties are for us. If they can control the rank-and-file, we are safe, if not we are gone." William A. Guthrie, a recent convert to the Populist Party from the GOP, opposed any curtailment in the university's funding, and Butler played a decisive hand in the crisis. Butler, a graduate of Chapel Hill, managed to persuade the state legislature to appropriate the necessary funds to the university, arguing that North Carolina needed more education, not less. One pro-university supporter breathed a huge sigh of relief that Butler had won the day for the university, explaining, "The influence of the University, exerted both directly on the Legislature and indirectly through her alumni who were Populist and Republican leaders, has prevented our State from becoming 'Tillmanized' and suffering the fate of our sister State to the South."[13]

The legislature's most important work was the enactment of a new election law and the restructuring of local and county government. The new election law addressed the Populist and Republicans' principal campaign issue of 1894 and also fulfilled the Populists' pledge to democratize the North Carolina political system and end the ring-rule of Democrats. The legislature threw out the 1877 anti-democracy legislation so that popularly elected local officials were the order of the day as opposed to appointed officials. This action was not a sign of a power-hungry political party. Rather, Populists merely made the political system fairer and more open. The Populists benefited from such actions because they were more representative of the people as opposed to the Democrats who blatantly used fraudulent tactics to remain in power. The outcry from the Democrats, big business, and merchants further underlines the progressive nature of Populists in the 1895 assembly.

In 1877, Democrats had passed an election law that required the election of state officers every four years. Every two years, Tar Heels went to the polls to elect members of the general assembly. The regulation of all elections was under the jurisdiction of boards of justices of the peace in each county. In 1879, the elective functions of the justices of the peace were transferred to county commissioners who were appointed by the legislature and who in turn appointed the justices of the peace. From 1876 until 1895, Democrats controlled the general assembly and, not surprisingly, Democrats chose a majority of Democratic county commissioners, who chose mainly Democratic justices of the peace, who in turn nominated Democratic registrars to oversee local elections. Therefore, there was a complete centralization of the election process and Democrats meticulously controlled the machinery of local government. The onus fell on the elector to prove that his name belonged in the election book. The time allowed to challenge the decision of the registrar was short, and as a result many non-Democrats were prevented from voting. In addition, there was no secret ballot. A voter had to hand his ballot to the judge (a Democrat), who then placed it in the ballot box. It was up to the judge to be honest in casting the vote. The election law was clearly unfair and designed to reinforce Democratic hegemony by making it very difficult for African Americans to vote. For over twenty years the law worked as Democrats envisioned. Even in African American or Republican districts the justices of the peace and election officials were white Democrats. Opposition to this election law was the central tenet of the cooperation movement between Populists and Republicans in the 1894 campaign. Each party hoped to smash the machine and ring-rule of the Democrats once and for all and return North Carolina to fair and honest elections. The Populists, in particular, saw this as the cornerstone of democracy, and they fervently pushed for a new election law. Opening up the electoral system was important because it allowed Populists to break up special interests' control over law making and, therefore, make public policy more responsive to the needs of the people. The Populists saw this as a strong link between reforming the political system and reforming the economic system. It was also a central element in the Populist campaign in 1894 and drew many grassroots activists into working earnestly for the People's Party and forming a cooperative arrangement with Republicans.[14]

Populists and Republicans worked together to repeal the Democratic election law and succeeded in passing their own into law on March 8, 1895. The new law offered a number of important provisions to ensure "honest" elections. The clerk of the superior court had the power to establish, alter, or create places of voting. Crucially, the position was now popularly elected, not appointed by the party that held power in Raleigh. The Populists and Republicans could have abused the system in the same way as Democrats had for the past twenty years, but they chose not to do so. There would also be a voting place for every 350 electors, assuring that the polling places were easily accessible to voters—a very important proviso in a rural state with poor transportation. Populists and Republicans realized that the selection of judges and registrars was vital in guaranteeing an honest election. As a result, the registrars and judges of the election would come from the three main political parties. One Populist, one Republican, and one Democrat would now sit at the polling stations. This is a clear indication of the progressive nature of the Populist-Republican alliance. Unlike Democrats, Republicans and Populists did not abuse their electoral power. They attempted to secure an election law that would guarantee representation to each party on election boards in subsequent elections. The law also allowed the use of ballots of any color. Thus, on Election Day each party would use a different color ballot. This clause aimed to help those electors who were either ignorant of the intricacies of voting or illiterate vote for whom they wanted based on the color of their ballot. Although Populists and Republicans did not bring in a secret ballot and the elector still handed his ballot to the judges for placement in the ballot box, there was a judge from each political party present at each precinct, ensuring that there was less chance for ballots to go missing or ending up the wrong ballot box. The law also allowed for the recasting of any miscast ballots in the election.[15]

In addition, the counting of the votes took place in front of the registrars, the judges, and the candidates from the three parties. This provision aimed to end the Democratic practice of throwing out votes in tight races. To prevent tampering with the votes, the judge of the superior court would seal and keep the ballots in a secure place. North Carolina had never witnessed these careful procedures to ensure fairness at elections. The Populists and Republicans also instigated a series of fines for anyone who intimidated voters or tried to assault them. North Carolina was notorious for heated Election Day activities, with many reports of bad language, threats of violence, rotten-egging, and even violence on some occasions. Although the law could not stop such activities, the possibility of heavy fines, Populists hoped, would deter Democrats from resorting to coercive practices. In addition, the law also provided that anyone who tried to bribe voters faced heavy fines. This was important because at a time of economic dislocation, many party officials and workers used money to influence a voter's decision. Candidates for office also had to fill in itemized records of campaign expenses and their contributions. Failure to do so would lead to expulsion from office. The Populists led the way on reforming the election law and local government in the 1895 legislature because the rank and file of the party as well as the leadership chafed under the practice of the Bourbon Democratic ring-rule. Populists based cooperation with Republicans on the premise that once in office North Carolina would benefit from fair and open elections. The cooperationists had broken one of the pillars of Democratic hegemony in North Carolina. As a testament to their progressive nature, Populists and Republicans did not continue the appointed practice, from which they would benefit in the 1896 elections. There is no doubt that Populists and Republicans wanted to safeguard their parties' interest in subsequent elections. Although there was a pragmatic reason for changing the laws, the result was an increased fairness in the election process.[16]

Coupled with the democratization of the North Carolina election law was the restructuring of local government. Under the Democratic system, the power of local government rested in the hands of justices of the peace, appointed by the Democratic-controlled legislature. The justices selected county commissioners who directed county affairs and levied local taxes. The Populists and Republicans saw nothing good in this law because it reinforced the ring-rule of the Bourbon Democrats. The new law passed in 1895 called for the election of justices at the township level every two years, beginning with the elections in 1896. In addition, voters would also elect three county commissioners. However, Populists and Republicans did not open up local government to complete local control because they feared the repercussions of such laws in majority-black districts. In order to prevent so-called Negro domination in the east, Populists urged the creation of additional commissioners. As a result, the law called for two additional commissioners appointed by the district's superior court judge if five electors petitioned for the additions on the basis that the "business of the county" would be "improperly managed" if such appointments were not made. Each petition had to be supported by two hundred voters, at least one hundred of whom must be freeholders. The two new commissioners could not belong to the party with a majority of the commission. In other words, both Populists and Republicans hoped to prevent all-black county commissioners in majority-black counties.[17]

The reaction to the 1895 state legislature and its new laws followed strict partisan lines. The Democratic press saw nothing good in any of the new laws. The *Wilmington Messenger* was particularly vitriolic in its appraisal of the assembly. It termed Populists and Republicans "rampant demagogues and ignoramuses." It termed the session "sixty days of folly, stupidity, madness, greed for office and extravagance."[18] The reaction of the Democratic press is important because it signifies the ways in which Democrats continually pounded at the cooperationists' weak points and areas of compromise. The issues that the Democratic press focused on in 1895 remained constant throughout the remainder of the decade. They accused the leadership of the Populist Party of corruption, characterizing them as mere office seekers who had no political principles.[19] The main focus of the Democratic press appraisal of the 1895 legislature was on the issue of race. The Democrats focused on the race issue in an attempt to discredit the Populist Party and to appeal to Populist voters to switch back to the Democratic Party, or, in the words of Democrats, the party of white supremacy. The Democrats tried to resurrect the "horrors of Reconstruction," focusing on one event in particular to portray Populists and Republicans as proponents of racial equality. This event became known as the Frederick Douglass Affair.

On February 21, 1895, William H. Crews of Granville County, one of only five African American representatives in the North Carolina state legislature, introduced a resolution to adjourn in honor of the nationally known African American Frederick Douglass, who had died. As if this was not outrageous enough in the minds of the Democratic press and party, what made matters worse was that on February 22, 1895, the legislature had not observed George Washington's birthday in any official capacity. According to Democrats, "a negro had been honored while Washington and Lee had been ignored." In actuality, Crews had not asked

for an entire day of observance, rather that the legislature cut short its deliberations. Regular adjournment occurred at 2:00 p.m. Despite Democratic claims,
the House *had* adjourned in honor of Robert E. Lee's birthday, and an African
American representative, James H. Young of Wake County, had proposed that
adjournment. Such facts mattered little to Democrats, who merely aimed to discredit the 1895 legislature by arguing that Populists and Republicans had opened
the flood gates of social equality between the races. According to Democrats, "If
anybody had suggested that when this great disciple of intermarriage should be
gathered to his fathers the Legislature of North Carolina would pass a resolution
to adjourn in his honor he would have been regarded as an insane or imbecile
person." The actions of Populists and Republicans disgusted the *Maxton Scottish
Chief.* It could not believe that the "mongrel" legislature adjourned for an African
American man who wanted "social equality and intermingling and intermarriage
of whites and blacks of the South, and who himself married a hard-up white
woman, and gave his last dying request that his body be taken to abolition cem-
etery where they bury the whites and blacks side by side." It implored the white
voters of Robeson County, "Shall these endorsers of social equality and intermarriage of the whites and blacks misrepresent us any longer?"[20]

The reaction of the Populist press was crucial here. Democrats were clearly trying to use the race card to split Populists and Republicans before their reform legislation became law. Butler led the Populists' response in the *Caucasian.* He argued
that Democrats merely engaged in fabrication, noting that the House did adjourn
in memory of Robert E. Lee and that James Young, a black representative, introduced the resolution to adjourn in honor of the Confederate hero. In an amazingly frank editorial Butler challenged the voters to ignore the "scarecrow" of race:

> For a quarter of a century the South has had its scarecrow. If Southern peo-
> ple have been wakeful and nervous and anxious for progress, along new lines
> demanded by new conditions, the old leaders of the lost cause have whispered
> in their ears 'Hush go to sleep, the nigger will get you.' If new leaders with
> new ideas and clearer vision have sought to lead their people forward, they
> have been stopped by fake prophets shouting 'nigger! nigger!' If honest men
> have demanded honest elections the answer has been 'nigger.' If intelligent
> men have pleaded for an increase in schools and more education as essential to
> progress of any kind, they have been silenced by the terrible scare-crow of 'nig-
> ger!' But yet when the poor darkey, feeling that his own condition was sadly
> in need of improvement, started to move away, these same scarecrow makers
> passed a law to keep him here. The scare-crow was too valuable loose.[21]

In this editorial, Butler used the controversy of the Frederick Douglass resolution to point to a larger issue facing North Carolina's poor farmers. Instead of

focusing on race, the proponents of reform would seek to improve the conditions of all Tar Heels. The "negro scarecrow" would not distract the Populists. Butler optimistically looked forward to the day when "the future historian will write down among the wild delusions, the temporary insanities that seem at intervals to possess mankind and deprive them of reason. It would be a comedy were it not so nearly a tragedy. But thank God, the farce is nearly ended." This passage seems amazing for its time. Butler looked beyond the privilege of his race and urged Tar Heels to break from the divisive race issue and move toward reforming the ills of society. Such optimism was perhaps unrealistic given the times and the continued vocal opposition of Democrats. But in this editorial, he espoused the long-term goals of the Populists in North Carolina.[22]

The Frederick Douglass Affair was not the only race issue exploited by the Democratic press in 1895. The Abe Middleton Affair was the second incident that could potentially strike an ill chord with the voters. A. R. Middleton, an African American Republican and chairman of the Republican Third Congressional District executive committee in 1894, was the assistant doorkeeper of the lower house—a very minor patronage position, but one that no doubt played well with African American voters. The *News and Observer* saw this appointment as a perfect illustration that Republicans and Populists favored blacks over whites, and to make matters worse, the paper falsely claimed that Middleton had unfairly displaced a disabled Civil War veteran, J. Reitzel of Catawba County. On the last day of the legislative session the Republican speaker, Zebulon Walser, urged the House to remain in session to keep a quorum until the House passed all the outstanding laws. Middleton was the assistant doorkeeper. Democrats R. B. Peebles and W. T. Lee demanded to be let out, but Middleton refused. A struggle developed and eventually the door opened and the Democrats departed. The *News and Observer* had a field day with the story; the headline claimed, "A Burly Negro Forcibly Detains Members of the House of Representatives." Although the facts of the case showed that Middleton was in the right and Democrats had caused the scuffle, the paper realized that such a report could anger the sensibilities of many white voters. For the *News and Observer* Middleton had transgressed the racial code by laying his hands on a white man, and this was symbolic of the Populists and Republicans breaking down the racial hierarchy and returning the state to the horrors of "negro rule."[23]

Despite the attempts by Democrats, the race issue did not catch fire in the way they hoped. Indeed, the race issue came to a close rather quickly after the state legislators departed from the capitol. However, it smoldered beneath the surface for the next three years. Populists remained especially sensitive to the restructuring of the county government system and feared the Democratic response to increased African American office-holding. Many rank-and-file Populists were opposed to African American office-holding, and the state leadership constantly grappled with the issue throughout the 1890s. It is also worth noting that the white Republican leadership and the white rank-and-file Republicans also opposed African American social equality and favored a very limited amount of African American office-holding. Populists exhibited no more racism than the Republican leadership, and certainly a lot less than Democrats. African Americans began to grow more vocal in their demands for more office-holding. As the majority element of the Republican Party, North Carolina's black citizens understandably hoped and demanded an improvement in their social and economic conditions now that the GOP was an equal power broker with Populists in state government. For over twenty years, African Americans had supported the party of Lincoln, but Democrats had always managed to gain power. In 1895 the situation was very different. In the eyes of the state's African Americans, office-holding by African Americans was the important first step toward achieving equality.

The legislators had passed a series of laws that certainly marked the first cooperationist legislature in a different light from its Democratic-controlled pre-decessors. The degree to which the Populist and Republican legislation would impact the lives of Tar Heels and the running of the state was in the future. But this did not prevent Populists from commenting on the work of their first leg-islative session in alliance with the GOP. The Populist reaction to the 1895 state legislature was extremely positive. The *Progressive Farmer*, for example, argued, "As a whole it was the best legislature that has assembled since the war." The paper did admit that the relative equal division between the three parties in the lower house caused some problem, but concluded that on the whole the legisla-ture produced excellent results. The paper praised the new election law, the local government law, and the new legal interest rate of 6 percent.[24]

Marion Butler welcomed the work of the state legislature. In the *Atlanta Constitution*, he wrote that the 1895 state legislature "was the tangible result of a political State revolution. It was the expression of a rebellion on the part of the people against a regime inaugurated and enforced in State and county govern-ment by the Democratic party." Despite the inexperience of the Populist legisla-tors, Butler noted they still passed a new election law, a county government law, a new educational policy, and other laws that would benefit the people of North Carolina. The *Caucasian* praised the work of the state legislature. Butler saw the session as the triumph of the people over the Bourbon Democratic oligarchy. The paper welcomed the new interest-rate law as a necessary relief measure for the average farmer. However, Butler was quick to show that the legislature's work did not meet only with his approval. In an attempt to show that the actions of the assembly pleased the Populist's grassroots constituents, the *Caucasian* printed letters from rank-and-file Populists on the work of the state legislature. According to a Populist from Yatesville, the legislature had "given to the people of North Carolina power at the ballot box to elect their justices of the peace and board of commissioners." He argued that Democrats were guilty of "malicious and slanderous falsehoods" on the Frederick Douglass adjournment. Lacing his letter with republican values, the Populist argued, "This is another piece of patch-work of bourbon demagogy to defeat the people at the next election, but my prayers to God and hearts desire are that North Carolina will continue to be saved." The farmer ended by saying that the People's Party platform was the greatest and would help all people. J. B. Carrol of Raleigh focused on the Frederick Douglass issue, noting that Democrats merely hoped to "prey on the ignorance of the poor, deluded, oppressed whites." But, he warned that a party that oppressed the working people of the United States would dismiss people from work on account of their voting tendencies. Carrol further admonished, "All the Fred Douglass matter dwindles into insignificance when I see the rights of manhood trampled in the dust by the Patricians. Wah! Fred will be the great hobby of 1896. . . . [W]e have greater problems to work than that. We will talk of financial matters, bond issues, the naked and starving millions."[25]

The Populists, in particular, succeeded in passing all their campaign pledges into law. A new election law, a new county government law, a legal rate of interest of 6 percent, increased appropriations for schools and state institutions, a stronger railroad commission, and the liberalization of the Alliance Charter were an impressive set of reforms. In comparison to the do-nothing Bourbon Democrats, the rank and file of the Populist Party could look with pride at their state representatives. In the long run, Populists hoped to become the main political party of the state. Far-reaching reforms, many Populists no doubt reasoned, would come once they were the majority party in the state and in the South. It is important to note that reforming the political system opened the way to economic reform. It was also good politics on the part of the People's Party because it was the one issue that Populists and Republicans had squarely in common, and any coalition wants to tackle those issues first and foremost. In addition, these issues mattered to the rank and file of both parties; and it makes sense, therefore, that Populists focused their attention on reforms in the election law and county government law first. To be too radical, too quickly could spell disaster for a young and fairly inexperienced party. The fact that Populists could even mount a serious election campaign in 1894 speaks to the commitment of the rank and file and the party leadership to the cause of reform. Populists looked to the 1896 state elections as the opportunity to augment their power base and hoped that the 1897 general assembly would offer them the opportunity to attack the trusts and monopolies of the state.

Although the 1895 state legislature was a success in the eyes of the Populist Party, the new party could not rest. Butler and the Populist leaders realized that Democrats would make an all-out assault throughout the remainder of the year and into 1896 to win back Populist voters before the national and state elections of 1896. Butler hoped that the daily *Caucasian*, with its circulation at fifteen thousand, would blunt this counterattack by the embattled Democrats. But his paper was very short of money. Advertising space was difficult to sell due to an economic depression, and the policies of the Populist Party hardly appealed to the business interests in the state, which gladly gave money to the Democratic press. On March 9, 1895, the paper's board of directors decided to suspend the daily edition of the paper at the end of the state legislative session. Thus, on March 13, 1895, the last daily *Caucasian* rolled off the presses. Although the paper promised to return soon, it never did. The disappearance of the daily paper meant Populists would never again have such an effective mouthpiece to espouse Populist political ideology and also to rebuke the constant stream of Democratic misinformation.[26]

The Populist Party in North Carolina also faced another potential problem. Butler, the state leader of the party, was now a United States senator. Although he had played a crucial role in the 1895 legislature, Butler could not be in two places at once. As Butler rose to national prominence, his grip on the Populist Party in the Old North State loosened. As a result, a second tier of leaders in the state would gain more power to control Populist state policy. Butler disliked power sharing, and his constant fear of losing power to a potential political rival would dog the party from late 1895 as other Populists leaders in the state took different political and strategic positions than Butler. Although the rank and file of the People's Party held Butler in very high esteem, he would never control policy and political maneuverings in quite the same way again. Indeed, one can see the beginning of Butler's reorientation to national issues and the beginning of his distance from state issues when he appointed Hal W. Ayer as the managing editor of the consolidated weekly *Caucasian*. Ayer was a former secretary of the North Carolina Agricultural Society, and because Butler would spend much of the next six years in Washington, Ayer, as editor of the largest Populist paper in North Carolina, had a large impact on the state party. Indeed, Ayer became one of the Populist Party's most prominent leaders in North Carolina. Other Tar Heel Populists began to play a more prominent role in state politics. Cyrus Thompson, S. Otho Wilson, William Guthrie, William H. Kitchin, James Mewboorne, and William Worth, as well as several other Populists, played an important role in the life of the Populist Party for the remainder of the decade.

CHAPTER SIX

THE BATTLE WON BUT THE WAR LOST

*Free Silver, Cooperation Blues, and the Unraveling
of the People's Party in 1896*

The success of the cooperation movement and the passage of key reforms in the 1895 state legislature invigorated Populists. To add to the list of legislative achievements, Populists could boast three U.S. representatives and a U.S. senator. Coupled with this, Populists elected scores of local and county officials: sheriffs, constables, registers of deeds, coroners, surveyors, and many other minor positions. With an energetic and ambitious state leader, the People's Party continued its endeavor to become the major party of North Carolina. Marion Butler sought to create a national reform coalition based on the free coinage of silver. But the silver movement was not the brainchild of Butler. Since 1893, if not before, the issue of free silver galvanized many voters in the United States. President Grover Cleveland's adherence to the gold standard in the wake of the economic downturn had not moved the economy out of recession, and, in fact, Cleveland's position had only succeeded in dividing the Democratic Party in the 1894 elections. The repeal of the Sherman Silver Purchase Act infuriated many voters who faced economic ruin and starvation and believed political leaders were in the pockets of the bankers and not responsive to their needs. As a result, a large section of the voters, particularly in the West and South, mired in poverty, turned to silver as the only cure for the economic conditions in America. Although many Americans did not understand the complexity of America's financial system, they believed that the only way to restore prosperity was to increase the money supply through the coinage of silver at the ratio of 16 to 1.[1]

Populists, Republicans, Democrats, and independents, particularly in the South and West, made up the American silver movement. Although there were many silverites in the two old parties, there was no agreement between the proponents of silver on a process to procure the coinage of silver. Some silverites hoped to enact monetary reform within the two main parties. Others decided to follow a more independent approach, and by March 1895 this group joined the National Silver Party, a party formed by the American Bimetallic League.[2]

North Carolina did not escape the heated and passionate debate over the silver issue. The cause of free silver produced deep factionalism within both the old parties in the state. For example, silver divided the Republican Party with notable state cooperationists, Judge Daniel L. Russell, Richmond Pearson, Oliver H. Dockery, and U.S. senator Jeter C. Pritchard (for a time), supporting the free coinage of silver, while other Republicans were less enthusiastic about the free coinage of silver. The Democrats also divided on the issue of silver in 1895. For example, Josephus Daniels, editor of the *Raleigh News and Observer*, forcibly pushed the cause of silver in the columns of his paper. Other Democrats remained staunchly for the gold standard and opposed to the free coinage of silver, a group that included ex-senator Ransom and editor Joseph Caldwell of the *Charlotte Observer*.[3]

The Populists had always supported the free coinage of silver at the ratio of 16 to 1. Not only was silver a central plank of their state platform, the leadership of the party was united on the need for the reform of the financial system in the United States and believed that a necessary component to achieve this was the coinage of silver at the ratio of 16 to 1. Marion Butler was especially attracted to the silver issue. As Butler prepared for the 1896 elections, he saw the growing silver movement as an opportunity to increase the strength of the Populists throughout the country, in the South, and also in North Carolina. As a result the *Caucasian* carried many editorials on the merits of the free coinage of silver as Butler endeavored to educate the voters on the financial issue. Butler hoped to use the silver issue as a rallying point for the Populist Party, but he did not give up on the other reform measures demanded by the People's Party. According to Butler the toiling masses in the United States wanted to restructure the entire financial system in the country, and free silver was merely the way to *begin* this process. Butler saw the silver issue as a symbolic political issue to galvanize the voters of the United States and a matter of practical politics for the People's Party.[4]

Not only did Populists envision the free coinage of silver as part of the solution to the monetary problems facing the common workers and farmers in the United States, they also saw it as good practical politics. Butler argued that Populists must fight for such changes because they were the most important and pressing reforms facing the United States, and just as crucially they "would draw from the old parties the greatest number of voters whose interests are identical, or nearly akin, to those who already compose the People's party." In an earlier letter, Butler argued that a political party had no excuse to live unless it differed radically from the other parties on the most vital questions of governmental policy.[5]

During 1895, various free silver groups in the Democratic Party, Republican Party, and People's Party began to coalesce around the idea of holding "non-partisan" meetings to push for the coinage of silver at the ratio of 16 to 1. In particular the monetary policy of Cleveland and the disastrous midterm elections propelled many Democrats to attend non-partisan meetings without incurring the wrath of the Democratic Party managers. One of the most important silver conventions was held in Memphis in June 1895 and attracted over two thousand delegates, including notable Democrats Ben "Pitchfork" Tillman of South Carolina, former Nebraskan U.S. congressman William Jennings Bryan, and Senator James K. Jones of Arkansas. Marion Butler also attended the convention with Populist representative Alonzo Shuford and Durham lawyer William A. Guthrie. The silver convention failed to settle the question of the nature of the silver movement and the resolutions adopted at the convention were vague and merely pledged that the various silver organizations would cooperate in the future.[6]

On returning to North Carolina, Butler hoped to enact cooperation with all the silver elements in the Old North State. Butler faced an uphill struggle in his task because although many Democrats in the state supported silver, these same Democrats also despised Butler and the Populists for deserting the party of their fathers and throwing the state to Republicans in 1894. In addition, many Democrats saw Butler's tactics on the silver issue as yet another attempt to disrupt the organization of the Democrats. In this Democrats were partly correct as Butler hoped to use the silver issue to transform Populists into the major political party in North Carolina, and they believed that such a move would lead to the disintegration of the Democratic Party, especially if the Democratic leadership and press remained loyal to President Cleveland or a goldbug successor. Although Democrats remained hostile, Butler continued to embark on the difficult task of forming a non-partisan silver coalition in the state. To that end, Butler urged the formation of "Honest Money Clubs" or "Free Silver Clubs" to help the organization of silverites in North Carolina, and he also proposed a statewide silver convention to marshal the forces of silver in readiness for the upcoming 1896 campaign.[7]

Populists in North Carolina varied in their attachment to the silver issue. James B. Lloyd, a close associate of Butler, wrote in the *Caucasian*, "The FINANCE QUESTION is now paramount to every other consideration; and should be made the sole issue." But Lloyd did not think that a new party for the free coinage of silver was necessary because, according to Lloyd, "the People's party has, for three years, fearlessly and ably championed the cause of silver and FINANCIAL REFORM." Other Populists were less happy about approaching Democrats on the silver issue. For example, Harry Hunt of Lawndale wrote to the *Caucasian* that the Democratic moves toward silver in North Carolina were merely an attempt to "offset the People's Party's success at the next election, by wedging in a facsimile board of their own to beguile the faithful." Hunt also argued that Democrats pretended to "hate old Grover" to trick Populists, and he continued, "[Democrats] are in a crooked path—floundering this way and that, endeavoring to strike a lick at random that will meet with Populist approval, or else terribly deceive them. Like a country patent doctor, they give first this medicine, then that, till finding it does no good; they try to vomit the patient to death on a preparation of green gourds."[8]

Throughout the summer of 1895, North Carolina witnessed many silver rallies and picnics as the leadership of the silver forces attempted to convert the Populist faithful and silverite sympathizers to the cause. For example, at Clinton on August 14, 1895, six thousand people attended a silver rally to hear speeches by Senator Butler, William Guthrie, James B. Lloyd, and others on the merits and urgency of the free coinage of silver. Such rallies and picnics with marching bands and huge spreads of food made for an enjoyable day out for the whole family. William Guthrie was particularly busy throughout the summer speaking on the merits of the free coinage of silver in order to save the people of America. On August 1, 1895, he attended a large rally of fifteen hundred people at Rialto in Chatham County and gave a two-hour speech that urged the voters to push for silver. At this rally mothers, wives, daughters, and sweethearts of the men of Chatham put on a wonderful meal for the vast gathering, and "Mr. Sid Henderson caught the popular fancy of the crowd by singing from the stand some old plantation melodies with guitar accomplishment."[9]

Marion Butler pushed forward a plan for a statewide convention of silver supporters, and this received support from notable Democrat Edward C. Smith. In early September, the *Caucasian* issued a call to Tar Heels to attend a non-partisan silver convention in Raleigh on September 25, 1895. But when the convention met, it was clear that Butler had failed to unite the silver forces of North Carolina. According to Hunt, of the 270 delegates who attended, about 240 were Populists. The *Caucasian* noted that just sixty Democrats and only forty Republicans attended, and many of these Democrats and Republicans were not even delegates. The convention was a complete failure for the silver movement and for Butler's hope to combine the silver forces in the Old North State into a non-partisan silver movement. The Democrat attendees refused to support a resolution that would force them to vote only for silver candidates. In reality, Populists had little chance of persuading Democrats to do as Populists wanted. Party loyalty was much stronger than that, and Butler overestimated his power to force Democrats to abandon Cleveland's policies in 1895.[10]

Thus, from the spring of 1895 to the end of the year, the Populist Party embarked on the silver movement. At no time did Butler and the other Populist leaders disavow the Omaha Platform. In addition, the silver movement did not mean the end of cooperation in North Carolina. Instead Butler's plan was to combine the supporters of silver outside of existing party organizations in order to realign politics. Butler also hoped to discredit Democrats on the silver issue and force silverite Democratic supporters to leave their party and join the only true supporters of silver, the Populists. The *Caucasian* portrayed Populists as the only real friends of silver who would fight for the free coinage of silver at the ratio of 16 to 1. Butler hoped that once the Populist press and People's Party speakers had educated the voters on the merits of free silver and monetary reform, the Populist Party would sweep to power in the South and in the nation in the 1896 elections. However, Butler's ambitious plan was full of risks. First, he assumed that the two old parties would never declare for the free coinage of silver and nominate a free silver man for president. Although this assumption was fair to make at the time, evidence in the South seemed to suggest that southern Democrats would support a silverite candidate and a free silver plank. Second, Butler assumed that voters would leave their old party and join another party. Such a belief was fanciful at best, and at worst it flew in the face of political tradition. Deserting a party on one issue ran the risk of social ostracism and personal attack on a voter. In 1892 Butler almost did not leave the Democratic Party, and to expect rank-and-file Democrats to leave their party on the issue of silver alone was rather naive. Third, Butler assumed that he could educate the masses on the silver issue and convince them that monetary reform would benefit all Americans. Here Butler hoped that the farmers of America would align themselves with industrial workers. This was a risky assumption to make.[11]

As the year drew to a close, politicians in particular found it difficult to determine what the new year would offer in cooperation politics and for the political future of the state. The Democratic press advocated some sort of cooperation in the upcoming year between Populists and Democrats. But Populists seemed in no mood to enact a rapprochement with the Democratic Party. For example, the *Wadesboro Plow Boy* noted that even though Democrats hoped to enact cooperation with Populists, the rank and file would not forget Democratic chiding at Populists as "anarchists and fools and rascals." The *Caucasian* took an even more caustic tone in response to rumors of cooperation between Populists and Democrats, and it reminded its readers that the voters had repudiated the Democratic Party in the last elections. It noted, "When the great people of North Carolina smashed the stinking stuffing out of the Democratic party, the remains of that party proved strong enough to concentrate a considerable stench as an aftermath." The paper lambasted the Democratic press for urging fusion between Populists and Democrats on principle. The *Caucasian* jabbed, "The Democratic press has the effrontery to talk about *principle*—talk about it as a thing which Democracy has practiced."[12]

As 1896 began, Butler believed that Populists must follow a new state policy for the upcoming election campaign. The cooperationist policy with the GOP had lost some appeal, especially as it seemed likely that Republicans would nominate a goldbug for president. Butler correctly realized that the national campaign would complicate the political spectrum in the Old North State. He guessed that leading Republicans in the state, especially Senator Pritchard and Representative

Thomas Settle, would find it virtually impossible to oppose the pro-gold position of the national GOP during the national election; and if this was the case, the North Carolina Populist Party would find it increasingly difficult to cooperate with the GOP without facing accusations from the Democrats of selling out its principles on the silver issue for the promise of office. From 1892 on, Populists had built their organization on the premise that they put principle above party gain and office; and, therefore, Butler's position on the silver issue in 1895 had the effect of tying his hands on cooperation with Republicans.[13]

Marion Butler sensed these dilemmas, but, ever the political trickster, he sought to find a middle way. He sought to avoid cooperation with Republicans and pursed a straight out Populist campaign. Indeed, it appears that Butler hoped to run a non-partisan silver ticket in the state that would preserve the Populist reform agenda at the state and national level. He also believed this would be in the long-term interest of the Populists, and thus in typical style he set out to convince his followers of the merits of such a policy through a series of open letters published in various Populist newspapers during the winter of 1895. Butler issued an address to all those "who are opposed to the single gold standard." Lacing his address in traditional republican values, Butler wrote, "Let those in North Carolina who are opposed to the gold combine waste no time in getting together and lining up for the greatest struggle we have ever had for American liberty and prosperity." Butler urged cooperation on principle in the same way that Populists and the GOP cooperated in 1894, but noted, "Co-operation last year was for principles on state issues. The coming fight is a Presidential one, and we must co-operate for principle on National issues."[14]

Butler's policy was fraught with serious misjudgments that would plague Populists throughout the entire year. Butler assumed that Democrats would not declare for silver, and thus his non-partisan plan would draw thousands of silverite Democrats into the Populist Party and so make his party the majority party in the state. Butler also had to keep his plan deliberately vague, especially on state candidates. As a result, he urged Populists to enter into a long waiting game until after the national conventions of the two other parties had declared their positions on the monetary question and nominated their presidential candidates. This meant that Populists were merely reacting to political events rather than shaping them. As a mass reform movement, many grassroots activists in the party did not want to sit around to wait for some backroom dealings between the political leaders. Populists reasoned that the vitality of their party flowed from their forceful and principled fight for reform and the activism of the people.[15]

The reaction of Populists in North Carolina throughout the winter of 1896 to Butler's plan illustrates the dilemmas and tensions at work. From 1892 until 1895, Marion Butler's policies *were* Populist policies, without question. However, after this time many Populists began to question Butler's strategic decisions.

Most critics questioned the ambiguity and vagueness of Butler's approach and did not want to wait around for Democrats and Republicans to set the agenda. The *Caucasian* indirectly admitted that the vagueness of the Populist position was causing concern in the ranks. But in an editorial the paper urged its readers to wait until the party's state executive committee had heard the views of the district and county organizations. Most Populists did support Butler's position on the silver presidential electoral ticket.[16]

Another group of Populists took a different position and argued that Populists must under no circumstance fuse with Democrats; rather, the People's Party should align itself with Republicans on the same basis as 1894. The *Progressive Farmer* contained numerous letters on the subject. For example, P. G. Rowland of Vance County wrote a lengthy letter to the *Progressive Farmer* that totally disagreed with Butler's plans. Rowland argued, "We want to turn every Democratic officer out from township constable to governor. They have deceived us. . . . We believe there is just as much principle in co-operation to save the results of the last election as there were to co-operate in 1894." But Rowland did not end there; rather, he finished his letter with a warning to the Populist voters that lambasted his state leader:

We believe that the last legislature passed just as good laws as would have been passed if we had a Populist majority. Therefore we are in favor of co-operation in 1896 with the Republican party on some fair and honorable basis to be agreed upon at our State convention and not before. We remember Senator Butler's course in trying to capture the Democratic party in 1892. We also remember that but for two or three counties sustained his course in the "Butler conference" although we had been led by him to believe that the State was practically unanimous for his plans. We also remember that he agreed to support the Democratic ticket after their convention in 1892, and we know further, pursing his plan in '92 we lost most of our leaders and at least 25,000 votes. He is now trying to capture both parties, it seems, and our opinion is we will lose everything if we follow his plan, and for ourselves we do not aim to do it, nor do we believe there are a dozen counties in the State that will.[17]

Such vocal sentiment against his plans should have sounded the warning bells for Butler and his policy of delay. However, Butler did not take criticism very well at the best of times, and he decided instead to pursue his own agenda.

The position of Butler provoked a response from Republicans. Senator Pritchard wrote a long letter to the *Caucasian* in which he pleaded for continued cooperation as the only way to defeat Democrats and for the principle of keeping intact local government and the rule of the ballot box. Pritchard praised the rank and file of the Populist Party in lavish terms. He wrote, "I honor the brave men who compose the People's party in North Carolina for their courage and patriotism in separating themselves from the Democratic party. The Republican party owes them a great debt of lasting gratitude for their services to the people of our State, local government and the enactment of an honest election law." Pritchard clearly hoped to fuel the disquiet of some Populists against Butler's policy and leadership.[18]

Marion Butler's newspaper also felt the effects of the disagreements over state election policy during the spring of 1896. J. D. Talley wrote the paper that free silver would save the people. He claimed, "Down with the goldbugs and straddle liars and rascals!" and he also urged Populists "to stay in the middle of the road and do no 'fusing' except on honest terms. Let's go by ourselves first. We are right." J. H. Cary of Greenville wrote that the People's Party could "whip them single handed any way. Let us fight like patriots—like men. We had rather suffer defeat than to have our principles mingled with old party damnation." In editorials Butler and Ayer continued to argue that the silver issue was the most important political issue for the People's Party in North Carolina. They argued that the party "would be delighted to cooperate on the Omaha Platform in full. But if we can't do that, then we want to cooperate on some principle in that platform." The paper also argued that it would not cooperate with Democrats because they had deserted the principles of Thomas Jefferson and resorted to ballot-box stuffing, intimidation, political corruption, and machine rule.[19]

Concomitant with the debate over state policy, the Populist Party attempted to reach out to African American voters in the Old North State. Butler believed that the goldbug policy of the national GOP ran counter to the worsening economic conditions facing all Americans, black and white. The pro-silver stance of the Populists, Butler reasoned, offered black voters the opportunity to improve their economic standing and perhaps break the divisive race issue in the South once and for all. The *Caucasian* noted, "What the great masses of colored people in North Carolina want is fair treatment and justice and this they ought to have." The paper also carried numerous letters from African Americans who urged their communities to vote the Populist ticket. As early as October 1895, one African American wrote, "I am glad to say that the people of this section have gotten so that they can see the light. The colored people in this place are solid for the People's party." The paper also quoted a lengthy letter from N. L. Keen of Halifax County in the Second Congressional District. Keen wrote that for the past seventeen years he had voted the Republican ticket, but this year he could not bring himself to vote for a goldbug. Rather he would now vote for the Populist ticket because "the People's Party is the only party to-day that is standing up and pleading for the people of the country." He also urged African Americans to subscribe to the *Caucasian* in order to educate themselves on the issues of the day and warned, "The colored people of each county in the State should stop going around howling 'straight Republican ticket.'" Such sentiment led to an editorial in the *Caucasian* in which the paper optimistically stated that the "cry of 'nigger' will never conjure the people of this State into making fools of themselves in the matter of voting again," and it noted that Republicans were "losing their conjuring power to make the colored men play the fool in voting." Populists attempted to build a biracial coalition on silver, and it seems they succeeded in some localities.[20]

By mid-winter, it was clear that the Populist rank and file was all at sea on state policy. Therefore, in an editorial in the *Caucasian*, Butler urged those rank-and-file Populists who were advocating mixed "and compromising fusion to stop and think a moment." He implored the rank and file to stick to principles so that those who were for a straightforward ticket did not have to apologize for compromise. In typical Butler style, he ended with a threat to those who continued to disagree with his opinion, "If you cannot stand for principle above every indication or promise of victory or office without principle, then, for Gods sake and for the sake of honesty get out of the People's Party and go back where you belong." Butler exaggerated the aspirations of those who disagreed with him. The fact that many rank-and-file Populists continued on the path to local cooperation with the GOP illustrates two things. First, the Populist Party was a movement of the people and the leadership of the party had great difficulty in keeping the rank and file in line. Second, the rank and file was keenly aware of local politics and the need for alliances. Although their state leader and U.S. senator were less enthusiastic about cooperation in a national election year, the local Populists could and did differentiate between national and local issues.[21]

In such an important election year as 1896, Butler realized that this state of affairs could not continue indefinitely, and he decided to call a meeting of the Populist executive committee for April 16 to finally settle the Populist state policy.[22] For three hours the committee listened to twenty-four speeches from various Populists who offered different views on the correct party policy and the views of their respective constituents. The Republican Party attempted to enact fusion by offering Populists the lieutenant governor, secretary of state, treasurer, superintendent for public instruction, and one state supreme court justice on their state ticket. At an executive session, Populists discussed the proposal until the early hours of the morning. The Populist leadership eventually decided to reject the offer by a very narrow margin of nine to eight, with Marion Butler favoring rejection. Thus Butler's policy of delay won out—but only just. Populists argued that any fusion or cooperation with another party depended on the silver issue. But not all leading Populists agreed with Butler, and, importantly, Butler's position faced vigorous opposition from the People's Party's two other notable leaders, Harry Skinner and Cyrus Thompson. Both argued that fusion with Republicans was desirable if Populists gained the governorship. Although

Butler's position won out, it was clear that he had failed to carry along leading Populists with him on electoral strategy, and the meeting also failed to alleviate tensions within the Populist ranks over policy for the upcoming state elections. In the long term, the tensions at this executive meeting would haunt Populists.[23]

After its state executive committee meeting had failed to set a new course for the upcoming state election, it was not surprising that the Populist Party continued its internal debate over the best strategy for the fall elections, and two opposing groups emerged. One group supported Butler's position on a non-Republican non-cooperative ticket. This group was made up of either those who believed that Populists should stick to the middle of the road and fight on their own for victory, or those who had not totally given up on their old party, the Democrats. The *Progressive Farmer*, in particular, favored an independent strategy because of the importance it attached to free silver. The paper printed letters from optimistic Populists who believed the party would garner significant numbers of African American votes in 1896 and thus ensure a Populist victory. W. O. Stratford summed up the position of the independent strand. He wrote to Butler, "It seems to me that we are damned if we do and damned if we don't," adding, "If we are to be a distinct political organization then the sooner we cease to think of coopera-tion or 'fusion' with the other parties the better, no cooperation with any party." Another faction of this group believed that the financial policy of Cleveland augured well for a sweeping election victory in the state.[24]

The second group of Populists favored the pro-Republican cooperative position of Thompson and Skinner. However, this group also believed that the coopera-tion of Populists and Republicans would prevent a Republican victory and there-fore help the cause of silver and preserve the election law. Cyrus Thompson urged Butler to resist a straight fight because Populists would die as a result, and if the party waited until after Republicans nominated their state ticket, Populists would not gain any offices. Thompson correctly discerned that a party needed offices to effect change in policy. Many members of this group feared that a Republican victory in the state without cooperation would lead to African American rule. A. J. Moye wrote to Butler that if this happened it would be "deplorable," and in the eastern portion of North Carolina Democrats would raise "such a howl of negro domination" and would "kill not a few negroes and some white republicans that there would be a veritable Hell here in our midst." He disclosed to Butler that at a recent meeting he had brought up the issue of cooperation with Democrats and "it raised a perfect storm not a single man in the room would for a moment entertain the proposition." He ended his letter to Butler by urging the senator not to trust the likes of Guthrie, William Peele, and especially William Buck Kitchin for "he hates the negro."[25]

From these private correspondences and newspaper reports it is clear that by early May 1896, the Populist Party in the Old North State was far from united on election strategy. Party unity was severely disrupted at a time when a united front was vital, and Butler did little to unify the party when such leadership was necessary. Rather than accept that local differences and local strategies were inevitable in 1896, Butler began to accuse his opponents within the Populist Party of unpatriotism and merely hoping to gain office. Butler sincerely believed that the majority of Populists supported his position, and he was determined to show his strength at a time of disagreement.[26]

There was another route open for Butler, as a lengthy letter from Cyrus Thompson suggested. Thompson urged Butler not to accuse Populists of disloyalty because they were fighting for what they believed in and because they hoped to gain local office. He believed that because local Populists hoped to gain office this did not mean they were unprincipled and opposed to reform, and he noted that in several locations the rank-and-file Populists would fuse with Republicans regardless of what the state committee mandated because "they fear the possibility of the return to power of the machine that we pictured and said would disfranchise them." Many Populists, Thompson reasoned, believed that if cooperation was for principle in 1894 it must also be for the same principle in 1896. If this was not the case, Thompson rhetorically asked Butler, was it not "a bold bit of prurient political whoredom, salaciously enacted in the public eye, the products of which are numerous robust official bastards walking the earth for two, four, or six years." Thompson knew Butler's answer already. However, despite the advice from Thompson, Butler believed that his actions were the best for the party. It is impossible to gauge the degree to which the grassroots of the party supported Butler's position and his criticisms of those who dared to oppose him. For example, the *Caucasian* only printed letters from Populists who agreed with Butler's policy. Only on one occasion did it give space to an opponent of Butler's, and this was to Populist congressman Harry Skinner. Skinner wrote that at the recent meeting of the state committee he had urged Populists to cooperate with the GOP on the state and local tickets so long as Populists gained the governorship. Skinner also noted that the People's Party was passing through a grave crisis and that the party could disintegrate unless the rank and file would settle the state policy at their conventions from the township level up to the state convention. In an implicit criticism of the state executive committee's decision, Skinner reminded the rank and file that the committee's decision was only a recommendation and only at the various meetings at the local, county, and state level could Populists agree on policy. In other words, Skinner laid down the gauntlet and challenged the rank-and-file Populists to push a policy they desired, which Skinner assumed was pro-Republican cooperation.[27]

The Republican Party observed the turmoil within the Populist ranks with particular concern. The GOP was almost totally behind cooperation with Populists on the state and local tickets, and Republicans were convinced that only continued cooperation would ensure victory for the reform movement and the defeat of the dreaded Democratic Party. Zebulon Walser, state speaker of the House in the 1895 session, argued that it was vital to have cooperation on state issues and postulated that "every man who opposes a united fight this year will be looked upon as an enemy or fool and will be smashed flatter than a pancake by the tread of patriots as they march grand on victory." The GOP argued that disagreements on national policy should be subsumed under state issues. When it became increasingly clear that Butler opposed Republican overtures at cooperation, Republicans attempted to encourage the pro-cooperation Populists to cooperate without the sanction of their state leader.[28]

On May 14, 1896, the Republican Party held its state convention in Raleigh. The GOP continued to hope that it could separate state and national issues as it sought a cooperative agreement with the Populists. The Republicans nominated Judge Daniel L. Russell for governor after a heated voting process. Russell was a well-known political figure in the Old North State who spoke his mind freely and regularly on controversial subjects as wide ranging as African American voting, the coinage of silver, and Democratic corruption at the ballot box. By the mid-1890s, Russell was a free silver Republican of the highest order, and he favored the pro-cooperation sentiment of the party with Populists. Thus in many ways Russell was a pro-Populist, and he displayed his Populist leanings on the anti-railroad trust issue and when he stated that he hoped Populists would fuse with Republicans. But Russell was a Republican and he also favored a protective tariff and the expansion of Republican influence in North Carolina. He also sought the votes of African Americans despite the fact that he had severely criticized the African American character for the past four years. However, as the GOP candidate, Russell appreciated the need for a solid black vote for his candidacy to succeed, and in his acceptance speech he began to heal his rift with African Americans. He stated that he had "been cradled in the lap of a negro woman and fed on her milk, both nutritious and plentiful," and declared he stood for the rights and liberties of African Americans. Republicans also only nominated one-half of their state ticket, inviting Populists to fill in the gaps.[29]

The Populist reaction to the Republican convention was crucial. The *Caucasian* continued to attack the GOP and its adherence to the gold standard, labeling both Russell and Senator Pritchard as goldbugs—Russell was not a goldbug and never had been. William Guthrie informed Butler that Russell could only hope to get two-thirds of the GOP vote and that Populists would gain the other third; and, therefore, he believed that the Populist vote would hold firm and lead the party to an overwhelming victory in November. At the same time, Harry Skinner and Cyrus Thompson continued to advocate cooperation with the GOP. In addition, local Populists continued to ignore the sentiments of their leader and negotiated with their local GOP counterparts on cooperation. Butler, however, stuck to his policy of waiting for the nominations and the financial planks of the platforms of the GOP's and Democrats' respective national conventions. He remained convinced that neither of the old parties would come out for free silver and Populists would garner hundreds of thousands of votes from disgruntled and disenchanted silverites.[30]

The Populist Party leadership was taken aback by the nomination of Russell, and the party was still rudderless by the end of May and early June on their state policy and the issue of cooperation with the GOP. Butler received numerous letters from his associates in North Carolina on the turmoil in the Populist ranks as he continued to play a waiting game. Many of these letters illustrated that Republicans hoped to enact local cooperation. For example, C. A. Nash noted that Republicans would do all they could to fuse with Populists on the county level so that the GOP could gain the governorship and the legislature. D. J. Hancock concurred with these views. He noted that in Cleveland County Republicans "are trying to bring about a discord among the Pops." A.D.K. Wallace wrote a lengthy letter to Butler on the situation in Rutherford County. He noted the arrogance of the GOP, but he also stressed the fact that by waiting Populists had merely strengthened Democrats who argue "that Mary Ann is coming back bringing the honest Pops. with him." All these Populists wanted a clear decision on state policy. Other Populists worried that the party was sending mixed messages to the voters. Other Populists wanted the People's Party to enter the field straight away or as soon as possible so that the party could play a proactive role in the state during the early summer months.[31]

Marion Butler also received public backing for his position in North Carolina. J. R. Sattenwaite, for example, wrote to the *Caucasian* that Populists in his county did not want cooperation with any party unless it was for the interests of the farmers and laborers of the country, and the only people who favored cooperation were office seekers. A Populist from Bladen County wrote that Populists there want to be "in the middle of the road," and they heartily endorse " 'Mary Ann' our gallant leader, in his honest defense of the poverty stricken people, and further we are gaining ground on the old parties as fast as the political wheel turns over." He also noted that the African American voters in Bladen "are solid for the Pops."[32]

The *Caucasian* finally responded to the letters from rank-and-file Populists. The paper advised its readers that national issues were the most pressing ones facing the people in 1896, and thus Populists should focus on gaining reforms at the national level. It further noted that the Republican cry of good state government was "a fakir cry" designed for "the relief of a few partisan officeholders of a successful party. These fellows (the GOP) would willingly sell out justice due to the people from the national government for local offices they hold if they could get the offices in no other way. So far as they are concerned the people might be d—d. Their own relief is what concerns them." The paper reassured its readers that the Populist Party would never resort to this approach, but rather would fight for national reform to gain relief and justice for all the people. Thus, the paper concluded, the only way to for Populists to win in 1896 was for the voters to vote for Populists. However, at the same time the *Caucasian* denied rumors that Populists would align themselves with Democrats because the policies of the Democrats were not for reform. The paper argued that Democrats were split on the financial issue and thus the Populists "WILL NEVER COOPERATE. We believe we speak the living truth when we say that before the Populists would consent to such a course, they would go HORSE FOOT, DRAGOON, RANK AND FILE BODILY INTO THE REPUBLICAN PARTY, AND DO WHAT THEY COULD to insure a Republican victory in the State of North Carolina."[33]

When the Democratic state convention met at Raleigh on June 25, 1896, they gave up on their past economic and political polices of the Bourbon era—at least in name. Instead, the state platform criticized monopolies, national banks, and trusts and even supported a graduated income tax. In other words, Democrats moved toward the principles of the Populist Party, and they capped such a fundamental policy change by endorsing the free coinage of silver. Democrats nominated a full ticket headed by Cyrus Watson for governor. They did not leave open any spots on the ticket for Populists.[34]

With state politics in flux, North Carolina Populists now turned their attention to the national political picture: What would happen? During the year, Butler played an increasingly pivotal role in the People's Party national leadership, and by the spring of 1896 he was a key member of the Populist national leadership. He remained convinced that both the old parties would nominate goldbugs for president and adopt an anti-silver plank in their platforms. Butler reasoned that this would cause a mass exodus from both the old parties that would in turn swell the ranks of the People's Party. Butler decided that a wait-and-see policy would lead to a rousing success for Populists and for the forces of free silver. At first everything seemed to go Butler's way. The Republican Party at their national convention in St. Louis in June nominated goldbug William McKinley for president. The party also endorsed a high tariff and other moderate reforms. Although McKinley secured the nomination on the first ballot, many western Republicans opposed the GOP's adherence to the gold standard. Silverite Republicans led by Senator Henry Teller of Colorado bolted the GOP in disgust. Butler and many leading Populists welcomed the exodus of silverite Republicans and envisioned Teller as an ideal presidential candidate for the silver forces.[35]

All eyes now turned to the Democratic convention at Chicago. The Populists believed that Democrats would likewise nominate a goldbug for president. But Populists had underestimated the strength of silver sentiment and the instinct for political survival in the Democratic ranks, despite early warnings that the pro-silver wing would not accept a goldbug candidate for president in 1896.

Many Democrats in the South and West refused to run another candidate with credentials similar to the repudiated sitting president, Grover Cleveland. A mighty battle ensued at the Chicago convention over the presidential nomination, and noted silverite William Jennings Bryan of Nebraska eventually received the presidential nomination on the fifth ballot. He gave a stirring speech on the merits of free silver that captivated the delegates. Bryan was not only an avowed silverite, but also a reform-minded politician on a host of other issues. Democrats nominated a little-known New Englander, Arthur Sewall, for vice president. The nomination of Bryan startled Populists and disrupted all the plans of Marion Butler for a silver movement led by Populists. Democrats now clearly held the silver mantle in the national campaign.[36]

The fallout from the Democratic convention plunged the Populist Party into turmoil just two weeks before its national convention. Populists held their national convention at St. Louis on July 22, 1896. The only course of events open to the national People's Party was to either endorse Democrat Bryan or name its own candidate and risk splitting the forces of silver. The mid-roaders at the convention, led by Thomas Watson and the Texas Populists, favored a straight Populist ticket, while western Populists favored supporting the Democratic ticket. Eventually, a compromise plan pushed by Butler emerged. Bryan would receive the nomination but the Democrats' vice presidential candidate, Arthur Sewall of Maine, would not. Butler hoped that this would save Populists and keep the silver issue at the forefront of the election. However, it was most unlikely that Democrats would drop Sewall. The political maneuverings at the St. Louis convention were complex. Over fourteen hundred delegates gathered; the largest delegations were from North Carolina and Texas. Butler advocated the compromise plan, arguing that it was vital that Populists remain a separate entity to prevent Democrats from returning to their old goldbug ways. The Populists rejected Sewall for vice president and instead nominated Tom Watson of Georgia for the spot, and he received the vice presidential nomination from the convention. Bryan received the presidential nomination, although there was no guarantee that he would accept it.[37]

At St. Louis Populists had taken a gamble in nominating Bryan and rejecting Sewall. In addition, the convention pointed to severe divisions between the mid-roaders and the other factions of the Populist Party. However, the party managed to hold together at a critical time. There is no doubt that the nomination of Bryan by Democrats had surprised Populists, and their convention was an indication that the 1896 election campaign would be one of the most complicated in memory. Despite the insistence of many historians, Populists had little option than to nominate Bryan. Although Populists were dismayed at the nomination of Bryan, their rhetoric gave them little option other than to support him. Indeed, if they had nominated another presidential candidate, Populists would have faced Democratic accusations of unprincipled actions and of throwing the election to a goldbug, William McKinley. Supporting Bryan was in keeping with the Populist reform agenda, and the rejection of Sewall and the nomination of the nationally known Populist Tom Watson was an indication that Populists were far from dismantling their party identity. Ultimately, Sewall remained on the ticket and Populist Tom Watson pulled out of the race after a public falling-out with Marion Butler.[38]

Following the national conventions, the Populist Party in North Carolina faced an incredibly complex political landscape. The state Republicans advocated cooperation and had nominated a silverite for governor. Democrats were less open to cooperation, but they had unequivocally declared for free silver before their national convention. At the national level the GOP was in favor of the gold standard while the Democratic Party embraced silver emphatically and nominated a genuine silverite for president. In addition, the national Populist Party had also nominated Bryan for president and a Populist for vice president. Even to the most seasoned politician such a state of affairs must have been bewildering. Populists remained as divided on policy as they were in the early months of the year. But now it was late July and the election campaign was drawing closer.

Due to national events, Butler, and probably many Populists, reasoned that they must align themselves with the Democratic electors or the state would vote for McKinley. In addition, Butler's pro-silver stance also meant that Populists should seek an alliance with Democrats on state issues. However, achieving such an agreement was fraught with difficulties. First, Democrats might not agree and choose instead to fight on their own. Second, many Populists could not bring themselves to vote for the hated Democratic Party on state issues. Third, many local Populists had already agreed on cooperation on the county and legislative tickets in many counties in the eastern section of the state.[39]

The Democrats divided on cooperation even though the new state chairman, Clement Manly, agreed to meet Butler to discuss cooperation before the Populist state convention. The Democratic state executive committee agreed to cooperation on the electoral ticket with Populists at a meeting in Raleigh on July 31. Republicans hoped to prevent a Populist-Democratic state fusion ticket and simultaneously endeavored to foster a Populist-GOP ticket. The GOP correctly reasoned that an alliance between the People's Party and Democrats spelled the electoral doom of the resurgent Republican Party. The GOP realized that many rank-and-file Populists despised the Democrats, not least because Butler and other Populist leaders had spent the past four years castigating Democrats as unprincipled, corrupt, fraudulent, and dominated by the machine.[40]

After the St. Louis convention, the Populist Party of North Carolina was still floundering. Butler's policy of waiting had only caused disagreement and uncertainty, and in some places outright disintegration and internal hostility and infighting. Most Populists could not bear the thought of aligning themselves with Democrats on the state ticket or for seats in the state legislature. As Butler moved ever closer to the Democrats, many Populists openly attacked him. For example, the *Progressive Farmer* and its editor, James L. Ramsey, rebelled against Butler. Ramsey accused Butler's policy of waiting and his move toward a non-partisan silver movement as ill thought out and most likely to lead to the disintegration of the People's Party in North Carolina. Ramsey argued that Populists should have had an early convention to pull Democratic silverites into the People's Party before their national convention at Chicago. Ramsey received support from notable Populists. Cyrus Thompson wrote to Ramsey that the warnings he had given Ramsey earlier on Butler's position had now come true. It is too easy to dismiss Ramsey's attack as one of sour grapes. It is true that Ramsey may have over-stressed the possibility that Democrats would stampede into the Populist Party, but his editorial illustrates that alternatives did exist for Populists during the early months of 1896, and Butler had made a serious blunder in misreading the political signals from the Democratic Party and enacting a wait-and-see policy. The Populist Party was a mass movement of common farmers who demanded far-reaching reforms. This pro-active group of activists disliked waiting around for their hesitant party leaders to make decisions on their behalf.[41]

With the political stakes increasing and tensions reaching fever pitch in the People's Party, Butler decided that he must control the Populist state convention. He also wanted to enact fusion with Democrats on presidential electors, congressional tickets, and state offices. On August 12, the day before the Populist convention, Butler and the Populist Party state executive committee offered a fusion package to Democratic state chairman Clement Manly. The Populists demanded five of the eleven presidential electors and Democratic support for a Populist governor, treasurer, superintendent for public instruction, and a state supreme court justice. The Democrats could fill the rest of the state ticket and elect a silverite U.S. senator to succeed Pritchard. However, Democrats rejected the offer and responded that they could only accept fusion on the presidential electors and congressional seats.[42]

The Populist convention began on August 13 at Raleigh and it quickly degenerated into a factional fight that mirrored the tensions in the Populist ranks throughout the year. The major dispute was between those Populists led by Butler who favored cooperation with Democrats and those Populists led by Harry Skinner who favored fusion with Democrats on the presidential ticket but with the GOP on the congressional, state, and county tickets. Butler and Skinner were the most respected Populist leaders in the state, and the fact that both chose different routes for Populism was emblematic of far-reaching problems within the Populist Party in 1896 and the cause of "free silver." First, the party had failed to become the major party in North Carolina as all Populists had hoped and claimed back in late 1894. As a result, Populists merely represented the balance of power within the state, and the tensions within the party were clear examples of the difficulties this position placed on the rank and file as well as the leadership of the party as they sought maximize the power of the party and balance the competing factions within the party on policy. Second, although Populists remained in a powerful position, there were deep personal disagreements in the leadership over election strategy, and because of the nature of southern politics, each group tended to mistrust the other deeply. Third, the silver movement, much heralded by Butler, had merely succeeded in converting Democrats to the free coinage of silver and, consequently, Populists lost much of their unique platform to Democrats.

Despite the apparent tensions and the fear of an acrimonious convention, the proceedings began quite peacefully as the delegates easily agreed on the various planks in the party platform. The North Carolina Populists adopted the national People's Party platform at St. Louis. The convention also praised the 1895 state legislature and, in particular, endorsed the new election law, the county government law, and the 6 percent legal rate of interest law. In addition, the convention reaffirmed the reform nature of the Populist movement by endorsing better schools, a non-partisan judiciary, a juvenile reformatory, and, importantly, the regulation of the state's railroads as well as the end of free passes. The Populists roundly condemned Governor Elias Carr's last-minute lease of the North Carolina Railroad to the Southern Railway Company for ninety-nine years. Thus, policy did not divide the Populist, only strategy did so.[43]

Although the convention could agree on the platform, Populists were deeply divided amongst themselves on how to politically achieve their agenda and who should lead the state fight. Butler gained the upper hand on election policy when his close associate, James Lloyd of Tarboro, nominated William Guthrie for the governorship. Guthrie was a former Republican who joined the Populists in 1894, an avowed silverite with a good reputation amongst his peers and known as a notable public speaker. As far as Butler was concerned, Guthrie would make an excellent candidate for governor and could draw both Republican voters disillusioned with Russell and Democratic voters who disliked the conservative Cyrus Watson. The pro-Republican faction of the Populist Party disagreed with this assessment, and they nominated Cyrus Thompson as their candidate for governor. Many pro-Republican Populists saw Thompson as one of the most charismatic Populists in the state, an original Populist, and an excellent stump speaker. They also reasoned that if, as they expected, Russell came off the ticket, Thompson was the best candidate to defeat Democrat Cyrus Watson. For several minutes delegates from the various counties voiced their support for either Guthrie or Thompson. However, Guthrie easily secured the nomination.[44]

After Guthrie's nomination, Butler sought to cement his hold on the convention. He personally nominated Republican Oliver H. Dockery, the "Old War Horse of Pee Dee," for lieutenant governor and called him "one of the most magnificent campaigners in the State. A man whose name commands the admiration of every citizen of the State." Butler also argued that Dockery was a pro-silver man. Dockery was an old-time Republican, but unlike Guthrie, he had not joined the Populists. Indeed, in May, Dockery narrowly and controversially lost the gubernatorial nomination to Daniel L. Russell at the stormy GOP convention. Why Butler nominated Dockery is unclear. Dockery hated the Democratic Party and that party despised Dockery. Perhaps Butler hoped to draw votes from the Republican Party during the election, especially the African American voters who were angry at Russell's nomination, or he hoped to appeal for moderate support. Whatever the motives behind Butler's actions, the nomination of Dockery certainly took the convention by surprise and brought a swift rebuttal from Harry Skinner. Skinner wanted to know if Dockery supported Bryan and Tom Watson at the national level, and he made it clear that he disliked the fact that a repudiated Republican would run for such a high place on the Populist state ticket. Skinner urged Populists instead to nominate a straight ticket and, with some justification, saw the nomination of Dockery as merely a tactic to divide Republicans and give the state to the Democrats. Skinner admonished, "Why take Russell or Dockery? We want principle, purity of the ballot box and silver. The nomination of Dockery means Democratic supremacy and the abolishment of our honest election law." Cyrus Thompson also supported Skinner's position on Dockery's nomination and stated that he would not vote for a "mongrel ticket" and opposed any attempt to "dicker" with the ticket for the benefit of Democrats. However, Butler was unperturbed by such opposition from leading Populists. Cashing in on his reputation and his personal power of persuasion, Butler personally worked the floor of the convention and met with many delegates and secured the overwhelming support of Dockery for the lieutenant governorship over the pro-Republican cooperationist, James Mewboorne. Butler realized that many Populists opposed his position on Dockery, and he urgently sought to mend political fences before the differences on personalities threatened to widen into a permanent split on policy. He endorsed Cyrus Thompson for the nomination as secretary of state, and this seemed to produce the desired effect when Skinner responded, "You may know that any ticket that has Cyrus Thompson on it meets with my approval." Butler also backed down from his attempt to nominate Republican silverite Zebulon Walser for attorney general after Harry Skinner again opposed the nomination of another Republican.[45]

The arguments within the convention did not end there. The next day the convention opened early in the morning and a new disagreement erupted over the position of a new state leader and a new state executive committee for the 1896 campaign. Butler was now the national chairman of the People's Party, and he could not remain the leader in North Carolina. However, Butler was determined that the new state chairman would be one of his close associates. Thus, the candidates for the committee reflected Butler's position on cooperation, and the nominated new members included A. S. Peace, Hal Ayer, and S. Otho Wilson, as well as Butler. This provoked opposition from Skinner and Thompson. Skinner argued that the new committee members were merely tools of Butler and that, in fact, the three men were merely one man. Skinner even called Butler a "Boss" in open convention, and he wanted to know why he, Thompson, and Guthrie were not on the committee. Butler denied the charges that the new committee men were his hirelings, and he made an impassioned speech to the convention in which he pleaded with the delegates that what hurt him the most was not the rotten eggs of his enemies but the insinuations against him from his friends. But Butler's speech could not silence Skinner, who became more annoyed with the convention's proceedings and chided, "I say that Mr. Butler is a party wrecker. His actions have caused our party to be a harlot between the old parties." This attack led to a swift response from the convention when several delegates started to hiss at the congressman and others called out for Skinner to shut his mouth. Eventually, the delegates voted on a new executive committee and it produced success for Butler's associates although Cyrus Thompson was also added to the committee in order to appease the pro-Republican Populists. Butler's initial success on the state ticket was complete, not least because Hal Ayer was named the new state chairman.[46]

The Populist convention was full of rancor and bad blood. It reflected the confusing nature of state politics and the difficult position the Populist Party found itself in by August. The blame for this state of affairs rests squarely with Butler and his supporters. By playing a waiting game and trying to fuse with first one party and then the other, Populists had severely weakened themselves. Thus, by the end of August Butler's plans lay in ruins, and to make the situation more confusing Populists nominated more Democratic-Populists and Republican-Populists and straight-out Republicans than Populists on its state ticket. The unity of the Populist Party from 1892 to 1895 was over. The party now entered a stage of disagreement and personal abuse at a time when the political landscape mandated a united political campaign.

To make the situation even more complex, the two other parties were not pre-pared to wait around for Populists to receive some sort of divine inspiration on election strategy. The GOP desired cooperation, and on August 15 the Republican executive committee met and decided to fill the gaps on their state ticket with the names of Populists without that party's sanction. However, the GOP did not take down their candidates for governor and lieutenant governor. In addition, the party endeavored to enact local cooperation with Populists without the sanction of the Populist executive committee. The GOP tactic worked, and by the end of August many counties renewed local Populist-Republican cooperation along the same lines as 1894. The majority of the Populist-Republican cooperation took place in the eastern section of the state, where each party needed the other in order to defeat Democrats. In addition, leading pro-Republican Populists Harry Skinner, Cyrus Thompson, and James Mewboorne came from the eastern section of the state. For example, Harry Skinner received the Populist nomination for the First Congressional District at Edenton in early August, and he quickly received the endorsement of the GOP. The rank-and-file Populists seemed far more willing to align themselves with the GOP regardless of the position advocated by Butler and Hal Ayer—grassroots Populists knew what they wanted.[47]

The Populist state leadership now faced the very real fact that the rank and file of their party was enacting cooperation despite the clear disapproval of their leader at the recent state convention. By September as many as fifty-three counties (60 percent of the counties of North Carolina) had adopted Populist-Republican cooperation, with most located in the eastern section of the state and in the lower Piedmont. In most counties and state senatorial districts the local Populists followed the same policy on cooperation with Republicans as in 1894. Whatever position the state leadership adopted, the rank and file and local leadership of the Populist Party discerned that only cooperation with the GOP could defeat Democrats. These Populists saw local issues and the laws passed by the state legislature as more important than an alliance with Democrats on silver. The large majority of these Populists and Republicans had not forgotten the machine rule of the Democrats over the past twenty years.[48]

In addition, matters were complicated still further by local Populist-Democratic cooperation in a few counties in the Fifth Congressional District, and the fact that this policy found support in Populist leaders William A. Guthrie and avowed racist William H. Kitchin. Local issues certainly played a part here. Guthrie hoped that the Democratic-Populist cooperation in the Fifth District would defeat goldbug incumbent Republican congressman Thomas Settle, and Kitchin hoped that a similar cooperation arrangement would hinder black candidates in his home district, the "Black Second." At the same time Butler hoped to enact cooperation with Democrats on congressional candidates, so it is not surprising that some Populists favored cooperation with Democrats. Local leaders seemed to ignore Butler and the state executive committee. Guthrie actively campaigned to defeat Populist nominee Dr. A. J. Dalby in the Fifth District. It was clear, however, that this situation could not last if the Populist state leadership wanted to keep some semblance of control over the rank and file.[49]

The Populist and Republican executive committees met on September 9 and 10 in Raleigh. Finally, both parties agreed to state cooperation, except on the governorship and the U.S. senator. Republicans promised to support the Populist congressional candidates in the First, Third, Fourth, Sixth, and Seventh Districts, while Populists could nominate their own candidates in the Second, Fifth, and Ninth Districts and the GOP would support the Populist candidates for secretary of state, auditor, treasurer, and superintendent of public instruction and for one associate justice of the state supreme court. The Populist leadership justified this agreement on the basis that it was the only way to maintain an honest election law and a fair system of local government. Ayer argued that the committee thought that the reforms of the past two years were worth preserving and that this depended on the defeat of Democrats in the state. The Populists also claimed that there was a tacit agreement that Russell would leave the ticket. Ayer seemed the most hostile to an agreement with Republicans, but he confided to Butler that it was the only way to defeat Democrats. Thus, despite all Butler's posturing and backroom dealings, political reality finally hit the Populist leadership in late September and they agreed on the same state ticket offered to them by the GOP back in spring. Indeed, the rank and file of the party had, to some degree, pushed the state leadership into taking such a position.[50]

To complicate matters still further the Populist leadership in North Carolina fused with the Democrats on presidential electors. The bargain, reached on September 21, gave five Bryan-Sewall electors to Democrats, five Bryan-Watson electors to the Populists, and one elector to the National Silver Party. Fusing on the presidential electors made sense to the Populist leadership now that Democrats had squarely endorsed silver. James Lloyd assured Butler that the rank and file of the party would accept cooperation with Democrats. The Populists now entered the remaining month and a half of the campaign in a cooperation agreement with Democrats *and* Republicans.[51]

Marion Butler played a less decisive role in the state campaign of 1896 than in 1894. Despite the cooperation agreement between Populists and Republicans on the state ticket, Butler still tried to enact a cooperation agreement with Democrats at the last minute in the hope that William Guthrie could become the governor of all the silver forces in North Carolina and thus defeat Daniel L. Russell. Butler hoped to force Democrats to agree to support Guthrie at a late stage in the campaign. Such actions were fanciful and ill-timed. Butler's motives may have been pure, but the fact that local Populist-Republican cooperation was in full force and the rank and file approved cooperation with the GOP, and Republicans endorsed five of the Populist congressional candidates, suggests that Butler was out of touch with the political reality of the state in 1896. Still, Butler believed that despite all the oscillations in the party's electoral policy and its inactivity during the past year, Populists could now once again totally reorient their campaign with just one month remaining before voting.[52]

As if the Populist predicament was not bad enough, Democrats, sensing that Republican-Populists would sweep the state, responded to Butler's initial overtures and offered cooperation on the state ticket. On October 12, 1896, Democrats sent a proposal for cooperation to Chairman Ayer. Democrats offered to divide the state offices and congressional seats equally. However, Democrats would not take down their gubernatorial candidate but offered instead to support Guthrie for the U.S. Senate or the lieutenant governor's spot. Ayer called a meeting of the Populist executive committee to discuss the latest proposal. The committee had now discussed more proposals than there were Populists in New England, and after some debate the committee overwhelmingly rejected the Democratic proposition.[53]

The Populist state leadership floundered through the complex world of cooperation politics like a fish out of water. At the same time, however, the local Populists enacted cooperation on local issues with either Republicans or, in a few cases, Democrats. Populists reasoned that the much-needed and lauded reforms of the 1895 legislature needed protecting from Democrats. Thus local issues played the primary motivating force in many rank-and-file Populist deliberations—local activists and local leaders ran the show. Cyrus Thompson's papers are full of letters from Populists who did not want to leave their cooperation agreements with the GOP. John Graham, for example, noted that although his sympathies were not Republican, he would "bitterly oppose breaking faith with them unless they are clearly at fault." William Worth wrote that it was not fair to Republicans to not let them know what was happening in the campaign, and if the Populists did align themselves with Democrats, the People's Party would lose its congressmen. But, Worth concluded, the majority of Populists would fuse with and stay with the GOP. In short, the Populist leadership could not control its rank-and-file members during the 1896 election campaign. This control, never easy, was made impossible by disagreements within the state leadership over election strategy, with some Populists advocating a straight ticket, while others advocated Populist-Democratic fusion on the silver principle, and still another group led urged that cooperation with the GOP was the only way to defeat the state Democratic Party.[54]

With the election campaign reaching its climax and with all three parties attempting to garner as many new voters as possible while simultaneously holding their core voters, the Populist Party suffered a huge setback on its state ticket to add to the already insurmountable odds it faced in the 1896 campaign. William Guthrie, the Populist candidate for governor, began his campaign with a series of robust speeches on the silver issue and an honest state government and a vigorous debate with his Democratic opponent on the stump, and in many ways he was a much better Populist candidate than Wyatt P. Exum in 1892. However, Guthrie expected that if Populists and Republicans aligned on the state and county tickets that Daniel L. Russell, the GOP's nominee, would come down from the ticket. But by October it was clear to Guthrie and the Populist leaders that Russell would not step down, and, indeed, it seemed likely that Russell would win the race to the governor's mansion in a three-way fight, and perhaps McKinley might even carry the Old North State. During October, Guthrie wrote incredibly long letters to Marion Butler on his predicament, and in many ways these letters had a pathetic ring to them as Guthrie began to withdraw from the campaign. Guthrie, never a supporter of Populist-Republican cooperation, determined that those local Populists who did favor such cooperation were mere office-hunters without true Populist-silver principles. On October 16, he wrote to Butler that Populist-Republican cooperation "has not only left me stranded as a candidate for governor; but has turned over substantially our party organizations to the Republicans." As a result, Guthrie began to move toward the Democratic Party. On October 27, he pleaded with Populists to vote the Democratic ticket. This came at the worst possible moment for the Populist Party and caused deep embarrassment for the party during the critical last few days of the campaign.[55]

Chairman Hal Ayer attempted to respond to Guthrie's bombshell. He accused Guthrie of selling out the Populist Party and insulting the Populist voters and urging them to vote for Democrats. Ayer claimed that Guthrie's action "ignores in State matters the firm determination and important principle of the Populists, that the State must not be again turned over to Democratic bringandage and spoliation." Ayer then claimed that although Guthrie was still the People's Party's candidate for governor, the vote for Guthrie should not and could not be accepted as an indication of Populist strength.[56]

As the campaign entered its final few days the Democratic Party, sensing its impending doom, once again reverted from discussing policy issues in a meaningful way and instead focused on the race issue in an attempt to hold voters in line and tempt wavering Populists back into the Democratic camp. Josephus Daniels led the way in the *News and Observer*, warning the voters that the black population would vote solidly for Russell and, therefore, the white population must vote solidly for Democrats lest North Carolina suffer a return to "negro rule" and Reconstruction.[57]

The Populists also responded vociferously to the Democrat's use of the race card. S. Otho Wilson's *Raleigh Hayseeder* led the way. In a series of editorials the paper noted that Democrats had once again taken up the race issue, and this merely showed "that the Democratic Party is now the same old hypocritical crowd it always was, this resort to old, worn out and discredited and disgraced tactics would prove it." Democrats had again resorted to their old staple and "as a hog returns to wallow in his mire," the paper chided "so do these Democrats return to their choice morsel—the cry of nigger!" The paper then broadened its attack on the Democrats by reminding its readers not to trust Democrats because, as in 1892, Democrats, if successful, would attack the Alliance charter, persecute Populist leaders, and rotten-egg its opponents. It urged all the voters to stand by cooperation and vote the Populist-Republican ticket in Wake County and do everything in the power of the People's Party to hold the balance of power. As the campaign came to a close Ayer issued a rallying cry to the People's Party voters. He argued that cooperation on the state ticket with Republicans was the correct policy and the only way to secure a large representation in the state legislature. Ayer noted that the state executive committee had acted earnestly and "this is much more than could have been secured by cooperation with any other party, and the sum total is a greater power and influence than could have been secured by any other arrangement that has at any time seemed possible."[58]

On November 3, 1896, the Populist-Republican forces swept the state. Bryan carried North Carolina by about 19,000 votes, and Populists increased their U.S. congressional representation to five. On the state ticket Populists gained several offices, including Cyrus Thompson for secretary of state, Hal Ayer as state auditor, and Charles Mebane as superintendent of public instruction. Walter Montgomery won re-election to a full term on the state supreme court and William Worth won re-election as the state treasurer. Guthrie's repudiation of Populist-Republican cooperation at the eleventh hour cost his candidacy many votes. Thus, many Populists voted for either Russell or Watson. Russell received 153,787 votes and carried forty-nine counties to Cyrus Watson's 145,266 votes and forty-six counties, with just 31,143 votes and one county (Sampson) for Guthrie. Russell's vote represented an increase for Republicans over 1892 of 57,103 votes. Thus it appears that the new election law passed by the 1895 cooperationist state legislature aided the GOP and, in particular, Russell's candidacy. For the first time since Reconstruction, Democrats lost the governor's mansion, and Daniel L. Russell became the first Republican governor since "Redemption."[59]

The Populists/Republicans out-numbered Democrats 43 to 7 in the state senate and 93 to 26 in the state lower house. Populists gained 39 seats in the lower house and 25 in the state senate. This made a total of 64 representatives, a decline of 2 seats from their representation in the 1895 state legislature. Republicans gained the most seats in 1896; in the lower house their representation increased to 54, and in the senate to 18, making a total of 72 seats. Democrats suffered a humiliating defeat. Their total representation stood at only 33 representatives, and in the state senate they had just 7 members. No one party gained a majority in the assembly, but crucially this time Republicans were the largest party.[60]

Explaining the Populist vote is difficult. Certainly, Populists polled 16,697 fewer votes for Guthrie than for Exum in 1892. However, it is erroneous to use this as an indication of Populist strength. Guthrie's political bombshell at the end of the campaign cost him and Populists dearly. What is clear though is that Populists had not expanded their electoral base in 1896. There were no more state representatives in 1896 than in 1894. Indeed, cooperation with Republicans had precipitated a decline in Populist strength in Chatham, Randolph, Richmond, and Robeson counties. However, one could argue that cooperation in these counties was not a sign of decline, but rather that Populists had to agree to share the ticket with Republicans. In 1896 Populists were the last party to enter the political campaign, and for two months they engaged in a game of political catch-up with the other two parties. Thus it is not surprising that

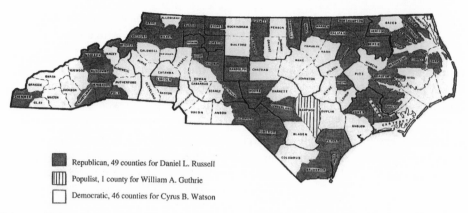

Republican, 49 counties for Daniel L. Russell

Populist, 1 county for William A. Guthrie

Democratic, 46 counties for Cyrus B. Watson

Gubernatorial election, 1896. R.D.W. Connor, comp. and ed., *North Carolina Manual*, issued by the North Carolina Historical Commission (Raleigh: E. M. Uzzell and Company, State Printers, 1913), 1005–1006.

Populists enacted cooperation on terms that were less favorable to them in 1896 than in 1894. However, if one analyzes the areas of Populist and Republican strength, it is clear that both parties benefited from the changes in the election law. For example, the cooperationists smashed the Democratic strongholds in the eastern section of the state. In 1894 Democrats carried nineteen counties east of Raleigh. In 1896, however, Democrats mustered just four. This was a sweeping victory for Populists and Republicans. Populists in particular swept through the eastern sections of the First and Third Congressional Districts, while the GOP managed to win ten of the majority-black counties.

In the national election, Republican William McKinley defeated Democrat-Populist, William Jennings Bryan by 271 to 176 electoral votes. In the popular vote, McKinley garnered 5,00,000 more votes than Bryan. McKinley won the election because he secured much of the Midwest vote, sweeping the states of Illinois, Iowa, Indiana, and Minnesota, and carried the Northeast. At the same time, however, the Populist Party did reasonably well throughout the country. Over twenty Populists would take their seats in the U.S. Congress, a higher number than in 1895.[61]

The Republican Party was overjoyed at the election results. Daniel L. Russell, the governor-elect, received numerous letters of congratulations. A. C. Swinson urged Russell to turn out all Democrats from state employment and appoint those friendly to cooperation. The attorney general–elect, Zebulon Walser, was overjoyed at victory and hoped that the party would once again win in four years time. H. B. Farmer concurred with Walser, and he hoped North Carolina would stay redeemed for a long time; and, noting the reform nature of the cooperation movement, he urged that "our election laws may be so amended as to

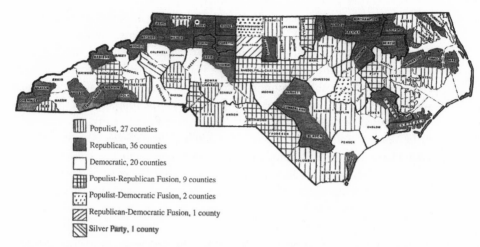

Populist, 27 counties

Republican, 36 counties

Democratic, 20 counties

Populist-Republican Fusion, 9 counties

Populist-Democratic Fusion, 2 counties

Republican-Democratic Fusion, 1 county

Silver Party, 1 county

State election to the North Carolina House of Representatives, 1896. D. C. Mangum, *Biographical Sketches of the Members of the General Assembly of North Carolina, Session 1897* (Raleigh: Edwards and Broughton, Printers and Binders, 1897).

prevent us for ever from having to go back under the Democratic *Punch* and *Judy* Ballot system that has prevailed in our state for so many years." Russell also received congratulations from one of the leading industrialists of North Carolina, Benjamin Duke. Duke invited Russell to spend a week in New York. In turn, Russell invited Duke and his father to come and visit Wilmington, and then they could rub Democrats' noses in the dirt. Russell playfully suggested, "We will walk around there and show the Bourbons that the Old State belongs as much to us as to them. We admit their partnership but we decline to acknowledge their superiority or mastery."[62]

Democrats were despondent over the election results. They had lost the presidency, all the state offices, two congressional seats (they now had just one), and in the state legislature they were the minority party by some distance. To make matters worse, they lost scores of county offices to the cooperationists. The press blamed Populists for their loss in the state and the People's Party's unprincipled fight for office over the cause of silver.[63]

The Populist Party in North Carolina achieved notable successes in the 1896 elections despite the convoluted nature of the campaign, the oscillations of the state leadership, Butler's ill-timed and continued bartering attempts that flew in the face of local cooperation, and William Guthrie's bombshell at the close of the campaign. But below the veneer of victory, the People's Party faced a number of difficult questions on policy and tensions within its ranks that needed resolving if they were to remain a viable political party in future years. First, the silver movement was not the political nirvana for Populists that Butler predicted in 1895 and 1896. The national elections produced an emphatic victory for Republican William McKinley over the avowed silverite William Jennings Bryan. The Populists had lost much of their unique appeal and strength once Democrats co-opted much of the Populist platform. The Populist national leadership began to squabble amongst themselves as their recriminations mounted after November. In North Carolina, Populists faced the prospect that Democrats now espoused much of the reform legislation of the People's Party.

In North Carolina, the Populist leadership had divided over election policy in 1896. Harry Skinner and Butler openly attacked one another in convention and many Populists chose to align themselves with either Butler or Skinner, producing two competing wings of the party. In addition, the party had not grown in numbers or in the number of state representatives as its supporters had hoped in 1895. Indeed, the Republican Party was now the leading party in North Carolina, not the Democrats. Although Populists now had several leaders in the state government, they were not the majority party and remained, instead, the party that held the balance of power in the state. Such a position had already caused much infighting and difficulties for the leadership in controlling the rank and file on local cooperation. Populists again faced the dilemma of supporting a state party (the GOP) that agreed with them on electoral reform or supporting the Democratic Party that now shared the Populist's financial policy. These questions were pressing, and Populists had little time to regroup after the exhausting election of 1896. They had to decide on their state legislature agenda for the 1897 session and the degree to which they would cooperate with the Republicans. In addition, the three parties faced the question of choosing a U.S. senator. How the parties aligned themselves on this tricky issue would set the tone for the next two years. It was unclear on the day after the election whether Populists would endorse a Republican candidate or seek to select their own candidate. What transpired during the first month of 1897 over the question of the U.S. senator would plague the People's Party for the remainder of its existence in the Old North State.

CHAPTER SEVEN

BOSSISM, FACTIONALISM, AND TURMOIL

The Disintegration of Populist and Republican Rule in 1897

The Populists, once again in cooperation with the GOP, routed Democrats in 1896. The cooperationists had not only captured control of the state legislature, but also filled all the state offices and could also make appointments to lower-level patronage positions throughout the state. During a time of depression these political appointments took on a double significance. Not only did they keep local leaders in line and cement party loyalty; they also offered hope to their other aspirants that the cooperationist experiment might lead to more appointments in the future. At first glance it seemed that the People's Party had successfully transformed itself from an oppositional party to a party of state government. However, the 1897 state legislative session promised to be far more turbulent for the cooperationist partners than in 1895. The 1896 election had propelled a Republican, William McKinley, into the presidency, and a wily GOP leader, Daniel L. Russell, into the governor's mansion in North Carolina. Populists campaigned against both candidates in the 1896 elections, and their leader, Marion Butler, was determined to reinvigorate the Populist Party. Butler was a good tactician and political manipulator, but he lacked a long-term vision for the People's Party of North Carolina, especially after the rise of William Jennings Bryan. During 1896, Butler had desperately tried to align Populists with their former arch-enemies, the Democrats. However, many other leading Populists in North Carolina did not agree with Butler. These leaders and many rank-and-file activists preferred continued cooperation with the GOP. Despite these sentiments or, indeed, because of them, Butler now moved to dictate the future of the People's Party in his home state. As a result, after a turbulent campaign, Butler declared himself against the re-selection of Republican senator Jeter C. Pritchard to a full six-year term in the U.S. Senate.

However, the Populist Party in North Carolina was far from united in the wake of a particularly difficult national and state campaign, and Butler's power was not without question from other Populist leaders and many of the rank and file. Butler and Harry Skinner had constantly squabbled with one another throughout the summer and fall of 1896 over election strategy and cooperation tactics. In addition, cooperation with the GOP in local and county elections and in the majority of U.S. congressional districts in the state severely tested the resolve of Populists. For some it now seemed that the GOP posed the most serious threat to Populist policy and the party, while other Populists, suspicious of Democrats, saw cooperation with Republicans as the only way for Populism to achieve its legislative agenda in the state. Through the columns of his newspaper, Butler openly opposed the re-election of Pritchard. As early as November 14, 1896, Butler issued an open letter that accused the Republican with changing his views on the currency question to such an extent that he could no longer support his former ally for re-election. Butler charged Pritchard with deserting the people in the great struggle against the money power and throwing his lot with "the money changers, who bleed and oppress the people." Once Butler issued this letter, it became clear to many political pundits in North Carolina that a political battle over Pritchard's election was in the offing. However, Butler's opposition to Pritchard was more personal and linked to his desire to rejoin Democrats on the silver issue. In following this line Butler showed tactical acumen but little long-term vision for Populists; they had only achieved power in North Carolina because they aligned themselves with Republicans.[1]

However, the Populist Party seemed on the brink of disintegration. The simmering feud between the Butler faction and the Skinner faction of the party was fast approaching a boiling point on the senatorial question. Butler could count on support from Populists who opposed Republican cooperation and those who respected Butler's political judgment and personal commitment to the Populist agenda. At the same time, however, Butler realized that some Populists opposed his electoral strategy. Many favored a closer alliance with the GOP, and others believed that Populists had promised Pritchard the longer senatorial term in 1897, as part of the cooperation deal in the senatorial election in the 1895 state legislative session. In addition, this group also contained Populists who disliked Butler's tendency to control the grassroots political movement. This faction found its leader in U.S. congressman Harry Skinner.

The historical record on the senatorial question is rather one sided. Butler's papers contain a vast number of letters hostile to the position eventually taken by Harry Skinner as well as to the GOP and cooperation in general. Although limited, there is some evidence that permits us to look at the contest from Skinner's point of view. In mid-November Skinner wrote a letter to his old ally Cyrus Thompson, the new secretary of state and former opponent of Butler's position in the 1896 state convention, urging the Onslow Populist to support him in his fight against Butler. Skinner argued that their policy for cooperation in 1896 would have brought a resounding success for Populists, and that now "Skinner and Thompson are the leading Populists in the state and we should confer together with our known friends both as to future policy of our party and as to the immediate action of the election of United States Senator." In addition, Skinner warned Thompson that he did not want the Populist Party to "be dominated any further by the desires caprices or ambitions of any one man." The final position taken by Thompson in the 1897 senatorial race was, therefore, crucial to both Skinner and Butler.[2]

In the face of significant opposition to his leadership in the state, Butler began a counter-offensive to shore up his power base and to restructure the People's Party in readiness for the 1897 legislative session and the selection of a U.S. senator. Throughout the last few weeks of 1896, Butler received correspondence from his supporters and local political workers throughout the state on the likely voting intentions of Populist legislators, their positions in the 1896 campaign on cooperation, and the attitude of the local rank-and-file Populists in a representative's county or senatorial district. Butler believed he was in the right and that the mass of the Populist Party supported his political position on the senatorial question. J. B. Schulken argued that if Populists voted for a goldbug, it would place the party "in a ridiculous attitude before the people, disrobe themselves of the respect, confidence and standing they now have, and so weaken their influence and strength that when another general election shall come the combined efforts of the Populists in North Carolina, then in use, would not be sufficient to elect a township constable."[3]

However, not all of Butler's reports were accurate. For example, U.S. congressman Shuford wrote Butler that Robert Parker of the Twenty-ninth Senatorial District and L. A. Abernathy of Lincoln County would "abide by the Populist caucus." (They did not.) Shuford, however, did admit that Republicans were "using every effort to tighten them, and neither have much experience in working with politicians." Claudius Dockery, son of Oliver Dockery, reported to Butler that Senator Odum of the Twenty-third District would now go into the Populist caucus, and that his support was no longer doubtful. (This also proved to be wrong.)[4]

As the new year opened, politicians, newspapermen, and many voters in North Carolina were aware of the divisions in the Populist Party over the senatorship. As the recently elected state representatives descended on Raleigh, everyone realized that the debate and election of a new senator would dominate the early proceedings of the assembly. At the same time the legislature had a far-reaching set of reforms to enact into law. For example, Populists had campaigned on a platform to reform education, reform state regulation and financial policies, and restructure county government. In addition, Populists aimed to reduce railroad rates, end free railroad passes, enforce the state's anti-trust laws, increase public spending on schools, and pursue other such reforms. Moreover, many Populists wanted to reverse the terms of the recent ninety-nine-year lease of the North Carolina Railroad to J. P. Morgan's Southern Railroad Company by Democratic governor Elias Carr. Butler believed that despite the senatorial differences Populists legislators would advance Populist proposals into law in 1897.[5]

Butler had dominated the 1895 assembly, and he was determined to do the same in 1897. He arrived early in January and sought to organize the Populist caucus and bind all Populist caucus members to vote against Pritchard. However, this time Butler's authority did not go unchallenged. Republicans, with Pritchard understandably taking an active role in his own candidacy, also met with Populist legislators in order to gain their support. For the next few days the state capitol was abuzz with the GOP and Populist leaders meeting individual legislators to shore up their respective camps in readiness for the crucial vote. What was clear to all concerned was that Pritchard needed the support of just fourteen "maverick" Populists (or Democrats) to succeed in gaining re-election to the U.S. Senate.[6]

Harry Skinner led the "maverick" Populists in their refusal to support Butler's position against Republican Pritchard for the U.S. Senate. Skinner argued that the senator must be a Republican of that party's choice. Skinner produced a letter from Senator Pritchard that he claimed reasserted the senator's support of the reforms championed by the Populist Party, and he urged Populists to vote for Pritchard. In the letter Pritchard described himself as a "staunch friend" of Populist financial reform. The senatorial issue came to a head at the Populist caucus on January 8. At the caucus Butler spoke for thirty minutes and urged Populists not to vote for Pritchard because he was not a silver man. He then called on Skinner to deny the truth of the statement that he had threatened to bolt the caucus. Skinner responded by arguing that there were enough Populists to elect Pritchard, and that he considered it a Populist obligation to vote for Pritchard above the decision of the caucus. At this point, according to reports, Skinner gave a "vehement speech" in which he called on the Populist senator to name his own candidate for the senate—which Butler declined. During a heated exchange in the Populist caucus the Skinnerites complained that they were not receiving a fair hearing from the rest of the caucus. Pandemonium then broke out when one state senator offered a resolution directly opposing Pritchard and resolutions then emerged from all corners of the caucus room. Eventually, Skinner led eighteen members of the Populist state representatives out of the Populist caucus and formed a bolting caucus. Cyrus Thompson did not join Skinner; rather, he implored the bolters to return to the caucus to preserve harmony in the party. However, the bolters refused and instead issued a lengthy resolution that essentially protested "the high-handed method of gag rule perpetuated . . . by the majority of the Populist caucus" on the views of the minority.[7]

Despite the formation of a new bolting caucus, the majority of Populists hoped that they could reach some sort of compromise on the senatorial question, and various meetings were hastily arranged between members of the bolting caucus and the Populist leadership of the majority caucus, including Butler, State Auditor Hal Ayer, Railroad Commissioner S. Otho Wilson, and Cyrus Thompson. For Butler the fight over the U.S. senatorship was more important than just the election of a senator. To Butler the fight was also over his legitimacy as state leader and the continuance of the Populist reform movement. The majority Populist caucus endeavored to bring the bolters back into the caucus, but the schism seemed too wide. The bolting caucus then adopted a resolution that stated, "We demand that each member of the caucus be left entirely free upon the senatorial question as his conscience tells him is the most honorable course to pursue." At this point there was little possibility of reconciliation.[8]

Concomitant with the internal dynamics of the Populist caucus, the political press of the Republican Party and Populist Party also jostled for dominance during the debates over the senatorial question. They, like Butler, realized that the fight over the senatorship had deep significance to the political future of the state. In 1897, the Republican Party founded its own daily newspaper, the *Raleigh Tribune*, to promulgate the GOP's position in the state legislature. An editorial in the paper on January 10 dismissed Butler's claims that Pritchard had switched from silver to the gold standard. The paper also printed letters from Populists who opposed Butler's position. For example, the paper quoted at length a letter from prominent Mecklenburg County Populist Walter Henry to Jeter Pritchard that promised his support to the GOP senator. According to Henry, Populists had promised the senatorship to a silverite Republican, and Pritchard was the "most eminent silver man in the field." Populists, Henry discerned, should also support Pritchard in order to "insure a continuance of cooperation in North Carolina between the Populist and Republican parties, thereby guaranteeing us against the political slavery at the hands of the intolerant Democracy." The Republican press supported Skinner at every opportunity and lambasted Butler.[9]

The African American press also joined in on the senatorial debate. The *Raleigh Gazette*, under the direction of Wake County representative James H. Young, wrote a lengthy editorial on the Populist Party. According to Young, African Americans in North Carolina welcomed the formation of the Populist Party in 1892 because it helped to liberate "our race from Democratic oppression and tyranny." Young warned his readers that the disintegration of the People's Party would be a catastrophe to the people of North Carolina, and Democrats would stop at nothing to destroy the Populists, even if this meant in the short-run giving Populists the senatorship. Young, therefore, argued, "The colored people of the State regard Senator Pritchard as their friend, and are very desirous of his re-election, and to such an extent that they would look with disfavor upon effects in the future to get them to support cooperation candidates of the Populist Party if he is defeated." He also believed "the Populists recognized the fact the colored voters, with few rare exceptions have been among their strongest, most zealous and potent allies in planning and carrying out co-operation in this State." Young hoped that friendly relations continued between Populists and African Americans and claimed, "The Populists have it in their power to make perpetual this relationship by helping to re-elect Pritchard, or greatly impair it by defeating him."[10]

A minority of Populist newspapers also supported Harry Skinner and the pro-Republican stance of the bolting Populists. R. A. Cobb of the *Morganton Populist*, G. D. Kestler of the *Concord Vestibule*, and T. W. Babb of the *Perquimans Record* argued that Populists had made an agreement to support Pritchard back in 1895 and insisted the most imminent danger facing Populists was from Democrats. Only a continuance of Populist-Republican cooperation, they contended, could keep Democrats out of power. In addition, they claimed Populists must also stick to their pledges and maintain their honor and integrity.[11]

The remaining Populist press, on the other hand, defended the position of Butler on the senatorial question. Butler's position in opposing Pritchard may have made good sense, but it took some explaining to rank-and-file members who had just voted the cooperation ticket in November. Butler took on the task with his usual zeal. However, the Populist leader did not have a daily newspaper for the 1897 legislative session. Nonetheless, Butler endeavored to respond to the political developments in Raleigh and the writings of the Republican press. For example, notable local Populist leader J. M. Cutchin from Whitakers wrote that Populists must oppose Pritchard because he did not stick to principle over monetary reform. He warned his fellow Populists that if Skinner consummated his deal with Pritchard and the GOP, "the Democratic Party [would] get the benefit in the next campaign," with the Populists divided.[12]

As early as January 8, 1897, after Skinner led the bolters out of the Populist caucus, it seemed that Pritchard would prevail in gaining re-election to the U.S. Senate. Despite the position, Butler used every political trick he could to delay a final vote in the hope that enough of the bolting Populists would return to the caucus. But despite his political power of persuasion, Butler could not convince the maverick Populists to return. He had met his match in Harry Skinner. Butler became increasingly desperate, and in one last throw of the political dice he nominated Cyrus Thompson as the official Populist caucus nominee for the U.S. Senate. But the bolting caucus did not return to the majority caucus. In an interview with the *Raleigh Tribune* on the nomination of Cyrus Thompson, Harry Skinner noted that Butler only hoped to destroy another prominent Populist and that there could not be two U.S. senators from the east. Populists, according to Skinner, "have had enough of Butler's tyranny." Skinner was still disappointed at the nomination of Thompson, whom he considered a potential ally in his fight against Butler. "I am sorry he has lent himself to Butler," he told a *Wilmington Messenger* reporter, "by which he is slaughtered."[13]

As the vote drew close, Butler believed he represented the position of true Populists. He received many letters from supporters for his position on the issue. John Duckett wrote Butler that he knew Skinner quite well and the old Democrat "is a great schemer, and often gets scared of his own schemes." Skinner was hoping, Duckett believed, to benefit from the fight over the senatorship, specifically by gaining control of federal patronage in the First Congressional District. However, he urged Butler to stand firm because Skinner was "easily scared, and if a lot of Populists were to write him or hold meetings in the 1st District condemning his support of Pritchard, it would scare him out of his boots."[14]

Despite all the voices of support for Butler and his position on the senatorial question, when the vote came for the U.S. senator on January 20, seventeen Populists voted for Pritchard. The official vote read thus: Pritchard, eighty-eight votes; Cyrus Thompson, forty-three votes; and Democrat Rufus Doughton, thirty-three votes. The victory for Pritchard was a crushing blow to Butler. Senator Pritchard then entered the general assembly with GOP governor Daniel L. Russell and Populist Harry Skinner. To thunderous applause Pritchard thanked those who supported his candidacy and vowed to work for the best interests of Tar Heels. He then turned to the Populist bolters and congratulated them for their votes: "Populists, you will never regret having voted for me on this occasion. I have been misrepresented, maligned and slandered." Daniel L. Russell then spoke and hoped that the fight over the senatorship would not cause Republicans and Populists to divide over crucial reform legislation facing the assembly. Harry Skinner then addressed the legislators. Skinner argued that Pritchard was a silverite Republican and it was in the best interests of the People's Party to have a GOP silverite in the Senate. Skinner denied that the deal would cause the disintegration of the Populists and insisted the bolters had voted for their contract with Republicans and "had done the best deed ever done for the Populist Party and the cause of humanity."[15]

Why did seventeen Populists support Pritchard and directly oppose the policy of their state leader? According to Butler and his supporters, the bolting Populists were promised lucrative (for the time) positions, such as postmasterships, and the promise that Republicans would support these candidates in the 1898 elections. For example, the *Caucasian* argued that Skinner wanted to build up his own power base in the First Congressional District, and to do this he wanted to put white Populists in postmaster positions rather than African Americans. Therefore, as part of the deal, the paper alleged, Pritchard would give Skinner the opportunity to build up his supporters in the northeastern section of the state. In addition, the paper reported that Republicans promised William Odum of the Twenty-third District the postmastership in Wadesboro if he voted for Pritchard.[16]

Harry Skinner wrote a lengthy piece detailing his actions on the senatorial question. According to Skinner, Pritchard had remained friendly to silver and thus he supported the senator. Importantly, Skinner, in an obvious attack on Butler's policy of enticing Democrats into the People's Party, argued that "old Populists" supported his position. Next, Skinner turned to the nub of the issue. He argued, "Without Republican assistance no Populist can have been elected to any state office, Congress or local office save an excepting two counties. Every man elected to the Legislature by Republican assistance was charged that if elected that he would vote for Pritchard." Skinner also noted that Butler was playing a complicated political game and in nominating Thompson he was merely trying to cover his back because the force of tradition meant that two senators could not come from the eastern section of North Carolina. Finally, Skinner turned on his U.S. senator with a damning critique: "As Populists we rebelled against . . . tyranny. Yet in the brief time of four years, we find the Senator of the party, owing his prestige to fighting tyranny, himself to the most reckless and unscrupulous tyrant, in compelling obedience to what he hitherto denounced, that no Senator in the State or nation has dared to suggest or approach; that is, by a small faction of the party to expel and excommunicate original Populists—the creators of the party and Butler, when they were assisting him to fight the friends that he now draws comfort and support from, and of which material he has constituted a majority of his central committee."[17]

In the final analysis, it seems that a combination of factors were at work in the bolting Populists' deliberations. First, many Populists concluded that Butler had too much power in a mass movement, and no doubt some Populists determined that this should end. Second, many Populists gained election to the state assembly on the back of an alliance with the GOP. In many counties Populists relied heavily on GOP support. In all good conscience many believed they could not vote for another Populist. Besides, many reasoned that they had promised to vote for Pritchard in 1895. At the heart of the turmoil was one of the central weaknesses of cooperation. Populists and Republicans needed one another to win power. However, each party had different policies and conflicting personalities. In a national election these issues became more pronounced. Butler, a skilled politician, knew the price Populists paid for cooperation. In 1896 the lines between the Republican Party and Populist Party blurred. As a result, after the election, when Butler tried to reconstitute the Populists, he faced a situation where earnest Populists wondered what on earth was going on. For the past two years the two parties had worked closely together and now suddenly their leader denounced his senatorial colleague in vehement terms.[18]

Third, personal hostilities in the People's Party also played a role, and personal ambition and promises of lucrative patronage positions cannot be discounted in the actions of some bolting Populists. But it is too simplistic to use personal ambition alone to explain the actions of the bolting Populists. The nature of cooperation politics, the bitter 1896 campaign, and the difficulty the Populist leadership had in controlling local rank-and-file supporters meant that such a showdown was inevitable at some juncture. While it is true that eight of the bolting Populists came from Harry Skinner's First Congressional District, in the end local factors seem to have propelled a majority of the seventeen Populists who voted for Pritchard. Local political realities outweighed the dictates of the caucus whip and the instructions of Butler. The senatorial race was the *occasion*, not the cause, of the divisions in the Populist Party. The difficulties of cooperation politics, the 1896 national election, personal differences among the leadership, and a disjuncture between grassroots activists and the backroom double-dealings of the leadership caused the disintegration of the Populists.[19]

More important than the individual reasons behind the actions of the bolting caucus members, however, was the reaction of Butler and the Populist majority caucus to the bolting caucus's actions on the senatorial question. Butler led the denunciation of the Skinner and the seventeen bolting Populists, going so far as calling Skinner a traitor. In private, Butler confided to his wife that he was fighting for the "very life and existence of my party in the state. I am fighting for *our* future and for the county's future." He believed that Pritchard gained election "by bribery and corruption." He lamented, "I would have whipped Pritchard had I not had the world, the flesh and devil combined against me"; but on an optimistic note he ended, "I am going to win by the grace of God and with the help of my wife's prayers." For Butler the senatorial defeat was his worst political and personal moment in five years.[20]

Butler did not stop at personally attacking Skinner and the bolting Populists. He decided he could not forgive their actions and decided instead to seek political retribution. His actions illustrate the disruption the Populists now faced. Butler, in an attempt to reassert his leadership, repudiated and expelled the bolters from the Populist Party. A week after the election of Pritchard the Populist legislative caucus met to decide the official party reaction to the schism in the party and to reconsider the party's relationship with the GOP. With Butler in command the caucus attacked the actions of the bolters and lambasted them as Republicans. Next, the caucus stated that only by expelling from the party false Populists could the People's Party maintain the integrity and independence of its organization. The caucus labeled Skinner a "Judas" of Populism. As a result, the majority caucus informed Skinner and the bolting state legislators that they were no longer Populists. The caucus then tried to renew cooperation with Republicans in order to push through the reform legislation. The Populist Party reeled from the senatorial question at the exact moment when the party needed to put up a united front during a difficult state legislative session.[21]

The senatorial fight poisoned the 1897 session of the state legislature. Populists remained divided throughout the session, and the minority faction (Skinnerites) tended to vote more with Republicans than with the majority Populists. The Republicans and the majority Populists remained divided over legislative reform. In addition, the 1897 legislative session was complicated still further by the presence and political agenda of Russell. On many issues the governor exhibited strong Populistic tendencies. For example, Russell favored the cancellation of Elias Carr's lease of the North Carolina Railroad, improvements in public education, and more effective railroad legislation. In an interview before his inauguration, the governor-elect challenged the legality of the ninety-nine-year lease and called on Populists to help him cancel it, a position that caused a great deal of worry in the ranks of conservative Republicans.[22]

As the Populist-Republican alliance crumbled, Russell took the oath of office as governor on January 12, 1897. Playing on Governor Zebulon Vance's famous speech, the old Greenback Republican claimed, "There is a retribution in history." Russell termed his election a victory for the "weak and oppressed" over the privileged and lawless. Russell called for a higher tax rate to support schools, large appropriations for the state university, protection of lawful public meetings, and a more efficient court system. He also urged the government "regulation of State and inter-state commerce by common carriers." Russell then showed his Populist leanings. He predicted the conversion of the railroads into "public highways, owned and controlled by the nation." Russell then turned to the lease of the North Carolina Railroad and urged state legislators to do all in their power to recover the railroad for the state. Despite the Populist overtones of his inaugural address, Russell had to negotiate the complex world of a collapsing cooperationist government and attempt to push through progressive legislation that would only further divide the already hostile parties.[23]

Although Butler was now in Washington, D.C., he still tried to direct Populist action in the state. Butler was determined, in the wake of the senatorial defeat, to push through the Populist reform legislation promised in the 1896 campaign. In the legislature the majority Populist caucus aimed to prevent discrimination against silver as legal tender, lower telegraph and railroad rates, and the make the railroad commission an elective body. However, because of the poisoned state of relations between Populists and Republicans, Populist attempts at monetary reform and corporate regulation failed. For example, on the silver bill Democrats supported the majority Populists but enough Skinnerites supported Republicans that the bill was effectively gutted in the lower house. In the face of opposition from Republicans, Democrats, and Skinnerite Populists, the Butlerites had an

Populists in 1897 Assembly

WHEN we dropped by the other day to see Frank Strowd, editor of the *Davie Record*, published in Mocksville, we observed this picture (on the opposite page) on the wall of his office. We immediately latched on to it.

It is a composite photograph taken by C. P. Wharton, photographer, of Raleigh. The caption at the top is "Populists who stood by the People's Party Principles During the Legislature of 1897."

In all probability, you'll recognize several of the names of these men, even though you did not know them personally. Here they are:

Populists in 1897 State Senate

1. J. W. Atwater, Chmn. Populist Caucus, Chatham.
2. Dr. J. B. Alexander, Mecklenburg.
3. George Butler, Sampson.
4. S. A. Earnheart, Rowan.
5. J. McF. Geddie, Cumberland.
6. G. L. Hardison, Craven.
7. J. E. Lyon, Durham.
8. J. F. Mitchell, Franklin.
9. R. G. Maxwell, Duplin.
10. A. J. Moye, Pitt.
11. Dr. William Merritt, Person.
12. D. A. Patterson, Richmond.
13. E. N. Roberson, Bladen.
14. A. Shaw, Robeson.
15. C. H. Utlery, Wake.
16. J. A. Walker, Rockingham.

Populist Representatives, 1897

17. W. T. Barrow, Franklin.
18. W. P. Craven, Mecklenburg.
19. V. B. Carter, Nash.
20. Slade Chapman, Pitt.
21. R. M. Crumpler, Sampson.
22. W. R. Dixon, Pitt.
23. W. W. Drew, Brunswick.
24. P. P. Foster, Rockingham.
25. J. M. Ferrell, Wake.
26. E. P. Hauser, Lenoir.
27. A. R. Holmes, Orange.
28. C. H. Johnson, Sampson.
29. John King, Granville.
30. D. B. McBryde, Robeson.
31. Y. C. Morton, Richmond.
32. L. Purgason, Rutherford.
33. J. N. Price, Union.
34. W. F. Platt, Clay.
35. Dr. R. T. Person, Wilson.
36. J. A. Reynolds, Montgomery.
37. J. B. Schulken, Columbus.
38. Maury Ward, Duplin.

Populists Who Were Present and Assisted the Legislators

39. Hal W. Ayer, State Auditor, Wake.

40. Marion Butler, U. S. Senator.
41. A. L. Byrd, Asst. Enrolling Clerk, Harnett.
42. L. C. Caldwell, Mayor of Statesville.
43. J. F. Click, Asst. Engrossing Clerk, Catawba.
44. W. E. Fountain, State Chmn. People's Party, Edgecombe.
45. J. B. Lloyd, Asst. Doorkeeper, U. S. Senate, Edgecombe.
46. V. J. McArthur, Doorkeeper of the Senate, Sampson.
47. A. H. Paddison, First Asst. Clerk of Senate, Pender.
48. Dr. W. Pearsall, Stationery Mail Keeper of the House, Duplin.
49. J. L. Ramsay, editor *Progressive Farmer*, Wake.
50. B. F. Scarborough, Asst. Engrossing Clerk, Lenoir.
51. J. H. Sherrill, Chmn. Populist Exec. Com. 7th Dist., Catawba.
52. A. C. Shuford, Congressman 7th Dist., Catawba.
53. John A. Sims, Chief Clerk to State Auditor, Wake.
54. W. F. Strowd, Congressman 4th Dist., Orange.
55. Dr. Cyrus Thompson, Secy. of State, Wake.
56. S. Otho Wilson, Railroad Commissioner, Wake.

Populists in the state legislature of 1897. Courtesy of the North Carolina Division of Archives and History, Raleigh, NC.

impossible task. At first Butler was suspicious of the new GOP governor, but gradually events would push the two men together, politically.[24]

During the 1897 assembly, the most important bill introduced before the legislature was the attempt to annul the lease of the North Carolina Railroad. Butler opposed the lease to the Southern Railroad and campaigned against the lease in the 1896 elections. Governor Russell also opposed the lease, and during the debate in the assembly on the lease the Butlerite Populists found themselves supporting the newly installed governor. Indeed, the governor had recruited a bipartisan group of politicians to plan his strategy for annulling the lease. However, most Republicans and Skinnerite Populists opposed annulment of the lease. The Republican press gave the bill a hostile reception. For example, the *Raleigh Tribune* warned the governor that capital was being frightened away from North Carolina by Russell's "revolutionary State legislation." Although the annulment bill passed the lower house by a narrow vote of sixty to fifty-four, it became bogged down in the state senate during February. Eventually, the bill was defeated by a coalition of conservative Republicans, Democrats, and Skinnerite Populists in the lower house after the senate offered a compromise measure. Politics certainly made strange bedfellows. Butler did all in his power to get the bill passed, but once the bill failed he concluded that the only way to change the situation was government ownership of the railroads.[25]

Although the Butlerite Populists achieved little in the 1897 legislature, the fight over the lease of the North Carolina Railroad did bring Butler and Russell together in a political alliance. Butler's brother, George Butler, a member of the 1897 session, wrote the senator, his brother, that Russell was now "virtually a Populist." The governor needed the support of the Butlerites, and Butler was determined to rebuild his party after the debacle of the senate race. Although such an alliance may have made good sense to the political chicanery of Butler, it proved another source of division in a badly divided Populist Party. The new Populist state chairman, William E. Fountain, seemed unimpressed by Russell. He urged Butler to take a bold stand and declare the Populist policy and purpose. Fountain also argued, "Treated as we have been by the republicans, and the policy pursued by the governor in his efforts to disorganize us, and seeking to take us under his wing, precluded any further alliance with them."[26]

At the same time that Russell and Butler began to form an alliance, the rest of the GOP state party began to attack the last vestiges of Redeemer rule. The Republicans were determined to overturn the last bastion of Democratic hegemony—the courthouse ring-rule—in many eastern cities. During his campaign for governor, Russell had promised the taxpayers of municipalities protection from misrule by the property-less and ignorant—code words for African Americans—and after the election the governor sought the power to appoint city aldermen in eastern cities such as Wilmington and New Bern. Republicans introduced the bill to give Russell this power. The Democratic press complained that Russell had committed a political U-turn on his promise of home rule by demanding the right to appoint city aldermen, and they also claimed that Republicans planned to install "negro rule and domination" in the eastern section of North Carolina. However, white Republicans were not willing to give the eastern cities over to African American rule. Indeed, African Americans complained that their communities were ignored through enactment of the bills to give the governor appointive power on city government. The bill to give Russell appointment power in the cities of Wilmington and New Bern passed with a solid Republican vote with aid from the Skinnerite Populists. The majority Populists and Democrats, fearing black rule in the eastern section of North Carolina and a white backlash in majority-black districts, opposed the bills.[27]

Republicans also pushed to make adjustments in the 1895 election law. The key section of the bill would decentralize the machinery of elections and place it in local hands. The county board of elections, instead of the chairman of the state executive committee, would appoint judges and registrars. The new election commission consisted of each county's clerk of the superior court, register of deeds, and chairman of the county commissioners. As a result, in majority-black districts the election machinery could "fall into the hands" of African Americans. Russell, sensing that this might prove the occasion to show his Populist credentials and form a binding alliance with Butlerite Populists, Russell Republicans, and some reform-minded Democrats, opposed the bill. He saw the bill's details and possible effects as "unfair and dangerous." The GOP governor, in a clear overture to Populists, worried that the People's Party would be deprived "of any representation" in the election process. If cooperation did not continue, Russell warned, Populists would return to the Democrats, and thus he opposed the bill. Butler and his supporters agreed with Russell. They worried that it would mean the end of Populist registrars and the possible return of illegal activities on Election Day. In addition, Populists worried that having large numbers of African American officials in the eastern section of the state might open them up to the charge by Democrats of supporting social equality between the races. The Populists' political strength lay in the eastern section of the state, and these same Populists were especially sensitive to the race issue. Russell's position on the election law and his other Populistic leanings outraged many Republicans. Despite the opposition of Russell and the Butlerites to the election bill, it passed into law with the help of the Skinnerite Populists.[28]

Although a new alliance between the Russell and Butler seemed to offer hope to some Populists, many Populists welcomed the adjournment of the legislature on March 9, 1897. The session was a complete disaster for the Populists. The party remained badly divided over the senatorial question, the political fallout over the treatment of the Skinnerites, and the alliance between many of the

Skinnerites and conservative Republicans. Republicans themselves divided over the policy initiatives of their governor. The cooperationist government in 1897 seemed a total failure. Many Populists, with some justification, could place much of the blame at the feet of Republicans who decided to consolidate their own power rather than advancing cooperation. At the same time, however, the divisions in the Populist Party and the backroom dealings of Butler did little to iron out the problems in the cooperation experiment.[29]

The Populists remained deeply divided in the early months of 1897. Butler received worrying news from across the state that pointed to party disintegration. A local Populist from Winston wondered if the Populists could now survive in the state, and he asked Butler if the party was "dying as fast as possible? Is it not gasping for its last political breath?" He continued, "To many of the rank and file of the Party, it begins to look as if they will be compelled to find homes in one of the other of the old parties again. They are discouraged by the bickering of their Party leaders and feel that the Party is rapidly disintegrating." J. Z. Green reported, "Our party is getting into a desperate condition and unless wisdom in the future exceeds that of the past rapid disintegration seems to be inevitable." Green, like so many other Populists, asked Butler the all-important question: "Do you see any way out of it? "[30]

The Populist press also exhibited similar factionalism on the future of the People's Party. The *Wadesboro Plow Boy* described itself as a mid-roader, but it also supported the actions of Butler. Butler could count on the strongest support from his paper, the *Caucasian*, the *Salisbury Carolina Watchman*, and J. F. Click's *Hickory Mercury*. Click seemed to favor harmony with Democrats, but the *Hickory Mercury* also poured scorn on the Democrats. It attacked the free-silver Democratic editors who were "continually heaping abuse on the Populists and Populist leaders." The paper also stated that although the Populists were willing to harmonize with honorable men of all parties on reasonable terms, they "will never harmonize with the wild shrieking hyenas and untamed jackasses. If the Democrats want harmony they should call off their dogs."[31]

During the remainder of 1897, Butler began to move ever closer to Russell, as the maverick Republican continued to vigorously oppose the ninety-nine-year lease of the North Carolina Railroad to the Southern Railway. He appointed anti-lease men to the North Carolina Railroad board of directors and asked the Railroad Commission to reduce railroad rates to consumers and to increase railroad taxes. In late September 1897, Russell removed James W. Wilson and Populist S. Otho Wilson from the Railroad Commission so that the commission would serve the will of the governor. Under the complicated rules governing the commission, the governor could suspend a railroad commissioner who held stocks, bonds, or any kind of interest in a company subject to the commission's jurisdiction. Russell justified the removal of the Wilsons because they held an interest in a hotel called Round Knob House that served the North Carolina Railroad. However, political considerations fueled the commissioner's removal as much as a conflict of interest on the part of the Wilsons. Russell wanted his chosen men in the commission. In removing S. Otho Wilson, however, the governor ran up against a leading Populist, one suspected of harboring sympathies with Harry Skinner. Thus, the removal of the railroad commissioners only worsened the split within the Populist Party.[32]

Butler and Russell remained in constant touch on these issues throughout the spring and summer. For example, a Populist close to Russell informed Butler that S. Otho Wilson did hold an interest in the railroad hotel and this might affect his vote on the governor's plan to reduce rates and increase taxes. Russell hoped the reduction of railroad rates would pass, but when it failed he removed the Wilsons and replaced them with a Democrat, John Pearson, and a Populist, L. C. Caldwell. S. Otho Wilson had, in fact, voted to reduce railroad rates, but that did not stop his expulsion. Butler supported both of these Railroad Commission replacements. Such actions by Russell and Butler hurt the Populists. The party, already in a state of disintegration, now divided still further. S. Otho Wilson was a leading Populist and an important leader in the Fourth Congressional District. Wilson's treatment by Russell and Butler outraged him, and through his newspaper, the *Raleigh Hayseeder,* he began to openly and vehemently attack the Populist senator. For example, the paper charged that S. Otho Wilson had done more than anyone else to make Marion Butler who he was, and yet now Wilson "has been stabbed in the back by Russell and Butler . . . right in his own house and by his bosom friends." Butler had now created two powerful Populist opponents, Harry Skinner and S. Otho Wilson. Although Butler may have discerned that a strong alliance with Governor Russell was more beneficial to the success of the Populist Party, by creating hostilities with two important and politically savvy leaders, Butler now had to constantly watch his political flanks.[33]

Marion Butler, sensing that control of the Populist Party was slipping from his iron-like grasp, went on the counter-offensive throughout the summer and autumn of 1897. He discerned that the health and future of the Populist Party was best served by launching a new campaign for reform, and many leaders of the Populist Party agreed with this idea. Hal Ayer, for example, urged that the Populist executive committee meet in the summer to set policy for the party and to devise a plan as quickly as possible to improve the condition of the party in the state. A sense of desperation was now creeping into the correspondence flooding into Butler. Although an aggressive campaign made political sense, Butler had done little to patch up the political differences with the Skinnerite faction of the party, nor had he fully articulated his strategy of aligning with Governor Russell. Coupled with this, Populists were now on the political defensive. In 1894 Populists could build up their party by lambasting the machine rule and undemocratic governance of Bourbon Democrats. In 1897, however, Butler had to constantly defend his actions as a cooperationist partner in a government that was torn by dissent.[34]

In August 1897, the state Populist executive committee met and issued an address to the voters of North Carolina that praised the party's success in achieving fair election laws, local self-government, improvements in education and schooling, and improvements in charitable and penal institutions. The committee also urged harmony in the Populist ranks to achieve success through united action and persistent action. Butler also took over the editorial reins of the *Caucasian* and set out to tour the state to deliver a series of addresses to the voters of North Carolina. Public speaking had served Populists well in 1894 and 1896, and Butler reasoned that an energetic series of speaking engagements would, firstly, reinvigorate the rank-and-file members of the Populist Party and, secondly, draw reform-minded Democrats and Republicans to the ranks of the People's Party. During the speeches he attacked Democrats and the Skinnerites in the state legislature. Using familiar rhetoric, he also portrayed Democrats, Republicans, railroads, trusts, and Wall Street as the enemies of the people. He warned the people that the railroads planned to control the next general assembly and even the schools and churches of the state. In an attempt to build up his idea of bipartisan reform movement, Butler argued that he was not making a party fight but a fight for principles and for cooperation between those who supported these principles. The *Hickory Mercury*, for example, praised the content and quality of the speeches; and "it shows," according to the paper, "that he has a power and influence with the masses unequaled by any other man or half dozen men in the State."[35]

Butler also hoped to form a close relationship with reform-minded Democrats in the Tar Heel state. During the early months of the year Butler found some cause for optimism. Josephus Daniels at the *News and Observer* seemed to support Russell's war on the railroad lease and Butler's position on free silver. During the 1897 assembly some reform-minded Democrats voted with the Butlerites, and many Democratic papers admonished the actions of the Skinnerites. But Democrats remained badly divided over their poor showing in the state in 1896, and many personality conflicts existed between Butler and the Democratic leadership. In addition, a more worrying development for Butler and his Populist followers emerged during the final few months of 1897. The divided Democratic Party began to focus on the biracial aspects of the cooperation experiment. The Democratic press began to complain more vocally of ignorant voters controlling the state (code for African Americans). Gradually, it seemed, Democrats began to focus their political campaign for reelection in 1898 on the race issue.[36]

Butler was wary of the increased number of columns in the Democratic press given over to the race issue. In 1897, he argued as he had since the formation of the People's Party that the real struggle was the economy and the people. The issue of race was just a scarecrow used to divide people. The *Caucasian* argued, "White supremacy is being used for a different and ulterior purpose." During his speaking tour Butler denounced the increased emphasis on race. At Clinton he exclaimed that he was a friend of African Americans and proclaimed that African American rights must be protected in the way that every citizen's rights must be protected. He also addressed the issue of white supremacy. Butler argued that white supremacy was safe under cooperation rule because African Americans were only a minority of the state's population, and even if the African Americans were in the majority, whites would remain in power because "of their superior intelligence." At Rocky Mount, Butler also claimed that Democrats exaggerated black crimes and "outrages" for their own political ends. He even charged Democrats with actually wanting more "outrages" because this served their selfish ends. According to the *Lenoir Topic*, Butler claimed, "If colored men commit outrages the Democrats pretend to be terribly shocked in public, but when they get behind a wall they laugh until they grow fat." Some Democratic papers stated that Butler claimed that Democrats had hired African Americans to commit such outrages.[37]

Democrats reacted angrily to Butler's claims and saw his comments as slanderous. The Democratic press argued that Butler claimed Democrats had actually contracted black men to commit such outrages. The word "outrage" meant the rape of white women. This struck a raw nerve in the Tar Heel State because it hit at one of the pillars of white supremacy. White supremacy was built, in part, on white fears that African Americans wanted to rape white women, and, therefore, white men had to protect their women from such outrages. The image of the white woman became identified by white men with the state, and therefore any attack on a woman was an attack on the white southern way of life. Butler immediately denied that he had said Democrats funded rapes by blacks of white women. Clearly now on the defensive, Butler gave an interview: "I have declared positively and unequivocally in favor of white supremacy and Anglo-Saxon rule. I have further declared that every good citizen, not only of the white race, but of the colored race should favor it; . . . and that the class of citizens, if there were such, either white or black, who attempted to stir up race prejudice for the purpose of calling attention from and defeating great economic reforms that concern the welfare of our population, were the worst and most dangerous element of society."[38]

The Populist press argued that Democrats were lying over the issue and Butler could not have said such things about Democratic-sponsored "outrages." The *Hickory Mercury*, for example, argued, "The Populists will not be turned to the right or left by the cry of 'nigger.'" In the short term the Rocky Mount speech kept the race issue in front of the voters and gave a clear indication on a central theme in the 1898 campaign. It also suggested that Populists and Democrats had a long way to go to enact any cooperation or fusion.[39]

As 1897 came to a close there seemed no hope of reconciliation between the Skinnerites and Butlerites at all. The party also had failed to enact any of its campaign planks into law during the 1897 session and, indeed, many Republican laws passed by the assembly ran counter to the reformist ideology of the People's Party. Personal animosities seemed even more strained than at the beginning of the year. Butler did little to alleviate the problem in the ranks of the party. As the leader of the Populists he chose instead to form an alliance with a GOP governor who was alienated from his own party on the railroad lease issue and reform-minded Democrats who had not promised to support him. Coupled with this, the national Populist Party was at sea on electoral strategy. It was clear to many political pundits that Democrats would focus on the race issue in 1898. The question now was what form a race-based campaign would take and how would Populists respond to a white supremacy campaign. Butler and his cadre of leaders believed that by focusing on class issues and his reform platform he could once again circumvent race issues. But in 1898 the Populists were badly divided and in the first stages of total disintegration. The Republicans, not the Populists, now led the battered cooperation forces in the Old North State. With increased GOP power came the fear from many Democrats of black rule in the eastern section of North Carolina.

CHAPTER EIGHT

THE CHICKENS COME HOME TO ROOST

The White Supremacy Campaign in North Carolina

The Populist Party breathed a sigh of relief as 1898 began. The 1897 state legislative session was the worst moment in the life of the young party. During the previous year the Populists divided into many factions, and bitter personality clashes indelibly marked the minds of the rank and file of the party. In 1892 Populists presented themselves as something new in politics. They opposed the backroom political dealings of a small cadre of ambitious office seekers in the Democratic Party. But now Populists were guilty of the same charge. Perhaps political leaders had little choice but to engage in such chicanery. However, the rank and file of the Populists seemed outraged at such internal backstabbing and name calling. Many Populists began to question their adherence to their party and remained susceptible to the rhetoric of the other political parties. Marion Butler, perhaps sensing this sentiment in his party, began to move Populists toward Governor Russell and reform-oriented Democrats.

Butler continued to pursue this realignment in the early months of 1898. He hoped to secure an alliance of reform-minded politicians, irrespective of party affiliations, for the upcoming state and congressional elections. Butler earnestly believed that Populists could align themselves with either the reform-minded faction of the Democrats or the entire Democratic Party on the need for financial reform. Thus he urged the Populists to call an early state convention and propose cooperation with the Democrats. At the same time, defeated Democratic presidential candidate William Jennings Bryan issued a statement to the voters of the United States urging unity and cooperation among all the opponents of the gold standard and monopoly. In Butler's mind, Bryan's address would force Democrats to fuse with Populists in the upcoming state campaign. At the same time that Butler appealed to the Democrats to fuse with the People's Party, he also tried to further the apparent disintegration within the Democratic Party. He called on the rank and file to oppose the actions of the Democratic state executive committee if it opposed cooperation with Populists, urging them to follow the policies of William Jennings Bryan and the cause of free silver.[1]

There was, however, a significant problem with Butler's strategy. The Populists were far from united on the issue of cooperation with Democrats in the upcoming state campaign. In fact, many Populists directly opposed Butler's plan, while other Populists favored continued cooperation with the Republicans. For example, S. Otho Wilson's *Raleigh Hayseeder* attacked Butler's position on cooperation and claimed that Butler only wanted to fuse with Democrats for his office and aggrandizement. According to Wilson, Democrats would disfranchise poor whites if they gained office, and in order to avoid this, the paper supported continued cooperation with the Republican Party. The *Chatham Citizen* also opposed cooperation with the Democratic Party. It worried that Democrats would merely use Populist votes to win election and then once in office oppose and throw out Populist reform-minded legislation. The paper's editor, R. B. Lineberry, wrote a scathing editorial on cooperation: "There is no common ground on which the Populists and Democrats can unite in North Carolina. They are not agreed on one solitary State issue," and cooperation would mean "death and dissolution of the Populist Party." Turning to the reasons behind talk of cooperation, the paper rhetorically asked, Who in the People's Party favored cooperation? Lineberry then answered his own question: "It springs from the avarice, the itching palms, and the love of office, of the politicians in our party." Lineberry implored, "And shall the rank and file of the party permit the carcass of populism to be laid down by the same politicians and used as a stepping stone to office?" These newspapers probably epitomized the views of the rank and file.[2]

On the other hand, some Populist papers did support Butler's position. The *Hickory Times-Mercury* supported cooperation with Democrats. Editor J. F. Click saw Butler as trying "to do fair and reasonable things of the cardinal principles" of the People's Party. Click did admit, however, that divisions existed in the People's Party. "For some time" he noted, "there has been in this State an undercurrent in the Populist party, to destroy the strong and general confidence existing between Butler and his party—the voters." Nevertheless, Click heaped lavish praise on the U.S. senator: "Butler keeps in touch with the sentiments and feelings of the most conservative elements of the party, those who think and act from purely unselfish motives, and he is governed accordingly. The voters love him for what he has done." From the editorials of the Populist newspapers it is clear that Butler's position on cooperation with the Democrats or with the reform wing of that party evoked strong reactions from his followers, and it seems that talk of cooperation only had the effect of dividing Populists still further.[3]

Butler's position on state cooperation with Democrats also provoked a flurry of private correspondence in the first few months of 1898. These letters illustrate the various sentiments in the party. Some Populists favored a straight fight.

For example, J. Dalton of Forsyth County wrote Butler that Populists had achieved little by fusing with the GOP, and he warned Butler that he could not persuade voters to cast their lot for Populists because the rank and file believe that "*all your leaders is after office.*" Others directly opposed cooperation with Democrats. George T. Jones argued, "Co-operation in N.C. between the Dem party and the Pop party is an 'irredescent [*sic*] dream' *It won't work*, they (the Dems) will nominate so called Silver Democrats in all the districts and then ask us (the Pops) *What more do you want?* They have been so abusive to the Populists that the pop rank and file *will not vote solidly* for Democrats." Thomas H. Sutton wrote what would turn out to be an accurate description of the Democratic campaign strategy in 1898:

> That plan is this—they will ignore everything except the color issue, and try to thus seduce the Populists to come back with them, and in more than one county I know of, they have offered the Populists every single office if they will give the Democrats the *next Legislature*—with that they will safely and for all time to come entrench themselves in power, by passing an election law, and they will under skillful manipulations, give them the election machinery, for the election of 1900, and then they will call a convention and before 1900 amend the Constitution by planning an election similar to that now prevailing in S.C. and Miss. (I mean an educational qualification), after which they will have no odds of any people, whether they be Populists or Republicans.[4]

Although Butler was careful to solicit the views from a cross-section of the People's Party, the responses he received illustrated a worrying lack of unity on campaign strategy.[5]

Opposition toward Butler's policy of cooperation with Democrats crystallized in an informal conference of Populists in Raleigh in mid-March 1898. Populists largely from the eastern section of the state, including Cyrus Thompson, Hal Ayer, S. Otho Wilson, and William Worth, attended the meeting. Of the fifty-two Populists at the meeting only twelve to fifteen were Butlerites. It seems that the Skinnerite wing of the party dominated the meeting. Many of these men advocated continued cooperation with Republicans. This was a worrying development for Butler because the eastern section of North Carolina was the Populist stronghold in the state. The convention rejected Butler's idea for state cooperation with Democrats and also demanded a Populist paper that focused on state issues rather than a national perspective. This was a slap in the face to the pre-eminent Populist and a sign of major divisions within the state party.[6]

Despite the opposition from many Populists toward his policy of cooperation with Democrats, Butler now determined his policy would win the day. Thus he sought an early meeting of the state executive committee to formulate such a strategy and to call an early Populist state convention. When the Populist state executive committee meeting convened on April 5, 1898, it acceded to Butler's wishes, calling the Populist state convention for May 17, 1898, eight days before the Democrats scheduled their convention. In an editorial in the *Caucasian*, Butler outlined his position on state policy ahead of the Populist convention. He argued that Populists must make a "proposition to cooperate to be fair and just that no honest man in any party can object to it."[7]

However, Butler's position still faced stiff opposition from many Populists. The *Charlotte People's Paper* gave a lukewarm response to Butler's position. It felt that cooperation could only work if the Bryan Democrats would "drive all the gold-bugs out of their party, and then relegate the silver plated goldbugs to the rear." The *Progressive Farmer* also opposed Butler's strategy. Indeed, the paper became more outspoken against Butler. In a scathing editorial it asked a series of questions. The paper wondered if cooperation with Democrats was based solely on free silver. If that was the case, the paper argued, Populists should not fuse with Democrats because the People's Party reform platform was not based only on free silver. Although the people of North Carolina needed free silver, the paper noted that "Chairman Butler wishes us [the Populists] to fall down at the knees of Democratic party, get a promise of free silver and a soft place for a few leaders and then go off and die." The *Progressive Farmer* then admonished, "We respectfully decline to be carried off in such a shape, and because we do this, we are said to have gone over 'horse, foot and dragoon to the gold and monopoly enemy.'"[8]

Nowhere was Butler's power questioned more openly than in Wake County, where the Populist county convention favored cooperation with the GOP. It seems that Butler's enemy, S. Otho Wilson, was in charge of the convention at Wake. Such a flagrant disregard for Butler's position certainly outraged the senator. However, J. J. Rodgers wrote a stirring defense of Wilson: "I beg to say that the Populists of this county remember the unjust abuse, slander, persecution and prosecution heaped upon Otho Wilson by the concentrated action of organized Democracy. They also remember his hard fought battles during and since 1892 for the Populist party."[9]

The Republican Party was determined to stymie Butler's movement toward the Democratic Party. The Republican press, for example, pointed out the threat to reform legislation if Populists discontinued the cooperation experiment. Most Republican leaders hoped that Harry Skinner and S. Otho Wilson would secure the leadership of the state Populist Party and cement cooperative links once again with the GOP. The *Winston Union Republican* once again advocated cooperation on the same lines as 1894 and 1896.[10]

Republican governor Daniel L. Russell took a very different path from the rest of the GOP. Russell and Butler drew ever closer politically, and Russell became further estranged from many in the Republican Party. Throughout the early months of 1898 Russell continued to fight for lower railroad rates in the state, against

S. Otho Wilson's opposition after his removal from the Railroad Commission, and against the lease of the North Carolina Railroad to the Southern Railway. Russell managed to defeat Wilson when the U.S. Supreme Court upheld Wilson's removal from the Railroad Commission. Russell, however, did not have as much success with the rest of his agenda when the courts did not overturn the lease of the railroad. Russell also lost out on the rate issue when the Railroad Commission voted to stop the decreases in passenger rates. However, Russell took comfort in the hope that he and Butler would form a new reform party.[11]

Butler now closely aligned himself with the Populistic GOP governor. He had supported the removal of S. Otho Wilson from the Railroad Commission, which created a bitter enemy in the process; urged a fight against the lease, which failed; and advocated the reduction of railroad rates, which also failed. Indeed, Butler was furious when his handpicked commissioner, L. C. Caldwell, voted against the rate decrease. Butler did not blame Russell for the defeats on the lease or the rate issue because he hoped to build a solid reform movement. Russell and Butler remained in constant touch with one another. Butler hoped to build an inter-party coalition based on reform, confident that a combination of Populists, Russellites, and Bryan Democrats would carry the 1898 elections. Russell seemed in-tune with such a policy. He wrote Butler that he would work for a silver coalition and attempt to convert pro-Republican Populists to Butler's course. He did, however, admit "there will be great difficulty in getting Democratic fusion on the county tickets." But he did note that he had stopped some of "their mouths" and "brought them over to the right side." Although this might have been the case, Butler's close work with a Republican governor and his overtures toward Democrats and opposition to the GOP did not make political sense and weakened Populists even further.[12]

Not only did many Populists and Republicans oppose Butler's strategy, the U.S. senator had no idea if the reform-minded Democrats would accept his offer to fuse in the state campaign. One group of Democrats favored the position taken by William Jennings Bryan advocating fusion of all silver forces in the state. Another group of Democrats supported the gold standard and believed that Democrats should not align themselves with any other party. Despite a vocal faction of Democrats supporting cooperation and free silver— which stoked Butler's engine for cooperation—many other Democrats opposed any agreement with Butler. Many leading Democratic newspapers, such as the *Charlotte Observer*, the *Raleigh Morning Post*, and the *Wilmington Messenger*, opposed cooperation—totally. The *Wilmington Messenger* was particularly vehement toward Butler. According to an editorial, "Some of the Populists are very, very tired of Marion Butler and his management. The State at large is even sicker of him and his blatherskite blowing and insane politics more than any of the Populists can be."[13]

With the Populist Party in turmoil, the rank and file gathered in Raleigh for their state convention. The Populists met first in the round of summer conventions. Both Butler and Harry Skinner marshaled their respective forces in readiness for a battle in the convention. Skinner's support came from many original Populists who disliked the moves toward the Democrats. These Populists feared that Democrats would merely use Populists to gain power, and once in office they would overturn the reform legislation of the Populist-Republican legislatures. In addition, this group believed that the future of the People's Party remained tied to a close alliance with Republicans. Although it is difficult to determine the strength of the Skinnerites, it seems that they made up about one-third of the People's Party. Their strength resided in the First and Fourth Congressional Districts and also to a lesser degree in the Sixth Congressional District, where the Populists relied on the GOP to gain office. It was clear to political pundits that both leaders wanted to control the convention's deliberations, and each worked to drum up support for their respective position on cooperation and the 1898 campaign.[14]

As the convention opened on May 17, 1898, Harry Skinner immediately challenged Butler's leadership, and a heated contest ensued over the organization of the convention. Both Skinner and Butler received support from notable Populists, but as the deliberations progressed it was clear that Skinner would not succeed in seating many of his delegates from contested counties. This outraged Skinner and he interrupted Butler at every opportunity. However, once again Skinner failed to defeat Butler. Cyrus Thompson, now opposed to the actions of Skinner, gained the permanent chairmanship of the convention. Skinner tried to wrestle the initiative away from the Butlerites as he gave a speech to the delegates in which he implored them to oppose any proposition to Democrats because it would only put the Populist Party in a terrible position in the state campaign. Other Populists then took the floor and opposed Skinner's position. Butler finally addressed the conference. He denied the rumors that he hoped to lead the People's Party into the Democratic Party or that he hoped for a cabinet seat or to succeed himself as U.S. senator. Butler then directed a successful resolution which, although it did not make a specific appeal to Democrats for cooperation, called for the "co-operation of all the free silver forces in North Carolina." Clearly, the aim was to offer a proposition to Democrats. The convention also resolved that any political cooperation would mandate free silver congressmen, non-partisan superior court judges and solicitors, and the election of an anti-monopoly legislature. The convention appointed a committee to discuss cooperation terms with any "accepting" organization. Skinner opposed the resolution, but he lost as it passed by 675 to 285 votes.[15]

Butler remained in control of the People's Party for four reasons. First, Butler's popularity was still high in the party, he was the most famous Tar Heel in the nation, and he used his state and national fame to sway wavering voters. Second,

Butler was a skilled tactician, and he was well aware of the subtle ways to persuade delegates to support his position. He used backroom tactics, flattery, and perhaps even threats, to persuade Populists to support his position in the convention. He also loaded the committees in his favor, and this greatly helped him to stamp out any internal opposition. Third, many Populists remained suspicious of Harry Skinner's agenda. Many felt Skinner was in the pocket of the conservative element of the GOP and would lead Populists into the Republican Party and thus end the organizational independence of the People's Party. Fourth, Butler and his supporters controlled the majority of the Populist papers, and, therefore, he could disseminate his views on cooperation and state policy to the rank and file of the party. The convention also adopted the previous platforms of the Populist Party as well as criticisms of the ninety-nine-year railroad lease, support for a referendum on the lease, and the need for better education. The convention also elected Cyrus Thompson as the new party chairman and passed a resolution praising the work of Russell for giving "to the people of North Carolina a clean and economic administration of the State government and more especially for the brave fight he is making to secure for them just and reasonable railroad fares and freights." The convention had not unified the two factions of the party; indeed, it had only further divided the Skinnerites and Butlerites.[16]

The Democratic convention was scheduled to meet on May 27, 1898, just one week after the Populist convention. Thus, the political situation reached a new height of tension and uncertainty. The Butlerite Populists now moved to make Democrats a formal offer for cooperation. Chairman Thompson called a meeting of the party committee in Raleigh on May 25, 1898. The proposal drawn up by the committee desired cooperation in order to elect a non-partisan judiciary, free silver and anti-monopoly congressmen, and an anti-monopoly legislature. Populists also wanted an end to the ninety-nine-year lease, the continued use of the cooperation election law and local government law, and reduced railroad and telegraph rates—all of which were central Populist tenets. Populists delivered their proposal to Democratic chairman Clement Manly on the evening of May 25. Such a lengthy proposition was difficult for Democrats to accept. Not only did it call on Democrats to reject a white supremacy campaign and the ninety-nine-year lease signed by a Democratic governor, it also called on Democrats to support election laws that the Democratic press had lambasted for the past three years. Indeed, Butler received a warning from James B. Lloyd that Democrats might reject the offer. He wrote, "From the sentiment that now prevails it is very evident that the convention will reject our proposition to cooperate on principle. The RR attys [railroad attorneys] and hirelings are in control of the convention."[17]

All eyes now turned to the Democratic Party. At their convention on May 27, Democrats rejected the Populist cooperation proposal. Robert Glenn led the way for those who opposed cooperation. In a "ringing speech" he argued that the Democratic Party would carry the state on its own and the supreme issue was "white supremacy." Chairman Manly presented the Populist proposition and the convention rejected the offer. No Bryanite/Silverite Democrat bolted the convention, and even Josephus Daniels refused to oppose the majority of his party. Rather, he decided to remain within the party, and, significantly, all the pro-silver Democrats followed Daniels. As a result, the conservative element, led by a younger group of Democrats, such as Charles B. Aycock, held sway over the party and the upcoming campaign. Although the convention covered its bases with an endorsement of Populistic planks on an income tax, an end to free railroad passes, and the direct election of U.S. senators, more threateningly, perhaps, to Populists, the Democrats did not endorse the 1895 election law or the local self-government law, the reduction of the legal rate of interest to 6 percent, or a non-partisan judiciary, and it did not condemn the ninety-nine-year lease. Significantly, Democrats raised the specter of black rule. The convention denounced the laws that turned over several towns and cities to "negro domination" and placed "negroes on committees to supervise white schools." Democrats vowed to overturn these laws and to reinstate "rule by the white men of the state," signaling that they intended to exploit the race issue in order to undermine the Populist appeal. It was clear that the conservative element of the Democratic Party was in total control. The race line was drawn by the Democrats and the battle would begin.[18]

If Populists could agree on little else, they could agree on what they saw as the outrageous actions of the Democratic convention. A common theme in the Populist papers' criticisms of the Democratic convention was the feeling that the lawyers and railroads now dominated the Democratic Party. The *Charlotte People's Paper* argued that Democrats had stolen the Populist platform and then made their state committee up of "dyed in the wool goldbugs and railroad lawyers, and they ask the Pops to walk in." But the paper claimed Populists would not return.[19]

If Populists roundly condemned the actions of the Democratic Party in public, in private Populists did not know what they should do over the next few months. Morrison Caldwell warned Butler that Democrats would make their campaign solely on the cry "for 'the *white man's* rule,'" and he worried that Populists would lose scores of voters to Democrats. Many Populists now wondered if they should align themselves with Republicans. With the Republican state convention scheduled for late July, North Carolina entered a period of political tension.[20]

The Populist Party entered another period of internal friction—at the precise moment when unity was paramount. Butler decided to reassert his leadership over the Populist Party in light of a heated People's Party convention and the rejection of cooperation from the Democratic Party. In particular, Butler aimed to snuff out Harry Skinner's attempt to gain reelection in the First Congressional District. Although this strategy endeared him to his close associates, it was hardly the cure for the internal divisions in the Populist Party. Indeed, Butler's actions only had the effect of hindering Populist campaigning in the various congressional and legislative districts. Butler targeted Skinner for the majority of his animosity, seeking to place his own choice as the Populist candidate. However, many Populists supported their native son in the First District. W. H. Standin of Gates County wrote a scathing letter to Butler that lambasted the senator for trying to return the Populist Party back to the Democratic Party.[21]

Although Butler sought to expend a great deal of time and energy to crush Harry Skinner, many Populists began to drift toward cooperation with the Republican Party. State chairman Cyrus Thompson issued a circular that seemed to preclude any cooperation with Democrats. Thompson wrote that no Populist should accept the nomination at the hands of the Democratic Party. Thompson argued, "If we are not good enough to be co-operated with as a party, upon principle, it would seem that no Populist who regards his party or respects himself can afford to lend a hand to the Democratic party in its efforts to break down our organization." Many Populists now reasoned the party only held the balance of power, and it would no longer grow in number. Local Populists decided that without cooperation the party would have little or no influence in the campaign, and because Democrats had shut off any chance of cooperation, Populists must look toward the GOP.[22]

Butler received more worrying news for his election strategy of trying to fuse with Democrats at the local level. In the Seventh Congressional District in the Piedmont section of the state, Populist incumbent congressman A. C. Shuford lost his bid to gain the nomination of the People's Party to Morrison Caldwell. James H. Sherrill, a close associate of Butler, was "mortified" at the result and believed that the Skinnerites were now in charge of the district. He was disgusted that Republicans seemed to control the People's Party in the section, and although Caldwell was an earnest Populist, the fight over the nomination might cripple the Populists in the upcoming campaign. Rumors also circulated that Republicans hoped to defeat the election of incumbent Populist congressman John Fowler in Butler's backyard of the Third Congressional District because the young Populist closely aligned himself with the U.S. senator.[23]

The sentiment of the rank-and-file Populists was not lost on the state GOP. Sensing the mood of the voters and the resurgence of the Democrats, the Republican state convention on July 20, 1898, openly offered cooperation to the Populist Party. The rancorous 1897 legislative session was clearly on the minds of many Republicans, and thus the justification for cooperation in the convention was merely to keep the election law and the local government law in place—which made sense, given the Democratic agenda. Thus the GOP viewed cooperation as a defensive strategy against a resurgent Democratic Party, and as such Republicans offered little in the way of reform legislation that Populist voters could find appealing. In many ways, the Republican convention illustrated how the GOP had overplayed its hand in 1897 as it sought short-term gains over Populists.[24]

For the rest of the summer many local Populists moved closer to the Republicans. This was particularly evident in the First, Fourth, and Sixth Congressional Districts. Butler did not agree with such sentiments. Rather, he regularly attacked both the Democratic and Republican parties, and he endeavored to control local nominating conventions to place Populists friendly toward local Populist-Democratic cooperation on the ticket. This scheme was driven by Butler's fear of the Skinnerite wing of the Populist Party—a fear that was overblown. The result of such a strategy was, however, to confuse Populists on the direction of the party's campaign in the remaining four months. If Populists exhibited a growing sense of localism and factionalism in preparation for the election campaign, political pundits turned their attention to the Democratic Party. Throughout the early months of 1898, it seemed that Democrats were gradually coalescing around the issue of race for their campaign theme in the upcoming election.[25]

With a divided Populist Party and a discredited GOP, Democrats had the opportunity to mount a serious campaign to recapture the state legislature and county positions. Democrats made their first move by appointing Furnifold Simmons as the new chairman of the state executive committee. Simmons was a wily campaigner and an avowed racist. He also had a great deal of experience in organizing political campaigns and was a conservative-minded Democrat on economic issues. His appointment came as a severe blow to Populists. Democratic leaders from the old landed families in the state and the emerging industrial elite worried at the changing nature of politics in the state, and they feared African American social equality. These Democrats were determined that North Carolina would follow its southern brethren in moving to curtail black political power, and thus they sought to smash an alliance of blacks and whites and demolish the reform-minded Populist Party. Democrats appealed to the capitalist classes of the state by denouncing the cooperationists' increased taxation of big business and attempts to regulate key industries such as the railroads. Through secret meetings, old-time Democrats, such as Thomas Jarvis, garnered large sums of money from industrialists for the Democratic state campaign, with the assurance that the party would not regulate businesses and would, indeed, roll back the reform legislation of the cooperationists.[26]

However, the old political elite in the state was discredited in the minds of the voters. Thus, the political campaign fell into the hands of the younger Democrats. Three of these new leaders, Furnifold Simmons, chairman of the state Democratic Party, Charles B. Aycock, a lawyer from the eastern section of North Carolina, and Josephus Daniels, the editor of the state's largest Democratic daily, the *Raleigh News and Observer*, met in the summer of 1898 to plan a campaign strategy to bring about Democratic success in November. Appealing to white racism, they formulated the concept of "home protection" for white women and an end to so-called black rule in the eastern section of the state. Thus it was to the votes of Populists that the white supremacy campaign made its primary appeal. Democrats accused Populists of betraying their race and opening the way to black rule and anarchy in the state. This was an effective way for Democrats, who were accused by Populists of catering only to special interests, to appear to promote the interests of the white people of North Carolina. Democrats successfully latched onto *the* issue that common whites cared deeply about. In many ways it was more Populist than free silver or anti-monopoly reform.[27]

During the summer of 1898, Democrats campaigned on the interlocking themes of home protection and black rule. The *Wilmington Morning Star*, for example, urged that "every white man," regardless of class, should take up arms to defend "the sanctity of home and extend protection to wives and daughters." Using these themes, Democrats aimed to pull enough white Populists into their old party to defeat the cooperation experiment. The Democratic leaders traveled across the state to whip up a racist frenzy. Francis D. Winston led the way by forming White Government Leagues to galvanize white voters into supporting the white supremacy campaign. Democrats exaggerated and even lied about so-called African American outrages against white women, even though crime was not on the increase during this period. However, this did not matter to Democrats. As Glenda Gilmore notes, "The rape scare was a politically driven wedge powered by the sledgehammer of white supremacy." With an overwhelming superiority in newspaper circulation and money in their campaign coffers, the rape scare was a politically effective tool calculated to appeal to white racism, split the cooperation alliance, and defeat the Populists.[28]

One strand of the campaign was played out in the press. Josephus Daniels published gross fabrications of "Negro atrocities" daily in his *News and Observer*. Day in and day out the paper was full of stories of attempted rapes of white women by African American men, of "uppity" black women refusing to "respect" social norms, and of actual rape and violence against white women. For example, a story circulated in the Democratic press of a black woman who refused to give way to white women on the sidewalk. After a white woman shoved her out the way, the black woman raised her umbrella and began to strike the white woman. According to the *News and Observer*, a black man shouted, "That's right; damn it, give it to her." This story outraged the editor of the paper, Josephus Daniels, who retorted, "Such exasperating occurrences would not happen but for the fact that the negro party is in power in North Carolina." These stories came from the eastern section of North Carolina, the heavily black section of the state, but Furnifold Simmons and Daniels made certain that these stories were spread throughout the majority-white areas of the Piedmont and the western mountains to frighten white Populist voters into voting for Democrats. In speech after speech, Democrats lambasted Populists

for allowing black men increased power and the opportunity to commit outrages against white women. Another infamous example for white consump-
tion occurred when a U.S. congressman, African American George H. White,
accompanied by several black women, attended Sparks's circus at Tarboro and
took seats in the white section. They only moved after two policemen were
called, and then they chose to leave rather than sit in the black section.[29]

The racist message was plain and direct. According to a Democratic paper,
"Negro supremacy means negroes in every office, mixed schools, intermarriage, and social equality." Democrats also charged that the cooperationists had
advanced "negro supremacy" by placing "hordes" of blacks in political office and
making white politicians dependent on black votes. Cooperation rule had led to
an increase in the number of African Americans in local office, but blacks did not
dominate state and local offices. Populists and white Republicans realized that the
white population would never stand for this and, thus, limited the number and
type of offices that went to African Americans. Thus, although African Americans
held positions as registers of deeds, postmasters, clerks, registrars, county commissioners, and even some statewide officers, whites held the vast majority of
positions. The charge of black rule was nothing new. But what was new was the
coordinated and effective manner in which the charge of black rule was delivered
by Democrats. Chairman Simmons led the campaign by equating state patriotism
with violent racism. He also made this bigotry seem pleasurable and even enjoyable by organizing lavish picnics, barbecues, and parades with the theme that only
Democrats stood for whites, white womanhood, and white supremacy.[30]

The Democrats also distributed white supremacy buttons, held mass meetings, and continued to issue numerous campaign documents to make the white
supremacy campaign into a noble crusade. Daniels's *News and Observer* led the
way with terrible cartoons depicting cooperationists as fools and sycophants
and blacks as members of a barbaric race and sexually deviant. Daniels rehired
political cartoonist Norman E. Jennett from New York to draw these cartoons.
In a state with a high number of illiterate white men, the lurid and provocative
political cartoons were an important tool in creating the fear of black dominance and the threat to white womanhood. Throughout the last two months of
the campaign, Furnifold Simmons, with all the money he needed from big businesses, delivered forty thousand papers to independent voters and fifty thousand
four-page supplements and over two million other documents, cartoons, and
broadsides to wavering Populist and Republican voters, imploring them to save
the state from black rule and to protect white womanhood.[31]

Race prejudice had to be tapped most forcibly in public meetings. Political
campaigns thrived on public speeches in the 1890s. In an isolated rural setting
the political meeting was an occasion for the whole family to enjoy a day of
socializing and entertainment. Democrats found their most effective spokesman

in Charles B. Aycock, whom many scholars regard as one of the most articulate speakers of the white supremacy campaign. He traveled the state, whipping up local white farmers and city folk into a state of hysteria. Before he spoke, horseback processions of white men and young white women, dressed all in white, with banners proclaiming their support for white supremacy, set the tone for the day. But the speaking engagements were not all spectacle. Aycock was there to whip up support. For example, at a debate with Cyrus Thompson in early September 1898, in Wilson County in the eastern section of the state, he asked how the African American James H. Young could be placed in charge of the deaf, dumb, and blind children at the state's institution. These white children who are so close to God, he pleaded, cannot be overseen by "an infamous negro." Next, he moved onto the issue of white womanhood in the state. He argued that only Democrats could protect white women because "the goddess of North Carolina Democracy is the white womanhood of the State.... In the name of the goddess I come to the white people of Wayne County and I demand that protection for the womanhood of the State.... I call upon you white men, Democrats, Populists, Republicans, to rally to the cause of Democracy this year and let us put an end forever to this strife, this outrage, this wrong." In Aycock's mind the cooperationist experiment had jeopardized the safety of white women, and he argued that only the Democratic Party could protect the honor of white women and so end black rule in the eastern section of the state. White women appeared at scores of Democratic rallies, and many demonstrated in support of white supremacy. Aycock was not the only Democratic speaker to play the race card. Robert Glenn, Alfred Waddell, Claude Kitchin, W. W. Kitchin, Locke Craig, and Cameron Morrison also gave vehement racist speeches in the eastern section of the state.[32]

The question for Populists was how they could respond to such a coordinated and well-funded Democratic white supremacy campaign. At the outset, Populists fought back on their own. They hoped they could run a normal campaign that focused on political and economic democracy—the real issues, in their estimation. In the past such an approach had led to good results. With a complex set of reform issues to articulate to the electorate in 1898, a successful Populist campaign demanded a reasonably ordered and respectful campaign and a deliberative and lengthy set of public engagements. But the 1898 election did not offer such an opportunity to the People's Party leaders and stump speakers because Democrats had "begun a campaign of prevarication, misrepresentation and abuse that is repulsive to honorable men."[33]

The Populist press, divided over Populist campaign policy, managed to unify in its condemnation of the Democratic campaign. The *Raleigh Home Rule* ridiculed the call from Democrats to Populists to return home. The paper noted, "This one takes the cake.... Why every man that dared express himself as a

Populist was ridiculed, bemoaned and slandered, and by whom? Many of the same crowd that now appeal us to come back home. The Democratic Party of today is the same machine ridden, rotten concern it was when we left." The *Chatham Citizen* argued that the Democratic speakers were trying to deceive Populists on the race issue. In an editorial on a speech by Thomas Jarvis, the paper noted, "His entire speech was full of abuse to the Populists, charging them with the whole responsibility for this great scare-crow, 'nigger domination' and in the next breath appeal to the Populists to come back home."[34]

The Populist press was one avenue of response to the Democratic white supremacy campaign, but Populists suffered from a declining number of newspapers. As a result Populists relied on their public speakers to get their message across to the voters—this was their strength in the past. However, Populists still did not know how to formulate their campaign strategy. But the party did possess some charismatic orators of its own. Their most notable speaker was Cyrus Thompson, and in the early months of the campaign Thompson met Charles Aycock in a series of debates on the election issues of 1898. At a debate in Wayne County, Thompson directly responded to Aycock's call for white men to protect white womanhood in North Carolina. Thompson argued that he would never do anything to dishonor a woman and, turning Aycock's rhetoric on its head, he used Populist reform ideology to get his message across: "I never would do anything that would dishonor her off-spring, the bright blue eyed children that God lays in her lap, and so help me God, as the way offers itself I will fight monopoly, I will fight the gold standard . . . because I know that curse lies still upon the country robbing womanhood of the luster of eye and the rosiness of cheek, pulling the suckling the bread and nourishment from which it should grow." For Thompson the biggest threat to white womanhood in the Old North State was not African American men, but the economic degradation of monopolies and the gold standard. These were strong words, and in a normal election they would surely have resonated with the voters. But 1898 was not a typical election.[35]

Cyrus Thompson had opened the Populist campaign to a fanfare in Butler's hometown of Clinton in late August. In an electrifying speech he attempted to galvanize the rank and file of the party. He poured over the history of the People's Party and reminded the party faithful that Populists fought oppression, economic degradation, machine rule, the goldbug policies of Grover Cleveland, and the right for everyone to reap the fruits of their labor. He lambasted Democrats for selling-out free silver and Bryan to the railroads and monopoly interests of the state. As his speech drew to a close Thompson directly addressed the race issue, asking the crowd: "You remember the campaign of 1876 was largely upon the issue of 'nigger.' It was then the cry of negro equality, now it is the cry of 'negro domination.' I state here that the Democratic Party does not desire to rid itself of the negro in politics. When the Democratic Party in North Carolina removed the negro from politics in North Carolina, the Democratic Party goes out of existence in North Carolina." Thompson argued that from 1876 to 1895 Democrats could have removed blacks from politics but they needed African Americans for the purpose of future campaigns. He continued, "It [the Democratic Party] has always howled the nigger, and yet it has given the negro office when it could notwithstanding the howl." Thompson then ended, "What hypocrites these Democrats be. It is astonishing to me that God Himself lets them live. It is a wonder he does not start out and blast them for their hypocrisy." Thompson outlined all the themes in the Populist campaign against Democrats. First, Populists argued that Democrats merely focused on the race issue to avoid a discussion of economic issues and thus mask their conservative economic position. Second, Populists characterized Democrats as hypocrites. Populists noted that Democrats had routinely used black votes in the past and appointed African Americans to local offices in the eastern section of the state. Third, Populists were the party of white metal and white supremacy in North Carolina.[36]

Although Populists began a vigorous response to the white supremacy campaign, it was clear they could not take a lone stand in the election, especially now that the issues were defined so narrowly by Democrats. Thompson faced the cooperation issue head on in late August: "What course shall we pursue in this campaign? Shall we go in the middle of the road for a straight fight, or shall we cooperate with the Republicans? If we go in the middle of the road, which might be the best course for us to pursue if we could pursue it and live as an organization, the canvass will be made against our candidates by the Democratic party that 'you have no chance for election. Our candidates will be elected or the Republicans will be. You are simply not in it.' . . . The cooperation has been mutually advantageous, and the advantage so far as numbers were concerned has largely been on our side. I think we can fuse with the Republicans."[37]

The white supremacy campaign forced the Butlerite Populists to fuse with Republicans—a move they had resisted for months. In actuality many local Populists had already read the signals back in June and July and effected cooperation in scores of counties. Populists bowed to the inevitable, and by the end of August the executive committees of the Republican Party and the Populist Party formally agreed on cooperation of the two parties along the same lines as 1894 and 1896.[38]

For a brief period it looked as though the campaign might revert to real issues. Populists and Republicans did all they could to end discussion of the race issue or show the hypocrisy of Democrats. Butler, still one of the most revered speakers in the state, engaged in an extensive tour to wrestle the spotlight from Aycock and his cronies. In his speeches the senator argued with some justification that the race issue was used to distract the public from the Democrats' conservative economic policies. At Clinton he held up a copy of the Democrats' campaign book and chided, "I have read it through. As I read it my heart sank with pity and sorrow and disgust. Here it is. Here is the first page. Is there anything about free silver and the dangers of monopolies and trusts? No. What is on the first page? My fellow citizens, what is their creed and doctrine today? On the first page there is but one thing. What is it? 'Nigger.'" Throughout the campaign book, Butler noted, Democrats only referred to "Niggers and Coons."[39]

Populists were hindered in their reaction to the Democratic campaign. Due to their white supremacist attitudes, they merely charged Democrats with using the race issue to avoid discussing economic issues. In an attempt to focus attention away from the race issue, Populists endeavored to get black politicians off the local and county tickets and in areas of black political strength some Populists aligned themselves with Democrats. However, even though white Populists and white Republicans tried to limit black office-holding in 1898, they disagreed with Democrats on the nature of the campaign. They consistently opposed the violent nature of the campaign and the focus on race and lambasted the Democrats for their virulent campaign speeches and political cartoons. Democrats were momentarily pushed on the defensive by Populists reactions to their campaign. The Populists' charge that Democrats planned to disfranchise poor illiterate whites caused Democrats to pause for a moment. Democrats hurriedly issued a denial against Populist accusations.[40]

However, the Populists were limited in their reaction to the Democrats' white supremacy campaign for two main reasons. First, they remained divided between the Skinnerite and Butlerite factions. Even after the GOP and Populists fused in early September, the local issues behind cooperation tended to disrupt the party as each faction sought to place its own candidates in line for the party's nomination. Second, Populists only really mounted a defensive campaign. Many Populists in the eastern section of the state opposed black office-holding, and thus many Populists endeavored to defeat black candidates. This sent mixed signals to other Populists throughout the state. If Populists in the east voiced their concerns against black office-holding, many other Populists wondered if, in fact, Democrats were correct in their speeches and editorials on the danger of black assertiveness, threats to white womanhood, and black office-holding.[41]

The tendency of the Skinnerites and Butlerites to oppose one another found its greatest sentiment in the First and Fourth Congressional Districts. In the First District, Butler first attempted to prevent the nomination of his archrival Harry Skinner for the cooperationist slot. After he failed to prevent Skinner's nomination, Butler began a series of letters to the Democratic candidate, John H. Small, with the effect of aiding a Democrat to defeat a Populist. Indeed, it appears that Butler did all he could to furnish Small with names of wavering Populist voters or issues that the Democrat could use to discredit Skinner. It also appears that Butler wrote to Populists in the district and pleaded with them to vote for Small. Butler's determination to seek personal revenge against Skinner destroyed the unity of the Populists in the First Congressional District.[42]

In the Fourth District, Butler was also determined to defeat S. Otho Wilson's chances at the congressional nomination. For the past year Wilson had been a thorn in the side of Butler. Butler wanted incumbent congressman William F. Strowd to gain the nomination. But in the convention neither Wilson nor Strowd secured the nomination. Instead, a Skinnerite, J. J. Jenkins, won the nomination. Butler had clearly lost control of the party by this stage. However, the nomination of Jenkins infuriated John W. Atwater, a key Populist leader from Chatham County. Atwater announced his own independent candidacy and invited the support of Democrats. Furnifold Simmons accepted Atwater's invitation, and Democrats fell in behind a Populist as they attempted to divide the cooperation elements and send Democrats to the state legislature from the district. In the Fourth District, Populists disintegrated into factional disarray.[43]

Many Populists in the eastern section opposed black office-holding, and this led to a curious development in the majority-black Second Congressional District. James B. Lloyd, the Populist congressional nominee, led Populists in a decidedly white supremacy manner. Lloyd faced off against African American incumbent George H. White. Lloyd urged Populists not to support any Republicans in the Second District because it would lead to black office-holding. Lloyd wrote Butler, "I have all along strenuously opposed any cooperation if negroes were to be on the tickets but my advice was not heeded." Lloyd felt that the presence of African Americans on the ticket would throw the district to Democrats, and he opposed black office-holding, and he offered to resign if Populists and Republicans effected cooperation. When Populists bowed to the inevitable in August and offered to fuse with the GOP, Lloyd offered his resignation to the Populist leadership. The Populists rejected Lloyd's offer, but William Fountain resigned as chairman of the Populist Party in the Second Congressional District and then announced his own candidacy as an independent and urged all Democrats to vote for him in November. In the Second District, Butler had also lost control of his party and even two of his closest associates did not heed the advice of their leader. Butler was furious at the action of Fountain because he saw him as a tool of the Democrats. But in reality Butler's oscillating position throughout the year had done little to crystallize campaign strategy, and this contributed to this factionalism.[44]

African Americans saw the white supremacy campaign from a different perspective. If Populists and Republicans saw it as an indication of the hypocrisy of Democrats and an attempt to avoid the real issues facing the people of the state, African Americans understood that they had the most to lose if Democrats won office. In addition, some African Americans directly challenged the Democratic strategy of interlocking the protection of white womanhood and black rule. This opposition found its spokesman in Alex Manly, the articulate black editor of the only African American daily newspaper, the *Wilmington Record*. Manly, the illegitimate son of a white North Carolina governor and an African American woman, published a provocative editorial defending his race and assailing white men who brutalized black women. Manly was responding to an article by Rebecca Felton, a prominent white Georgian, who had advocated the lynching of African American rapists. Manly asserted, "[White women] are not any more particular in the matter of clandestine meetings with colored men than are the white men with colored women." Recoiling at the idea of white purity, Manly counseled white women, "Tell your men that it is no worse for a black man to be intimate with a white woman that for a white man to be intimate with the colored woman. You set yourselves down as a lot of carping hypocrites, in fact you cry aloud for the virtue of your women, when you seek to destroy the morality of ours." He then admonished, "You leave your goods out doors and then complain because they are taken away. Poor white men are careless in the manner of protecting their women." Although he did not intend to do so, Manly stoked the fires of the Democrat's campaign strategy by directly assaulting white men's patriarchy.[45]

Manly's editorial had equated the morals of poor white and poor black people and suggested that some white women freely chose black men as lovers. Manly wrote, "Every negro man lynched is called a 'big, burly, black brute,' when in fact many of those who have been thus dealt with had white men for their fathers and were not only not 'black and burly' but were sufficiently attractive for white girls of culture and refinement fall in love with them is well known to all." This directly attacked white self-image and the fundamental ideas that underlay white supremacy. All white women were pure, according to white southerners, regardless of their class. All black men were animals or children, regardless of their class. Therefore, in the minds of the white supremacists, no white woman could prefer a black man to a white man.[46]

If Populists had momentarily thrown Democrats on the defensive, Manly's editorial gave them a way back into the campaign. Pointing to what they saw as a chilling example of black assertiveness, Democrats revived the race issue, turning it with a new ferocity on Populists and Republicans. They increased the number of stories of "outrages" in the Democratic press and held larger social gatherings, and the number of incidents of intimidation and violence against Populists and African Americans multiplied. The *News and Observer* ran a story that African American state senator W. Lee Person had urged Africans to go to the polls armed. While the story was false, it did not matter to the Democratic press as it focused exclusively on the race issue.[47]

Democrats used Manly's editorial to great effect for their own political capital. For the next three months the editorial appeared every day in the Democratic *Wilmington Messenger*. Manly's statement outraged white Democrats, and many called it a dirty defamation, a great slur on the white people of the state, or "a sweeping insult to all respectable white women who are poor." In Wilmington tensions ran especially high as rumors circulated that the whites would burn Manly's press and lynch him. Alfred Waddell, a leading white citizen of Wilmington, was furious at the increased black political presence in the port city and saw Manly's editorial as the opportunity to resurrect his political career. Waddell illustrated his determination to end African American political rule in the largest city of North Carolina with a plea to a crowd of white Democrats: "We will not live under these intolerable conditions. We will never surrender to a ragged raffle of negroes even if we have to choke the current of the Cape Fear with carcasses." Waddell and his associates secretly planned to use force after the state elections to oust the cooperationist city government. Waddell received support from so-called respectable elements of white society. Rebecca Cameron of the Church Periodical Club, and a cousin of Waddell, wrote the former U.S. congressman, "We have been arranged, confounded and bitterly ashamed of the acquiescence of the men of North Carolina at the existing conditions; and more than once we asked *where are* the white men and the shot guns? . . . I never thought to be ashamed of the manhood of North Carolina but I am ashamed now." She urged Waddell to engage in killing to redeem the state: "You go forward to your work bloody tho' it maybe with the heartful approval of *any* good woman in the State." Threats were made against individual cooperationists in Wilmington, and reports circulated that if the cooperationist ticket remained a riot would occur. Russell was deeply worried that his home city would descend into chaos, and after much backroom dealing he secured an agreement to persuade the GOP ticket for New Hanover County to withdraw from the canvass. Only the congressional and state ticket remained in place.[48]

As the campaign entered its final month, the southeastern section of North Carolina witnessed bands of Red Shirts, armed with Winchester rifles and other weapons, who aimed to intimidate voters into casting their ballot for Democrats or keep them from attending political rallies. It is unclear when the Red Shirts appeared, but their presence increased after Manly's editorial was circulated by Democrats throughout the state. The Red Shirts appeared in small towns and villages, shooting their rifles into the air and terrifying the local African American population and any pro-cooperation activists. They also appeared at political rallies organized by the cooperationists and did their utmost to disrupt political speakers. The *Raleigh Home Rule* noted that the Red Shirts were active in the counties of Richmond and Robeson. It argued that disorder and violence were now in evidence because Democrats recognized "that they are already defeated if we have an honest and free election." The Democrats also asked the notorious Ben Tillman, who as governor of South Carolina had led a successful disfranchisement movement in the Palmetto State, to speak in North Carolina to whip up more support for the white supremacy campaign. On October 20, 1898, a large political rally of between seven thousand and ten thousand people at Fayetteville witnessed over three hundred Red Shirts riding in a parade along with Tillman. As he began his speech, Tillman whipped his audience into a racist frenzy, urging, "Why don't you kill that damn nigger editor [Manly] who wrote that? Send him to South Carolina and let him publish any such offensive stuff, and he will be killed." Democrats also disrupted Populist and Republican meetings in the eastern section, rotten-egged speakers, and threw others back on trains. In such a violent atmosphere no Populist or Republican could hope to mount a serious campaign.[49]

North Carolina now teetered on the brink of a race war. The heated nature of the campaign and the vehement rhetoric of the Democratic speakers and newspapers, as well as the intimidation and violence of the Red Shirts in the southeastern section of the state, forced Governor Russell to issue a proclamation to the people of North Carolina. Russell exclaimed that no turbulent mob using weapons of intimidation and violence should usurp the authority of the courts. He stated that he had received reports of lawlessness in certain counties; that certain counties lying along the southern border of North Carolina had been actually invaded by armed and lawless men from South Carolina; that political meetings had been broken up and dispersed by these armed men; that citizens had been fired upon from ambush and taken from their homes at night and whipped; and that peaceful citizens were afraid to register to vote. After such a litany Russell called on all ill-disposed persons to desist from unlawful and turbulent conduct and on all law-abiding citizens to resist the calls to their passions and prejudices. He then ordered all those who had entered the state to foment conflict to leave instantly.[50]

Russell's proclamation fell on deaf ears. Indeed, Democrats openly and defiantly snubbed the governor. For example, the *News and Observer* characterized Russell's proclamation as a stump speech. Josephus Daniels reacted angrily to Russell's pronouncement: "It seeks to place at the door of white men the crimes of which men of his party are guilty. There has been no bad feeling in the State except such as has been engendered by Republican demagogues who have sought to inflame the passions of the negroes." On October 28, 1898, led by Chairman Simmons, Democrats organized a huge white supremacy rally in Goldsboro. The railroads offered free transportation to the rally and over eight thousand people gathered. One of the chief speakers was none other than William Guthrie, the Populist gubernatorial candidate in 1896. Democrats welcomed the political turncoat into the fold, and they saw this as a clear indication that the Populists were flocking to the party of white supremacy. The Democratic leadership was also much in evidence. The names of those present read as a who's who of the white supremacy campaign: Charles B. Aycock, Alfred Waddell, Thomas Jarvis, James

In this cartoon, Populist state chairman Cyrus Thompson is portrayed as having no control over his own actions and, instead, has sold out all his principles to the Republican Party, portrayed by State Chairman Alfred Holton. Indeed, according to the Democratic newspaper, Thompson was in favor of the gold standard, trusts, and "Negro Rule." In fact, none of these charges were true. *News and Observer*, September 18, 1898.

Pou, Cyrus Watson, and Furnifold Simmons. At the rally Democrats contended that African Americans held one thousand offices in the eastern section of the state, that scores of towns were turned over to black rule and anarchy, and that the sanctity of white womanhood was endangered, business was paralyzed, and property values were in a state of decline. Rumors also circulated that Pritchard and Russell would request President McKinley to send in federal troops to maintain peace in North Carolina. This gave Democrats even more ammunition to charge the cooperationists with throwing the state into anarchy. Ironically, it was Democrats, not cooperationists, who placed the state on the verge of chaos, and they did so intentionally.[51]

In the closing days before the election Populists attempted once again to shift the political advantage from Democrats. They printed letters from Populist women who lambasted Democrats for the use of the race issue and the defense of white womanhood in the state. The Populists printed an address from Mrs. Sarah E. Mitchell to the Bertie County Farmers' Alliance. In the address Mitchell touched on all the issues Populists addressed in their campaign. She wondered why Democrats had used black votes in the past and why Democrats only resorted

In this cartoon, the Goddess of Democracy (a white woman) is seen as congratulating white men as they leave the Populist Party and Republican Party and return to the Democratic Party. This cartoon represents quite nicely the Democrats' interlocking themes of white supremacy and protection of white womanhood in the virulent campaign of 1898. *News and Observer*, September 16, 1898.

to the "negro scarecrow" at election times. She did not fear African Americans and felt the real issues facing the Tar Heel State were economic. The *Hickory Times-Mercury* printed the address, called Mitchell a "respectful lady of the East," and praised her for arguing that women "realize that the cry of 'negro supremacy' is used by hypocritical politicians for the sole purpose of boasting themselves into office." But these efforts were too little, too late, and too restricted.[52]

In desperation Populists decided to issue their own set of cartoons at the end of the political campaign as they desperately sought to defuse the clamor for white supremacy. These pathetic cartoons were no match for those in the *News and Observer*, but they illustrate the predicament of the Populist Party. All Populists could do was to accuse Democrats of the same crimes that Democrats accused the cooperationists of committing. The "Election Supplement" in the *Progressive Farmer* and the *Caucasian* accused Democrats of placing white girls at work with African American men in Alamance County. In a clear attempt to discredit Aycock's notion that only the Democratic Party could protect white womanhood, Populists printed a sworn affidavit which stated that "Mattie Pugh," a nineteen-year-old white woman, had worked in a ditch on a county work detail in Alamance County with black men because she committed a minor offense. The paper also accused the Democratic commissioners of Warren County of hiring out a white woman to an African American man. If these cartoons seem rather incongruous, it is important to remember that the People's Party supported white supremacy. They believed in the natural superiority of white people, and they did not support social equality between the races. But Populists believed that conservative economic and political interests (i.e., the Democrats) used the race issue to mask the real issues of economic reform that they discerned would benefit all people in North Carolina. In addition, Populists campaigned on the defensive in 1898, and because they had fused with Republicans, they could only counter the Democrats' propaganda by accusing Democrats of the same "crimes."[53]

The day of the election in North Carolina was tense. Democrats were armed to the teeth with Winchester rifles in many small towns in the eastern section of the state. Reports circulated that Red Shirts intimidated black voters in the border counties. On Election Day in Robeson County, according to Robert Russell, an African American newspaper man, the Red Shirts blocked every road leading to Maxton and drove back African Americans who wanted to vote by brandishing their rifles and firing "in the direction of fleeing voters." The violent nature of Election Day affected Russell. He was determined to vote despite threats on his life if he entered Wilmington. On his return to Raleigh via train he was almost lynched at Maxton when an angry mob of Red Shirts boarded the train looking for the governor. He only avoided detection by hiding in the baggage car. Although reports of actual violence on Election Day were scarce, Democrats and their Red Shirt supporters succeeded in keeping many voters away from the polls, thus reducing the "need" for actual violence. Nevertheless, tensions ran high throughout the eastern section of the state.[54]

On Election Day the success of the white supremacy campaign was clear. Democrats, after four years in the political wilderness, had smashed the biracial coalition of Populists and Republicans. A sophisticated organization, an overwhelming superiority in campaign funds and newspaper circulation, the interlocking themes of the protection of white womanhood and an end to black rule, and widespread intimidation and violence in marginal districts and border counties ensured a sweeping Democratic victory. In the state legislature Democrats won 134 out of 170 seats. Although Democrats won just 52.8 percent of the vote in a turnout of 84.2 percent, it was enough to secure an overwhelming majority in the state legislature. Populists suffered heavy losses. Their representation in the legislature dropped from over 60 in 1896 to just 6 in 1898, a humiliating loss. Republicans also suffered heavy losses with a decline from 72 legislators in 1897 to just 30 in 1898. Democrats scored victories in scores of local elections in the counties. To make the result even worse for Populists and Republicans, Democrats won all but 4 of the U.S. congressional seats. The Populists lost the relatively safe Third and Seventh Districts to the Democrats. Harry Skinner lost out to Democrat John

Table 8.1. Decline in Populist Vote in North Carolina							
	1896			1898			
County	Populist	Democrat	Majority	Populist	Democrat	Majority	Populist Decline, 1896–98
Columbus	1784	1245	539	1520	2106	586	264
Duplin	1981	1578	403	1849	2112	263	132
Jones	905	604	301	827	833	6	78
Richmond	2830	1839	991	1680	2728	1048	1150
Union	1872	1767	105	1296	2520	1224	576

Source: Records of Election, Columbus, Duplin, Jones, Richmond, and Union counties, North Carolina Division of Archives and History, Raleigh, NC.
Note: These five counties are in eastern and southeastern North Carolina.

H. Small in the First District, while Oliver H. Dockery, the Republican-Populist candidate, lost the violent Sixth District to Democrat John Bellamy. Ironically, in a virulent white supremacy campaign, African American incumbent congressman George H. White managed to hold onto his seat in the Second Congressional District as the white vote split between Populist James B. Lloyd and ex-Populist William Fountain. Only in the Fourth District did a Populist, John W. Atwater, gain election, and even here the candidate was an independent who received the backing of Democrats. It is impossible to estimate how many Populists left their party and joined the Democrats, but it is clear that thousands of Populists did vote the Democratic ticket or decided to stay at home (see table 8.1). The Democratic white supremacy campaign was a brilliant success. Intimidation and violence also produced a decline in the number of cooperationist votes in the eastern section of the state. All across the eastern section of the state Populists and their Republican counterparts lost large numbers of votes to the Democrats. This is suggested by table 8.1, which charts the waning of Populist support and the resurgence of Democratic turnout in five previously strong Populist counties.[55]

The sweeping victory overjoyed Democrats. Chairman Simmons was ecstatic at the result. The *Wilmington Messenger* cheered, "Our State Redeemed: Negroism Defunct." In private, Democrats began to talk of ways "to eliminate the negro question from politics as fast as it can be done." Some favored a constitutional amendment to rid the state of black voting for "his sake, as well as ours." Thus, although state chairman Simmons and other leading Democrats denied that they planned to disfranchise any man, as soon as the election results came in they began to crow that disfranchisement was inevitable.[56]

The highly charged and violent white supremacy campaign reached its nadir just a day after the election. White Democrats in Wilmington, led by

Alfred Waddell, perpetuated a coup d'etat or, perhaps more accurately, a racial pogrom in the port city. Tensions had reached the boiling point throughout the summer and fall of 1898, and they exploded on November 10, 1898. In the minds of many white Democrats the African American community exhibited a growing indifference toward whites and so challenged the racial hierarchy in the state. In addition, Manly's editorial had outraged many whites. Others saw a violent massacre as an opportunity to resurrect their political careers or to rid the city of its cooperationist government before municipal elections in 1899. Whatever the motivating factors behind the bloodshed, the targets of white Democratic fury are clear. After burning down Manly's press, white Democratic mobs with retribution in their eyes engaged in a murderous assault in the city, killing innocent African American men and attacking black women. Estimates of the numbers of African Americans killed vary, ranging from about ten to forty. In a sickening display of racial hatred, prominent whites led by William Rand Kenan drew a machine gun through the black neighborhoods of the city to intimidate residents. Whites also burned down middle-class African American establishments and forced many others to flee for their lives. Sympathetic whites, such as Populist chief of police John Melton, were also forced to leave the city. Alfred Waddell and his cronies forced the cooperationist aldermen to resign, and Waddell installed himself as the new mayor of Wilmington. White supremacy had come home to roost.[57]

Populists reacted angrily to the election, arguing that North Carolina had now descended into anarchy and basic freedoms and rights were ignored. The *Hickory Times-Mercury* admonished Democrats for their campaign: "The hate and revenge engendered during the campaign is to be deplored. It has been fearful. . . . This thing of putting ropes around white men's necks and driving them from their homes . . . or advising as the Charlotte Observer virtually has of killing white men who dared to differ in politics, does not speak well of boasted civilization and is a sad commentary on our modern Christianity."[58]

In private Senator Butler was furious at the Democratic campaign, and he argued they had "won by the most contemptible and infamous methods." He lamented that if the real issues had taken up the campaign debates, Populists would have won easily. He regretted the Populist-Republican cooperation and argued that this hindered the party and caused many Populists to leave. Butler argued that he preferred a straight fight and naïvely believed that, had Populists fought alone, thousands of Democrats and Republicans would have joined the People's Party. He felt that the Populist executive committee had allowed the campaign to drift, and this made him "sick" to the point of almost leaving the campaign. But Butler was optimistic that Democrats would show their true colors in the 1899 legislative session and that Populists could rise again once education and political organization was effected with the rank and file of the party. The sense of optimism was clear, but the political landscape was now very different.[59]

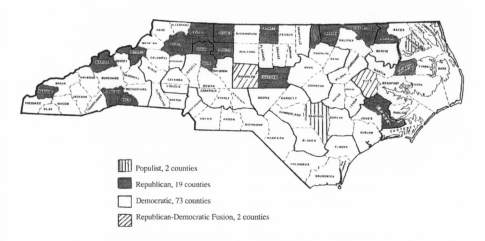

State election to the North Carolina House of Representatives, 1898. C. Beauregard Poland, *North Carolina's Glorious Victory, 1898: Sketches of the Democratic Leaders and Statesmen* (Raleigh: n.p., 1898).

As the tumultuous year of 1898 closed, the Populists faced the real prospect of total and irreversible disintegration. The Democratic white supremacy campaign had smashed the plans of Butler and Russell to create a reformist movement in the state based on Populists, silverite Republicans, and Bryanite Democrats, at best a noble dream and at worst a naïve proposition. Butler, his Populist supporters, and Russell had failed to shift attention from race issues to economic issues. Once the Democratic Party turned down the offer of Populist cooperation at their state convention in May 1898, the issue of race and the protection of white womanhood alone determined party loyalty and voting patterns in North Carolina. Many cooperationists, Republican and Populist, black and white, were not allowed to vote or their votes were not counted. Other Populists caught up in the racist frenzy of the closing months of the campaign answered the Democratic call to prejudice and passion and left their party in enough numbers to throw the election to Democrats. Cooperationists could not find another issue in the campaign to force the race issue off the front burner—race trumped everything, or so it seemed. As a result the eastern section of the state was left to the mercy of the Red Shirts, the White Government Leagues, marauding bands of vigilantes, and prominent Democrats who secretly planned and carried out scores of illegal activities to end cooperation rule and usher in the restoration of Democratic white hegemony. The evidence suggests that the white supremacy campaign was not a revolt of the rednecks but a coordinated strategy by many of the wealthiest and most respected white citizens in the Old North State.

Chapter Nine

THE DEATH OF LIBERTY AND THE PEOPLE'S PARTY IN NORTH CAROLINA, 1899-1901

The white supremacy campaign of 1898 left Populists in disarray; and, coupled with the internal divisions within the People's Party and the decline of the national organization, its existence remained in serious jeopardy. The Democratic control of the state legislative session of 1899 further threatened to smash the remnants of the Populist Party as the leadership of Furnifold Simmons, Charles B. Aycock, and others sought to replace the reformist legislation of the 1895 and 1897 sessions with conservative laws. The Democratic legislative agenda effectively killed off any chance for the Populist Party to re-launch themselves in the Old North State.[1]

Democrats determined that they would permanently defeat the Populist Party and end the opportunity for the triumph of cooperation. Democrats had barely taken their seats in the state legislature before they overturned the cooperationists' election law and local government law. A notable group of Democrats led the Democratic-controlled legislature, many of whom had played a significant role in the 1898 white supremacy campaign. For example, the county and municipal government committee included "White Union League" leader Francis D. Winston and white supremacy orator George Roundtree. Winston and Locke Craig, an avowed white supremacist campaigner, sat on the election law committee. On the constitutional amendment committee sat Roundtree, Winston, and Lee S. Overman. Judge Henry Groves Connor gained election as speaker of the House. Not a single Republican or Populist sat on any committee in either the lower house or senate. Significantly, a majority of the Democratic leaders came from the eastern section of North Carolina, the area that had shaped the racialized 1898 campaign. It is not surprising, therefore, to note that many of these Democrats replaced Populists as county representatives in the 1899 legislature. All the Democratic leaders were either members of the landed elites in North Carolina or hirelings of the railroads and the new manufacturing industries, and they represented the conservative economic and white supremacist attitudes of the Democratic Party and big business interests of the state. This group of politicians would dominate the political actions of North Carolina for the next generation.[2]

These conservative Democrats also changed the cooperationists' local government laws so that the general assembly would once again select magistrates who in turn would appoint county commissioners in areas of Republican or Populist strength, or in so-called black rule areas. These new Democratic laws were especially complex. The provisions varied from county to county, but in the end Democrats left the governance of only thirty-two counties untouched by the new laws. Restrictions in the other sixty-five counties went far beyond abridging the potential of black rule in the sixteen majority-black counties in the eastern section of the state, though in these counties Democrats made doubly sure that white Democrats controlled local government. By fundamentally altering local governance, Democrats succeeded in destroying opposition leadership in areas where Democrats remained in the electoral minority. In addition, Democrats succeeded in perpetuating the centralization of their party and the rule of Democrats for years to come by again appointing hand-picked partisan officials in sixty-five counties. Democrats railroaded this legislation through the legislature in time for it to take effect prior to the 1900 elections.[3]

Perhaps of greater significance to the immediate political future of the state and the Populists, Democrats sought to control the election machinery at the state level. They threw out all the cooperationist laws and instigated a centralized set of voting rules that directly benefited Democrats. By centralizing the registration law in the hands of the Democratic state officials, Democrats restored one of their central mechanisms of hegemony that Populists and Republicans had swept away. The laws were very complicated, but in essence the assembly appointed a state election board, which in turn chose county election officials and local registrars, all of who were Democrats. To further Democratic control, the legislature passed a law that made registering to vote more complicated. The registration records would note the race of a voter and also allow challenges to voters on Election Day. They also ended the use of colored ballots and other laws passed by the cooperationists to ensure an honest and fair election and aid the large number of illiterate voters to cast their vote properly.[4]

The importance of such changes in the election law and local government law was clear. Democrats, led by Simmons, Winston, and Roundtree, also introduced a law to put before the voters of North Carolina a constitutional amendment redefining the right of suffrage. Winston, a member of one of the oldest landed families in the state, cared little for the political rights of poor whites and African Americans. He and the Democratic elite designed this amendment to cement their hegemony in the state and to place North Carolina alongside many other southern states in opposing the principle of universal manhood suffrage. The amendment required all voters to pass a literacy test and to pay a poll tax. In a state with a rate of over 30 percent adult illiteracy, this constitutional amendment would lead to the disfranchisement of both poor whites and poor blacks. In addition, the amendment included a "grandfather clause" to allow persons registered before December 1908 to avoid the literacy test if they, or their lineal ancestors, had registered to vote before 1867. Democrats all but copied this law from Louisiana, and they believed that the amendment circumvented the Fifteenth Amendment of the U.S. Constitution that prohibited the denial of the right to vote based on race, color, or previous condition of servitude. By changing the cooperationist election law and local government law, Democrats stacked the odds in their favor on the passage of the amendment in 1900. To make their chances even better, Democrats passed a resolution that divided the elections in North Carolina into two separate campaigns. Fearing federal interference, Democrats scheduled the regular congressional and presidential votes for November, while the referendum on the constitutional amendment and the state and legislative election would take place on August 2, 1900.[5]

Democrats designed the disfranchisement of African Americans and perhaps some poor whites to ensure that a coalition of reform-minded Populists and Republicans, black and white, could never again successfully challenge Democratic hegemony. By eliminating over half the votes of the opposition, Democrats could ensure that their power was permanent. By stacking the local government law and the new election law in their favor, Democrats made it almost certain that Populists and Republicans could not defeat the constitutional amendment in the August election. The *Wilmington Messenger* gave a good indication of Democratic attitudes on the amendment and its desired effect: "Negro supremacy in North Carolina is of the past. The Anglo-Saxon will hence forth be master of this state and all white folks and negroes who do not like that prospect and declaration would do well to pull up, and leave for their sake and for the good of the state."[6]

The other legislation passed by Democrats was also decidedly conservative. They filled all the offices, such as the corporation commission, with very conservative Democrats and did not raise new taxes to support education and charitable institutions because the state had collected sufficient funds under the cooperationist plan in 1895 and 1897. They abolished the Railroad Commission and replaced it with a Corporate Commission filled with pro-business Democrats. They also passed a Jim Crow car law. Winston led the way on laws to provide "separate but equal" accommodation in railroad cars and steamboats. Winston lost, however, because the railroads did not want to go to the expense of providing such accommodations for African Americans. Eventually, the railroads and legislators reached a compromise that meant African Americans would receive separate and unequal services on railroads. The Democratic-controlled legislature adjourned in early March 1899, after repealing fifty-three sections of the North Carolina code and

153 of the laws passed between 1895 and 1897 by the cooperationists. However, the legislature arranged to meet again in June 1900 to rewrite the laws and amend others. In just three months Democrats succeeded in destroying every discernible cooperationist reform of the previous four years.[7]

During 1899, Marion Butler began to move toward directly opposing the constitutional amendment. At first many Populists exhibited mixed feelings on the amendment issue. But by the end of the year, however, many followed Butler in opposing the constitutional amendment. As Hunt notes, Butler believed the amendment would not advance white supremacy, would not prevent Democrats from using the race issue, would not aid Populism, and that the grandfather clause was unconstitutional. Although Butler began to work earnestly to oppose the amendment, not all Populists seemed to support his position. Morrison Caldwell, the defeated Populist congressional candidate in the Seventh District, warned Butler that "some of the best Populists I know, say they will vote for it to get rid (as they put it) of the negro, so that a man can be a Populist without being called a 'white negro.'" Caldwell hoped that Populists could fight an aggressive campaign, but he remained skeptical that the amendment would provide the rallying point for the People's Party in the August election. Many Populists no doubt reasoned that the race issue merely obscured real economic issues from the voters, and they hoped that without the race issue Populists could successfully challenge and defeat Democrats on economic issues.[8]

As if this was not bad enough for the grassroots organization, it was clear that Populists remained badly demoralized. J. J. Jenkins of the Fourth Congressional District urged "an aggressive campaign" to defeat the amendment. Morrison Caldwell likened Populists "to a flock of sheep—badly demoralized by defeat." Many Populists also wondered if such a reasoned debate over the amendment was now possible. Remembering the violent nature of the 1898 campaign, Hal Ayer candidly discerned that the Democratic plan for victory "does not mean argument or discussion; it means riot, slander, abuse, physical violence and general anarchy. Their plan is to red-shirt every town in the state, and to terrorize voters through the means of such characters as can be hired to wear red-shirts, drink mean whiskey and raise commotion generally." Ayer also argued that Butler and the Populist leadership should carefully appraise the political situation in North Carolina if they hoped to reverse their fortunes in 1900. Ayer concluded his frank letter, "If we cannot succeed in effecting an organization that is both willing and able to suppress such tyranny and terrorism by physical force if necessary, then our fight will be something like of the billy goat who showed enough spunk to try and put a steam-engine off the track." In this, Ayer was right.[9]

In early 1900, Butler took an unequivocal position on the constitutional amendment. In February he addressed the U.S. Senate on the proposed suffrage amendment in North Carolina. Earlier in the year Republican senator Pritchard introduced a resolution proposing that the grandfather clause was a violation of the Fourteenth and Fifteenth Amendments, and if it passed, North Carolina would no longer have a republican form of government. Pritchard's amendment led to an interesting debate between southern U.S. senators who favored disfranchisement and Pritchard and Butler, who opposed it. Senators H. DeSoto Money of Mississippi, Benjamin Tillman of South Carolina, Samuel D. McEnery of Louisiana, and John T. Morgan of Alabama spoke against Pritchard's resolution. For the past two years, Butler and Pritchard's relations had remained severely strained over the financial policy of the McKinley administration and the fight over the U.S. senatorship in the 1897 North Carolina legislative session. However, both senators realized that they needed one another if the anti-amendment forces hoped to defeat Democrats. In light of these developments Butler addressed the U.S. Senate on February 6, 1900, carefully articulating his position against the amendment. Butler focused much of his time on the constitutionality of the grandfather clause. He believed that it was, indeed, unconstitutional because it would not "operate equally, impartially, and uniformly upon both races and upon those formerly free and formerly bond." Butler then argued that if the literacy test remained after the Supreme Court ruled the grandfather clause unconstitutional, thousands of poor whites would lose the right to vote.[10]

Butler then turned his attention to political considerations. No doubt realizing that his speech would receive wide publicity in the Old North State, he argued that the literacy test would disfranchise "the sturdy yeomanry" of North Carolina who exhibited "honesty, integrity, industry, and patriotism." He noted that many of these men had fought in the Civil War and in the recent war against Spain in Cuba. Butler then reasoned that "these men, who compose some of the very best and most substantial citizens of my State, would be disfranchised . . . while the town negro dude would vote and be eligible to hold office."[11]

Butler's position on the amendment clearly illustrated the Populist predicament on the suffrage question. Butler showed that Populists favored constitutional government and believed that African Americans had a constitutional right to vote. Although Butler and the People's Party held a paternalistic attitude toward African Americans and they believed in the natural superiority of "Anglo Saxons," unlike the Democratic Party, which opposed the right of blacks to vote, Populists did favor universal manhood suffrage. Butler was more concerned with protecting the right of poor, illiterate whites to vote, and he believed that the U.S. Constitution would not support the grandfather clause, and thus a literacy test would disfranchise the yeomen of North Carolina. In reality Butler's speech in the Senate, along with Pritchard's, was a rallying cry to those who opposed the amendment in North Carolina.[12]

Butler did receive some notable support for his position on the amendment. J. E. Marshall congratulated Butler on opposing the amendment and believed the western section of the state would vote against it. Republican John C. Dancy, the African American collector of customs at Wilmington, wrote Butler a letter full of praise. "You display rare political wisdom and astuteness," he wrote, and "your courage and boldness are half the battle. You have put every freeman whose citizenship is threatened under renewed and lasting obligations to you, which none will withhold from you when it is his to grant you the full benefit of their suffrage which you seek to perpetuate." Butler's position endeared him to many black leaders in the state, many of whom had distrusted the Populist leader over the past six years.[13]

Letters of support, however, did not translate into effective organization. Cyrus Thompson epitomized the worsening political scene for the party; he was deeply dispirited and discouraged and noted that the party was in financial turmoil. He echoed Hal Ayer's earlier candor, predicting, "This campaign resolves itself into a question of physical force, and we have nothing in sight with which to make the struggle." Thompson went further and asked, "If you can find a more hopeful and active man to relieve me of the Chairmanship I should gladly give way to him." Later in March, Thompson informed Butler that a fight on the amendment would only lead to the defeat of the People's Party, and the only way for the Populists to defeat the Democrats "is to prevent the solidification of their voters, and that there is no way tp [sic] prevent this except by leaving the question of the Amendment open for individual action." He believed that whatever Populists tried to do, Democrats would "howl of negro domination." And howl they did.[14]

In the 1894 and 1896 campaigns, grassroots activism was the Populists' trump card, and Butler determined that the only way Populists could successfully oppose Democrats was if they reorganized and took a bold path. The Populist executive committee, led by an energized Butler, set April 18, 1900, as the date of the People's Party state convention. More importantly, perhaps, Butler used the executive committee meeting as the venue to articulate his position on the amendment. He denounced the new election law and the amendment because he believed that Democrats aimed to disfranchise poor whites as well as African Americans. At the same time Butler sent out anti-amendment literature to wavering voters. In an open letter in the *Caucasian*, Butler carefully argued his position against the amendment, and he used these themes throughout the remaining six months of the campaign. He argued that the amendment would not remove the race issue, that the amendment was unconstitutional, and that it would remove from the electorate over one hundred thousand voters, black and white, who opposed the "reactionary" policies of the Democratic Party. He argued that in other southern states that introduced disfranchisement clauses, such as Louisiana, the number of white voters declined significantly. He believed that Simmons and other Democrats had lied in the last campaign on the disfranchisement question. Butler also wrote, "I believe in manhood suffrage and the freedom of speech and conscience. I believe that the good people of the State will never endorse, but will ever condemn ballot box stuffing and election frauds." He hoped the people would "band themselves together and fight until these evils are removed and the red shirt mob is driven from power." Butler also remarked that if Democrats were merely afraid of "negro domination," they would pass a law that barred blacks from office. The Populist state executive committee endorsed Butler's position and decided to print fifty thousand copies of the public letter for circulation to rank-and-file voters. Butler also wanted reliable Populists to distribute campaign literature, reasoning that such an approach would once again bring success to the Populists and to those who opposed the amendment. He also discerned that by directly appealing to individual Populists he could negate the overwhelming numerical superiority of Democratic campaign literature.[15]

Despite the vigorous leadership shown by Butler and the support of the Populist executive committee, many Populists noted that the party remained in serious organizational trouble. For example, Fernando Ward of Greenville, in the eastern section of the state, warned "that the Populists of our County are very much disorganized, and hardly know what course to pursue," and he continued by noting that Populists had no idea what position to take on the amendment. Many Populists worried that Democrats would once again resort to fraud and violence to carry the elections. Clearly, the Populist leadership had their work cut out to convince earnest Populists on the merits of fighting against Democrats on the amendment.[16]

Some Populists, on the other hand, remained optimistic for the upcoming election. For example, J. J. Jenkins noted that in a debate with a Democrat, Frank Spurill, on the election law and amendment, "four fifths of the crowd were with me . . . . The people can't be scared by the negro racket like they were two years ago." But these reports remained in the minority, and clearly the Populist Party was not in the best of health to fight a political campaign of such magnitude. Butler decided that he would marshal the Populist forces in the upcoming campaign. As the Populist state convention approached, his supporters sent encouraging news that the Populist rank and file now realized the importance of a coordinated political campaign against Democrats. N. R. Dixon of Chatham wrote that the county was "O.K." and that Populists would "register our men and see that they vote and that the vote is counted as cast if we have to wade in blood."[17]

Notwithstanding some reports of Populist optimism and organization, the People's Party at best faced an uphill struggle to defeat Democrats in the August election. Democrats had shrewdly loaded the political dice in their favor in 1899. The changes in the election and local government laws gave them an advantage for the political campaign in 1900, and they were determined that they would use this advantage to good effect in the August election. In reality the 1898 election had settled the question on Democratic white rule in North Carolina, but the

1900 election was important to the leadership of the resurgent Democratic Party. Voters would not only cast their ballot on the constitutional amendment; they would also elect new state officers and a new state legislature that would select a new U.S. senator. Leading Democrats keenly eyed these positions. Josephus Daniels in his *News and Observer* once again led the propaganda charge for Democrats. Because Butler had taken up the leadership role for the anti-amendment forces, he would feel the full force of Democratic vitriol throughout the campaign. The election campaign engineered by Democrats would be slanderous, violent, and full of racism, intimidation, and fraud. Democrats would not allow reasoned debate to undermine their hegemony again. Chairman Simmons began the Democratic campaign early. After the adjournment of the 1899 state legislative session, he flooded the state with campaign literature in favor of the amendment. Democrats once again procured large sums of money from big business and prominent Democrats to fund their campaign. Democrats accused Populists and the GOP of using federal offices to fund their anti-amendment campaign. As early as January 1900, Democrats sent out speakers such as Aycock and Robert Glenn to whip up support for the constitutional amendment and to intimidate those white voters who might oppose the passage of the amendment.[18]

Democrats also engaged in personal intimidation and misrepresentation. Simmons asked Democrats to furnish names of leading men who might oppose the amendment or who wavered in their decision. He sent out a poll book that local Democratic leaders could use to classify every voter in their precinct. Democrats also organized white supremacy clubs, and Simmons sent fifty thousand red white-supremacy buttons to these clubs so that Democrats could identify white supremacy members. Daniels engaged in flagrant misrepresentation in his paper. He asked for the names of prominent anti-amendment leaders in the counties so he could publish their names in his paper. Importantly, Democrats instigated all these tactics months before their state convention in April 1900, and it illustrates the degree to which Democrats once again organized themselves into a coherent political unit and forced the badly demoralized Populists onto the defensive even before the campaign opened.[19]

Democrats met in convention first on April 11, 1900. Determined to swell the passions and prejudices on the race issue in the Old North State, they made certain that the conservative leadership of the successful 1898 campaign remained in place. Furnifold Simmons reminded the delegates that just two years before over one thousand African Americans held office, but Democrats had ended black rule. Now, Simmons argued, it was time to end the race issue once and for all through disfranchisement. Charles B. Aycock, the avowed racist campaigner and leading orator of the 1898 white supremacy campaign, received the nomination for governor. Aycock directly attacked cooperation rule and argued that Republicans had allowed black rule because the party depended on the votes of

African Americans. But Democrats, he argued, were not beholden to black votes and therefore opposed manhood suffrage with their endorsement of the suffrage amendment at their convention. In an endeavor to steal the Populists' thunder and appear progressive on other issues, Democrats supported an income tax, the direct election of U.S. senators, and a four-month school term and criticized the gold standard, militarism, free passes, and imperialism. However, the Democratic position on education was a cynical attempt to rectify the illiteracy of poor whites in time for the expiration of the grandfather clause in 1908.[20]

In the weeks leading up to the Populist Party convention it was clear that the party was in a terrible condition. Led by Hal Ayer and later by James B. Lloyd, Populists coalesced around the idea that blacks should be barred from office rather than from voting in elections. In a lengthy article in the *Caucasian*, Lloyd argued, "I think I can safely assert that there would be no danger or fear of so called 'negro domination' if the negro could not hold a political office; and the old slogan that rallies men to the standard of the dominant party would no longer be effective." Lloyd and other leading Populists perhaps saw this as a way to prevent Democrats from relying on the race issue in the upcoming election. However, what it clearly illustrates is that Populists no longer shaped political discourse in the state and that Democrats had completely changed the parameters of debate.[21]

The Populist convention met on April 18, 1900. The *Caucasian* described Populists as the true adherents of Jeffersonian democracy. It argued, "A more intelligent representation of the sturdy yeomanry of the State never assembled in Raleigh for any convention." Populists, the paper argued, were not lawyers, "pie-hunters" from the cities and towns, but were sent "by the boys in the ditches, those who are interested in good and economical government." The Populist platform supported the national party's 1896 platform and instructed delegates to the Sioux Falls convention to support William Jennings Bryan. Populists condemned the 1899 election law as "glaringly unjust" and blasted the poll tax. They supported self-government in white counties, white control in black counties, better schools, and other Populist policies. Most importantly, Populists decided to not *officially* oppose the amendment. Fearing Democratic attacks on the party as a supporter of black rule, Populists made the amendment an issue for "individual" choice rather than a "party question." This illustrates the degree to which Populists had lost control of the political debate and their purely defensive position during 1900. However, at the same time, the party believed the amendment was wrong and decided it would educate the populace on the evils of the amendment, believing the rank-and-file Democrats would also oppose the amendment. Further, Populists proposed that because the U.S. Constitution's Fifteenth Amendment prohibited the disfranchisement amendment, it would be better to amend the state constitution by providing that no African American "to the third generation inclusive" could hold office. To show that the party remained a solid entity, Populists named a full state ticket with Thompson as their gubernatorial candidate. However, the excitement of the early 1890s was gone, and the race issue and the amendment, rather than economic issues, took up most of the party's platform.[22]

With Butler taking over the reins of the Populist state organization, Populists also took an important strategic position for the upcoming election. In late March and throughout April, local Populist county conventions and nominating conventions began to organize for the campaign. Although they did not know this, the campaign would be the last hurrah for Populists. The Populists decided that as the "white man's party" *they* would lead the fight *against* the amendment. Republicans were tied too closely to the African American voters, and both the GOP and the People's Party quickly realized that only the Populists could withstand the expected Democratic onslaught of a racialized campaign. This was perhaps a naïve position, but there was little choice. Therefore, Populists and Republicans could not and did not name joint tickets so that Democrats could not charge Populists with using black votes to gain office in most counties. Local Populists did not nominate candidates for the state legislature or local offices until later in the campaign.[23]

In the face of mounting odds, Butler, a wily campaigner and excellent public speaker, tried to regain the initiative. On April 20, 1900, Butler challenged Simmons for a series of joint debates between himself, Simmons, Aycock, and Thompson on the constitutional amendment. In the past, the two parties and political leaders had engaged in such debates, and Thompson and Butler were excellent debaters. But Simmons, sensing the Democratic advantage, flatly refused. Butler realized that this would hurt Populists, and he snapped back that the honest people of the Old North State would not "submit again to ruffianism, red-shirtism, and wholesale debauchery of the ballot box" that Simmons instigated in the last campaign. Butler called Simmons a coward for refusing to debate and labeled him a man of the white feather rather than of white supremacy. He argued that a debate was the only opportunity for illiterate white men to hear all the issues and that Democrats were "afraid of the results" of such meetings. He lamented that Democrats would steal the election and that the whole law was "more odious and outrageous than the infamous Federal Force Bill."[24]

In light of the political developments, Democrats began a well-coordinated and sophisticated campaign to carry the amendment. Aycock and Glenn led the stump speakers throughout the state. Simmons continued to compile lists of voters and to garner money from sympathetic business interests. Other Democratic speakers toured their locales drumming up support for the amendment. The Democratic campaign was a carbon copy of the 1898 white supremacy campaign. Simmons realized that Butler had now engineered a well-organized response to Democrats and that the senator had made some headway in convincing voters that the amendment was indeed unconstitutional. To counter this, Simmons sent out a circular signed by 175 North Carolina lawyers arguing that the amendment was indeed constitutional. Worried that Butler might convince illiterate whites that the amendment would disfranchise them, Simmons sent out a flood of literature to local Democratic leaders arguing that the amendment would not disfranchise poor whites. Simmons did admit that the amendment would "disfranchise the ignorant negroes," but he made clear to the voters that the upcoming special session of the state legislature would prevent any poor whites from losing the right to vote. Josephus Daniels sent out the *News and Observer* at reduced rates to convince poor whites that only Democrats would protect them from black rule.[25]

Butler received worrying news that Democrats were making a successful fight on the amendment and that the People's Party remained in difficulty on the amendment. Many Populists implored their leader to send speakers quickly to combat the overwhelming Democratic propaganda. H. W. Caswell of Pamlico County in the eastern section of the state warned Butler that only the U.S. senator could "heal the wounds" in the party and that "we must" have speakers. William J. Leary of Chowan concurred with the need for organization. "The speakers will do much towards evoking a proper sentiment among the people + fixing them in their political faith," he believed, but the party needed real organization. Populists had their work cut out if they hoped to prevent the passage of the amendment.[26]

In June 1900, Butler returned to North Carolina and began a vigorous campaign to defeat the amendment. Although Populists had little money and Democrats would not participate in debates, Butler determined that the best chance to defeat the amendment was by a coordinated campaign in the western section of the state. Butler believed that Democrats would inflate their majorities in the eastern section, as they had done so in 1898, and that the majority of illiterate whites, those most likely to oppose the amendment, lived in the western section of the state. Butler organized an extensive series of campaign stops for himself in western towns and crossroads. He also scheduled appointments for Cyrus Thompson, Hal Ayer, H. F. Seawell, and Alonzo Shuford in the western section of the state. Butler hoped that personal appearances by notable Populist orators would stem the effectiveness of the Democratic stump speakers and Simmons's campaign literature. Butler was the consummate organizer. He sent out letters on regularly, asking local Populist leaders who had registered to arrange for poll holders to petition Democratic election officials for appointment of Populist election judges and to organize the party as thoroughly as possible. Butler used his personal friendship with local Populists to help organize the party in areas of Democratic strength.[27]

Butler also used the *Caucasian* as his mouthpiece against the amendment and the Democratic 1899 legislature. Week after week, Butler lambasted Democrats for their partisan election law, for ruling by party machine, and for threatening the liberties of the people of North Carolina. The paper argued, "When a white man has lost his political rights he has become a slave. It is the purpose of the Simmons-Ransom machine to establish permanently in North Carolina a system of political slavery and to do this their plan 'to work the nigger racket for all its worth' and thus endeavor to hide their damnable perfidy and treachery towards the illiterate white voters." The paper printed a large number of letters from politicians and lawyers who claimed the amendment was unconstitutional. The paper also asserted, "The infamous scheme to disfranchise good, honest, brave white men because they cannot read and write is now understood by these good citizens of the State, and when election day comes they will bury with their ballots the Simmons ballot-box stuffers. The people of this State love liberty."[28]

Butler also hoped to enact local cooperation with Republicans for the state legislature. Some Republicans and Populists had already combined in the aftermath of the state conventions. However, in some counties disagreements between the two parties continued to surface as both tried to gain the lion's share of the nominations. The GOP leadership implored Butler to send Populist speakers to the eastern section, the heart of white supremacy intimidation and violence, even after Butler and his cohorts had canvassed the western section against the amendment. Butler's shoulders now carried the heavy load of organizing, campaigning, writing, and political dealing for the anti-amendment forces. In many ways, he single-handedly carried out the work done by Aycock, Daniels, and Simmons for Democrats.[29]

As if this did not make matters worse, Populists realized that they could not match the efforts of Democrats. Thomas Babb, a former Skinnerite enemy of Butler, wrote from the First District, "There is no organization of the Populist Party in this district and no effort at organization." Q. F. Pool, the Populist chairman of Alexander County, advised Butler that the "failure of Populist speakers to show up" has injured the party. To make the situation worse for the People's Party, many leading Populists did not have the stomach for a fight along the same lines as 1898.[30]

In the face of a determined Butler and news that Populists were reorganizing, Democrats decided to crank up their campaign. On June 12, 1900, Democrats reconvened the general assembly for a special extra session, which served as another portion in campaign. The Democrats shot down any lasting vestiges of fairness in the new election law and registration process. Now Populists, Republicans, and African Americans would find it even more difficult to register to vote. More importantly, perhaps, Democrats also added a clause to the constitutional amendment that made the grandfather clause inseparable from the literacy test. The assembly planned to reconvene and remain in session until just before the August election in order to prevent the cooperationist state supreme court from interfering with the new legislation.[31]

Democrats did not stop with legislative shenanigans; they also campaigned throughout the eastern section of the state, drumming up support for the amendment with the same organizational tactics from 1898. Democrats appealed to the trusted rhetoric of "black rule" and the threat of violence by black men against white women. Democrats organized lavish picnics and barbecues to give a festive feel to the disfranchisement campaign. White supremacy rallies, featuring white women and young girls dressed in white, greeted Charles Aycock as he traveled the eastern section of the state whipping up Democrats into a racist frenzy. Red Shirts escorted the Democratic gubernatorial candidate in town after town as brass bands played patriotic music. In a speech to a group of Democrats at Whiteville, Alfred Waddell, the leader of the Wilmington pogrom, advised and even urged his party "to kill the leaders of the opposition to the amendment." In a speech in the east in mid-July, future Democratic governor Robert Glenn implied that Butler had "suggested whipping them (the white men) out of the State"; and the Democratic racist reminded his audience "how the older men could shoot in the Civil War and the young men had doubtless learned since," and, if necessary, they must stand up and shoot, and "when they went into business to shoot to hit and to shoot to kill." It is no surprise, therefore, that the 1900 election would become one of the most notorious in the state's history.[32]

Democrats not only mounted a well-coordinated series of parades, stump speeches, barbecues, picnics, and demonstrations, they also made certain that their opponents would find it difficult to vote against the amendments. One way to do this was to make it more difficult for Populists and Republicans to register to vote. With the changes in the election law in 1899, Democrats certainly made the registration process extremely complicated for non-Democrats. Voters had to register with a Democratic registrar. This involved answering a series of questions to the satisfaction of this partisan official. The questions included age, residence, and employment. Registrars used technical loopholes to exclude scores of non-Democrats. Some registrars also asked questions not allowed in the statute in order to prevent the registration of many non-Democrats. For example, at Kenansville Democrats refused to register a local Populist leader "unless he would go and get one of two Democrats who he named to come and swear with him." In addition, Democrats would not register any African Americans at Kenansville. The effect of these tactics was clear. One Populist wrote Butler, "The negroes are so completely frightened by threats that we find it impossible to get them to try to register and many that has been refused registration we can't get them to file their affidavit." Butler received scores of letters from Populists informing him that Democrats abused the registration process and that Democrats barred many African Americans from registering. The problem seemed most acute in the eastern section of the state. But in the Piedmont similar problems occurred for Populists and African Americans. The situation was depressing for local Populist leaders. One

Populist lamented "that if our success depends upon the voters reregistering, the probability of our defeat (I am afraid) is evident." In the face of Republican hesitancy, Populists found themselves organizing the anti-amendment forces in the state and instigating the registration of African Americans in the eastern section. GOP state chairman A. E. Holton reminded Butler, "You must stir your people to get them to see that the colored folks are registered." Without such organization, Holton believed, the amendment would pass in August. Thus, in the face of outright illegal activities, Republicans admonished Butler to organize his forces more fully when the real issue was the Democratic intransigence at the registration books. Butler believed that African Americans had the right to vote, and because he realized that African Americans' votes would decide the fate of the amendment, he demanded "the arrest of every registrar at once who refused to register qualified voters." Ultimately, dozens of registrars were arrested, but many Populists opposed arresting registrars because it would only outrage the Democratic white supremacists—though it is hard to see how this could be worse. Although Butler had a political reason for supporting the rights of African Americans, the fact that he pushed such a policy during the virulent white supremacy campaign nevertheless illustrates his commitment to equal political rights.[33]

Evidence of Populist organization and Democratic vitriol and violence at the local level is hard to come by. However, contested election testimony concerning the Third Congressional District in the November election does include some evidence of the type of local campaign instigated by those in support of and those against the constitutional amendment in the summer. From the surviving testimony, it is clear that the Democratic speakers enflamed passions, stirred hatred, and condoned violence that demoralized and depressed Populists, poor whites, and African Americans and prevented them from showing up at the polls on Election Day.[34]

Duplin County was in the heart of the Red Shirt violence. J. W. Mallard testified that over two hundred Red Shirts were armed and active before the August election in his area. The fifty-seven-year-old Populist stated, "I saw as many as thirty together at Rose Hill at one time. . . . [T]hey were armed with pistols and rifles to their teeth." Other Populists noted that Red Shirts threatened to whip those that voted against the amendment. Local Populist leaders were shouted down by the Red Shirts. For example, Maury Ward, a noted local Populist, was prevented from speaking at Warsaw when a train arrived from Clinton full of Red Shirts with pistols, and they "hollered out 'Take him down! Take him down!'" According to a witness, this caused the crowd to disperse. The effects were clear; it scared the voters and caused consternation for the local organizers at the grassroots. One local leader, R. C. Seawell, a former justice of the peace, was harangued by Red Shirts as he registered in Cypress Creek. The hollering for the Red Shirts made his mule nervous, and as Seawell left, a Red

Shirt "stepped from the crowd and pointed toward me and said: 'Yonder goes a black-hearted negro.'"[35]

There was also plenty of evidence of inflammatory speeches from Democratic leaders. J. W. Mallard noted, "I heard a member of the Democratic State executive committee say that they were going to carry the election if it took blood to do it and said also that they were going to clear the registrar at Rose Hill if it took blood to do it." Aycock was known as a particularly violent speaker. Sam B. Newton, a Populist and member of the Duplin county commission, testified that a week before the August election the gubernatorial candidate spoke with over six hundred Red Shirts in attendance, half of whom were armed with pistols, and stated "that if any of the registers were arrested before he was inaugurated governor that we would appear for them, and after he was inaugurated governor he would get the attorney general to appear for them." As if this was not inflammatory enough, Newton continued that Aycock urged the crowd "that if any lawyer appeared for any registrar that he wanted you (the crowd) to take him and give him 39 lashes," and Newton felt that the cheers meant the crowd would do so. Future governor Robert Glenn matched Aycock's venom. According to C. C. Vann, at a speech in Cypress Township in Duplin County, Glenn was so abusive toward Populists and Republicans that even Democratic leaders said it was not safe for Populists to speak. Apparently, Glenn exhorted that he "wanted them to shoot and he wanted to tell them how to shoot. He wanted them to shoot twice to everybody else once—shoot to hit, shoot to kill—not to shoot the poor ignorant negro, but shoot the white men, their leaders."[36]

African Americans were often the target of the Red Shirts in the eastern section of the state. Duplin County saw a lot of activity in this regard. According to Populist A. J. Ward, a gang of Red Shirts fired over thirty times at a group of African Americans in the country outside of Magnolia. Ward found the frightened group of blacks in a cotton patch. Moses Judge from Cyprus Creek concurred that the Red Shirts "produced a good deal of excitement, and they (African Americans) were scared to go to the polls." Some African Americans were so fearful that they hid during the run up to the election. For example, Dave Kennedy, an African American voter in Duplin, testified that he, his brother, and a friend hid in Grove Swamp in fear of their lives. Tim Middleton of Kenansville was directly threatened by a Red Shirt Democrat, Dr. Herring, not to vote. Under oath, Middleton testified that Dr. Herring stated, "You colored people better not vote, for we are better prepared with guns now than we were at the last war, and we are going to cut you down as you go to the polls." Not surprisingly, this scared Tim Middleton.[37]

In the face of such activities it was clear that Populists had their work cut out to stop the election from turning into a farce. The Populists could not run a separate state and legislative ticket and hope to carry the state in 1900. Populists did not have the votes to win a three-cornered fight in such a troubled election. Besides,

Butler and the Populist leaders discerned, the amendment issue was the preeminent issue in the campaign because if the amendment passed the Populist Party was dead. In addition, many Populists and Republicans had already fused along the same lines as in 1894, 1896, and 1898. In the eastern section of the state, Butler argued, Populists had gained about 75 percent of the legislative nominations. On July 18, 1900, Butler wrote to the Populist county chairmen to sound out their position on cooperation with the GOP at the state and county level. Butler wrote that there was no sense in running two distinct tickets when "human liberty is at stake." On July 24, 1900, the Populist and Republicans formalized an agreement. In an open letter to Populists, Cyrus Thompson announced he was resigning as the Populist candidate for governor. Thompson believed that cooperation could help to carry the western section and the Piedmont. He also asserted that the eastern section of the state was lost to "the Simmons Democratic machine." He urged Populists to support the joint ticket so that "the cause of liberty will win in North Carolina without 'fraud,' without 'force' and without law (?) obtained by 'force or fraud,' which after all is but legalized fraud." Simultaneously, Butler and GOP state chairman A. E. Holton arranged a joint state ticket.[38]

Marion Butler decided that as the preeminent Populist, he must take an active role on the stump to fire up his supporters in preparation for the election on August 2, 1900. Without a daily newspaper or the opportunity to debate Democrats, Butler discerned that he must address the public along with other Populist leaders. Throughout the closing months of the campaign Butler received scores of letters pleading with him to give rousing speeches to the party faithful. Although Populists also found the speeches of Thompson, Seawell, and others uplifting, it was Butler they wanted to hear. Butler gave as many speeches to the Tar Heels as he could. As state chairman of the People's Party he spent much of his time organizing the party from its headquarters in Raleigh. However, he did travel throughout the state and address the amendment issue head-on to large crowds of voters. He espoused the same themes from his speech to the U.S. Senate in February. He accused Democrats of hypocrisy, treachery, and cowardice and asserted that the amendment was unconstitutional and would disfranchise poor whites. In late June at Morganton, Butler picked up an eleven-year-old boy from the audience who was wearing a white supremacy button and brought him to the platform. He announced that the button was a lie and that white supremacy was dangerous to the liberties of the people in North Carolina. He argued that in the future the boy would find himself "on a plane lower than the town negro." In Butler's mind the amendment would end political liberty in North Carolina for poor whites and, indeed, for anyone who opposed Democrats.[39]

The Populist response to the Democrats forced Simmons, Daniels, and Aycock to alter their campaign strategy in the closing months of the campaign. After Democrats reconvened the state legislature in June, they began to counter

Populist claims that the amendment would disfranchise thousands of poor illiterate whites. Although Democrats never gave up on the claim that black rule threatened North Carolina, and they continued to campaign in the eastern section on the importance of the disfranchisement amendment, they realized that Populists might convince enough whites in the west to vote against the amendment and scupper its passage. Therefore, Aycock canvassed the western section of the state in July to reassure illiterate poor white voters that their future was safe with Democrats. Aycock watered down his virulent attacks on black officeholding and promised white voters that Democrats would not disfranchise any white child in 1908 because of the lack of education. Aycock pledged that he would abolish illiteracy in North Carolina, and in the four years of his administration he would build up the schooling in the state and endeavor "for every child in the state to get an education." Although Aycock campaigned on an educational platform, it is important to note that this was plain political expediency. None of the Democratic white supremacists had mentioned the education of poor whites until Populists focused on the potential disfranchisement of sixty thousand illiterate poor whites under the constitutional amendment.[40]

Democrats also turned their focus onto Populists. Butler received the brunt of Josephus Daniel's criticisms in the *News and Observer*. Daniels delighted in portraying Butler as a friend of "the negro." The paper mocked the senator's speeches on the amendment and even argued that the young boy Butler grabbed at Morganton was a mulatto and not a white boy. According to the paper, Butler could not tell the difference between whites and blacks because he favored black rule. In a direct attempt to ridicule and undermine the credibility of the Populist leader, the *News and Observer* printed lurid cartoons that depicted Butler as a pawn of the GOP leadership who took his campaign instructions from African Americans. The paper also argued that Butler had no principles but would rather do anything to stay in office. In other words Butler was guilty of treachery to the white man, of backroom political dealings and hypocrisy. Democrats directed these cartoons and editorials at the most articulate spokesman of the anti-amendment forces precisely because Butler's arguments carried such weight.[41]

In the last few weeks of the campaign armed bands of Red Shirts again appeared in the eastern section of North Carolina to intimidate the opponents of the amendment. As noted earlier, Duplin County was a hive of activity, with intimidation and violence common. But there were many other areas that witnessed their fair share of tumult. Reports circulated from local Populists that Democrats had large stores of arms, that they threatened Populist speakers with death, and that cooperation mail was broken into. The Red Shirts appeared in scores of small towns and villages and disrupted the activities of Populist organizers. Many Populists feared that the Red Shirts would destroy cooperation ballots or interrupt voting. Other Populists also noted that the Red Shirts shot at

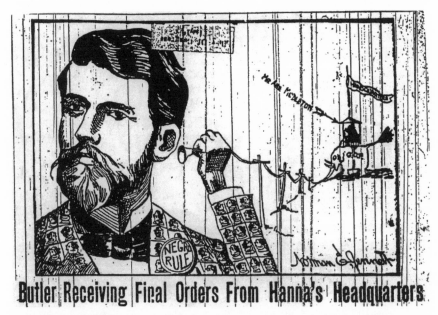

In the highly racialized campaign of the summer of 1900, Senator Marion Butler is portrayed in these cartoons as blinded by "Negro Rule" (*News and Observer*, June 19, 1900) and as a hireling of the Republican Party and notable black leader Abe Middleton (*News and Observer*, July 29, 1900).

African Americans in order to prevent them from registering. Richmond County was a hotbed of Red Shirtism, and here Nelson McAskill noted that few people dared speak their sentiment on the amendment. Populists also believed that "the democrats are going to force the white men to vote the democratic ticket or scare them away. They say they have plenty of rifles . . . and if any white man try to instruct a negro they will shoot them."[42]

Intimidating white and black leaders was commonplace. One of the most infamous occurred in Duplin County. A notable black leader, former Republican county chairman, and member of the state executive committee, A. R. Middleton, found himself the target of Red Shirt ire. Although Middleton did not speak publicly or canvass in 1900, he was still the target of Democratic and Red Shirt threats. On the night before the August election, Middleton testified that there was a lot of shooting around his home—more than normal. On the day of the election, Middleton received word that an eighteen-inch "pasteboard coffin" was placed in his garden—a popular form of intimidation. Although he ignored the threatening news, Middleton was, in fact, quite angry about it, noting, "What the devil do I care about that coffin. I don't care about that, for when I am trying to do right and behave myself then can't be treated right what in devil do I care about the coffin." However, many members of the black community did not ignore this development and crowded around to get a glimpse of the coffin that "read 'Abe Middleton. At rest.'" Middleton noted that several other black leaders had also received a delivery of a coffin in their gardens. This was corroborated by Lafayette Hussy, who noted the use of pasteboard coffins to intimidate black leaders and voters. The locals knew what the coffins meant, as they read, "Your time next."[43]

Democrats also committed acts of violence against the opponents of the amendment. Red Shirts delighted in preventing Populist speakers from getting off trains or, if they managed to get off the train, from speaking to their audience. The Red Shirts even prevented Butler from speaking at Warsaw and other locations in the eastern section of the state by not allowing the U.S. senator off his train. When Butler did make it off the platform, the Red Shirts "tossed" him "back bodily to the platform. All the while shouts of no complimentary nature hit the air." The Red Shirts forcibly broke up a Populist meeting in Warsaw with the threat of "blood." The Red Shirts also gave a Populist activist in Charlotte a ducking because he opposed the amendment. As if this was not enough, the Red Shirts also instigated a riot at Smithfield when they pulled a Populist speaker off the stump. In Duplin County, for example, O. L. Ward testified that Captain Davis was prevented from speaking at Warsaw because the Red Shirts put him back on the car, and in Cypress Creek the local Populist leaders were not allowed to speak. Ward even admitted that he advised Thompson to not speak in Duplin because he felt "it unsafe for him." Henry Faison, the former chairman of the Populist Party in Duplin County, heard that speakers were threatened that if they spoke against the amendment they "should 'be tarred and feathered.'" Few brave souls spoke in public.[44]

The actions of the Democrats and their violent associates depressed Populists and kept many from going to the polls. Butler received warnings from several local Populists that the party remained demoralized and badly beaten in many eastern sections of the state. James Mitchell of Winston wrote Hal Ayer that Populists in his county had "*completely surrendered.*" He also exclaimed, "Nothing but a company of U.S. troops to stand over the poll and see the vote counted will save this county." W. R. Dixon epitomized Populist sentiment when he candidly wrote, "I think now that the Democrats will carry the State by a large majority. It seems to me that our people are so thoroughly intimidated as they were in '98 . . . a good many of the Populists have not registered, and I expect that this is the case in a good many of the Eastern counties." In Duplin County, for example, scores of testimony reiterates the point that many poor whites and blacks did not register and could not vote.[45]

Despite these private letters showing the huge difficulties the Populist Party faced, Butler wrote a call to all opponents of the amendment to go out and vote on Election Day. Hoping for a high turnout, Butler once again argued that the amendment was unconstitutional and that those that faced disfranchisement held the balance of power in the state. However, in keeping with the heightened tensions and violence in the closing month of the campaign, the newspapers focused on a public attack made by Congressman John D. Bellamy on Butler in which the Democrat called Butler "the most despicable and contemptible creature in this state," who should be "forcibly expelled" from the state. This letter outraged Butler and for the first time he exploded with indignation. In a damning public letter he lashed out at Bellamy with all the frustration he must have felt over the last two years: "Do you mean that you feel it is your duty to forcibly expel me from the State, or do you mean that some one else should do it? Do you mean than one man should undertake it, or that a cowardly lawless mob should do it? Now if you think I should be expelled from the State, I suggest that you undertake the job yourself. You are one man, and I am one man. If you mean what you say, and have any courage (except when you have a mob of Red Shirts behind you) I suggest that you proceed to Raleigh, and begin this expelling business at once. If you have not the courage to undertake this job, I suggest that you have the decency to keep your mouth shut."[46]

By this stage, the cause was lost. The Democratic campaign of character assassination, hypocrisy, lies, intimidation, and violence tested the patience of many Populists. The party no longer set the agenda for the state and did not have the means to combat the well-coordinated Democratic white supremacy campaign. Populists did not support African American rights. Thus, the party found itself caught in the rapidly shrinking middle ground between the politics of white supremacy and civil rights for all people. Populists had failed to shift North Carolina and southern attitudes on the primacy of race and racial politics and did not end the deep-seated racism in the South. Populists themselves believed in the inferiority of African Americans, and they chose to attack Democrats for using the votes of blacks in the past, for appointing black officials in many counties, and for using black workers at Democratic campaign headquarters. Butler's main criticism of the amendment was that it would disfranchise sixty thousand illiterate poor whites while fifty thousand blacks would remain as voters. In addition, Populists themselves fueled the racist nature of the election by adopting a resolution to bar blacks from office. Thus, even though Populists supported the right of blacks to vote, they did not want blacks to have equal civil rights. At the same time, however, Populists correctly maintained their argument that Democrats used the race issue to obscure the economic issues in the state and the region as a whole. They believed Democrats used the mask of race to push through conservative economic policies to maintain the power and privilege of the planter elite, the big business interests, and the railroads. Time and time again, Butler argued that universal manhood suffrage for whites prevented political slavery and the death of liberty. Populists positioned themselves as the protectors of the liberty of the poor and illiterate white man, and they argued that the amendment would remove the lower classes of whites from the political process and thus place power in the hands of the "town ringster." Whatever the position the Populists adhered to in the campaign in 1900, Democrats controlled the agenda, the resources, and the guns in the election.[47]

The August 2, 1900, election produced an overwhelming victory for Democrats. The amendment passed by a majority of 53,932 votes, with 182,217 votes for and 128,285 votes against, or 58.7 percent for and 41.3 percent against, and carried sixty-six counties. A sign of the future, however, was evident in that the voter turnout dropped to 74.6 percent. This number would decline markedly over the next ten years. Democrat Charles B. Aycock gained election as governor by an even larger margin of 186,650 votes to 126,296 votes for Republican Spencer B. Adams (or 59.6 percent for Aycock to 40.4 percent for Adams). With seventy-three counties voting for Aycock, the virulent white supremacist carried even more counties than the amendment. Adams received the lowest percentage of the vote for a Republican gubernatorial candidate in over a generation. However, the amendment cut across party lines in some counties. Interestingly, the counties that voted against the amendment were located in the western and upper central portion of the state. But these counties did not provide large enough majorities to defeat the amendment statewide. Even the Populist stronghold of Chatham defeated the amendment by just 268 votes. The only exceptions in the east to this were Butler's home county of Sampson, Brunswick County, the home of Daniel L. Russell, and Camden County, which gave a majority of just one against the amendment. The legislature returned an overwhelmingly Democratic majority. In the 1901 session the assembly would see 140 Democrats, 27 Republicans, and just 3 Populists writing legislation. The solid votes for the amendment came from the eastern section of the state, as Populists had feared. In one county, New Hanover, with a majority-black population of 50.5 percent, Republican support dropped from over 2,600 votes in the violent election of 1898 to just 3 votes in 1900, and just 2 votes against the amendment. In eleven of the thirteen precincts in the county Democrats received all the votes. In the new county of Scotland, with a black majority of 53.5 percent, the opponents of the amendment numbered just seven. In Richmond County, a center of Red Shirt activism, the vote for the amendment stood at 1,636 for and 193 against, with several townships casting just a single vote against the amendment. In Robeson County, another Red Shirt area, the amendment passed by an overwhelming 4,015 votes to 704. Estimating the number of Populists who voted for the amendment is difficult. J. Morgan Kousser estimates that 37 percent of Populists voted for the amendment and 42 percent voted against the amendment. Although Kousser's findings may be correct, it is important to remember that Democrats may have inflated their majorities in several counties that had a tradition of Populist activism from 1892 to 1898. Thus it is not surprising that the vote for the amendment was so large in many white counties in the eastern section of the state.[48]

In counties with a black majority the amendment passed by huge majorities. The examples of New Hanover and Scotland were the most extreme, but every other black-majority county followed their lead. Only in one county, Caswell, did the proponents of the amendment carry the day by a small majority of just 150 votes. More egregious was the count of 6,280 votes for the amendment and just 899 votes against in Halifax County. Thus, if one believes the "official" returns, 73 percent of African Americans voted to disfranchise themselves in the 1900 election.[49] Indeed, in the black counties the amendment passed by a majority of 27,133 votes, over half the amendment's overall majority. More likely, the repercussions of the Wilmington pogrom, the Democratic election law of 1899, the difficulty in registering, the intimidation, Red Shirt violence, and the barring of voters on Election Day skewed the majority for the amendment in the black counties, if not elsewhere.[50]

If one analyzes the results more closely, it is noticeable that the Populist message that poor whites could face disfranchisement did have some effect in some counties of the western and central section of the state. For example, the majority of voters in Alamance, Orange, Moore, Davidson, Graham, Jackson, and Haywood counties voted for Aycock for governor but did not vote for the amendment. However, in many of these counties the vote against the amendment was only slightly higher than the vote of those who favored it. In addition, several counties that returned Democrats in 1898 did not vote for the amendment in 1900. What is clear is that the eastern section of the state, as Populists and Republicans feared, went solidly for Democrats and the amendment. Indeed, the white counties of the east returned a majority for the amendment of 23,073. Only three counties east of Raleigh voted against the amendment, whereas in 1898 eight counties voted against Democrats. Thus, the total majority vote in the eastern section for the amendment stood at 50,206 votes, just 3,728 votes short of the amendment's overall majority.[51]

The Populist leadership realized that illegal activity by Democrats and their Red Shirt supporters inflated Democratic majorities. Before the election Butler asked Populists to record the vote for a future challenge in the courts. The reports he received from local Populist leaders and activists illustrate the extent to which the August 2 election was not a real election. Butler received reports that Democrats put blacks in jail or forced them to vote for the amendment while other blacks found themselves prevented from voting. In other areas Red Shirts whipped and shot blacks. For example, in Bertie County, a black-majority county in the eastern section of the state, "a colored man was shot three times the ball passing through his face, and the man, a democrat, who shot him, was brought before [the local mayor's court] and fined one cent."[52] White Populists also faced difficulty in voting. Scores of letters detail the wholesale frauds committed by Democrats against white voters throughout the state.

The news of such fraudulent elections throughout the state outraged Populists. In a stinging editorial Butler wrote that Democrats did not really win the election because "the majority, which the Democrats are claiming, was secured through violence, intimidation, and rascality, after the registration books closed." Other Populists expressed similar sentiments to their state leader. The *Hickory Times-Mercury*, for example, wrote that both Populists and Republicans "made a campaign on which any party may be proud." The paper echoed the views expressed in the *Caucasian* by arguing that "with thousands of their voters intimidated and kept from registering and voting by redshirts in the East; with the other thousands of voters denied registration by partisan registrars; with the election machine practically in the hands of the opposition, and with no representation in the election boards in many precincts, they made gains in nearly all the white counties."[53]

If the outcome of the election outraged Populists, the results overjoyed Democrats. The *Charlotte Observer* rejoiced over the result and claimed that "ignorance and race prejudice are to disappear, and in their stead we are to have enlightenment, charity and breadth of mental vision." What this meant was the triumph of white supremacy and the end of African American voting rights. Anyone who stood against Democrats was portrayed as an enemy of the white race. Butler received particular condemnation for opposing the amendment. Democrats in Clinton burned an effigy of the U.S. senator and the *News and Observer* chided that Butler had committed the "unpardonable sin" of depending on black votes. One Democrat expressed these sentiments directly to Butler during the latter stages of the election campaign. D. K. Blue wrote a damning letter, insisting, "I am a white man and a Democrat, and therefore I forbid you to send me any of your filthy corrupting papers, misnamed 'Caucasian.'" He continued, "Your attitude on the Constitutional Amendment places you in the ranks of the 'accused of God' the Ethiopians." Blue then blasted, "Your objections are based on one of two things, you are trying to ride into office on the *negro* vote and are against the amendment for policy, while you really care nothings for the negro. If that is the case, there is only one other reason. *You have more respect for the Negro race than the White Race.* I speak the truth and you know it."[54]

The North Carolina People's Party virtually collapsed after the August elections. Butler hoped to organize a legal challenge to the election and to galvanize Populists, and the *Caucasian* filled its pages with information on voting irregularities throughout North Carolina. Indignation meetings convened throughout the state and at first they rallied some Populists. Such optimism was misplaced, however, and by the end of October, the Populist leaders abandoned the idea of a lawsuit challenging the fraudulent election. Many Populists probably saw such a lawsuit as hopeless. After the plans for a lawsuit collapsed, the People's Party all but withered and died.[55]

The North Carolina Populist Party played only a minor role in the November elections. Although some local organizations remained intact, the majority of Populists either voted for the Republican Party or the Democrats, or stayed at home. Only in the Third Congressional District, the home of Butler, Thompson, and several other Populist leaders, did Populists maintain their organization. However, this was the exception. In the remaining eight congressional districts the party played at best a minor role. But even in the Third Congressional District Democrats made sure that Populists could not regain power. In the Third Congressional District, former Populist congressman John Fowler, though very sick, ran for Congress in an attempt to defeat Charles R. Thomas and give a political black eye to the resurgent and cocksure Democrats. Although Fowler lost, apparently by 1,909 votes, it seemed that there was widespread fraud, intimidation, and violence in that congressional election. Although it was only a minor blip in the restoration of Democratic control, it is further evidence of the extent to which Democrats sought to destroy their opponents. What is amazing is that Populists and African Americans continued to push for their voting rights after the constitutional amendment carried in August.[56]

The August disfranchisement amendment election ended any hope for the People's Party to play a discernible role in the politics of North Carolina. Populists had no response to Democratic organization and control of the political debate in 1900. The Democrats stacked the election law in their favor in readiness for the 1900 election. They also had a superior campaign fund and a

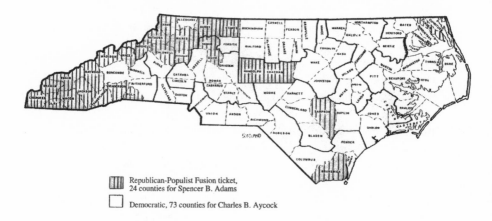

Republican-Populist Fusion ticket, 24 counties for Spencer B. Adams

Democratic, 73 counties for Charles B. Aycock

Gubernatorial election, 1900. R.D.W. Connor, comp. and ed., *North Carolina Manual*, issued by the North Carolina Historical Commission (Raleigh: E. M. Uzzell and Company, State Printers, 1913), 1005–1006.

powerful daily press. The People's Party had little to counter these odds. In addition, the People's Party did not support equal rights for African Americans, and thus they campaigned on the premise that the amendment was unconstitutional and would only succeed in disfranchising poor and illiterate white yeomen. This position placed Populists on the defensive throughout the campaign. Democrats used the new election law, intimidation, violence, and fraud to pass the amendment and gain office in August 1900. There was little Populists could do to prevent the amendment's passage. Political liberty was dead in North Carolina. In the face of such an election the People's Party had nowhere to turn. In just a few years the Populist leadership joined the lily-white Republican Party while the rank and file of the party returned to the party of their fathers, voted Republican, or decided that there was nothing to vote for and thus joined the increasingly large number who abstained from voting.[57]

The Populist Party was dead in North Carolina because, fatally weakened by the national election of 1896 that essentially ended it as a vibrant party, it had failed to overcome the force and violence of the campaigns engineered by Democrats in 1898 and 1900. Populists could not find a suitable response to the heated white supremacy campaign in 1898, and the party's debacle in that election essentially sealed its fate. Internal divisions, demoralization, and disintegration racked the People's Party at the time the party needed a united front to withstand the Democratic onslaught. But the reform party failed to transform itself from an oppositional party to a party of governance. In addition, Populists in North Carolina failed to become a majority party. As a result they remained the party that held the balance of power. This position was not an enviable one. The party spent too much time trying to broker cooperation at a time when the middle ground between white supremacy and economic reformism turned into political quicksand. The politics of cooperation with the GOP had only further exacerbated the cleavages within the People's Party as Democrats shot arrow after arrow at the cooperationist Achilles' heel of race and black office-holding. In addition, Populists failed to persuade enough voters in the Old North State that economic questions outweighed the race issue in the South. The decline of the People's Party after 1898 was swift and in many ways painful. Democrats succeeded in holding the reins of power as they had never done before, and for the next sixty years the Old North State remained a one-party state. Butler perhaps best summed up the feeling of North Carolina Populists at the end of 1900 when he wrote, "The claim is made that 'the Constitution follows the flag.' Perhaps it has gone to the Philippines or to China—it has certainly departed from North Carolina." North Carolina would wait until the civil rights movement in the 1960s before a new political alignment, universal suffrage, and civil rights for all, black and white, would supplant the era of Jim Crow, lynchings, and disfranchisement.[58]

EPILOGUE

As the twentieth century opened, the Populist Party in North Carolina withered and died. The disfranchisement campaign killed off the floundering party once and for all. With just three state legislators and a lame duck U.S. senator, the party had little chance to revive itself into a political organization now that Democrats had loaded the political dice in their favor with a new election law and a disfranchisement amendment. After 1897, the People's Party steadily declined as factionalism, personality clashes, and serious divisions over campaign strategy wrecked the reform party. This state of affairs disoriented and demoralized the rank and file that the People's Party relied on to mount successful political campaigns. Once Democrats mounted a well-funded and well-organized white supremacy campaign in 1898, the People's Party had nowhere to turn. White supremacy only exacerbated the problems within the Populist Party, and once Democrats co-opted much of the Populists' state policies, which they jettisoned after gaining office, many of the recent converts to the Populists fled back to the Democrats under the umbrella of white supremacy.

North Carolina entered the new century with the forces of racism, conservatism, and Democrats in the ascendancy. Indeed, the state witnessed a period of one-party rule that would last well into the 1960s. What happened, therefore, to the Populist leaders and the rank and file of the party? Although this study focuses on the Populist movement of the 1890s, it is important to note, albeit briefly, the aftermath. Essentially, Populists followed three paths. For some Populists it is clear that the nature of the Democratic take over and the virulent racism and violence signaled the end of political engagement and action. Many Populists, particularly African American members, could no longer vote, and it is probable that some began the trek to the North during the Great Migration. Some white Populists could not or would not vote for either the Democrats or the Republicans.[1]

A second group of Populists succumbed to the racist arguments of the Democrats, the violence and the politics of fear, and returned to the party of their fathers. Many recent converts followed this path. Perhaps the biggest loss for the Populists was the transformation of the *Progressive Farmer* under the editorship of Clarence Poe from a strong Populist newspaper to a mouthpiece of the Democrats; indeed, Poe came out in support of the disfranchisement amendment in 1900—Leonidas Lafayette Polk probably turned in his grave at this. It is impossible to determine how many Populists followed the path of the *Progressive Farmer*, but it is clear that in many eastern counties, such as the "Black Second," the Sixth Congressional District, and the area in the Piedmont, many Populists returned to the Democrats.

However, from the surviving evidence, it does seem clear that the majority of Populists did not return to the Democrats. In fact, the vast majority of the Populist leadership entered the Republican Party; they had simply been abused too much by the Democrats, encountered too much violence, and knew that the Democratic leaders, particularly Aycock, Simmons, and Glenn, were not Progressives at all and cared little for the plight of farmers and the poor in the state. Harry Skinner led the move toward the Republicans in 1901, becoming U.S. attorney for eastern North Carolina. Cyrus Thompson also joined the Republicans and later became a Progressive and something of a local leader in eastern North Carolina. However, he spent most of his time as a doctor, helping the rural folk of his area. Other Populists, such as James Mewboone, J. F. Click, and H. F. Seawall, also became Republicans. What is interesting to note about North Carolina is that the vast majority of Populist leaders became Republicans; this was not replicated in other southern states. Perhaps the reason was the experience of cooperative rule and the decidedly vitriolic nature of the campaigns of 1898 and 1900. Butler did not join the Republicans as speedily as other Populist leaders. However, after some hesitation, he finally joined the GOP in 1904—having formed friendly relations with Jeter Pritchard and the new GOP president, Theodore Roosevelt. Butler became a Progressive of the Roosevelt mold, rather than that of Woodrow Wilson. Butler tried to build a grand alliance of white Populists, farmers, manufacturers, and Republicans; and for a time it seemed to offer a chance for success, but internal squabbling over patronage and power, personal disputes, and sour memories, plus differences over economic policy and a strong Democratic Party, doomed the experiment. The Progressives were not Populists, and the radicalism of the People's Party was noticeably absent from the Progressive wing of the GOP. Many rank-and-file Populists followed Skinner, Thompson, and then Butler into the Republican Party. Sampson County, the home of Butler, became a Republican stronghold, and there were pockets of Republican activity and strength, reinforced by the presence of Populists, in many eastern counties and also in the Piedmont section of the state. The Republican Party became lily-white as it saw the disfranchised African Americans as a lost cause, and therefore the party shifted to the right. The "Progressive" Democrats kept taxes low, cut appropriations to state institutions, gerrymandered districts, passed partisan election laws, elected the Southern Railroad's candidate to the U.S. senate in 1903, elected a corporation lawyer to the governorship in 1904, and did nothing to protect workers or trade unions as North Carolina industrialized.[2]

In the face of such a racialized society of the 1880s and 1890s, what is remarkable is that the Populist insurgency occurred at all. But as C. Vann Woodward reminds us, "forgotten alternatives" did exist after the end of Reconstruction. While it is true that Populists wanted power in the state, they wanted this power to reorient society in a more progressive and democratic direction. Populism in North Carolina did not suffer from poor leadership or an overcautious attitude on the part of the leadership of the Farmers' Alliance. Indeed, the leadership in conjunction with the rank and file built a cooperative movement that formed the crucial stage in the emergence of the Populist Party. North Carolina had a vibrant and politically active Farmers' Alliance, and the Populists also had some of the most gifted leaders in the South. The death of Polk left a reluctant Marion Butler at the head of the Populists in 1892, but he did not remain reluctant for long. Butler's moves toward cooperation with Republicans and later with Democrats may have caused him to moderate some of the more radical elements of the Populist program in order to gain votes, but he never deserted the Omaha platform. In addition, the People's Party was a movement of the people, and the rank-and-file members were the life and sinew of the party. The Tar Heel Populist Party was no more conservative in its economic, social, and political policies than any other of its counterparts in the southern states, but the major difference was that Populists actually gained state office in a cooperation alliance with Republicans.[3]

The Populist Party was a *movement* of the people, it was the "people's party" and was not just a political party run by the dictates of a small cadre of leaders. Populists saw their party as something different than the old parties. A constant theme in the study of North Carolina Populism is the difficulty that party leaders such as Butler and Skinner had in keeping the rank and file in order and following the lead of their party leaders on state policy and campaign strategy. Indeed, in many cases the rank and file pushed electoral policy in the state and the moves toward cooperation at the local level, particularly in the eastern counties of the state, where Populists realized that only an alliance with the GOP could possibly end the machine rule of Democrats. In the short term, the actions of the rank and file made for a vibrant mass movement that succeeded in joining with the GOP, overthrowing Democrats, and electing a progressive-minded state legislature that both reformed the election laws of the state and increased public spending in the notable areas.

In the long term, however, the independent actions of the rank and file caused consternation amongst the cadre of leaders in Raleigh and in the

U.S. Congress. Butler, the great political trickster, could not control the party during his complex cooperation negotiations with the Democratic Party during the campaign of 1896 and again in 1898—probably no leader could have done so. The fact that Butler had some control illustrates his excellent leadership skills. Rank-and-file members in scores of counties refused to follow the edicts of Butler as he vainly sought a cooperation agreement with Democrats based on free silver and financial reform. As a result, two wings of the party developed: One followed Butler, his moderate reform agenda, and his attempts to align with the state Democratic Party. The second followed Skinner, who favored a contin-ued alliance with Republicans to preserve the life of the Populists in the state and to reinforce North Carolina's new election and county government laws. These tensions existed because Populists failed to supplant Democrats in the state.

The Populists' attitudes toward African Americans in North Carolina also mirrored the contradictory and oscillating attitudes of Populists in the Upper South in the 1890s. In no southern state did Populists argue for the social equal-ity of the two races. But Populists earnestly fought for equality of opportunity and for political and economic reforms that would benefit African Americans. In North Carolina, Populists' attitudes toward African Americans changed dur-ing the decade. In 1892, Populists made overtures toward black voters in the state, and in some majority-black counties the party even nominated African Americans for office. However, this appeal to African Americans remained short-lived. Believing that they would supplant the Democrats in the state, Populists appealed to the core Democratic constituency—white men. Further complicating matters, the vast majority of African Americans remained loyal to the GOP. Throughout the 1890s, African Americans continued to vote for Republicans and gained scores of local offices. Thus, when Populists joined a cooperative movement with Republicans, they no longer had to appeal to the black vote. At the same time, however, cooperative arrangements led African Americans and whites to vote for one another in 1894, 1896, and even during the white supremacy campaign of 1898. When Democrats tried to focus on the race issue in 1894 and 1896, Populists responded quickly and strongly by accusing Democrats of using the "scarecrow" of race to obscure the real economic issues. This approach worked well for the Populists for three years. However, in 1898, a united, resurgent, and well-financed Democratic Party mercilessly focused on race and forced Populists onto the defensive for the remainder of the decade. Race triumphed over class *precisely* because Populists threatened the class inter-ests of the wealthy elites in North Carolina. If North Carolina Populists were really that conservative, this position was certainly lost on the business leaders who financed the Democratic white supremacy campaign.

The long-term legacy of the People's Party is difficult to assess. In terms of hastening the emergence of Jim Crow laws and the disfranchisement of

African Americans and poor whites, Populists and African American voters gave Democrats all the excuses they needed. The political insurgency of the Populists also awakened the Bourbon Democrats from their comatose state and forced them to react to the threat of a long-term political realignment in the state. Democrats found their answer to this threat by cranking up the race issue. The Populists failed to reorient society to what they considered as the real issues facing southern farmers, namely, the gold standard, monopoly capitalism, and an undemocratic form of government. That Populists failed to achieve this is perhaps not that surprising given the time in which the Populist revolt transpired. The politics of race had trumped reform and so ended North Carolina's fleeting experiment in biracial rule and democracy. Although there were internal problems with the cooperation experiment, both Populists and Republicans attempted to instigate a new form of coalition politics. To be sure, the Populists and GOP hoped to use the cooperation arrangement to bolster their respective party's power base, but the fact that whites and blacks voted for one another and served together to transform the political culture of the state was unique in the South in the 1890s. The cooperation experiment only lasted a few years, and therefore it is impossible to assess the potential long-term implications of the cooperation experiment. The cooperationists did not have that chance. Democrats resurrected the scarecrow of race to great effect in 1898, and the Red Shirts made certain that enough voters remained away from the polls to guarantee Democratic victory. With the demise of the cooperation experiment in North Carolina, the South entered a period of strident Jim Crowism and racial violence. It would take an African American-led civil rights movement to usher in a new era of politics and integration in the South. But from 1894 until 1898 Populists gave the rest of the United States an object lesson in biracial politics. It was also a party of earnest rank-and-file activists who often risked social ostracism, their jobs, and even their lives in campaigning and casting their ballot for the "party of the people."

NOTES

INTRODUCTION

1. William R. Lindsey to *Websters Weekly*, published July 19, 1892, quoted in the *Winston Union Republican*, July 28, 1892.

2. Woodward, *Origins of the New South*, 75–106; Woodward, *The Strange Career of Jim Crow*, 54. Carl Degler carried out a comparative analysis of opposition to Democrats in *The Other South*, where he argued that a tradition existed in the South from 1820 to 1900 of southern "Dissenters" opposed to the dominant political line in the South. See also Hahn, *The Roots of Southern Populism*; Hyman, *The Anti-Redeemers*; McKinney, *Southern Mountain Republicans*; Hair, *Bourbonism and Agrarian Protest: Louisiana Politics*; Hart, *Redeemers, Bourbons, and Populists: Tennessee*; Rogers, *The One Gallused Rebellion: Agrarianism in Alabama*; Sheldon, *Populism in the Old Dominion*. Other studies focused on the Southern Farmers' Alliance and its impact on the Democratic Party in the South, the most important of these was Robert McMath's work on the Southern Alliance as a vanguard of the People's Party, but since McMath's work, there have been many state histories on the Alliance in the 1880s and 1890s: McMath, *Populist Vanguard*; Barnes, *Farmers in Rebellion*; Saloutos, *Farmer Movements in the South*. Also see Hicks, *The Populist Revolt*; Woodward, *Origins of the New South*, 235–290; Hofstadter, *The Age of Reform*; Durden, *The Climax of Populism*; Goodwyn, *Democratic Promise*.

3. Several books mention the Readjusters: Woodward, *Origins of the New South*; Degler, *The Other South*; Dailey, *Before Jim Crow*.

4. Hamilton, *History of North Carolina since 1860*, 270, 280. Woodward's analysis of southern Populism gave only fleeting attention to the defeat of the Tar Heel Democrats. He saw the actions of the Populists in the state as only part of the southern Populists' efforts to achieve power at all cost and did not analyze in any detail the cooperation government in North Carolina. Woodward even argued that African Americans were politically apathetic, and, as Craig Thurtell notes, this "may have led him to doubt that anything worthy or notable could result from their supposed manipulation by cynical white politicians." Woodward, *Origins of the New South*, 277–278; Woodward, *Strange Career of Jim Crow*, 51, 59, 69–70; Thurtell, "The Fusion Insurgency in North Carolina," 5.

5. Edmonds, *The Negro and Fusion Politics in North Carolina*. Other studies tend to be rather short. See Lefler and Newsome, *North Carolina*; Billings, *Planters and the Making of a "New South"*; Escott, *Many Excellent People*; Kousser, *The Shaping of Southern Politics*; Ayers, *The Promise of the New South*.

6. Goodwyn, *Democratic Promise*, 341, 410, 442–445. James L. Hunt's excellent biography of Marion Butler has corrected this argument. See Hunt, *Marion Butler and American Populism*. Hunt provides a lot of details on North Carolina Populism, and for this I am thankful. Throughout my study, I use a great

detail of facts from Hunt's dissertation, "Marion Butler and the Populist Ideal." The dissertation was significantly altered and abbreviated for Hunt's book; thus most citations come from the dissertation.

7. Palmer, *"Man Over Money,"* 143–144; Woodward, *Tom Watson*; Gerald Gaither, *Blacks and the Populist Revolt*; Shaw, *The Wool-Hat Boys*. For more on the debate on Populism and African Americans, see Abramowitz, "The Negro and in the Agrarian Revolt," 89–95; Abramowitz, "The Negro in the Populist Revolt"; Goodwyn, "Populist Dreams and Negro Rights"; Saunders, "Southern Populists and the Negro"; Simms-Brown, "Populism and Black Americans"; Anderson, *Race and Politics in North Carolina*.

8. Steelman, *The North Carolina Farmers' Alliance*.

9. Hunt, *Marion Butler*. Hunt also tends to hold a too glowing opinion on Butler. Butler was a great tactician, but he does not seem to have a long-term vision for the party or a strategy for success in the long term. There are other dissertations that briefly touch on Populists in North Carolina: Bromberg, "Pure Democracy and White Supremacy"; Redding, "Making Power: Elites in the Constitution Disfranchisement in North Carolina"; Steelman, "The Progressive Era in North Carolina"; Wooley, "Race and Politics." Philip R. Muller's dissertation on Populism in North Carolina begins well enough with an analysis of the Populist's attitude toward the New South creed and industrialization. But his work lacks detailed analysis of the development of the party, and it breaks down after 1892 with scores of factual errors and little analysis of the politics of cooperation or the actions of the rank and file of the party. Muller, "New South Populism: North Carolina, 1884–1900."

10. The theoretical influences on this book are too numerous to mention here. In short, my thinking of the Populist insurgency is informed by the work of Althusser, *Lenin and Philosophy*; Barthes, *Mythologies*; Bocock, *Hegemony*; Eagleton, *Ideology*; Edwards, *Angels in the Machinery*; Ellis, *American Political Cultures*; Foucault, *The History of Sexuality*; Geertz, *The Interpretation of Cultures*; Gramsci, *Selections from the Prison Notebooks*; Jameson, *Postmodernism, or the Logic of Late Capitalism*; Rosenberg, *Disorderly Conduct*; Scott, *Gender and the Politics of History*; Thompson, *The Making of the English Working Class*; Williams, *Marxism and Literature*. The dovetailing of these rather divergent theoretical positions helped me make sense of the political culture of Populists; the worldview of the grassroots activists; the nature of power relations; the public and private spheres; the meshing of sexuality, gender, race, and white supremacy; and the notion of hegemony and counter-hegemonic struggle.

11. It is important to note that throughout this book the term *cooperation* will be used for the alliance between Populists and Republicans. At no time was fusion enacted. Both parties maintained their own organization, platform, and activists. The term *fusion* was coined by the Democrats as an attempt to discredit the Populists and point out their illegitimacy. I will only use the term *fusion* if it is an actual quote.

12. I am indebted here to the work of Gilmore, *Gender and Jim Crow*. But even Gilmore's work does not explicate the nature of the Populist insurgency and the effect on the Democrats and the politics of North Carolina.

CHAPTER ONE. THE ALLIANCE BROTHERHOOD: THE ORIGINS OF THE POPULIST PARTY IN NORTH CAROLINA

1. Wright, *The Political Economy of the Cotton South*; Ransom and Sutch, *One Kind of Freedom*; Fite, *Cotton Fields No More*; Ritter, *Goldbugs and Greenbacks*; Steelman, *The North Carolina Farmers' State Alliance*.

2. McMath, *Populist Vanguard*, 35.

3. Saloutos, *Farmer Movements in the South*, 87.

4. McMath, *Populist Vanguard*, 47.

5. Goodwyn, *Democratic Promise*, 144–145; McMath, *Populist Vanguard*, 54–58.

6. *Progressive Farmer*, April 28, 1887.

7. *Caucasian*, December 5, 1889; Escott, *Many Excellent People*, 170–180; Steelman, *The North Carolina Farmers' State Alliance*, chapter 1; Muller, "New South Populism," 18.

8. Mitchell, "A Forgotten Institution" 24–49; Wright, *The Political Economy of the Cotton South*; Ransom and Sutch, *One Kind of Freedom*; Fite, *Cotton Fields No More*.

9. Department of the Interior, *Eleventh Census, Agriculture*, 168–171, 118. Only 1.1 percent of these owners were planters, and 3.3 percent owned large farms. Tenants numbered 10,500, and sharecroppers 50,000. Department of the Interior, *Eleventh Census, Agriculture*, 169.

10. For all the complex details on the formation, see Steelman, *The North Carolina Farmers' Alliance*; Hicks, "The Farmers' Alliance in North Carolina," 162–187, 170; *Proceedings of the Fourth Annual Session of the North Carolina Farmers' State Alliance, Held in the City of Asheville, N.C. August 12, 13, 14 and 15 1890* (Raleigh, NC: Edwards and Broughton, Printers and Binders, 1890); *Proceedings of the Fifth Annual Session of the North Carolina Farmers' State Alliance, Held in the City of Morehead, N.C. August 11, 12, and 13 1891* (Raleigh, NC: Edwards and Broughton, Printers and Binders, 1891).

11. Evangeline Usher to Polk, December 25, 1889, LPP, SHC; Escott, *Many Excellent People*, 253; Steelman, *The North Carolina Farmers' State Alliance*, 17–20.

12. John Flintoff, April 8, 1890, John Flintoff Diary, NCDAH; Hicks, "The Farmers' Alliance in North Carolina," 172.

13. *Progressive Farmer*, February 16, 23, March 20, May 1, 22, June 12, July 31, 1888.

14. It is worth noting that Alexander turned down the lieutenant governorship once Fowle gained the gubernatorial nomination. The lieutenant governorship went instead to Thomas Holt. Governor Fowle died in office. Had Alexander accepted the lieutenant governorship, he, rather than Holt, would have succeeded Fowle. It is also worth noting that of the eleven southern states, by 1889, seven had railroad commissions. *Progressive Farmer*, August 14, 1888, March 26, 1889; Hicks, *The Populist Revolt*, 144–146; Steelman, *The North Carolina Farmers' State Alliance*, 54.

15. For the Democratic use of the Election Law and County Government Act, see Billings, *Planters and the Making of the New South*.

16. J. A. Long to Matt Ransom, January 31, 1890, Matt Ransom Papers, SHC.

17. McMath, *Populist Vanguard*, 88–98; Goodwyn, *The Populist Moment*, 90–113.

18. Zebulon Vance to E. C. Beddingfield, May 18, 1890, Zebulon Vance Papers, SHC; Steelman, *North Carolina Farmers' Alliance*, 67–95; Bromberg, "The Worst Muddle Ever Seen in North Carolina Politics."

19. *Progressive Farmer*, July 6, 1890; William Justice to Zebulon Vance, July 12, 1890, Zebulon Vance Papers, SHC; *Raleigh News and Observer*, July 26, August 14, September 2 and 3, 1890; Noblin, *Leonidas Lafayette Polk*, 229–260, 246; Lefler and Newsome, *North Carolina*, chapter 38; Steelman, *The North Carolina Farmers' State Alliance*, 59–96; E. Chambers Smith to Matt Ransom, September 10, 1890, Matt Ransom Papers, SHC.

20. E. Chambers Smith to Matt Ransom, September 10, 1890, Matt Ransom Papers, SHC; *News and Observer*, August 16, 21, and September 6, 9, 1890; Steelman, *The North Carolina Farmers' State Alliance*, 86.

21. The seventeen majority black counties in 1890 were Bertie, Carteret, Caswell, Chowan, Craven, Edgecombe, Granville, Halifax, Hertford, New Hanover, Northampton, Pasquotank, Pender, Richmond, Vance, Warren, and Washington. For more details on the Republican Party in the period 1888–1890 and the role of the white leadership and their relationship with African Americans, see Hershman, "The North Carolina Republican Party," 1–17; Edmonds, *The Negro and Fusion Politics*, 14–20.

22. J. J. Mott to E. W. Walford, July 14, 1890, Benjamin Harrison Papers, quoted in Hershman, "The North Carolina Republican Party," 64; *News and Observer*, May 24, 1890. The reporting of this cannot be taken at face value. The history of the paper in the 1890s is littered with half-truths and blatant lies.

23. *The Congressional Record: Fifty-first Congress, First Session*, June 28, 1890 (Washington: Government Printing Office, 1890), 21: 6688–6692.

24. *News and Observer*, October 5, 1890. For more details on the GOP, see *Winston Union Republican*, October 2, 1890; *News and Observer*, October 7, November 1, 1890; *Asheville Citizen*, October 30, 1890; Hershman, "The North Carolina Republican Party," 63–73.

25. Steelman, *The North Carolina Farmers' State Alliance*, 96–123.

26. David Schenck, November 4, 1890, David Schenck Letterbooks, SHC; *Union Republican*, February 5, March 12, 19, April 2, 16, 1891.

27. Elias Carr to Zebulon Vance, November 20, 1890, Zebulon Vance Papers, SHC. For more on Ocala and the Alliance platform, see McMath, *Populist Vanguard*, 107–109; *Raleigh News and Observer*, November 6 and 10, December 3, 4 and 5, 1890; Hunt, "Marion Butler and the Populist Ideal," 98.

28. *Caucasian*, January 15, 1891; Steelman, *North Carolina Farmers' Alliance*, 96–139; Hunt, "Marion Butler and the Populist Ideal," 56–160; Noblin, *Leonidas Lafayette Polk*, 229–260; Lefler and Newsome, *North Carolina*, chapter 38. For more on the debate among Alliance members over Vance's reselection, see *Caucasian*, January 15, 1891.

29. Noblin, *Leonidas Lafayette Polk*, 252–253; Boyette, "The North Carolina Alliance Legislature of 1891," 202–203; *Raleigh News and Observer*, January 5 to March 8, 1890; Hunt, "Marion Butler and the Populist Ideal," 100–103, 104–109.

30. Boyette, "The North Carolina Alliance Legislature of 1891"; Steelman, *The North Carolina Farmers' State Alliance*, 125–171.

31. See, for example, John Graham to Edward A. Thorne, May 23, 1891, Edward A. Thorne Papers, Duke University; *Progressive Farmer*, February 24, March 3, July 7, 1891; *Caucasian*, July 2, 1891. For the importance of education, see Mitchell, *Political Education in the Southern Farmers' Alliance*.

32. John Graham to E. A. Thorne, May 23, 1891, E. A. Thorne Papers, Duke University; *Caucasian*, January 7, 1892; *Raleigh News and Observer*, March 16, May 20, 21, and 22, 1890; *Raleigh Signal*, September 26 and October 15, 1891. For more details on Polk's attitudes, see Noblin, *Leonidas Lafayette Polk*, 268–271. For more on the Cincinnati convention, see McMath, *Populist Vanguard*, 114–115.

33. *Caucasian*, May 28, July 2, September 10, October 10, 1891. See also *Carolina Watchman*, July 30, 1891; *Proceedings of the Fifth Annual Session of the North Carolina Farmers' State Alliance*. Details on the voting are scarce. See Thomas B. Long to Polk, August 3, 1891, LPP, SHC; *Raleigh News and Observer*, July 26, 1890; Steelman, *The North Carolina Farmers' State Alliance*, 185–187; Hunt, "Marion Butler and the Populist Ideal," 120; *Raleigh Signal*, November 19 and December 3, 1891; *Tarboro Farmers' Advocate*, September 2, October 21, November 4, 1891; *Progressive Farmer*, March 15, 1892.

34. *Progressive Farmer*, April 28, May 5, June 16, 23, August 4, 1891; *Tarboro Farmers' Advocate*, July 8, 1891.

35. Thomas B. Long to Polk, August 3, 1891, L. Polk Denmark Papers, NCDAH.

36. For more details, see James B. Lloyd, "Marion Butler," in *Biographical History* 8 (1906): 81–90; Carl Snyder, "Marion Butler," *Review of Reviews* 14 (1896): 429–433.

37. Steelman, *The North Carolina Farmers' State Alliance*, 181–195; Polk to James Denmark, February 3, 8, 17, 1892, LPP, SHC. For Polk's speech, see *Progressive Farmer*, March 15, 1892.

38. The figures for the largest organizations at the convention are as follows: Southern Farmers' Alliance, 246; Colored Farmers' Alliance and Co-operative Union, 97; the Knights of Labor, 82; Patrons of Husbandry, 75; the Farmers' Mutual Benefit Association, 53; and the National Farmers' Alliance, 46. Noblin, *Leonidas Lafayette Polk*, 273.

39. *Tarboro Farmers' Advocate*, March 16, 1892; *Caucasian*, February 25, 1892; *Progressive Farmer*, February 16, March 1, 1892; Steelman, *North Carolina Farmers' State Alliance*, 191–193; Bromberg, "Pure Democracy," 479; Hicks, *The Populist Revolt*, 223–229; McMath, *Populist Vanguard*, 130–131.

CHAPTER TWO. "WE HAVE PUT OUR HANDS ON THE PLOW AND WE WILL NOT LOOK BACK": THE PEOPLE'S PARTY AND THE ELECTION OF 1892

1. *Wilmington Messenger*, March 4, 1892; C. Dowd to Vance, March 23, 1892, Zebulon Vance Papers, SHC; John S. Henderson to Mrs. Henderson, March 28, 1892, Henderson Papers, SHC; *News and Observer*, February 28, 1892.

2. Steelman, *North Carolina Farmers' Alliance*, 182–200; Hicks, "The Farmers' Alliance in North Carolina," 180–183.

3. *Caucasian*, March 31, April 28, May 5, 1892; *Progressive Farmer*, March 22, 1892; Steelman, *North Carolina State Farmers' Alliance*, 182–184; Hunt, "Marion Butler and the Populist Ideal," 131–132.

4. *Progressive Farmer*, March 22, May 3, 1892; J.D. Uzzell to Polk, April 22, 1892, LPP, SHC; Salisbury *Carolina Watchman*, May 5, 1892. Wilmington *Messenger*, March 16, 1892.

5. Quoted in the *Wilmington Messenger*, April 26, 1892; Abbott Swinson to Polk, April 10, 1892. T. B. Lindsay, secretary of the Rockingham County Farmers' Alliance, also argued in a letter to Polk, "I fear that North Carolina is making a big mistake in not unfurling the People's banner at once. We are gaining nothing by waiting." T.B. Lindsay to Polk, April 22, 1892, LPP, SHC. J. D. Thorne of Pancea Springs concurred with the sentiments of Swinson. He congratulated Polk on his stand for the people and called for a new party because "the day of compromise is past." Later, in April, Thorne elaborated on his views to Polk. According to Thorne, "The Democratic party has been trying to exterminate the Alliance by absorption. The Rads. are playing the same game on the negro alliances and will (the latter) probably succeed. . . . The cause seems to be swiftly growing in interest to the masses and well it may for upon its success depends the welfare, safety and perpetuity of our system of government." J. D. Thorne to Polk, April 12, 18, 1892, LPP, SHC.

6. Hunt, "Marion Butler and the Populist Ideal," 135; S. F. Telfair to J. Bryan Grimes, April 25, 1892, J. Bryan Grimes Papers, SHC; Steelman, *North Carolina Farmers' Alliance*, 193–196; Elias Carr to Polk, April 8, 1892, LPP, SHC.

7. James H. Pou to E. Chambers Smith, February 29, 1892, James H. Pou Papers, NCDAH; Thomas Jarvis to E. C. Smith, April 5, 1892, Edward C. Smith Papers, Duke University; *Charlotte Observer*, May 17, 1892.

8. Thomas Sutton to Samuel A'Court Ashe, March 28, 1892, Samuel A'Court Ashe Papers, NCDAH; *Wilmington Messenger*, May 7, 1892.

9. Polk to J. W. Denmark, April 29, May 10, 1892, LPP, SHC.

10. *News and Observer*, May 19, 1892; *Fayetteville Observer*, May 26, 1892; *Caucasian*, June 9, 1892; *Progressive Farmer*, May 24, 1892; *Charlotte Daily Observer*, May 18, 1892. On the one hand, James Hunt, in "Marion Butler and the Populist Ideal," argues that there was no formal agreement on the governor and that Butler's Alliancemen favored George W. Sanderlin, the current state auditor and a noted supporter of the St. Louis platform (138). Muller, on the other hand, argues that Polk and Alexander were approached on the gubernatorial candidacy, but they both turned it down. This left only Elias Carr as the possible candidate with sufficient statewide recognition. See Muller, "New South Populism," 69. Polk admitted in a private letter that he should go for the governorship. See Polk to J. W. Denmark, April 26, 1892, L. Polk Denmark Papers, NCDAH.

11. *News and Observer*, May 19, 1892; *Charlotte Observer*, May 19, 1892; *Carolina Watchman*, May 19, 1892; Steelman, *North Carolina State Farmers' Alliance*, 209–210; Hunt, "Marion Butler and the Populist Ideal," 139–140.

12. *Progressive Farmer*, May 24, 1892. The delegates to Omaha, according to the Republican *Raleigh Signal*, consisted of Harry Skinner, Alonzo C. Shuford, D. H. Gill, Dr. A. J. Dalby, George Hunt, and V. N. Seawall. First District, M. G. Gregory of Elizabeth City; Second District, A. B. Yorke of Rocky Mount;

Third District, Rev. E. J. Edwards of Fayetteville; Fourth District, S. Otho Wilson of Raleigh; Fifth District, J. B. Smith of Durham; Sixth District, M. K. McKinnon of Rockingham; Eighth District, P. H. Rich of Lenoir; and Ninth District, J. C. Brown of Asheville; see the *Raleigh Signal*, May 19, 1892. James Hunt argues that these earliest Populists were little known in the state Alliance. However, S. Otho Wilson, A. C. Shuford, and even Abbott Swinson were well known in Alliance circles. Hunt, "Marion Butler and the Populist Ideal," 143. In addition, according to the *Signal*, congressional conventions for June 11 were called at the first meeting. This questions Hunt's claim that the Populists only decided to field congressional candidates on May 23. See also Steelman, *North Carolina Farmers' Alliance*, 216–218; *News and Observer*, May 24, 1892.

13. Wilson quoted in Collins and Goodwin, *Bibliographical Sketches of the Members of the General Assembly of North Carolina*, 15; *Charlotte Observer*, March 15, 1892.

14. *Winston Union Republican*, May 26, 1892. See also *Elizabeth City North Carolinian*, June 1, 1892.

15. *Progressive Farmer*, May 24, 1892; Polk to ?, May 31, 1892, LPP, SHC; Hunt, "Marion Butler and the Populist Ideal," 143–146.

16. *News and Observer*, June 12, 1892; Noblin, *Leonidas Lafayette Polk*, 277–298.

17. At the Fifth District convention Patton was nominated for Congress. In the Seventh District, D. C. Thorne received the nomination for Congress. In the Sixth Congressional District, a small convention met, including two African Americans, but there was no nomination for Congress. *Raleigh Signal*, June 16, 1892; *Progressive Farmer*, June 21, 1892.

18. *News and Observer*, June 19, 1892; C. B. Aycock to Matt Ransom, June 27, 1892, Matt Ransom Papers, SHC.

19. See Merrill, *Bourbon Leader*, 158–161; Steelman, *North Carolina Farmers' Alliance*, 219–220; *Hertford Perquimans Record*, June 29, 1892.

20. *News and Observer*, July 5, 1892; *Charlotte Observer*, July 6, 1892; Steelman, *North Carolina Farmers' Alliance*, 219–221. According to the *Progressive Farmer*, the numbers of delegates per county were as follows: Anson, 6; Cabarrus, 5; Franklin, 8; Johnston, 10; Mecklenburg, 5; Nash, 8; Pitt, 9; Pender, 6; Richmond, 7; Robeson, 10; Sampson, 8; Union, 6; Vance, 7; Wake, 19. Clearly, the Populist Party organized across the state, though the majority of the delegates came from the eastern and southeastern section of North Carolina. This reflects the nature of the Alliance. The state Alliance was strongest in the eastern section of the state, the area of the state with poorer farmers. *Progressive Farmer*, July 19, 26, 1892; *Tarboro Farmers' Advocate*, July 16, 1892; *Salisbury Carolina Watchman*, July 7, 1892; *Hertford Perquimans Record*, June 15, 1892; *Red Springs Comet*, July 28, 1892. For the Omaha convention see Hicks, *The Populist Revolt*, 229–236, 439–445; McMath, *Populist Vanguard*, 195; Goodwyn, *The Populist Moment*, 167–168; Clanton, *Populism*, 82–84; McMath, *American Populism*, 166–169.

21. *Caucasian*, July 14, 1892; Hunt, "Marion Butler and the Populist Ideal," 148–152.

22. *Caucasian*, July 21, 1892. Hunt argues that Butler had subtle reasons for staying in the Democratic Party and opposing the Populists. This may be true, but it does seem that Butler worried more about his own political career than the Populists. Butler, ever the politician, waited to the last minute to make a decision and sounded out all the possible permutations and political alliances involved in any move. This tendency would dog his Populist career throughout the 1890s. Hunt, "Marion Butler and the Populist Ideal," 152.

23. John G. Shaw to Matt Ransom, July 28, 1892, Matt Ransom Papers, SHC; Hunt, "Marion Butler and the Populist Ideal," 154–156.

24. *Caucasian*, July 28, 1892; *News and Observer*, July 23, 1892; *Charlotte Observer*, July 24, 31, 1892; Steelman, *North Carolina Farmers' Alliance*, 224; Hunt, "Marion Butler and the Populist Ideal," 153–154.

25. *Winston Union Republican*, July 28, 1892.

26. Daniels, *Tar Heel Editor*, 387; Hunt, "Marion Butler and the Populist Ideal," 156–159.

27. *Caucasian*, August 11, 1892; *Raleigh Signal*, August 11, 1892.

28. *Charlotte Observer*, August 4, 1892; *Wilmington Messenger*, August 4, 1892; *Wilmington Messenger*, August 5, 1892; *Raleigh Signal*, August 5, 1892; *Elizabeth City North Carolinian*, August 10, 1892; *News and Observer*, August 7, 1892; James H. Pou to Matt Ransom, July 6, 1892, and Samuel A'Court Ashe to Matt Ransom, July 17, 1892, Matt Ransom Papers, SHC.

29. The convention named the following to the committee of permanent organization: B. Scarborough, W. H. Smith, Y. B. Smith, R. A. Cobb, B. Stilley, A. J. Gordon, S. B. Swain, J. M. Parks, G. E. Boggs. The convention then named the following to the committee on platform: J. M. Bateman, Marion Butler, R. A. Cobb, H. B. Collier, A. J. Dalby, W. P. Exum, D. H. Hill, J. E. Kimel, W. H. Malone. Hunt, "Marion Butler and the Populist Ideal," 166.

30. *Mecklenburg Times*, August 19, 1892.

31. *Wilmington Messenger*, August 17, 1892; *News and Observer*, August 17, 1892.

32. *Wilmington Messenger*, August 17, 1892; *Mecklenburg Times*, August 19, 1892; *Charlotte Observer*, August 17, 1892; *Henderson Goldleaf*, August 18, 1892; *Lenoir Topic*, August 24, 1892.

33. R. A. Cobb of Burke received the nomination for lieutenant governor, and William H. Worth, a prominent Quaker from the Piedmont and former business agent of the state Alliance, received the nomination for state treasurer. The convention began with nominations for secretary of state. Delegates nominated Dr. L. N. Durham of Cleveland and Marion Butler for the position. Butler stated, however, that although he was flattered by the nomination, he would rather not be a candidate because, in his words, he wanted as president of the North Carolina State Farmers' Alliance to get as many Alliancemen to join the People's Party as possible. Durham received the nomination. For state auditor, Thomas B. Long, a former Republican from Buncombe County in the western section of the state, received the nomination, and the convention nominated him by acclamation. R. H. Lyon received the nomination for attorney general. *Wilmington Messenger*, August 17, 1892; *Mecklenburg Times*, August 19, 1892; *Charlotte Observer*, August 17, 1892; *Henderson Goldleaf*, August 18, 1892; *Lenoir Topic*, August 24, 1892; *Winston Union Republican*, August 18, 1892; *Elizabeth City North Carolinian*, August 24, 1892.

34. Hunt, "Marion Butler and the Populist Ideal," 167–168.

35. *Caucasian*, August 25, 1892; *Salisbury Carolina Watchman*, August 18, 1892.

36. See also Hunt, "Marion Butler and the Populist Ideal," 169–171.

37. *Whitakers Rattler*, August 6, 1892. Unfortunately, only a single copy of this local Populist paper survives.

38. Hunt, "Marion Butler and the Populist Ideal," 171; *Progressive Farmer*, September 6, 27, October 11, 1892; *Salisbury Carolina Watchman*, September 29, 1892; *Hickory Mercury*, September 14, 1892. Jones, in "The Gubernatorial Election of 1892 in North Carolina," claims that Populists engaged in a campaign devoid of state issues. He is wrong here and in that Populists never refuted the attacks made by Democrats. *Progressive Farmer*, September 13, 20, October 11, 25, 1892.

39. *Caucasian*, September 22, 1892. Thompson cut his teeth on the 1892 election, and his reputation was held in esteem by supporters and enemies alike for the remainder of the decade.

40. *News and Observer*, August 20, September 15, 1892; *Hickory Mercury*, September 14, 1892; *Salisbury Carolina Watchman*, September 8, 1892; *Raleigh Signal*, September 22, 1892; *Progressive Farmer*, September 27, 1892; *Charlotte Observer*, October 28, 1892; *Wilmington Messenger*, August 20, October 28, 1892; *Lenoir Topic*, November 2, 1892. Interestingly, Aycock escaped censure for his actions—one can assume that he was as much to blame for this fracas. Hunt, "Marion Butler and the Populist Ideal," 175–176. Exum was not the only candidate who embarrassed the Populists. Thomas B. Long, the Populist candidate for state auditor, was accused by the *Lenoir Topic* of stealing funds from the North Carolina Railroad and of refusing to pay for goods bought on credit. Long resigned from the race in disgrace. The Populist candidate for lieutenant governor, R. A. Cobb, was accused of stealing the Populist candidate for secretary of state, Capt. L. N. Durham's hogs, and, purportedly, Durham caned Cobb in public for the offense. Cobb argued that he bought the hogs. The *Lenoir Topic* took great delight in publishing the

story and claimed that such news disgusted the voters of North Carolina. *Lenoir Topic*, September 21, 1892. The Democratic press was skillful in character assassination.

41. Circulars from Furnifold Simmons, October 13, 24, 1892, Marmaduke Hawkins Papers, Duke University; circulars from Furnifold Simmons, October 29, 31, 1892, Marmaduke Hawkins Papers, NCDAH; *To the People of North Carolina from the State Democratic Executive Committee* (Raleigh, NC: n.p., October 6, 1892), 5, 7–8; Steelman, *North Carolina Farmers' Alliance*, 232–244; Schlup, "Adlai E. Stevenson and the 1892 Campaign in North Carolina," 16–34.

42. *Red Springs Comet*, September 22, 1892; Hunt, "Marion Butler and the Populist Ideal," 182–187.

43. See *Fayetteville Observer*, September 15, 29, October 6, 26, 1892; *News and Observer*, October 20, 29, 30, 1892; *Charlotte Observer*, October 6, 8, 1892; *Red Springs Comet*, October 27, 1892; Hunt, "Marion Butler and the Populist Ideal," 182–187.

44. *News and Observer*, August 23, September 25, November 6, 1892; Hunt, "Marion Butler and the Populist Ideal," 182–187; *Henderson Goldleaf*, October 13, 1892; *Lenoir Topic*, October 12, 1892; Steelman, *North Carolina Farmers' Alliance*, 232–244.

45. A. A. Sherrill to Matt Ransom, September 10, 1892, Matt Ransom Papers, SHC.

46. *Raleigh Signal*, March 17, 1892. For more details, see Steelman, "Vicissitudes of Republican Party Politics," 430–442. For the role of Daniel Russell, see Crow and Durden. *Maverick Republican in the Old North State*, 45–48.

47. As late as July, the *Raleigh Signal* argued, "We are inflexibly opposed to the nomination of a state ticket because it will greatly damage and embarrass the People's Party in the effort to harmonize their party in this State. The men of the People's Party can and will see to a free election and an honest count." *Raleigh Signal*, July 21, 1892; Hunt, "Marion Butler and the Populist Ideal," 182.

48. D. M. Furches to Thomas Settle, July 29, 1892, Thomas Settle Papers, SHC; *Winston Union Republican*, July 28, September 29, 1892; *Elizabeth City North Carolinian*, September 7, October 12, 1892.

49. *Raleigh Signal*, September 22, 1892.

50. Steelman, *North Carolina Farmers' Alliance*, 245–250.

51. *Progressive Farmer*, October 4, 1892; *Caucasian*, September 29, 1892; *Tarboro Farmers' Advocate*, October 5 1892; *Lenoir Topic*, October 12, 1892.

52. *Caucasian*, September 29, 1892; *Progressive Farmer*, October 4, 1892; Hunt, "Marion Butler and the Populist Ideal," 170–171.

53. *Caucasian*, October 27, 1892; Hunt, "Marion Butler and the Populist Ideal," 171–175.

54. *Progressive Farmer*, August 30, 1892; *Caucasian*, September 1, October 27, 1892.

55. *Caucasian*, August 25, 1892; Butler, quoted in Hunt, "Marion Butler and the Populist Ideal," 178–179.

56. *Progressive Farmer*, October 4, 1892.

57. *Lenoir Topic*, October 26, 1892. The irony of the Democrats on this issue is beyond words. *Mecklenburg Times*, October 21, 1892. See also *Charlotte Observer*, November 3, 1892; *Lenoir Topic*, November 2, 1892; Daniels, *Tar Heel Editor*, 502–503.

58. For example, in Sampson County a tight race between the three gubernatorial candidates gave Exum 1,585 votes or 37.6 percent of the vote. In Chatham County, on the other hand, Exum received 2,240 votes or 52.1 percent of the vote. Steelman, *North Carolina Farmers' Alliance*, 257–259; *Records of Election*, Sampson County, 1892; Hunt, "Marion Butler and the Populist Ideal," 187–188.

59. A. E. Holton to Thomas Settle, October 5, 1892; B. C. Sharpe to Thomas Settle, n.d., 1892; R. P. Hughes to Thomas Settle, October 11, November 3, 1892; W. B. Brogden to Thomas Settle, November 10, 1892, all in Thomas Settle Papers, SHC; *Winston Union Republican*, December 15, 1892; *Records of Election*, Chatham County, Jones County, and Craven County, 1892.

60. Kousser, *The Shaping of Southern Politics*, 185; U.S. Bureau of Census, *Negro Population in the United States, 1790–1915* (Bureau of the Census, Washington, DC, 1918), 784–785.

61. In Vance County, African Americans made up 59 percent of the voters, and in Warren they made up 64 percent of the voters. In Wake blacks made up 45 percent of the voters and the Populists garnered 37 percent of the vote; in Franklin black voters stood at 36 percent and Exum gained 31 percent of the vote, and in Franklin African Americans made up 44 percent of the vote and Exum garnered 35 percent of the vote. For details, see Department of the Interior, *Eleventh Census, Report on the Productions of Agriculture* (Bureau of the Census, Washington, DC, 1895); Cheney, *North Carolina Government*, 1405.

62. Bromberg, "Pure Democracy," 508–510; Steelman, *North Carolina Farmers' Alliance*, 268–272; Kousser, *The Shaping of Southern Politics*, 185–186; Edmonds, *The Negro and Fusion Politics*, 8–29; Escott, *Many Excellent People*, 245–247; Bromberg, "Pure Democracy," 505–510.

63. *Records of Election*, Brunswick County, Chatham County, Sampson County, and Wake County, 1892.

64. *News and Observer*, November 9, 1892; Daniels, *Tar Heel Editor*, 503.

65. William E. Clarke to Cyrus Thompson, November 20, 1892, CTP, SHC; *Progressive Farmer*, December 13, 1892.

66. *Caucasian*, November 17, December 1, 1892; Hunt, "Marion Butler and the Populist Ideal," 188–189.

CHAPTER THREE. THE PEOPLE'S PARTY TRIUMPHANT: THE POLITICS OF COOPERATION IN 1894

1. Hunt, "Marion Butler and the Populist Ideal," 194–197; *Caucasian*, March 2, 9, 30, 1893; *Progressive Farmer*, February 21, 28, 1893.

2. *Wilmington Messenger*, January 19, 1893.

3. *Wilmington Messenger*, March 29, 30, 31, 1893; *Caucasian*, March 30, 1893; *Lenoir Topic*, April 5, 1893.

4. *Caucasian*, January 5, 1893; Hunt, "Marion Butler and the Populist Ideal," 213–220.

5. *Caucasian*, January 12, 1893.

6. *Caucasian*, January 12, May 25, 1893.

7. *Caucasian*, May 25, 1893.

8. *Caucasian*, May 25, 1893.

9. Hunt, "Marion Butler and the Populist Ideal," 212–215.

10. M. B. to Richmond Pearson, February 16, 1893, Richmond Pearson Papers, SHC; R. P. Hughes to Thomas Settle, April 14, 1893, Thomas Settle Papers, SHC.

11. *Proceedings of the Seventh Annual Session of the North Carolina Farmers' State Alliance, Held in the City of Greensboro, N.C. August 8, 9, and 10, 1893* (Raleigh, NC: Barnes Bros., Job Printers, 1893), 6.

12. Ibid., 27, 29–35.

13. Ritter, *Goldbugs and Greenbacks*, 45–47, 152–207; Livingston, *The Origins of the Federal Reserve System*; Gourevitch, *Politics in Hard Times*.

14. *Caucasian*, January 5, February 9, March 16, 23, 30, May 4, 18, 25, September 7, 14, October 5, 1893, November 23, 30, 1893; Hunt, "Marion Butler and the Populist Ideal," 200–220; Steelman, "Republican Party Strategists and the Issue of Fusion."

15. A. R. Kindill to Zebulon Vance, September 29, 1893, Zebulon Vance Papers, SHC.

16. Bromberg, "Pure Democracy," 512–542.

17. R. L. Abernathy to Zebulon Vance, November 1, 1893; and Harry Skinner to Zebulon Vance, October 11, 1893, both in Zebulon Vance Papers, SHC. The infighting only ended with the death of Vance.

18. *Caucasian*, January 4, 1894.

19. Ibid., January 11, 1894.

20. Ibid., January 11, 1894.

21. *Hertford Perquimans Record*, May 16, 1894; R. H. Lane to Cyrus Thompson, April 2, 1894; and J. W. Carpe to Cyrus Thompson, April 2, 1894, CTP, SHC.

22. *Caucasian*, February 15, 1894.

23. Ibid., March 15, 22, 1894.

24. *Hertford Perquimans Record*, March 23, 1894; *Caucasian*, March 29, 1894.

25. Marion Butler to Richmond Pearson, January 22, 1894, Richmond Pearson Papers, SHC; M. B. to Thomas Settle, January 24, 1894; and Richmond Pearson to Thomas Settle, January 31, 1894, Thomas Settle Papers, SHC; Hunt, "Marion Butler and the Populist Ideal," 225–228.

26. *Caucasian*, March 22, 1894; *Winston Union Republican*, April 5, 1894; J. B. Eaves to Thomas Settle, 1894; J. B. Eaves to Thomas Settle, April 19, 1894; J. B. Eaves to Richmond Pearson, March 2, May 28, 1894, Richmond Pearson Papers, SHC.

27. R. P. Hughes to Thomas Settle, February 7, 1894; James H. Young to Thomas Settle, April 16, 1894; S. B. Delanor to Thomas Settle, April 18, 1894, Thomas Settle Papers, SHC.

28. James Cheek to Thomas Settle, April 16, 1894; R. Amis to Thomas Settle, April 18, 1894; D. W. Patrick to Thomas Settle, April 19, 1894; J. B. Fortune to Thomas Settle, April 19, 1894; G. W. Crawford to Thomas Settle, April 20, 1894, Thomas Settle Papers, SHC.

29. James B. Lloyd to Cyrus Thompson, June 5, 1894; John McDuffie to Cyrus Thompson, June 21, 1894, CTP, SHC; *Caucasian*, June 28, 1894.

30. Julian S. Carr to Matt Ransom, February 20, 1894, Matt Ransom Papers, SHC.

31. *Progressive Farmer*, April 24, 1894.

32. Dewill C. Pessy to Matt Ransom, June 7, 1894; G. W. Blackwall to Matt Ransom, July 31, 1894, Matt Ransom Papers, SHC.

33. *Wilmington Messenger*, August 1, 1894; Hunt, "Marion Butler and the Populist Ideal," 230.

34. The convention then named the following to the committee of permanent organization: John Brady, W. H. Palmer, W. E. Hill, E. W. Timberlake, William Merritt, W. W. Dree, Jno. Beard, W. E. White, and William Bumgarner, all activists in the party. Hunt, "Marion Butler and the Populist Ideal," 231–235.

35. *Caucasian*, August 2, 1894; *Wilmington Messenger*, August 2, 1894; Hunt, "Marion Butler and the Populist Ideal," 231–235.

36. *Caucasian*, August 2, 1894. See also *Hertford Perquimans Record*, August 9, 1894; *Progressive Farmer*, August 7, 1894.

37. *News and Observer*, August 2, 1894; *Charlotte Observer*, August 26, 1894.

38. *News and Observer*, August 8, 1894.

39. *Caucasian*, August 30, 1894.

40. *Wilmington Messenger*, August 18, 1894.

41. *Winston Union Republican*, September 6, 1894; Bromberg, "Pure Democracy," 544.

42. *News and Observer*, August 31, 1894; *Charlotte Observer*, September 1, 1894; *Mecklenburg Times*, September 6, 1894.

43. *Hertford Perquimans Record*, September 12, 1894; Hunt, "Marion Butler and the Populist Ideal," 238–240.

44. Circulars printed in *Caucasian*, November 1, 1894; *News and Observer*, October 20, 1894.

45. Circular from Marion Butler at the office of the People's Party State Executive Committee, August 18, 1894, CTP, SHC; circular from Marion Butler at the headquarters of the People's Party State Executive Committee, August 20, 1894, CTP, SHC.

46. For more details on speeches, see *Caucasian*, September 13, October 11, 25, 1894; *Charlotte Observer*, September 18, 1894; *Mecklenburg Times*, September 20, 1894; *News and Observer*, October 4, 10, 12, 1894; *Sampson Democrat*, October 25, 1894; Ingle, "A Southern Democrat at Large."

47. *Wilmington Messenger*, September 13, 1894.

48. See the circulars from James H. Pou, September 13, October 26, 31, and November 3, 1894, Marmaduke Hawkins Papers, NCDAH; Bromberg, "Pure Democracy," 552; *Wilmington Messenger*, September 12, October 2, 1894.

49. *Wilmington Messenger*, September 11, 1894; *Charlotte Observer*, October 11, 1894; *Southport Leader*, October 25, 1894.

50. *Wilmington Messenger*, October 4, November 3, 1894; *Lenoir Topic*, October 24, 1894. Hunt gives more examples of the character assassination of Butler in "Marion Butler and the Populist Ideal," 253–254.

51. *News and Observer*, October 3, 1894.

52. The long quote is from *Hertford Perquimans Record*, October 31, 1894. See the same paper for other examples, September 26, 1894. For the *Caucasian*, see September 13, October 11, 1894.

53. Helen Edmonds notes that 23 counties returned Republican majorities, 33 returned Populist majorities, and 34 returned Democrat majorities, while 4 supported Republican-Populist fusion, 1 supported Republican-Democrat fusion, and 1 supported Republican-Prohibitionist cooperation. Six of the majority–African American counties, Bertie, Edgecombe, Halifax, Hertford, Northampton, and Pender, returned Democrats where the Democrats managed to use internal fighting within the Republican Party over black office-holding as well as the Democrat's usual tactics of fraud, bribery, and exploitation to gain seats in the general assembly. In New Hanover, the Republicans fused with the Democrats in order to carry the county.

54. Although the Populists performed well in the election, their margin of victory varied between counties. For example, in Cumberland County the two Populist representatives received 2,274 and 2,338 votes, or 51 and 52 percent of the vote, respectively. In Sampson County, where a three-horse race developed, the Populist candidates won with 1,929 and 1,926 votes or 45 percent of the vote. In Duplin County the Populists won 56 percent of the vote. *Records of Election*, Cumberland County, Duplin County and Sampson County, 1894; Edmonds, *The Negro and Fusion Politics*, 17, 40.

55. *Caucasian*, November 8, 22, 29, 1894; *Lenoir Topic*, November 14, 21, 1894; *Wilmington Messenger*, November 9, 1894; *Charlotte Observer*, November 10, 1894.

CHAPTER FOUR. "EQUAL RIGHTS TO ALL AND SPECIAL PRIVILEGES TO NONE": GRASSROOTS POPULISM IN NORTH CAROLINA

1. J. Morgan Kousser's work is an exception to this, but his analysis did not center on Populism per se. In a brief discussion of North Carolina Populism, Kousser uses complex statistical analysis to argue that the Populist Party in North Carolina was not a sizable party. Rather, the Populists played an important role because they held the political balance of power between the Democrats and Republicans. However, Kousser may have underestimated the strength of the Populists. Kousser bases his statistical analysis of Populists on the votes garnered by the Populist gubernatorial candidates in the elections of 1892 and 1896. In doing this, it seems that Populism reached a high point in 1892 and declined thereafter. This was not the case. The high point for Populism was 1894. In addition, the reliance on gubernatorial votes is potentially misleading. For example, in the counties that made up the Third District, Populist gubernatorial candidate Exum polled 6,888 votes in 1892. In 1894, Populist Cyrus Thompson officially received 9,705 votes (there was a Republican candidate in this election, and thus no cooperation). This was an increase of 2,817 votes for the Populist candidate in an election that overall witnessed 638 fewer votes than 1892. Kousser, *The Shaping of Southern Politics*, 183–195.

2. Historians of North Carolina and southern history have for too long failed to utilize these sources to full effect. Indeed, it would seem that the existence of such sources remains unknown in some states. No other detailed study of North Carolina politics in the 1890s utilizes the testimony in the contested election results, even though contested election cases provide, perhaps, the only possible entry point into

the politics of Populism at the local level. A few mention the contested election cases with reference to African Americans. But even here historians have yet to decipher the wealth of information in the reports. E. Anderson, *Race and Politics in North Carolina*. An exception to this is the work of Shaw, *The Wool Hat Boys*.

3. *Contested Election Case of Cyrus Thompson vs. John G. Shaw from the Third Congressional District of the State of North Carolina, 1895* (Washington, DC: Government Printing Office, 1895); *Contested Election Case of Charles H. Martin vs. James A. Lockhart from the Sixth Congressional District of the State of North Carolina, 1895* (Washington, DC: Government Printing Office, 1895). Hereafter cited as *Charles H. Martin vs. James A. Lockhart*, Lewis N. Jones, 176–178. A version of this article originally appeared in the *North Carolina Historical Review* (used with permission).

4. *Charles H. Martin vs. James A. Lockhart*, Lewis N. Jones, 176–178.

5. Daniel L. Russell's actions in this contested election case have gone unnoticed by historians. Russell's biographers, Crow and Durden, make no mention of the case or the pivotal role played by Russell in securing a positive result for the Populist contestant. This is a key historical fact that merits close attention and analysis. It seems clear that Russell's role was in keeping with his attitude in the 1892 state campaign and his sympathy with the Populists' political and economic agenda. Russell was a shrewd politician, and his actions might explain why Butler and other leading Populists held Russell in high esteem.

6. *Progressive Farmer*, January 8, 1895; Clanton, *Congressional Populism*, 10–11. House Report, No. 2002, *Congressional Record: Fifty-fourth Congress, First Session, 1895–1896* (Washington: Government Printing Office, 1896), 27: 1.

7. Caucasian, August 30 and September 13, 1894; *Cyrus Thompson vs. John G. Shaw*, 9.

8. *Charles H. Martin vs. James A. Lockhart*, Thomas B. Russell, 127–129; Nathan Andrews, 134–135; Isaac T. McLean, 122–123.

9. *Cyrus Thompson vs. John G. Shaw*, Andrew Melton, 174–175; George Robert Ventus, 166–167; Henry Murrell, 168.

10. *Cyrus Thompson vs. John G. Shaw*, Thomas M. McLean, 107–110.

11. *Cyrus Thompson vs. John G. Shaw*, T. B. Newberry, 44–45; Arthur Dixon, 87–88.

12. *Charles H. Martin vs. James A. Lockhart*, John G. Brown, 108; Harry H. Sampson, 111–113.

13. *Charles H. Martin vs. James A. Lockhart*, Edward Cole, 23; Harry Covington, 29; Sol Covington, 30; Jacob Roberts, 29; Henry Terry, 33; Elijah Leak, 80–81.

14. *Charles H. Martin vs. James A. Lockhart*, Dock Covington, 18. Fletcher Leak echoed these sentiments. Counsel for the contestee asked Leak, "What are your politics?" to which Leak replied, "Populist and Republican." The contestee's counsel, sensing an opportunity to show confusion among the cooperationist voters, jabbed, "Are there any differences in the principles of the Populist and the Republican parties?" Leak, now on the defensive, replied that in one instance there was, and that the Populists and Republicans did not agree on everything; however, he continued, "I don't know" what the difference is. Ibid., Fletcher Leak, 82.

15. *Charles H. Martin vs. James A. Lockhart*, Lemuel Simmons, 21; H. W. Pope, 344; Elias M. Thompson, 345; D. L. Maultsby, 346; Enoch McCallum, 120–121; Marsh Roper, 78; Edmonds, *The Negro and Fusion Politics in North Carolina*, 17; E. Anderson, *Race and Politics in North Carolina*; Gaither, *Blacks and the Populist Revolt*; Haley, *Charles N. Hunter and Race Relations in North Carolina*; Gilmore, *Gender and Jim Crow*; Logan, *The Negro in North Carolina, 1876–1894*; Prather, *Resurgent Politics and Educational Progressivism in the New South*; Rabinowitz, *Race Relations in the Urban South*; Mabry, "Negro Suffrage and Fusion Rule in North Carolina." At the master's and PhD level, see Elmore, "North Carolina Negro Congressmen"; Paoli, "Marion Butler's View of the Negro"; Reid, "A Biography of George H. White"; Wooley, "Race and Politics."

16. *Cyrus Thompson vs. John G. Shaw*, Archie McNeill, 90; Henry Cox, 90; George Maxwell, 91; Ben Taylor, 91; Charles Bogan, 91; F. P. Wilston, 92; Clint Hall, 93; Jas Bradley, 94; Owen Brown, 96; Louis Gill, 96; Isaac Bain, 97; Robert Hill, 98; Herbert Brown, 103; Peter Handon, 105; Andrew Jackson, 106;

George Moore, 112; J.F.K. Simpson, 112; Wiley Goodwin, 115; Peter Patterson, 117; Louis Holmes, 119; Louis Hoskins, 122; Sam Lord, 130; and many others. *Cyrus Thompson vs. John G. Shaw*, Evander Smith, 48; Wm. Smith, 48; L. L. Hoyt, 202–204.

17. E. Anderson, *Race and Politics in North Carolina*; Edmonds, *The Negro and Fusion Politics in North Carolina*; Mabry, "Negro Suffrage and Fusion Rule."

18. *Charles H. Martin vs. James A. Lockhart*, John McKinnon, 54–59. See also ibid., A. D. Spivey, 70–73.

19. *Charles H. Martin vs. James A. Lockhart*, Thomas B. Russell, 127–129; *News and Observer*, October 17, 1894; *Charles H. Martin vs. James A. Lockhart*, Duncan McBryde, 124–127; *Progressive Farmer*, November 27, 1894; *Charles H. Martin vs. James A. Lockhart*, James T. Martin, 161–163; L. D. Kirby, 163–164; E. W. Flake, 164–67; Albert V. Harrington, 395–396.

20. *Records of Election*, 1894 and 1892, Cumberland County.

21. *Cyrus Thompson vs. John G. Shaw*, J. K. Kinlaw, 50–56 and 66–69; Thomas H. McLean, 107–110.

22. *Cyrus Thompson vs. John G. Shaw*, J. K. Kinlaw, 50–56 and 66–69.

23. *Cyrus Thompson vs. John G. Shaw*, Thomas H. McLean, 107–110.

24. *Wadesboro Plow Boy*, February 13, 1895. See *Caucasian*, March 29, 1894. Marion Butler's paper also mentions the founding of a Populist newspaper that has not survived to the present day, the *Granville County Reformer* at Oxford.

25. *Progressive Farmer*, January 8, 1895.

26. House Report, No. 1635, *Congressional Record: Fifty-fourth Congress, First Session, 1895–1896* (Washington: Government Printing Office, 1896), 27.

27. House Report, No. 2002, *Congressional Record: Fifty-fourth Congress, First Session, 1895–1896* (Washington: Government Printing Office, 1896), 27. This report outraged congressional Democrats, and they proceeded to produce a minority report on June 10, 1896. In their conclusion the minority report agreed that discrepancies existed in the returns for the Sixth Congressional District. However, they argued that the 40 votes added to the contestant at Lilesville were wrong because the majority report misapprehended the testimony of B. K. Jones. In addition, the minority claimed, it was wrong to take away votes in Red Springs and Rockingham from the contestee. Instead of a majority of 330 for the contestant, the minority report claimed that the contestee should have a majority of 256 votes. House Report No. 2002, Part 2, *Congressional Record: Fifty-fourth Congress, First Session, 1895–1896* (Washington: Government Printing Office, 1896), 27.

28. *Maxton Scottish Chief*, May 7, 1896. There is a wealth of information on the 1898 campaign in North Carolina; see Gilmore, *Gender and Jim Crow*, 1–118; Cecelski and Tyson, *Democracy Betrayed*.

CHAPTER FIVE. "EVER TRUE TO THE PEOPLE'S CAUSE, TRUE TO COUNTRY, TRUE TO HOME": THE COOPERATIONIST LEGISLATURE OF 1895

1. *Caucasian*, January 17, 1895; *Wadesboro Plow Boy*, January 30, 1895; Hunt, "Marion Butler and the Populist Ideal," 265–272.

2. Collins and Goodwyn, *Biographical Sketches of the Members of the General Assembly of North Carolina, 1895* (Raleigh: Edwards and Broughton, Printers and Binders, 1895).

3. Ibid.

4. Ibid.

5. Ibid.

6. Daniels, *Editor in Politics*, 126–130. Josephus Daniels notes that as editor of the *News and Observer* he wanted to find out the disagreements and "hot" debates in the joint caucus. Democratic reporters sometimes pretended to be "Fusionist" legislators to gain entry to the meeting, or some hid under the tables in the meeting rooms to scribble down the discussions. Others climbed trees outside to see what was going on.

Later in the session the reporters, posing as the general public, would buy the legislators beer at Denton's Bar, opposite the assembly building, and talk politics with the unsuspecting Populists.

7. At the joint caucus meeting on January 16, state senator John Fowler of Sampson placed Butler's name before Populist and Republican legislators, and the Populist leader received the nomination by acclamation for the full term in the U.S. Senate. *Caucasian*, January 17, 1895; Hunt, "Marion Butler and the Populist Ideal," 265–273.

8. There has been a debate about what was actually promised here. Republicans claimed that Butler promised the GOP the shorter term on the condition that he and the Populists would support the reselection of a Republican (presumably Pritchard) senator after the two years were up. In other words, there would not be another Populist while Butler was a senator. Daniels, *Editor in Politics*, 131; Hunt, "Marion Butler and the Populist Ideal," 269–270.

9. *Caucasian*, January 3, 24, February 23, 1895; Hunt, "Marion Butler and the Populist Ideal," 269.

10. Daniels noted that the *Caucasian* was very effective at opposing his *News and Observer* and "roasting the filibustering Democrats." Daniels, *Editor in Politics*, 131; Hunt, "Marion Butler and Populist Ideal," 260–263.

11. B. N. Duke to M. B., January 2, 1895; M. B. to B. N. Duke, January 14, 1895; B. N. Duke to W. H. Worth, January 19, 1895; W. H. Worth to B. N. Duke, January 19, February 13, 18, 1895; Josephus Daniels to B. N. Duke, January 28; B. N. Duke to James Ramsey, January 7, March 5, 1895, all in Benjamin Duke Papers, Duke University; Hunt, "Marion Butler and the Populist Ideal," 260–263.

12. *Caucasian*, January 24, February 21, 28, 1895; *Progressive Farmer*, March 19, 1895. For a useful overview of the state legislature, see Trelease, "The Fusion Legislature of 1895 and 1897"; Edmonds, *The Negro and Fusion Politics*, 41. For an amazing diatribe against the Fusion-controlled legislature, see *History of the General Assembly of North Carolina, January 9–March 13, 1895* (Raleigh, EM Uzzell Printer and Binder, 1895).

13. Edwin Alderman to Cornelia Spencer, January 17, 1895; George T.? to Cornelia Spencer, April 9, 1895; both in Cornelia Spencer Papers, NCDAH. For an interesting overview of the battle over the university from a Democratic perspective, see Daniels, *Editor in Politics*, 105–111; Hunt, "Marion Butler and the Populist Ideal," 272.

14. Edmonds, *The Negro and Fusion Politics*, 67–81, gives an excellent overview of the workings of the old and new election law in North Carolina and the impact on African Americans.

15. Interestingly, the Democratic press was outraged at this. They had the gall to claim that the Republicans and Populists would out-number Democrats in majority-Democratic counties. This was certainly a case of the pot calling the kettle black. In addition, Democrats challenged Populists on this issue. Democrats thought it odd that Populists did not bring in the secret ballot and reasoned that Populists planned to commit fraud at elections.

16. Hunt, "Marion Butler and the Populist Ideal," 267–269; Edmonds, *The Negro and Fusion Politics*, 70–79; *History of the General Assembly of North Carolina*, 23–27 and 45–49.

17. Spier Whitaker to Thomas Settle, February 12, 1895, Thomas Settle Papers, SHC; Hunt, "Marion Butler and the Populist Ideal," 267–269; Daniels, *Editor in Politics*, 132–134.

18. The *Maxton Scottish Chief* attempted to portray the legislature as merely a place of bluster and squabble, and it characterized the new laws in negative terms. According to the paper, "The people are now considering and weighing the acts of the late General Assembly, and the more they think the more disgusted they become." *Maxton Scottish Chief*, March 21, 1895; *Wilmington Messenger*, March 15, 1895.

19. *Wilmington Messenger*, March 6, 1895; *Lenoir Topic*, February 20, 1895.

20. *History of the General Assembly of North Carolina, 1895*, 37, 50, 63. According to Helen Edmonds, even with Crew's resolution the House did not adjourn until thirty-seven minutes past two o'clock. Edmonds, *The Negro and Fusion Politics*, 42; *Maxton Scottish Chief*, February 28, 1895.

21. *Caucasian*, March 14, 1895.

22. Ibid.

23. *Charlotte Observer*, January 12, 1895; *News and Observer*, March 13, 14, 1895; *History of the General Assembly of North Carolina*, 23.

24. *Progressive Farmer*, March 19, 1895.

25. *Caucasian*, March 21, 1895; letters to editor, *Caucasian*, March 30, 1895; *Caucasian*, April 4, 1895; J. B. Carrol to editor, *Caucasian*, March 28, 1895; *Caucasian*, April 4, 1895; *Caucasian*, January 31, February 7, 28, April 4, 1895.

26. Caucasian Publishing Company to B. N. Duke, March 5, 1895, Benjamin Duke Papers, Duke University; Hunt, "Marion Butler and the Populist Ideal," 279–281.

CHAPTER SIX. THE BATTLE WON BUT THE WAR LOST: FREE SILVER, COOPERATION BLUES, AND THE UNRAVELING OF THE PEOPLE'S PARTY IN 1896

1. Ritter, *Goldbugs and Greenbacks*, 152–206. The currency debate is extremely complex and the subtleties are not needed for the history of North Carolina Populism. However, it is important to note that this issue became the predominant policy difference between Republicans and Populists in North Carolina and exacerbated the cooperative tensions at the heart of the 1894 victory.

2. Ritter, *Goldbugs and Greenbacks*, 178–194.

3. For more details on the various positions within the GOP and Democratic Party on silver and gold in North Carolina, see Hunt, "Marion Butler and the Populist Ideal," 292–309.

4. *Caucasian*, April 18, June 20, July 4, 18, August 1, 8, 15, 22, 1895; Hunt, "Marion Butler and the Populist Ideal," 292–300.

5. *Caucasian*, May 2, 23, 1895.

6. Faulkner, "North Carolina Democrats and Silver Fusion," especially 242–243; *Progressive Farmer*, June 11, 25, 1895; Hunt, "Marion Butler and the Populist Ideal," 298–301.

7. See B. O. Flower to M. B., May 8, August 24, 1895; Henry Jones to M. B., May 31, 1895; R. N. West to M. B., June 5, 1895; J. Erwine to M. B., July 16, 1895; W. E. Fountain to M. B., August 13, 1895, all in MBP, SHC.

8. James B. Lloyd to the editor, April 30, 1895, in *Caucasian*, May 9, 1895; Harry Hunt to the editor, June 15, 1895, in *Caucasian*, June 20, 1895.

9. *Caucasian*, August 8, 15, 22, 1895, *Caucasian*, August 8, 1895.

10. *Caucasian*, September 12, 26, 1895. It seems that Butler received a warning that trouble might come with the convention. See A. Whitaker to M. B., August 29, 1895, MBP, SHC. *News and Observer*, September 26, 1895; *Progressive Farmer*, October 1, 1895; *Charlotte Observer*, September 26, 1895; *Wilmington Messenger*, September 26, 1895; Faulkner, "North Carolina Democrats and Silver Fusion," 243–245; Hunt, "Marion Butler and the Populist Ideal," 303–305.

11. The details are messy but Hunt gives a nice evaluation. Hunt, "Marion Butler and the Populist Ideal," 300–327. Another controversy that caused disagreement between Populists and Democrats was over Cyrus Thompson's criticisms of the organized church. For more details, see *News and Observer*, August 18, September 8, 17, 18, 1895. Thompson's position was articulated through a series on letters and speeches contained in newspapers: *Progressive Farmer*, September 17, 1895; and *Caucasian*, September 19, 1895. See also Bode, *Protestantism and the New South*, 39–61; *Progressive Farmer*, September 17, 1895; J.P.R. to editor, July 4, 1895; and R.H.W. Barker to editor, June 20, 1895, letters to editor, *Caucasian*, October 10, November 7, 1895; Z. E. DeWitt to Cyrus Thompson, August 29, 1895, CTP, SHC; *Charlotte Observer*, October 16, 1895; *Caucasian*, September 5, 19, 26, October 10, 24, November 7, December 12, 19, 1895, January 9, 16, 1896. The best treatment is Creech, *Righteous Indignation*.

12. *Wadesboro Plow Boy*, September 18, 1895; *Caucasian*, November 14, October 17, 1895.

13. For details, see Hunt, "Marion Butler and the Populist Ideal," 328–342; W. R. Lindsay to M. B., n.d. [1896], MBP, SHC.

14. M. B. to W. R. Lindsay, December 30, 1895, MBP, SHC. See also *Caucasian*, January 30, February 6, 13, 1896; *Wadesboro Plow Boy*, February 12, 1896; M. B. to J. A. Simms, February 17, 1896, MBP, SHC; *Progressive Farmer*, February 4, 1896; Hunt, "Marion Butler and the Populist Ideal," 329–332.

15. *Caucasian*, February 6, 1896; Hunt, "Marion Butler and the Populist Ideal," 330–332.

16. N. Gibbon to M. B., January 10, 1896; C. A. Nash to M. B., January 9, 1896; E. J. Wakefield to M. B., January 9, 1896; H. E. Williams to M. B., January 11, 1896; A. J. Gordon to M. B., January 11, 1896, all in MBP, SHC; *Caucasian*, February 27, 1896; James B. Lloyd, in the *Caucasian*, February 20, 1896; Hunt, "Marion Butler and the Populist Ideal," 331–334.

17. P. G. Rowland in *Progressive Farmer*, February 18, 1896. See Hunt, "Marion Butler and the Populist Ideal," for more details.

18. *Caucasian*, February 13, 1896.

19. J. D. Talley to the editor, March 5, 1896, in *Caucasian*, March 12, 1896; W. E. Hill to the editor, March 14, 1896, in *Caucasian*, March 19, 1896; J. H. Cary to the editor, April 11, 1896, in *Caucasian*, April 16, 1896; *Caucasian*, March 5, 19, 1896; Hunt, "Marion Butler and the Populist Ideal," 334–338.

20. *Caucasian*, March 19, 1896; *Caucasian*, March 5, 1896; N. L. Keen to the editor, February 26, 1896, in *Caucasian*, March 5, 1896; P. T. Everitt to the editor, October 15, 1895, in *Caucasian*, October 24, 1895.

21. *Caucasian*, April 2, 1896; Hunt, "Marion Butler and the Populist Ideal," 334–338.

22. *Caucasian*, April 9, 1896; *Progressive Farmer*, April 7, 1896; *Wadesboro Plow Boy*, April 8, 1896; Hunt, "Marion Butler and the Populist Ideal," 334.

23. *Wilmington Messenger*, April 17, 18, 1896; *Progressive Farmer*, April 21, 1896; *Caucasian*, April 23, May 7, 1896; *News and Observer*, April 18, 1896; J. E. Fowler to M. B., April 20, 1896, MBP, SHC; Hunt, "Marion Butler and the Populist Ideal," 334–335.

24. W. O. Stratford to M. B., April 30, 1896; A. D. Spivey to M. B., April 30, 1896; W. H. Kitchin to M. B., April 20, 1896; H. F. Freeman to M. B., April 22, 1896; William A. Guthrie to M. B., April 30, 1896; H. H. Paddison to M. B., April 23, 1896; Y. C. Morton to M. B., April 30, 1896; R. B. Kinsey to M. B., May 1, 1896; all in MBP, SHC; *Progressive Farmer*, April 21, 28, 1896; *Caucasian*, May 14, 1896; Hunt, "Marion Butler and the Populist Ideal, 336–338.

25. Cyrus Thompson to M. B., May 2, 1896; A. J. Moye to M. B., April 30, 1896, both in MBP, SHC; Hunt, "Marion Butler and the Populist Ideal," 337.

26. *Caucasian*, April 30, 1896; Hunt, "Marion Butler and the Populist Ideal," 338.

27. Cyrus Thompson to M. B., May 2, 1896, MBP, SHC. See John A. Buck to the editor, *Caucasian*, April 23, 1896; J. P. Sossaman to the editor, *Caucasian*, April 30, 1896; J. H. McLean, Ralph Howland, and T. B. Gorforth to the editor, *Caucasian*, May 7, 1896; Harry Skinner's card in the *Caucasian*, May 7, 1896.

28. *Elizabeth City North Carolinian*, February 5, March 25, April 22, 29, 1896; Zebulon Walser, in *Elizabeth City North Carolinian*, February 26, 1896. See also H. L. Grant, in *Union Republican*, February 27, 1896; *Union Republican*, April 23, 30, 1896; William E. Clark to Thomas Settle, April 22, 1896, Thomas Settle Papers, SHC. This GOP tactic came after Butler's policy narrowly won.

29. Quoted in *Wilmington Messenger*, May 16, 1896. For a complete discussion of the various African American attitudes to Russell's candidacy and the question of fusion, see the excellent article by Jeffrey Crow, "Fusion, Confusion, and Negroism," 364–384. Crow and Durden, *Maverick Republican*, 60–65; Hunt, "Marion Butler and the Populist Ideal," 380.

30. *Caucasian*, May 21, June 4, 1896; Harry Skinner to Daniel L. Russell, May 29, 1896; J. A. Sims to Daniel L. Russell, May 26, 1896, both in Daniel L. Russell Papers, SHC; William A. Guthrie to M. B., June 7, 1896, MBP, SHC; Hunt, "Marion Butler and the Populist Ideal," 343–380, 381–382.

31. Henry Butler to M. B., May 1, 1896; C. A. Nash to M. B., May 1, 1896; D. J. Hancock to M. B., June 10, 1896; S. Otho Wilson to M. B., May 4, 1896; A.D.K. Wallace to M. B., May 20, 1896; J. A. Taylor to M. B., June 22, 1896; A. S. Pease to M. B., May 1, 1896; ? to M. B., May 9, 1896; H. K. King to M. B., May 5, 1896; all in MBP, SHC.

32. J. E. Brown of Union County echoed the writings of many Populists when he wrote that the Populist Party was the only party that would help the suffering millions. Therefore, Brown exclaimed, "Let every friend of good government arise and march forward in a solid phalanx, and crush the combines, trusts and all enemies of good government out of existence." J. E. Brown to the editor, June 18, 1896, in *Caucasian*, June 25, 1896. J. R. Sattenwaite to the editor, May 11, 1896, in *Caucasian*, May 21, 1896. See also E. D. Sifford to the editor, G. Davis to the editor, H. Hodge to the editor, and T. J. Chandler to the editor, all in *Caucasian*, May 16, 1896; W. W. Erwin to the editor and G. F. Kornegay to the editor, both in *Caucasian*, May 21, 1896; *Caucasian*, May 28, 1896. W. W. Russell of Onslow County concurred with these sentiments. He noted that the Populists were for the People's Party out of principle, and he also argued that the financial question was more important than any other question, including a few state offices. W. W. Russell to the editor, May 25, 1896, in *Caucasian*, June 4, 1896. See also the sentiments of Eddie Paul, T. N. Newberry, A. D. McLeod, and James Basnight in the same issue.

33. *Caucasian*, June 11, 1896.

34. The Democratic state convention met before the national Democratic convention at Chicago. This is something Hunt seems unclear on. He states that the Democrats were motivated by "a new national leadership." Hunt, "Marion Butler and the Populist Ideal," 382. It is not certain that was the motivation. For details on the convention, see *Wilmington Messenger*, June 26, 1896; Steelman, "The Progressive Era in North Carolina," 138–139; R. B. Davis to Edward C. Smith, June 3, 10, 22, 1896, Edward Chambers Smith Papers, Duke University; *News and Observer*, June 26, 1896.

35. W. H. Kitchin to M. B., June 5, 1896; W. A. Guthrie to M. B., June 23, 1896; J. J. Mott to M. B., June 21, 1896; M. B. to William J. Peele, July 1, 1896, all in MBP, SHC; *Caucasian*, June 25, 1896; Durden, *The Climax of Populism*, 17–18; Jones, *Presidential Election of 1896*, 91–98.

36. *Caucasian*, June 25, 1896; Paul W. Glad, *McKinley, Bryan, and the People*, 131–141.

37. There are many books on the Populist National Convention. Hunt, *Marion Butler and American Populism*, 92–106.

38. Durden, *The Climax of Populism*, 23–44; Hunt, "Marion Butler and the Populist Ideal," 358–379; Goodwyn, *Democratic Promise*, 470–492; Woodward, *Tom Watson*, 294–301; Jones, *Presidential Election*, 244–260. These issues dogged the Populists and caused the party's ultimate demise.

39. It is difficult to ascertain the political calculations (due to a paucity of sources), but it is clear that Populists considered all permutations and possibilities. Hunt, "Marion Butler and the Populist Ideal," 386–392.

40. *Wilmington Messenger*, August 1, 1896; *Elizabeth City North Carolinian*, August 1896.

41. *Progressive Farmer*, August 4, 1896; Cyrus Thompson to James L. Ramsey, August 7, 1896, L. Polk Denmark Papers, NCDAH; Hunt, "Marion Butler and the Populist Ideal," 388–390.

42. *News and Observer*, August 14, 1896; Hunt, "Marion Butler and the Populist Ideal," 390–391.

43. For details on the convention's platform, see *Caucasian*, August 20, 1896.

44. *News and Observer*, August 14, 1896; Hunt, "Marion Butler and the Populist Ideal," 393–394.

45. Oliver Dockery to M. B., August 10, 1896, MBP, SHC; *News and Observer*, August 14, 15, 1896. For a slightly different interpretation, see Hunt, "Marion Butler and the Populist Ideal," 394–395.

46. *Caucasian*, August 20, 1896; *News and Observer*, August 15, 1896; Hunt, "Marion Butler and the Populist Ideal," 395–396.

47. For details on local cooperation, see *Caucasian*, August 20, 1896; *Union Republican*, August 20, 27, 1896; *Elizabeth City North Carolinian*, August 19, 26, 1896.

48. The Populists and Republicans offered joint tickets in Buncombe, Chatham, Johnston, Mecklenburg, Onlsow, Pender, Pitt, Randolph, Richmond, Robeson, Rowan, Stanly, and Wake counties in order to defeat the Democrats. Meanwhile, Republicans endorsed scores of local Populists in the eastern section and supported Populist legislative tickets in Beaufort, Brunswick, Columbus, Duplin, Gates, Greene, Hyde, Jones, Martin, Pamlico, Pasquotank, Perquimans, Sampson, and Union counties. Hunt, "Marion Butler and the Populist Ideal," 400–401.

49. Hal Ayer to M. B., September 1, 4, 1896; W. O. Stratford to M. B, August 31, 1896; William Worth to M. B., September 1, 1896; J. J. Mott to M. B., September 2, 1896; all in MBP, SHC; M. N. Corbett to Thomas Settle, August 31, 1896, Thomas Settle Papers, SHC.

50. *Caucasian*, September 17, 1896; Hal Ayer to Cyrus Thompson, September 1, 1896, CTP, SHC; *Elizabeth City North Carolinian*, September 16, 1896; *Progressive Farmer*, September 15, 1896; *Union Republican*, September 16, 1896; *News and Observer*, September 11, 1896; Hal Ayer to M. B., September 11, 1896, MBP, SHC; Hunt, "Marion Butler and the Populist Ideal," 401–402.

51. James B. Lloyd to M. B., September 15, 19, 22, 30, 1896; W. R. Henry to M. B., September 23, October 2 and 20, 1896, all in MBP, SHC. For an interesting discussion of the complex nature of local Republican-Populist fusion in Mecklenburg County, see Greenwood, *Bittersweet Legacy*, 178–184; Hunt, "Marion Butler and the Populist Ideal," 403–404; Hal Ayer to M. B., October 6, 1896, MBP, SHC. Cooperation occurred in Catawba, Davie, Gaston, Forsyth, Iredell, Lincoln, Nash, and Yadkin counties. For an interesting analysis of the local Populist-Democratic fusion, see Garrett Weaver, "The Politics of Local Democratic-Populist Fusion in the Election of 1896." William E. Fountain to M. B., October 6, 1896, MBP, SHC; Hunt, "Marion Butler and the Populist Ideal," 403–404.

52. For evidence, see C. B. Aycock to M. B., October 19, 1896; M. B. to C. J. Faulkner, October 17, 1896; W. J. Peele to M. B., October 24, 1896; Hal Ayer to M. B., October 6, 1896; William Worth to M. B., October 8, 1896, all in MBP, SHC.

53. Ayer explained that Populists rejected the proposal because it was made too late in the campaign and because Democrats refused to take Cyrus Watson off their ticket and place Guthrie in his stead, and as a result Populists could not vote for the conservative Watson. Populists demanded the governorship, and because Democrats refused to yield on the issue, the committee had little choice, Ayer argued, but to reject the offer. Hal Ayer to M. B., October 6, 1896, MBP, SHC; *Caucasian*, October 15, 1896; *News and Observer*, October 13, 14, 15, 16, 1896; *Caucasian*, October 15, 1896; *Winston Union Republican*, October 22, 1896; Hunt, "Marion Butler and the Populist Ideal," 404–407.

54. Hal Ayer to M. B., October 6, 1896, and J. Z. Green to M. B., October 6, 1896, both in MBP, SHC; John Graham to Cyrus Thompson, October 14, 1896, and William Worth to Cyrus Thompson, August 29, September 4, 17, 1896, both in CTP, SHC; Hunt, "Marion Butler and the Populist Ideal," 407–409.

55. William Guthrie to M. B., September 29, October 4, 6, 16, 24, 1896, MBP, SHC; *Progressive Farmer*, October 29, 1896; William A. Guthrie, "Supplemental Address to the People of North Carolina," October 30, 1896, North Carolina Collection, Chapel Hill; *News and Observer*, October 28, 29, 1896; *Wilmington Messenger*, October 28, 29, 30, 1896; Hunt, "Marion Butler and the Populist Ideal," 407–409.

56. *News and Observer*, October 29, 1896. Guthrie's actions certainly threw an already convoluted and contentious election campaign into further uncertainty. The Democrats condemned the actions of Ayer but praised the actions of Guthrie. Republican state chairman Alfred E. Holton declared that as many as fifteen thousand Populist voters would now switch to Russell. Daniel Russell even ventured the opinion that Guthrie's bombshell would help him because "the great mass of the Populist party . . . are determined to keep the State from Democratic control."

57. *News and Observer*, October 29, 1896, for quote, and also see October 14, 15, 17, 18, 1896; *Raleigh Gazette*, October 31, 1896.

58. *Raleigh Hayseeder*, October 22, 1896; *Caucasian*, October 29, 1896.

59. *Manual of North Carolina: Issued by the North Carolina Historical Commission*, compiled and edited by R.D.W. Connor (Raleigh: E.M. Uzzell and Co., State Printers, 1913), 1005–1006.

60. Edmonds, *The Negro and Fusion Politics*, 59. Allen Trelease argues that there were thirty-seven Populists in the lower house. Trelease, "The Fusion Legislature of 1895 and 1897," 281. Muller erroneously argued there were fifty-eight Populists in the state legislature. Muller, "New South Populism," 122. Hunt, "Marion Butler and the Populist Ideal," 449. In the lower house the Populists carried the counties of Allegheny, Beaufort, Brunswick, Cabarrus, Caswell, Catawba, Clay, Columbus, Duplin, Franklin, Gates, Greene, Hyde, Jones, Lenoir, Lincoln, Martin, Montgomery, Nash, Orange, Pamlico, Pasquotank, Perquimans, Rutherford, Sampson, Union, and Wilson. Of these counties only Sampson produced two Populist representatives. The Populists also gained members of the lower house by sharing the ticket with the Republican Party in the following counties: Buncombe, Chatham, Granville, Mecklenburg, Pitt, Randolph, Richmond, Robeson, and Wake. Interestingly, in this category, the Populist strongholds in 1895, Chatham, Randolph, Richmond, and Robeson, produced two Populist representatives from each of these counties. Thus it appears that in some counties Populist strength was diminishing. Additionally, in the nine counties that effected Democratic-Populist fusion, only two, Rockingham and Wayne, produced a Populist (and a Democrat) representative. Interestingly, Populist strength was in the eastern and southeastern portion of the state. Only in a few counties in the Seventh and Fifth Congressional Districts did Populists secure legislative seats. In addition, it is worth noting that Populists again carried some majority-black counties: Caswell, Granville (in alliance with Republicans), Pasquotank, and Richmond (in alliance with Republicans). Given the larger number of black voters in these counties, it is clear that Populists garnered black votes in large numbers. The extent of Populist victories varied in each county. For example, in Sampson County the party garnered 66 percent of the vote, whereas in Duplin County the Populist gained 56 percent of the vote, and in Union County the Populist candidate squeezed home by a margin of just 105 votes, with a total share of the vote at 51 percent. From the available evidence the Populist share of the votes was 58 percent. However, Populist strongholds remained in Sampson, Chatham, and the Third Congressional District. Populists benefited greatly from the annihilation of Democrats in the eastern section of the state. D. C. Mangum, *Biographical Sketches of the Members of the Legislature of North Carolina, Session 1897* (Raleigh: Edwards and Broughton, Printers and Binders, 1897); Edmonds, *The Negro and Fusion Politics*, 58; *Caucasian*, November 19, 1896, January 14, 1897; *Records of Election*, Brunswick County, Cabarrus County, Columbus County, Jones County, Nash County, Richmond County, Sampson County, Union County, and Wake County. The victory in the eastern section would prove mightily important for the subsequent years.

61. Hicks, *The Populist Revolt*, 377; Glad, *McKinley, Bryan*, 189–209.

62. H. N. Falkener to Daniel L. Russell, November 6, 1896; A. C. Swinson to Daniel L. Russell, November 7, 1896; Zebulon Walser to Daniel L. Russell, November 7, 1896; H. B. Farmer to Daniel L. Russell, November 9, 1896; all in Daniel L. Russell Papers, SHC. See also B. L. Blackmore to Daniel L. Russell, November 10, 1896; E. C. Duncan to Daniel L. Russell, November 10, 1896; B. N. Duke to Daniel L. Russell, November 25, 1896; Daniel L. Russell to B. N. Duke, November 30, 1896, all in Benjamin Duke Papers, Duke University.

63. See, for example the Lenoir *Topic*, November 17, 24, 1896; *News and Observer*, November 27, 1896.

CHAPTER SEVEN. BOSSISM, FACTIONALISM, AND TURMOIL: THE DISINTEGRATION OF POPULIST AND REPUBLICAN RULE IN 1897

1. *Caucasian*, November 19, 1896; Hunt, "Marion Butler and the Populist Ideal," 453–454.

2. Harry Skinner to Cyrus Thompson, November 12, 1896; James Ramsey to Cyrus Thompson, November 6, 1896; R. L. Storr to Cyrus Thompson, November 9, 1896; A. S. Pease to Cyrus Thompson,

November 10, 1896; W. G. Hallwell to Cyrus Thompson, November 12, 1896, all in CTP, SHC; Hunt, "Marion Butler and the Populist Ideal," 456–460. S. Burners wrote Thompson a lengthy letter on the senatorial question. He argued that Thompson would make an excellent choice for the Senate, and he urged Thompson to do all he could to end Butler's leadership of the North Carolina Populists and argued that political honor meant that the Populists must support Pritchard because the voters of both the GOP and People's Party thought that Pritchard was to be elected. In these letters it is clear that some Populists viewed Butler as a "boss." Abbott L. Swinson to Cyrus Thompson, December 12, 1896, CTP, SHC; Abbott Swinson to Daniel L. Russell, November 7, 28, 1896, Daniel L. Russell Papers, SHC; M. Caldwell to Cyrus Thompson, November 14, 1896, CTP, SHC; S. Burners to Cyrus Thompson, December 3, 1896, CTP, SHC.

    3. L. C. Caldwell to M. B., November 25, 1896; J. B. Schulken to M. B., December 2, 1896, both in MBP, SHC. For example, Congressman William Strowd of the Fourth District argued that only "a *Bona Fide Free Silver Man*" could gain election to the Senate. William Strowd to M. B., November 21, 1896, MBP, SHC. See also P. W. Patton to M. B., November 21, 1896; W. E. Bower to M. B., November 20, 1896; George Hunt to M. B., December 3, 1896; John A. Sims to M. B., December 4, 1896, all in MBP, SHC.

    4. A. C. Shuford to M. B., November 27, 1896; Claudius Dockery to M. B., December 12, 1896, both in MBP, SHC.

    5. See, for example, *Caucasian*, December 10, 1896; Crow and Durden, *Maverick Republican in the Old North State*, 79–81; Hunt, "Marion Butler and the Populist Ideal," 459–460.

    6. *Caucasian*, January 7, 1897; Hunt, "Marion Butler and the Populist Ideal," 460.

    7. *Wilmington Messenger*, January 6, 1897; *Salisbury Carolina Watchman*, January 14, 1897.

    8. *Raleigh Tribune*, January 12, 14, 15, 16, 1897; *Wilmington Messenger*, January 9, 10, 12, 1897.

    9. *Raleigh Tribune*, January 10, 12, 1897; *Winston Union Republican*, January 21, 1897; Hunt, "Marion Butler and the Populist Ideal," 462–463.

    10. *Raleigh Gazette*, January 2, 1897.

    11. *Chatham Citizen*, February 18, 1897; *Winston Union Republican*, January 14, 1897; Hunt, "Marion Butler and the Populist Ideal," 462.

    12. J. M. Cutchin's letter in the *Caucasian*, January 7, 21, 1897; Hunt, "Marion Butler and the Populist Ideal," 463–465.

    13. James Hunt argues that Thompson opposed Skinner and Pritchard because "Pritchard did not stand for anything resembling Populism." However, it appears that Thompson did not feel that the issue warranted a further hemorrhaging of the Populist Party. Hunt, "Marion Butler and the Populist Ideal," 461; *Wilmington Messenger*, January 16, 1897; Harry Skinner's interview in the *Raleigh Tribune*, January 17, 1897.

    14. S. A. Edmunds to M. B., January 7, 1897. W. M. Bagwell concurred with Edmunds and urged Butler to continue on his "manly course" in the senatorial battle. The Republicans, Bagwell argued, hoped to draw all the Populist strength into their own party and then leave the People's Party to die. W. M. Bagwell to M. B., January 7, 1897, John Duckett to M. B., January 7, 1897, both in MBP, SHC.

    15. The following Populists voted for Pritchard: L. A. Abernathy of Lincoln, C. M. Babbitt of Pamlico, H. F. Brown of Jones, J. E. Bryan of Chatham, John G. Harris of Hyde, J. H. Parker of Perquimans, H. E. Hodges of Beaufort, T. H. Roundtree of Gates, J. J. White of Randolph, C. J. Yarborough of Caswell, Senator R.H.W. Barker of the Twenty-ninth District, Senator George H. Cannon of the Tenth District, Senator J. M. Early of the Third District, Senator T. E. McCaskey of the Second District, Senator John F. Newsome of the First District, Senator William H. Odum of the Twenty-third District, and Senator E. F. Wakefield of the Thirty-first District. *Caucasian*, January 28, 1897; *Wilmington Messenger*, January 21, 1897; *Elizabeth City North Carolinian*, January 27, 1897.

    16. *Caucasian*, January 21, 1897.

    17. *Raleigh Gazette*, February 13, 1897; *Elizabeth City North Carolinian*, January 27, February 3, 1897.

18. In the case of state senators E. F. Wakefield, R.H.W. Barker, T. E. McCaskey, John F. Newsome and state representatives J. E. Bryan, and J. J. White, these assemblymen owed their election directly to cooperation. In each of their respective districts a Republican was also elected on the same ticket. In addition, Populist senators G. H. Cannon and J. M. Early and representatives C. J. Yarborough and T. H. Roundtree gained election in non-Populist strongholds with the assistance of Republican votes.

19. This interpretation is highly contentious, but if one analyzes the local factors behind the voting patterns, a clear picture emerges. With perhaps the exception of Senator Odum, all the Populists had a local reason to vote for Pritchard, and these tendencies were exacerbated by the personal clash between Skinner and Butler. For more discussion, see Billings, *Planters and the Making of a "New South,"* 177–181. Hunt gives a different view. Hunt, "Marion Butler and the Populist Ideal," 460–467.

20. *Caucasian*, January 14, 21, 1897; M. B. to Florence Butler, January 25, 1897, Florence Butler Papers, SHC; M. B. to George Washburn, February 5, 1897, MBP, SHC.

21. *Wilmington Messenger*, January 21, 1897; Hunt, "Marion Butler and the Populist Ideal," 467–469.

22. Billings, *Planters and the Making of the "New South,"* 178–183; *Raleigh News and Observer*, December 1, 1896; Crow and Durden, *Maverick Republican in the Old North State*, 75–82; Hunt, "Marion Butler and the Populist Ideal," 469–470.

23. For details of the speech, see Crow and Durden, *Maverick Republican in the Old North State*, 81–83.

24. For details on the problems Butlerite Populists faced, see George Butler to M. B., January 29, February 18, 28, April 7, 1897; Walter Clark to M. B., January 30, February 11, 22, 1897; W. S. Pearson to M. B., February 14, 1897, all in MBP, SHC; Trelease, "The Fusion Legislature of 1895 and 1897," 280–309; Crow and Durden, *Maverick Republican in the Old North State*, 90; *Caucasian*, February 11, 18, 1897; Hunt, "Marion Butler and the Populist Ideal," 469.

25. *Raleigh Tribune*, February 6, 7, 1897; Crow and Durden, *Maverick Republican in the Old North State*, 85–89; Trelease, "The Fusion Legislature of 1895 and 1897," 301–304; J. F. Click to M. B., February 23, 1897; Thomas S. Sutton to M. B., January 30, 1897; George Butler to M. B., February 18, 1897; M. B. to J. H. Ferris, March 11, 1897, all in MBP, SHC; Hunt, "Marion Butler and the Populist Ideal," 470.

26. George Butler to M. B., February 18, 1897; William E. Fountain to M. B., April 2, 1897, both in MBP, SHC; Hunt, "Marion Butler and the Populist Ideal," 471–472.

27. For more details, see Crow and Durden, *Maverick Republican in the Old North State*, 91–93; Trelease "The Fusion Legislature of 1895 and 1897," 285–287; *Wilmington Messenger*, February 25, 26, 1897; *Raleigh Tribune*, March 3, 1897.

28. Crow and Durden, *Maverick Republican in the Old North State*, 94; interview in *News and Observer*, March 3, 4, 1897; Crow and Durden, *Maverick Republican in the Old North State*, 94–95; Edmonds, *The Negro and Fusion Politics*, 60–64, 74–81; *Wilmington Messenger*, March 2, 3, 4, 5, 1897.

29. *Progressive Farmer*, March 16, 1897; Hunt, "Marion Butler and the Populist Ideal," 471.

30. J. G. Parker to M. B., February 13, 1897; James A. ? to M. B., February 2, 1897; J. Z. Green to M. B., June 22, 1897, all in MBP, SHC.

31. *Wadesboro Plow Boy*, March 7, 14, April 28, 1897; *Salisbury Carolina Watchman*, June 10, August 12, 1897; *Hickory Mercury*, September 22, 1897; L. C. Caldwell to M. B., June 13, 1897; George Butler to M. B., December 12, 1897; R. C. Rivers to M. B., March 6, May 1, 1897; Hal W. Ayer to M. B., May 28, 1897, all in MBP, SHC; *Hickory Mercury*, September 8, 1897; Hunt, "Marion Butler and the Populist Ideal," 510–512.

32. The details on the affair are messy and not pertinent here. However, for a complete analysis, see Crow and Durden, *Maverick Republican in the Old North State*, 97–116; Hunt, "Marion Butler and the Populist Ideal," 512–513.

33. *Hickory Mercury*, September 29, 1897; *Raleigh Hayseeder*, October 14, 1897. For details on the Railroad Commission, see Crow and Durden, *Maverick Republican in the Old North State*, 97–116; John

Graham to M. B., April 17, 1897; Daniel L. Russell to M. B., May 5, June 12, July 24, December 20, 1897; J. H. Pearson to M. B., December 26, 1897, all in MBP, SHC.

34. Hal Ayer to M. B., July 6, 1897; W. E. Fountain to M. B., July 12, 1897; J. Z. Green to M. B., July 13, 1897, all in MBP, SHC; Hunt, "Marion Butler and the Populist Ideal," 514–515.

35. *Progressive Farmer*, August 17, 1897; M. B. to W. J. Peele, October 12, 1897, MBP, SHC; *Caucasian*, August 19, September 16, October 14, 21, 1897; *Hickory Mercury*, August 25, 1897; Hunt, "Marion Butler and the Populist Ideal," 514.

36. *Wilmington Messenger*, September 8, 1897.

37. *Lenoir Topic*, December 1, 1897, quoting *Charlotte Observer*, November 19, 1897; *Caucasian*, September 16, 30, October 7, December 16, 1897; B. F. Keith to M. B., November 29, 1897, MBP, SHC; Hunt, "Marion Butler and the Populist Ideal," 518–519.

38. M. B. quoted in Hunt, "Marion Butler and the Populist Ideal," 519–520; Gilmore, *Gender and Jim Crow*, 1–89; R. Edwards, *Angels in the Machinery*, 91–110; Cecelski and Tyson, *Democracy Betrayed*, 73–93, 143–162.

39. *Hickory Mercury*, October 6, 1897; G. Hardison to M. B., December 13, 1897; Z. M. Jeffreys to M. B., December 23, 1897, both in MBP, SHC; Hunt, "Marion Butler and the Populist Ideal," 519–520.

Chapter Eight. The Chickens Come Home to Roost: The White Supremacy Campaign in North Carolina

1. *Caucasian*, February 10, April 15, 28, 1898; Hunt, "Marion Butler and the Populist Ideal," 559. This was a very naïve approach by Butler. He failed to heed the warnings of the 1897 session.

2. *Raleigh Hayseeder*, January 20, 27, February 17, March 17, 1898; *Chatham Citizen*, April 27, 1898; Hunt, "Marion Butler and the Populist Ideal," 561. The *Progressive Farmer* was also very critical of cooperation with the Democrats. It argued that the talk of cooperation was wrong and furthered the decline of the party. The paper singled out Butler for blame. In a damning editorial the paper chided, "It seems to be the height of folly to expect reforms from a party that we were forced to leave on account of its insincerity, a party which has fought us at every point, that declined to give us a single reform when it had full power." Thus, a powerful segment of the party lined up against Butler and his plan for cooperation. These newspapers probably epitomized the views of the rank and file. *Progressive Farmer*, April 19, 1898.

3. *Charlotte People's Paper*, January 7, February 25, March 4, April 1, 1898; *Hickory Times-Mercury*, February 2, 9, 16, March 2, 23, 1898; Hunt, "Marion Butler and the Populist Ideal," 561–562.

4. Thomas H. Sutton to M. B., January 31, 1898, MBP, SHC.

5. J. Dalton to M. B., January 15, 1898. Others had no idea what to do. For example, J. A. Meares wrote Butler that he was totally unclear what strategy the Populists should pursue. He advised Butler that the Populists should not run an independent ticket because it would merely allow the Republicans to win office, but he also did not favor cooperation with the Republicans because of the GOP's treatment of the Populists in the 1897 state legislature. Cooperation with the Democrats, he warned, "would mean the utter destruction of our party," and he ended his letter, "Now Senator the way I look at it we are between the Devil and the Sea." J. A. Meares to M. B., February 16, 1898; George T. Jones to M. B., March 30, 1898, both in MBP, SHC. Other Populists worried over the continual infighting in the Populist Party and the negative impact this division had on the rank and file. Morrison Caldwell urged Butler that the "work of organization should begin *at once*," but he also warned that this "is going to be much more difficult than heretofore." Thus, by the middle of March 1898, Butler received numerous reports of the divisions in the People's Party and the variance of opinion on campaign strategy. Indeed, it seems that the vast majority of Populists, for a variety of reasons, perhaps many local in nature, opposed his position on cooperation. William J. Leary did not know with whom Populist should fuse, but he felt a three-cornered fight would only throw the state to the Democrats. If Populists did fuse with the Democrats, Leary

argued, it must be for the principles of the People's Party. See, for example, M. Oliver to M. B., January 22, 1898; J. M. Bateman to M. B., January 25, 1898; E. A. Moye to M. B., January 25, 1898; Morrison Caldwell to M. B., February 17, 1898; William J. Leary to M. B., March 11, 1898, all in MBP, SHC.

6. Many notable Populists attended: J. E. Bryan (Skinnerite), J. J. Jenkins (Skinnerite), R. B. Lineberry (Skinnerite), F. D. Koonce (Butlerite), H. E. King (Butlerite), A. H. Paddison, Angus Shaw, Spier Whitaker, J. J. Rogers, J. W. Denmark, W. H. Worth, and J. L. Ramsey. *Raleigh Hayseeder*, March 17, 1898; *Hickory Times-Mercury*, March 23, 1898; *Caucasian*, March 24, 1898; Morrison Caldwell to M. B., March 19, 1898; James H. Sherrill to M. B., March 25, 1898; J. F. Click to M. B., March 19, 1898, all in MBP, SHC.

7. *Caucasian*, April 14, 1898.

8. The *Raleigh Home Rule*, a new Populist paper edited by A. S. Peace and Joshua Skinner, openly opposed Butler's position on cooperation. It argued, "It is passingly strange to us how any self-respecting Populist can for a moment think of entertaining a proposition from a Democrat leading to fusion after the abuse they have heaped upon the Populists from their incipiency," and the editors mused, "Up to date they have been the Populists only political enemy in this State." *Charlotte People's Paper*, April 15, 1898; *Progressive Farmer*, May 10, 1898; *Raleigh Home Rule*, April 28, 1898. For more details on Butler's position during the first half of 1898, see: Hunt, "Marion Butler and the Populist Ideal," 558–570; Muller, "New South Populism," 131–135.

9. B. P. Uttley to M. B., May 6, 1898; J. J. Rodgers to M. B., May 6, 1898, both in MBP, SHC; *Progressive Farmer*, May 10, 1898; *Raleigh Home Rule*, May 12, 1898. For more evidence of divisions, see Morrison Caldwell to M. B., May 2, 7, 1898; M.V.B. Howard to M. B., May 6, 1898; W. B. Fleming to M. B., May 4, 1898; B. F. Keith to M. B., May 7, 1898; M. N. Sawyer to M. B., April 23, 1898, all in MBP, SHC.

10. Richmond Pearson to M. B., March 21, 1898, MBP, SHC; *Winston Union Republican*, March 17, May 5, 1898; Hunt, "Marion Butler and the Populist Ideal," 564–566.

11. Crow and Durden, *Maverick Republican in the Old North State*, 111–116; Hunt, "Marion Butler and the Populist Ideal," 565.

12. *Caucasian*, January 13, 20, 1898; Daniel L. Russell to M. B., April 20, 20, 1898, MBP, SHC; Hunt, "Marion Butler and the Populist Ideal," 566.

13. Walter Clark to M. B., April 28, 1898, MBP, SHC; see also J. Steelman, "The Progressive Era," 158–175; *Caucasian*, April 14, May 5, 12, 19, 1898; Hunt, "Marion Butler and the Populist Ideal," 567–569; *Wilmington Messenger*, May 12, 1898; *Caucasian*, May 5, 1898; *Wilmington Messenger*, March 15, April 6, 9, May 3, 1898.

14. Hunt, "Marion Butler and the Populist Ideal," 570.

15. All leading Populists attended the meeting. From the earliest moment it seemed that Butler had the majority of the leadership on his side. Skinner only had the support of the influential S. Otho Wilson, Walter Henry, and A. S. Peace. Butler could count on the support of Hal Ayer, Cyrus Thompson, William Worth, John E. Fowler, J. B. Schulken, William Fountain, James B. Lloyd, William F. Strowd, and many others. *Wilmington Messenger*, May 18, 1898; *Caucasian*, May 26, 1898; Hunt, "Marion Butler and the Populist Ideal," 570.

16. *Wilmington Messenger*, May 19, 1898; *Caucasian*, May 19, 1898; *Lenoir Topic*, May 25, 1898. Importantly, many Populist papers that had criticized movement to fuse with the Democrats or that had personally attacked Butler now welcomed the resolutions of the Populist convention. For example, the *Progressive Farmer* wholeheartedly approved of the resolutions and welcomed the criticisms of the ninety-nine-year lease. Only the *Raleigh Home Rule* opposed the actions of the convention on its plan for cooperation. The paper pleaded, "In case of Dem. Pop. fusion, it would not only be 'fusion' but *confusion* and *refusion* for Pops." The *Home Rule* would remain deeply hostile to Butler's position throughout the upcoming campaign. *Progressive Farmer*, May 24, 1898; *Raleigh Home Rule*, May 19, 1898.

17. Morrison Caldwell to M. B., May 23, 1898; James B. Lloyd to M. B., May 26, 1898, both in MBP, SHC; Hunt, "Marion Butler and the Populist Ideal," 573.

18. For more details on the Democratic convention, see *Wilmington Messenger*, May 27, 1898; *Progressive Farmer*, May 31, 1898; *Caucasian*, June 2, 1898; *Lenoir Topic*, June 1, 1898; Hunt, "Marion Butler and the Populist Ideal," 573–574.

19. *Caucasian*, June 2, 9, 1898; *Charlotte People's Paper*, June 3, 1898; *Chatham Citizen*, June 1, 1898.

20. Morrison Caldwell to M. B., May 30, 1898; James H. Sherrill to M. B., May 30, 1898; William Leary to M. B., May 27, 1898; J. Shook to M. B., June 1, 1898; J. J. Mott to M. B., June 3, 1898; W. C. Pearson to M. B., June 6, 1898; R. C. Rivers to M. B., June 6, 1898, all in MBP, SHC; Hunt, "Marion Butler and the Populist Ideal," 576–578.

21. J. H. Sherrill to M. B., May 30, 1898; J. F. Click to M. B., June 26, 1898; B. B. Lassiter to M. B., July 4, 1898; I. J. Dapy to M. B., July 5, 1898; Cyrus Thompson to M. B., June 3, July 21, 1898; W. F. Strowd to M. B., July 7, 21, 1898; E. A. Moye to M. B., June 20, 1898; B. F. Keith to M. B., July 8, 1898; J. C. Cutler to M. B., July 2, 1898, W. H. Standin to M. B., July 23, 1898, all in MBP, SHC; Hunt, "Marion Butler and the Populist Ideal," 576.

22. Circular in *Charlotte People's Paper*, June 17, 1898.

23. James H. Sherrill to M. B., July 15, 1898; G. Hardison to M. B., July 19, 1898, both in MBP, SHC. Anyone who opposed a Butlerite in local conventions seemed to be accused of being a sellout, even long-standing Populists.

24. *Elizabeth City North Carolinian*, July 27, 1898; Crow and Durden, *Maverick Republican in the Old North State*, 124–125; *Winston Union Republican*, July 28, 1898; Hunt, "Marion Butler and the Populist Ideal," 578.

25. J. L. Cooper to M. B., June 30, 1898, MBP, SHC; Hunt, "Marion Butler and the Populist Ideal," 578–579.

26. *Caucasian*, June 30, 1898; Hunt, "Marion Butler and the Populist Ideal," 580–584; Edmonds, *The Negro and Fusion Politics*, 138–139.

27. On the Democratic use of race and gender, see Gilmore, "Murder, Memory, and the Flight of the Incubus," in Cecelski and Tyson, *Democracy Betrayed*. There is a great deal of literature on the 1898 campaign: Crow and Durden, *Maverick Republican in the Old North State*, 117–137; J. Steelman, "The Progressive Era," 150–180; Edmonds, *The Negro and Fusion Politics*, 148–177; Wooley, "Race and Politics."

28. The Democrats did mention other themes such as corruption and scandals in the government of Daniel Russell, but these issues took a backseat to race. *Wilmington Morning Star*, August 9, 18, 1898; Gilmore, "Murder, Memory, and the Flight of the Incubus," 75. The number of political papers for each party is difficult to determine. Democrats had 145 state newspapers, the GOP had 20, and Populists had 36. Democrats had the only daily papers and also had the largest circulation.

29. *News and Observer*, September 8, 22, 1898, October 14, 1898; *Charlotte Observer*, September 7, 1898.

30. *News and Observer*, October 25, 26, 1898; *Wilmington Messenger*, July 23, 1898; Gilmore, "Murder, Memory, and the Flight of the Incubus," 73–94; Gilmore, *Gender and Jim Crow*, 31–118; Hunt, "Marion Butler and the Populist Ideal," 582–586.

31. Here are examples of broadsides: Dr. Thompson Butts His Head (n.p., 1898); Five Lessons for the Voters of North Carolina (n.p., 1898); White Man's Convention in North Carolina (n.p., 1898); Hunt, "Marion Butler and the Populist Ideal," 582–585.

32. *Caucasian*, September 29, 1898. For Populist reaction, see P. L. Parker to M. B., October 3, 1898, MBP, SHC; *Wilmington Messenger*, November 4, 1898. For an interesting appraisal of Democratic campaign speakers, see Daniels, *Editor in Politics*, 283–292; Hunt, "Marion Butler and the Populist Ideal," 584.

33. *Caucasian*, September 8, 1898; Hunt, "Marion Butler and the Populist Ideal," 586.

34. Quote from *Hickory Times-Mercury*, September 8, 1898; *Raleigh Home Rule*, August 4, 1898; *Chatham Citizen*, August 17, 1898.

35. Cyrus Thompson to M. B., August 11, 1898, MBP, SHC; *Caucasian*, September 29, 1898.

36. *Dr. Thompson's Great Speech*, party document, 20–21; *Caucasian*, September 1, 1898.

37. *Dr. Thompson's Great Speech*, 22–23.

38. *Progressive Farmer*, September 13, 1898.

39. M. B., quoted in *Caucasian*, Oct. 27, 1898. For details on the Democrats handbook, see *Democratic Handbook, 1898: Prepared by the State Democratic Executive Committee of North Carolina* (Raleigh: Edwards and Broughton, Printers and Binders, 1898); see also *People's Party Handbook of Facts, Campaign of 1898: Issued by the State Executive Committee of the People's Party of North Carolina* (Raleigh: Capital Printing Company, Printers and Binders, 1898); Hunt, "Marion Butler and the Populist Ideal," which gives more detail on the speech, 590–593.

40. G. L. Hardison to M. B., August 9, 1898; James B. Lloyd to M. B., August 11, September 29, 1898; James H. Sherrill to M. B., September 15, 28, 1898; all in MBP, SHC; *Charlotte People's Paper*, August 5, 19, 26, September 2, 9, 16, 30, 1898; *Hickory Mercury*, September 7, 11, 28, 1898; *Raleigh Home Rule*, October 20, 27, 1898; *Charlotte Observer*, September 25, 1898; *Wilmington Messenger*, September 18, 1898; *Charlotte Observer*, September 25, 1898; *News and Observer*, October 23, 25, 1898.

41. *Chatham Record*, September 24, 1898; *News and Observer*, September 30, 1898; John W. Smith to M. B., July 15, 1898, MBP, SHC; D. C. Newberry to Daniel L. Russell, October 17, 1898, Daniel L. Russell Papers, SHC.

42. Muller, "New South Populism," 135–136; John H. Small to M. B., October 17, November 2, 1898; E. A. Moye to M. B., October 21, 1898, both in MBP, SHC; S. B. Spruill to John H. Small, October 1, 3, 1898; W. J. Cross to John H. Small, October 1, 1898; P. Hunayan to John H. Small, October 1, 1898; H. Gibbs to John H. Small, October 4, 1898, all in John H. Small Papers, Duke University; Hunt, "Marion Butler and the Populist Ideal," 594.

43. Muller, "New South Populism," 136–137; W. F. Strowd to M. B., July 7, 1898; R. L. Strowd to M. B., September 12, 1898; R. C. Rivers to M. B., September 12, 1898; Daniel L. Russell to M. B., September 26, 1898, all in MBP, SHC. The Democrats wanted control of the state legislature.

44. James Lloyd to M. B., October 15, 1898, MBP, SHC. For more details, see *Caucasian*, November 17, 1898; James B. Lloyd to M. B., July 28, August 11, September 29, October 21, 22, 29, November 4, 1898; William Fountain to M. B., August 9, 1898, both in MBP, SHC; Muller, "New South Populism," 138; Anderson, *Race and Politics*, 252–279; Hunt, "Marion Butler and the Populist Ideal," 596–597.

45. Manly was the acknowledged son of Charles Manly, the Whig governor of North Carolina from 1849 to 1851. According to Prather, he could pass for white. He was born in 1866. He moved to Wilmington to look for work and became a local politician and a Sunday school teacher at a Presbyterian church. He served as a register of deeds until he bought a printing press. *Wilmington Record*, August 18, 1898; Gilmore, *Gender and Jim Crow*. In addition, prominent white men could not stand lack of deference from black women. White conductors on Wilmington's street cars (there was no legalized Jim Crow in 1898) refused to help black women onto the cars. Gilmore, "Murder, Memory, and the Flight of the Incubus."

46. *Wilmington Record*, August 18, 1898; Gilmore, "Murder, Memory, and the Flight of the Incubus."

47. *News and Observer*, September 22, 1898. See also *News and Observer*, October 1–November 9, 1898; *Wilmington Messenger*, October 1–November 9, 1898.

48. *Wilmington Messenger*, November 1, 1898. Waddell was born in 1834 and was a confederate veteran. He was a three-term U.S. congressman from 1871 to 1877, losing to Russell. He was unemployed in 1898. *Wilmington Morning Post*, October 28, 1898; Rebecca Cameron to Alfred Waddell, October 26, 1898, Alfred Waddell Papers, SHC; Crow and Durden, *Maverick Republican in the Old North State*, 130–132; McDuffie, "Politics in Wilmington and New Hanover County," 520–566.

49. For details on the Red Shirts, see Prather, "The Red Shirt Movements in North Carolina." *Raleigh Home Rule*, October 20, 1898; Joseph M. King to M. B., October 25, 1898; James Lloyd to M. B., September 23, 1898, both in MBP, SHC; *Raleigh Home Rule*, October 20, 27, 1898; *Fayetteville Observer*, October 22, 27, 1898; *News and Observer*, October 22, 1898.

50. Proclamation of Governor Daniel L. Russell, October 26, 1898, Governor's Papers, NCDAH.

51. *News and Observer*, October 25, 26, 29, 1898; *Wilmington Messenger*, October 29, 1898; *Lenoir Topic*, November 3, 1898.

52. *People's Party Handbook of Facts, 1898*, 94–96; *Hickory Times-Mercury*, September 28, 1898.

53. *Progressive Farmer*, October 25, 1898; *Caucasian*, October 27, 1898; *Raleigh Home Rule*, October 27, 1898.

54. *Contested Election Case of Oliver H. Dockery vs. John D. Bellamy from the Sixth Congressional District* (Washington, D.C.: GPO, 1899), testimony of Robert Russell, 350–360; *New Bern Daily Journal*, November 10, 1898.

55. Kousser, *The Shaping of Southern Politics*, 186, 187–189, 193–194. Records of election do not exist for every county in North Carolina at each election. Table 8.1 is a representative example of the decline in the Populist vote in certain eastern counties from 1896 to 1898. Escott, *Many Excellent People*, 258. For details on the election results, see *Caucasian*, November 10, 17, 24, 1898; *Records of Election*, Bladen County, Brunswick County, 1898; Crow and Durden, *Maverick Republican in the Old North State*, 135–137; Muller, "New South Populism," 131–140; Hunt, "Marion Butler and the Populist Ideal," 595–603; Edmonds, *The Negro and Fusion Politics*, 153–154.

56. *Wilmington Messenger*, November 9, 1898; W. W. Bond to Henry G. Connor, November 10, 1898; R. H. Brattle to Henry G. Connor, November 10, 1898, both in Henry Groves Connor Papers, SHC.

57. The Wilmington Riot has received a great deal of attention. It is not pertinent here to go into all the details about the riot. However, for more details, see Prather, *We Have Taken a City*; Cecelski and Tyson, *Democracy Betrayed*; Edmonds, *The Negro and Fusion Politics*, 158–177; Higuchi, "White Supremacy on the Cape Fear"; McDuffie, "Politics in Wilmington and New Hanover County." For more primary sources or recollections, see Keith, *Memories: "Truth and Honesty Will Conquer"*; Kirk, *Statement of Facts: Bloody Riot in Wilmington NC*; Jane Cronly, "Account of Race Riot in Wilmington," Cronly Family Papers, Duke University; Thomas W. Clawson, "The Wilmington Race Riot in 1898: Recollections and Memories," Thomas Clawson Papers, SHC; George Roundtree, "Memorandum of My Personal Recollection of the Election of 1898," Henry Groves Connor Papers, SHC.

58. See D. M. Bobbs to M. B., November 10, 1899; James H. Sherrill to M. B., November 11, 1898; James B. Lloyd to M. B., November 13, 1898; Chas Jervis to M. B., November 13, 1898; W. R. Dixon to M. B., December 12, 1898, all in MBP, SHC; *Hickory Times-Mercury*, November 16, 1898.

59. M. B. to J. S. Mitchell, November 15, 1898, MBP, SHC; Hunt, "Marion Butler and the Populist Ideal," 600–601.

CHAPTER NINE. THE DEATH OF LIBERTY AND THE PEOPLE'S PARTY IN NORTH CAROLINA, 1899–1901

1. *Democratic Handbook, 1900: Prepared by the State Executive Committee of North Carolina* (Raleigh: n.p., 1900).

2. Billings, *Planters and the Making of a "New South,"* 191; Edmonds, *The Negro and Fusion Politics*, 178; Mabry, "White Supremacy," 3–10.

3. *Wilmington Messenger*, January 11, 1899; Edmonds, *The Negro and Fusion Politics*, 187; Escott, *Many Excellent People*, 259; Mabry, "White Supremacy," 11–12.

4. Kousser, *The Shaping of Southern Politics*, 190–191; Hunt, "Marion Butler and the Populist Ideal," 622–623; Escott, *Many Excellent People*, 257–259; Edmonds, *The Negro and Fusion Politics*, 183–185.

5. *Wilmington Messenger*, January 13, 1899; Edmonds, *The Negro and Fusion Politics*, 179–180; J. Steelman, "The Progressive Era," 205–206; Mabry, "White Supremacy," 11–12.

6. *Wilmington Messenger*, February 19, 1899.

7. *Wilmington Messenger*, January 11, 1899; Edmonds, *The Negro and Fusion Politics*, 189–191, 193; Crow and Durden, *Maverick Republican*, 141.

8. *Caucasian*, August 24, 31, September 28, November 23, 1899; *Charlotte People's Paper*, October 6, 1899; Morrison Caldwell to M. B., December 20, 1899, MBP, SHC; Crow and Durden, *Maverick Republican*, 144–145; Hunt, "Marion Butler and the Populist Ideal," 628.

9. E. V. Robinson to M. B., December 11, 1899; J. J. Jenkins to M. B., December 12, 1899; Morrison Caldwell to M. B., December 20, 1899; Hal Ayer to M. B., December 30, 1899, all in MBP, SHC.

10. Edmonds, *The Negro and Fusion Politics*, 198; *Congressional Record, Fifty-sixth Congress, First Session, 1899–1900*, vol. 33 (Washington: Government Printing Office, 1900), in the North Carolina Collection, NCDAH, 1–3, 6; Hunt, "Marion Butler and the Populist Ideal," 634–640.

11. *Congressional Record, Fifty-sixth Congress, First Session, 1899–1900*, vol. 33, 8. For analysis on Butler's motivations, see Hunt, "Marion Butler and the Populist Ideal," 634–640.

12. Hunt, "Marion Butler and the Populist Ideal," 634–640. Despite Butler's utterances, the Populists remained on the defensive throughout the latter months of 1899 and into 1900 and divided over whether to support or oppose the amendment. In addition, many leading Populists no longer played an active role in politics. Other reformers seemed more in sympathy with the amendment. Democrats had succeeded in creating the ultimate wedge issue for the Populists. The *Charlotte People's Paper* came out in support of the amendment early in 1900. Editor J. P. Sossaman wrote, "So long as the negro scare crow is held up before the people it will be out of the question to get the people—the masses—united for reform." Such sentiment in the leadership made it difficult for a united fight in the upcoming elections—divide and conquer was working. *Charlotte People's Paper*, February 9, 1900.

13. J. E. Marshall to M. B., January 19, 1900; John C. Dancy to M. B., January 20, 1900, both in MBP, SHC.

14. Cyrus Thompson to M. B., January 9, 22, March 13, 1900, MBP, SHC.

15. *Senator Butler's Position on the Proposed Constitutional Amendment and the Simmons-Goebel Election Law*, January 1, 1900, North Carolina Collection, Wilson Library; *Caucasian*, January 4, 1900; *Progressive Farmer*, January 23, 1900; *Hickory Times-Mercury*, January 24, 1900; E. C. Pencous to M. B., February 22, 1900; M. B. to Dear Sir, January 22, 1900, both in MBP, SHC; *Caucasian*, January 25, February 1, 8, 1900; Hunt, "Marion Butler and the Populist Ideal," 681–683.

16. Fernando Ward to M. B., March 10, 1900; W. Clarke to M. B., February 23, 1900; James S. Wentdeem? to M. B., March 12, 1900, all in MBP, SHC.

17. J.T.B. Hoover to M. B., March 14, 1900; J. J. Jenkins to M. B., March 15, 1900; E. M. Wellborn to M. B., April 2, 1900; P. G. Pritchett to M. B., April 4, 1900; R. B. Elliott to M. B., April 4, 1900; N. R. Dixon to M. B., April 5, 1900, all in MBP, SHC; Hunt, "Marion Butler and the Populist Ideal," 683.

18. Furnifold Simmons to Dear Sir, December 16, 18, 1899, Furnifold Simmons Papers, Duke University; Hunt, "Marion Butler and the Populist Ideal," 676–677.

19. Hunt, "Marion Butler and the Populist Ideal," 676–678.

20. *Charlotte Observer*, April 12, 1900; *Caucasian*, April 12, 1900; Edmonds, *The Negro and Fusion Politics*, 198–199; Hunt, "Marion Butler and the Populist Ideal," 683–684.

21. *Caucasian*, April 12, 1900.

22. The rest of the ticket was A. C. Shuford for lieutenant governor, J. B. Schulken for secretary of state, incumbent William Worth for treasurer, incumbent Hal Ayer for auditor, and H. F. Seawall for attorney general. *Caucasian*, April 19, 1900; *News and Observer*, April 18, 19, 1900; *Hickory Times-Mercury*, April 25, 1900; *Progressive Farmer*, April 24, 1900; Edmonds, *The Negro and Fusion*

Politics, 199; Hunt, "Marion Butler and the Populist Ideal," 686. For the Republican convention, see *Caucasian*, May 3, 1900; *Elizabeth City North Carolinian*, May 10, 1900.

23. Cyrus Thompson to M. B., March 13, 1900; J. B. Price to M. B., April 10, 1900; B. F. Keith to M. B., February 26, 1900, all in MBP, SHC; *Caucasian*, March 29, April 5, 1900.

24. "Some Correspondences Between the State Chairmen of Two Political Organizations," North Carolina Collection; Marion Butler to Furnifold Simmons, April 30, 1900, MBP, SHC; *Caucasian*, April 26, 1900; *Hickory Times-Mercury*, May 9, 1900; *News and Observer*, April 17, 22, 1900. Hunt gives more details on the exchange between Butler and Simmons. Hunt, "Marion Butler and the Populist Ideal," 689–690.

25. *Opinion of About One Hundred and Seventy-Five North Carolina Lawyers that the Amendment is Constitutional* (n.p., June 1900, North Carolina Collection, Wilson Library; Hunt, "Marion Butler and the Populist Ideal," 692–693.

26. H. W. Caswell to M. B., May 1, 1900; William J. Leary to M. B., May 2, 1900, both in MBP, SHC.

27. N. Reid to M. B., June 6, 1900; B. F. Keith to M. B., June 2, 21, 1900; W. H. Hoover to M. B., June 25, 1900; R. B. Davis to A. B. Bradley, June 15, 1900; Ralph Bender to M. B., June 28, 1900; Felix Mahoney to M. B., June 25, 1900, all in MBP, SHC; Hunt, "Marion Butler and the Populist Ideal," 694.

28. *Caucasian*, April 19, 26, May 10, 17, 25, 31, June 7, 14, 21, 28, July 5, 12, 19, 26, 1900.

29. Zebulon Walser to M. B., June 4, 1900; George Bryson to M. B.; R. B. Davis to M. B., June 11, 1900; A. C. Shuford to M. B., June 22, 1900; J. B. Schulken to M. B., June 28, 1900; J. B. Lloyd to M. B., June 18, 1900; A. E. Holton to M. B., May 18, 1900, all in MBP, SHC.

30. Thomas Babb to M. B., June 7, 1900; Q. F. Pool to M. B., June 9, 1900, R. B. Davis to M. B., June 9, 1900, all in MBP, SHC. Morrison Caldwell, for example, wrote that he was too busy to campaign outside his county, and even if he was not too busy, he was too poor. Morrison Caldwell to M. B., June 16, 1900, MBP, SHC.

31. J. Steelman, "The Progressive Era," 310; Claude Bell to M. B., June 29, 1900; H. C. Foster to M. B., June 18, 1900, both in MBP, SHC; Edmonds, *The Negro and Fusion Politics*, 201–203; Hunt, "Marion Butler and the Populist Ideal," 696.

32. J. J. Jones to M. B., July 26, 1900; Maury Ward to M. B., July 16, 1900; J. J. Lewis to M. B., July 18, 1900, all in MBP, SHC.

33. R. C. Carr to M. B., July 3, 1900, MBP, SHC. On issues facing African Americans, see James D. Thomas to M. B., July 3, 1900; William J. Leary to M. B., July 3, 1900; B. B. Lassister to M. B., July 3, 1900; J. S. Basnight to M. B., July 3, 1900; William Powell to M. B., July 6, 1900, D. M. Hall to M. B., July 16, 1900; D. G. McLellan to M. B., July 16, 1900; P. B. Lockerman to M. B., July 16, 1900; J. W. Lee to M. B., July 16, 1900; J. R. Hines to M. B., July 16, 1900; W. D. Longhorn to M. B., July 16, 1900; J. K. Gore to M. B., July 18, 1900; J. W. Canadam to M. B., July 18, 1900; W. D. Bartlett to M. B., July 18, 1900; W. R. White to M. B., July 14, 16, 1900; "The Law on Registration and Challenges," July 23, 1900; circular, July 24, 1900, all in MBP, SHC; For example, P. H. Bright of Kinston wrote to Hal Ayer that the registrars "are acting outrageously in the matter of registering negroes. Not more than a third who apply are allowed to register." P. H. Bright to Hal Ayer, July 12, 1900; G. L. Williams to M. B., July 4, 1900; R. R. Harris to M. B., July 2, 1900; D. M. Konegay to M. B., July 16, 1900; A. E. Holton to M. B., July 17, 1900, all in MBP, SHC; "Instructions to Judges of Election," 1900, NCDAH. Hunt gives the number of registrars arrested as forty. Hunt, "Marion Butler and the Populist Ideal," 698–699.

34. *Contested Election Case of John E. Fowler vs. Charles R. Thomas from the Third Congressional District of North Carolina, 1901* (Washington, DC: Government Printing Office, 1902).

35. *John E. Fowler vs. Charles R. Thomas*, J. W. Mallard, 32–34; Z. J. Quinn, 123; C. C. Vann, 154; R. C. Seawall, 168.

36. *John E. Fowler vs. Charles R. Thomas*, J. W. Mallard, 33; Sam B. Newton, 150–151; C. C. Vann, 154.

37. *John E. Fowler vs. Charles R. Thomas*, A. J. Ward, 158; Moses Judge, 166; Dave Kennedy, 124; Tim Middleton, 125.

38. Marion Butler to W. R. Dixon, July ?, 1900, MBP, SHC; *Caucasian*, July 26, 1900; Hunt, "Marion Butler and the Populist Ideal," 700–705.

39. Zebulon Walser to M. B., June 16, 1900; J. H. Quinn to M. B., June 7, 1900; H. F. Seawell to M. B., June 16, 1900; R. Dodd to M. B., July 7, 1900; William Creek to Hal Ayer, July 11, 1900; J. E. Carpenter to Hal Ayer, July 11, 1900; R. E. Creech to M. B., July 12, 1900; C. C. Fagan to Hal Ayer, July 13, 1900; all in MBP, SHC; *Caucasian*, July 5, 1900; Hunt, "Marion Butler and the Populist Ideal," 703–704.

40. Edmonds, *The Negro and Fusion Politics*, 204–205.

41. *News and Observer*, July 15, 26, 28, 28, 31, 1900.

42. Maury Ward to M. B., July 16, 1900; B. F. Keith to M. B., July 24, 1900; J. H. Fussell to M. B., July 14, 1900; C. Casteen to M. B., July 19, 1900; G. F. Walker to M. B., July 20, 1900; Nelson McAskill to M. B., July 24, 1900; H. F. Seawell to M. B., July 26, 1900, all in MBP, SHC.

43. *John E. Fowler vs. Charles R. Thomas*, A. R. Middleton, 118–120; Lafayette Hussy, 137; Sanders Middleton, 138; and J. S. Hamilton, 146.

44. *Hickory Times-Mercury*, August 1, 1900; *Charlotte People's Paper*, July 13, 1900; Maury Ward to M. B., July 26, 1900; A. B. Winner to M. B., July 25, 1900; R. W. Blackman to M. B., July 28, 1900, all in MBP, SHC; *John E. Fowler vs. Charles R. Thomas*, J. C. Summerlin, 149; O. L. Ward, 190; Henry J Faison, 194; Hunt, "Marion Butler and the Populist Ideal," 708.

45. W. P. Lyon to M. B., July 25, 1900; James Mitchell to M. B., July 25, 1900; W. R. Dixon to M. B., July 30, 1900, all in MBP, SHC; *John E. Fowler vs. Charles R. Thomas*, Duplin County, 29–200.

46. M. B. to John D. Bellamy, August 1, 1900, MBP, SHC; *Caucasian*, July 26, August 2, 1900.

47. *Caucasian*, June 28, August 2, 1900; Hunt, "Marion Butler and the Populist Ideal," 704–706.

48. Connor, *North Carolina Manual*, 1005–1006, 1016–1018; *Records of Election*, Sampson County, Brunswick County, New Hanover County, Richmond County, 1900; *Progressive Farmer*, August 19, 1900; Kousser, *The Shaping of Southern Politics*, 193–195. Although Kousser's work is excellent and is the most detailed analysis of voting patterns, a detailed analysis of township and precinct patterns at the local level might produce a more accurate indication of the number of Populists who voted for the amendment. It is important to remember that all the leaders of the People's Party campaigned against it, including Marion Butler, Cyrus Thompson, Harry Skinner, James Mewboorne, H. F. Seawall, Hal Ayer, A. C. Shuford, J. E. Fowler, J. J. Jenkins, J. B. Schulken, William J. Leary, A. S. Peace, R. B. Davis, J. F. Click, J. Z. Green, M. N. Caldwell, J. B. Lloyd, Z. T. Garrett, E. A. Moye, and many other Populists. In 1904 the turnout dropped to 50 percent. See also Hunt, "Marion Butler and the Populist Ideal," 712.

49. McDuffie, "Politics in Wilmington and New Hanover County," 801.

50. See Prather, *Resurgent Politics*, 194–196.

51. The debate over the significance of fraud and violence is interesting. Mabry, in his article "White Supremacy," argues that despite "some irregularities in the conduct of the election" the white voters voted solidly for the amendment." However, an examination of the votes supports the view that Democrats inflated their majorities in the majority black and white counties in the entire eastern and southeastern section of the state.

52. L.M.M. Morgan to M. B., August 3, 1900; Wheeler Martin to M. B., August 4, 1900; C. C. Vann to M. B., August 4, 1900; Harrison Freeman to M. B., August 4, 1900; C. B. Capps to M. B., August 4, 1900; A. S. Reynolds to M. B., August 4, 1900, all in MBP, SHC.

53. H. F. Seawell to M. B., August 6, 1900; J. B. Overman to M. B., August 6, 1900; G. H. Gibson to M. B., August 6, 1900; George Hunt to M. B., August 6, 1900; William Merritt to M. B., August 6, 1900, all in MBP, SHC; *Caucasian*, August 2, 1900; *Hickory Times-Mercury*, August 9, September 12, 1900.

54. *Charlotte Observer*, August 5, 1900; *News and Observer*, August 3, 1900; Edmonds, *The Negro and Fusion Politics*, 210–211; D. K. Blue to M. B., July 25, 1900, MBP, SHC; Hunt, "Marion Butler and the Populist Ideal," 712–715.

55. *Caucasian*, August 9, 16, 23, 30, 1900; D. A. Long to M. B., August 13, 1900; B. C. Congleton to M. B., August 23, 1900; William H. Hoover to M. B., August 24, 1900; Jno. Skinner to M. B., August 24, 1900; W. A. Reinhardt to M. B., August 24, 1900; T. H. Casey to M. B., August 23, 1900; N. W. Dixon to M. B., August 28, 1900; J. D. Parker to M. B., August 29, 1900; C. Jones to M. B., August 29, 1900; J. J. Jenkins to M. B., August 31, 1900, all in MBP, SHC.

56. *Progressive Farmer*, November 20, 1900; *Hickory Times-Mercury*, October 10, 1900; *John E. Fowler vs. Charles R. Thomas*, see, in particular, the testimony from Craven County, 201–678.

57. Kousser, *The Shaping of Southern Politics*, 238–265.

58. Letter to the *New York Independent*, August 16, 1900, published in *Caucasian*, August 30, 1900.

EPILOGUE

1. Hunt, *Marion Butler and American Populism*, 185–212. There are several studies on the post-1900 period in North Carolina and what happened to the insurgency. See J. Steelman, "The Progressive Era"; Roller, "Republican Party in North Carolina."

2. Kousser, *The Shaping of Southern Politics*, 195; J. Steelman, "The Progressive Era," 237–248, 300–721; Roller, "Republican Party in North Carolina." The best summary of the role of Butler from 1904 to 1912 is Hunt, *Marion Butler and American Populism*, 186–231.

3. Woodward, *Origins of the New South*; Goodwyn, *Democratic Promise*, 442–445, 341, 410. Hunt, in "Marion Butler and the Populist Ideal," makes this point clear.

BIBLIOGRAPHY

ABBREVIATIONS

CTP   Cyrus Thompson Papers
LPP   Leonidas Lafayette Polk Papers
M. B.   Marion Butler
MBP   Marion Butler Papers
NCDAH   North Carolina Division of Archives and History
SHC   Southern Historical Collection

PRIMARY SOURCES

MANUSCRIPT COLLECTIONS

Southern Historical Collection, Wilson Library, University of North Carolina at Chapel Hill

Florence Faison Butler Papers
Marion Butler Papers
Julian S. Carr Papers
Walter J. Clark Papers
Thomas Clawson Papers
Henry Groves Connor Papers
Charles L. Coon Papers
Theodore Davidson Papers
Augustus W. Graham Papers
Bryan Grimes Papers
John Steel Henderson Papers
Jones and Patterson Family Papers
Theodore Kingsbury Papers
Claude Kitchin Papers
Mathias Manly Papers
Stuart Noblin Papers
Richmond Pearson Papers
William J. Peele Papers

Leonidas Lafayette Polk Papers
James Graham Ramsay Papers
Matthew W. Ransom Papers
Rosset Family Papers
Daniel L. Russell Papers
David Schenck Diaries and Journals
Thomas Settle Papers
Southern Oral History Project
Cyrus Thompson Papers
Zebulon Vance Papers
Alfred Waddell Papers
William Wallace White Diary
Zebulon Walser Papers
Robert W. Winston Papers

Manuscript Department, Perkins Library, Duke University, Durham, North Carolina

A. I. Butner Papers
Albert Coble Papers
William A. Couch Papers
Cronly Family Papers
Benjamin N. Duke Papers
Addison Gates Papers
Marmaduke Hawkins Papers
Charles N. Hunter Papers
Jamestown, North Carolina, Alliance Minutes
Duncan McLaurin Papers
John Nichols Papers
Edward A. Oldham Papers
John Osborne Papers
Furnifold Simmons Papers
John Humphrey Small Papers
Edward Chambers Smith Papers
Edward A. Thorne Papers
Bryson Tyson Papers

Manuscript Section, North Carolina Division of Archives and History, Raleigh, North Carolina

Samuel A'Court Ashe Papers
Charles B. Aycock Papers
Charles B. Aycock Governor Papers and Letterbooks
Richard B. Creecy Papers
Delmar Collection
L. Polk Denmark Papers
John Flintoff Papers
Marmaduke Hawkins Papers
Harry A. London Papers
Isaac S. London Papers

BIBLIOGRAPHY

Elizabeth Moore Collection
George Norwood Collection
Old Arm Chair Club Minutes
William Parker Papers
James Pou Papers
John T. Revell Diary
Governor Daniel L. Russell Papers and Letterbooks
Robert W. Scott Papers
Edmund Smithwick Papers
Cornelia Spencer Papers
Richard White Collection
Whitfield Papers
William Worth Papers

East Carolina Manuscript Collection, J. Y. Joyner Library, Greenville, North Carolina

Elias Carr Papers
William E. Clarke Papers
Elizabeth A. Fearrington Papers
Celeste McClammy Logan Papers
William Blout Rodman Papers
Herbert F. Seawall Papers
Elihu A. White Papers

NEWSPAPERS

Charlotte Mecklenburg Times (Democrat)
Charlotte Observer (Democrat)
Charlotte People's Paper (Populist)
Clinton Caucasian (Populist)
Clinton Sampson Democrat (Democrat)
Dunn Central Times (Alliance-Democrat)
Elizabeth City North Carolinian (Republican)
Fayetteville Observer (Democrat)
Greensboro North State (Republican)
Henderson Gold Leaf (Democrat)
Hertford Perquimans Record (Populist)
Hickory Mercury and *Times-Mercury* (Populist)
Lenoir Topic (Democrat)
Maxton Scottish Chief (Democrat)
Pittsboro Chatham Citizen (Populist)
Pittsboro Chatham Record (Democrat)
Raleigh Caucasian (Populist)
Raleigh Gazette (African American, Republican)
Raleigh Hayseeder (Populist)
Raleigh Home Rule (Populist)
Raleigh News and Observer (Democrat)

Raleigh Progressive Farmer (Populist)
Raleigh Signal (Republican-profusion)
Raleigh Tribune (Republican)
Red Springs Comet (Democrat)
Rockingham Anglo-Saxon (Democrat)
Rockingham Rocket (Democrat)
Salisbury Carolina Watchman (Populist, Democrat)
Sanford Express (Democrat)
Scotland Neck Democrat and *Commonwealth* (Democrat)
Snow Hill Great Sunny South (Democrat)
Southport Leader (Democrat)
Tarboro Farmers' Advocate (Populist)
Trinity College Country Life (Alliance)
Wadesboro Plow Boy (Populist)
Whitakers Rattler (Populist)
Wilmington Messenger (Democrat)
Wilmington Morning Star (Democrat)
Wilson Times (Democrat)
Winston Union-Republican (Republican)

North Carolina State Documents and Miscellaneous Records

House Journal, 1891, 1893, 1895, 1897, 1899, 1901.
Public Documents, 1893, 1895, 1897, 1899, 1901.
Public Laws, 1889, 1891, 1893, 1895, 1897, 1899, 1901, 1903.
Senate Journal, 1891, 1893, 1895, 1897, 1899, 1901.
Records of Election, Anson County, Bladen County, Brunswick County, Cabarrus County, Catawba County, Chatham County, Columbus County, Craven County, Cumberland County, Duplin County, Franklin County, Harnett County, Jones County, Mecklenburg County, Moore County, Nash County, New Hanover County, Onslow County, Pender County, Richmond County, Robeson County, Sampson County, Wake County.

Autobiographies, Biographies, and Memoirs

Ashe, Samuel A'Court. *Biographical History of North Carolina*. Greensboro: Van Noppen, 1906.
Ashe, Samuel A'Court, and General E. McCrady Jr. *Cyclopedia of Eminent and Representative Men of the Carolinas of the Nineteenth Century*. Madison: Brant and Fuller, 1892.
Bellamy, John D. *Memoirs of an Octogenarian*. Charlotte, NC: Observer and Printing House, 1942.
Collins and Goodwin. *Bibliographical Sketches of the Members of the General Assembly of North Carolina, 1895*. Raleigh: Edwards and Broughton, 1895.
Connor, R.D.W., and Clarence Poe. *The Life and Speeches of Charles Brantley Aycock*. New York: Doubleday, Page and Company, 1912.
Daniels, Josephus. *Tar Heel Editor*. Chapel Hill: University of North Carolina Press, 1939.
———. *Editor in Politics*. Chapel Hill: University of North Carolina Press, 1941.
Dowd, Clement. *The Life of Zebulon B. Vance*. Charlotte: Observer Printing and Publishing, 1897.
Keith, Benjamin F. *Memories: "Truth and Honesty Will Conquer."* Raleigh: Bynum Printing Company, 1922.

Mangum, D. C. *Biographical Sketches of the Members of the Legislature of North Carolina, Session 1897.* Raleigh: Edwards and Broughton, Printers and Binders, 1897.

Poland, C. Beauregard. *North Carolina's Glorious Victory, 1898: Sketches of the Democratic Leaders and Statesmen.* Raleigh: n.p., 1898.

Sinclair, D. F. *Biographical Sketches of the Members and Officers of the General Assembly of North Carolina, Session 1889.* Raleigh: n.p., 1889.

Tomlinson, W. F. *Biography of the State Officers and Members of the General Assembly of North Carolina, 1893.* Raleigh: n.p., 1893.

Waddell, Alfred. *Some Memories of My Life.* Raleigh: Edwards and Broughton Printing Company, 1908.

PARTY DOCUMENTS, PAMPHLETS, AND BROADSIDES OF NORTH CAROLINA

Agricultural Depression: Its Causes—The Remedy: Speech before the Senate Committee on Agriculture and Forestry, April 22, 1890. Raleigh: Edwards and Broughton, 1890.

Ayer, Hal W. *To the Populist Voters of the Eighteenth Senatorial District.* Populist instructions from the chairman of the Populist State Executive Committee. N.p., n.d.

Butler, Marion. *Address of Marion Butler.* From headquarters of the Populist Party State Executive Committee. N.p., August 20, 1894.

———. *Senator Butler's Position on the Proposed Constitutional Amendment and the Simmons-Goebel Election Law.* Washington, DC, January 1, 1900.

———. *Manhood Suffrage in North Carolina and the Proposed Constitutional Amendment.* N.p., February 6, 1900.

Butler, Marion, and Cyrus Thompson. *Addresses of Marion Butler, President, and Cyrus Thompson, Lecturer, to the North Carolina Farmers' State Alliance at Greensboro, N.C., August 8, 9, and 10, 1893, at Its Seventh Annual Session.* Raleigh, NC: Barnes Bros., Books and Job Printers, 1893.

Carr, Julian S. *Issues of the Campaign Stated in an Open Letter to Van B. Sparrow, Patterson Township.* N.p., October 24, 1898.

———. *The Problem of the Hour: Will the Colored Race Save Itself from Ruin?* Address delivered by Julian S. Carr at the Commencement Exercises before the Trustees, Faculty, and Students of the North Carolina College of Agriculture and Mechanic Arts for Negroes. Greensboro, NC, May 1899.

———. *Letter to Ex-Confederates.* Wentworth, NC, May 7, 1900.

———. *Julian S. Carr for Senator.* Durham, NC, August 25, 1900.

Chairman Simmons Says the Democrats Made No Promises on the Suffrage Question in 1898. N.p., 1900.

Comments by the State Democratic Committee on the Handbook Issued by the People's Party State Executive Committee. N.p., n.d.

Connor, R.D.W, comp. and ed. *North Carolina Manual.* Issued by the North Carolina Historical Commission. Raleigh: E. M. Uzzell and Company, State Printers, 1913.

Democratic Broadside. *Plot Exposed: The Liberties of the People in Danger.* N.p., 1892.

Democratic Broadside. *Not Dead Only Sleeping.* N.p., 1892.

Democratic Broadside. *Dr. Thompson Butts His Head.* N.p., 1898.

Democratic Broadside. *Five Lessons for the Voters of North Carolina.* N.p., 1898.

Democratic Broadside. *Whiteman's Convention in North Carolina.* N.p., 1898.

Democratic Broadside. *The Negro Smith Scores Populist Johnson.* N.p., 1900.

Democratic Broadside. *Opinion of About One Hundred and Seventy-Five North Carolina Lawyers that the Amendment is Constitutional.* N.p., 1900.

Democratic pamphlet. *The Negro and His White Allies*. Raleigh: n.p., June 1900.

Democratic Handbook, 1894: Prepared by the State Democratic Executive Committee. Raleigh: E. M. Uzzell, Printer and Binder, 1894.

Democratic Handbook, 1898: Prepared by the State Democratic Executive Committee of North Carolina. Raleigh: Edwards & Broughton, Printers and Binders, 1898.

Democratic Handbook, 1900. Prepared by the State Democratic Executive Committee of North Carolina. Raleigh, NC, 1900.

Guthrie, William A. *Supplemental Address to the People's Party of North Carolina*. Raleigh, NC, October 30, 1896.

———. *Opinion of a Lawyer on the Constitutionality of the Proposed Amendment to the Constitution of North Carolina*. N.p., April 21, 1900.

History of the General Assembly of North Carolina: January 9–March 13, 1895, Inclusive. Raleigh, NC: E. M. Uzzell, Printers and Binders, 1895. (Democratic pamphlet.)

Is the Democratic Party Honest? A Statement of Facts Issued by the People's Party State Executive Committee, 1898. N.p., 1898.

Kirk, J. Allen. *Statement of Facts: Bloody Riot in Wilmington N.C.* N.p., 1898.

People's Party Broadside: Instructions to the Judges of Election and the Law. Prepared by Able Counsel and Published by the People's Party State Executive Committee for August Election, 1900.

People's Party Broadside: What May Occur on the Day of Election. N.p., [1898].

People's Party Broadside: The People of Sampson County Indignant. N.p., [1900].

People's Party Broadside: A Property Qualification Next. N.p., [1900].

People's Party Handbook, 1896. Raleigh, 1896.

People's Party Handbook, 1900. Raleigh, 1900.

People's Party Handbook of Facts, Campaign of 1898: Issued by the State Executive Committee of the People's Party of North Carolina. Raleigh: Capital Printing Company, Printers and Binders, 1898.

Proposed Suffrage Amendment. The Platform and Resolutions of the People's Party. N.p., April 18, 1900.

Proposed Suffrage Amendment. Some Constitutional Discussions with Declarations from Vance, Saunders, Ransom, Scales, Fowle. N.p., n.d. (Populist/Republican broadside.)

Proceedings of the Fourth Annual Session of the North Carolina Farmers' State Alliance, held in the City of Asheville, N.C. August 12, 13, 14 and 15, 1890. Raleigh, NC: Edwards and Broughton, Printers and Binders, 1890.

Proceedings of the Fifth Annual Session of the North Carolina Farmers' State Alliance, Held in the City of Morehead, N.C. August 11, 12, and 13, 11891. Raleigh, NC: Edwards and Broughton, Printers and Binders, 1891.

Proceedings of the Sixth Annual Session of the North Carolina Farmers' State Alliance, Held in the City of Greensboro, N.C. August 9, 10, and 11, 1892. Raleigh, NC: Edwards and Broughton, Printers and Binders, 1892.

Proceedings of the Seventh Annual Session of the North Carolina Farmers' State Alliance, Held in the City of Greensboro, N.C. August 8, 9, and 10, 1893. Raleigh, NC: Barnes Bros., Job Printers, 1893.

Proceedings of the Eighth Annual Session of the North Carolina Farmers' State Alliance, Held in the City of Greensboro, N.C. August 14 and 15, 1894. Raleigh, NC: Barnes Bros., Job Printers, 1894.

Proceedings of the Ninth Annual Session of the North Carolina Farmers' State Alliance, Held in the City of Cary, N.C. August 13, 14, and 15, 1895. Raleigh, NC: Barnes and Bros., Job Printers, 1895.

Proceedings of the Tenth Annual Session of the North Carolina Farmers' State Alliance, Held in the City of Hillsboro, N.C. August 10, 11 and 12, 1896. Raleigh, NC: Capital Printing Company, 1896.

Proceedings of the Fifteenth Annual Session of the North Carolina Farmers' State Alliance, Held near Hillsboro, N.C. August 13, and 14, 1901. Raleigh, NC: Alfred, Bynum and Christopher Printers, 1901.

Republican Party Handbook, 1892. Raleigh, 1892.

Some Correspondence Between the State Chairman of Two Political Organizations. Issued by Marion Butler. Marion Butler, Populist, to Furnifold Simmons, Democrat, May 18, 1900.

Thompson, Cyrus. *Cyrus Thompson to the Voters of Carteret County.* N.p., 1894.

———. *Dr. Cyrus Thompson's Great Speech, Delivered in Clinton, North Carolina, August 19, 1898.* N.p., 1898.

———. *Address from the Headquarters of the People's Party State Executive Committee.* N.p., March 24, 1900.

To the People of North Carolina from the State Democratic Executive Committee. Raleigh, NC: n.p., 1892.

CONTEMPORARY BOOKS, PERIODICALS, AND MISCELLANEOUS ITEMS

Bland, Thomas A. *People's Party Shot and Shell.* Chicago: C. H. Kerr, 1892.

Butler, Marion. "The Hours Need." *University Magazine* 3 (March 1886): 157–161.

———. "Why the South Wants Free Coinage of Silver." *Arena* 15 (March 1896): 625–632.

———. "Trusts; Their Causes and the Remedy." *Arena* 19 (March 1898): 289–299.

———. "The People's Party." *Forum* 28 (February 1900): 658–662.

———. "Election in North Carolina." *Independent* (August 16, 1900): 1953–1955.

Diggs, Annie. "The Farmers' Alliance and Some of Its Leaders." *Arena* 28 (1892): 590–604.

———. "The Women in the Alliance Movement." *Arena* (July 1892): 160–179.

Donnelly, Ignatius. *Caesar's Column: A Story of the Twentieth Century.* Chicago: Schulte & Co., 1890.

———. *The Golden Bottle: or, Ephraim Benezet, of Kansas.* New York: Merrill, 1892.

———. *The American People's Money.* Chicago: Laird and Lee, 1895.

———. *The Bryan Campaign for the American People's Money.* Chicago: Laird and Lee, 1896.

Drew, Frank M. "The Present Farmers' Movement." *Political Science Quarterly* 6 (1891): 282–310.

Howe, Charles. *Songs of Industry: A Choice Collection of Songs for the Farmers' Alliance.* South Allen, MI: Charles Howe, 1891.

McVey, Frank L. "The Populist Movement." *Economic Studies* 13, no. 3 (August 1896): 135–194.

Skinner, Harry. "The Hope of the South." *Frank Leslie's Illustrated Weekly Newspaper* 59 (November 30, 1889): 290.

Watson, Thomas B. *The People's Party Campaign Book.* Washington, DC: National Watchman Publishing Company, 1892.

Weaver, James B. *A Call to Action: An Interpretation of Its Sources and Causes.* Des Moines: Iowa Publishing Group, 1892.

OFFICIAL FEDERAL PUBLISHED REPORTS

Congressional Record: Fifty-fourth Congress, First Session, 1895–1896. Washington: Government Printing Office, 1896. Vol. 28.

Congressional Record: Fifty-fourth Congress, Second Session, 1896–1897. Washington: Government Printing Office, 1897. 29.

Congressional Record: Fifty-fifth Congress, First Session, 1897. Washington: Government Printing Office, 1897. 30.

Congressional Record: Fifty-fifth Congress, Second Session, 1897–1898. Washington: Government Printing Office, 1898. 31.

Congressional Record: Fifty-fifth Congress, Third Session, 1898–1899. Washington: Government Printing Office, 1899. 32.

Congressional Record: Fifty-sixth Congress, First Session, 1899– 1900. Washington: Government Printing Office, 1900. 33.

Congressional Record: Fifty-sixth Congress, Second Session, 1900– 1901. Washington: Government Printing Office, 1901. 34.

Contested Election Case of Charles H. Martin vs. James A. Lockhart from the Sixth Congressional District of the State North Carolina, 1895. Washington: Government Printing Office, 1895.

Contested Election Case of Cyrus Thompson vs. John G. Shaw from the Third Congressional District of the State of North Carolina, 1895. Washington: Government Printing Office, 1895.

Contested Election Case of John E. Fowler vs. Charles R. Thomas from the Third Congressional District of the State of North Carolina, 1901. Washington: Government Printing Office, 1901.

Contested Election Case of Oliver H. Dockery vs. John D. Bellamy from the Sixth Congressional District of the State of North Carolina, 1899. Washington: Government Printing Office, 1899.

Department of Commerce, Negro Population in the United States, 1790–1915. Washington, DC, 1918.

Department of the Interior, Eleventh Census, Report on the Productions of Agriculture. Washington, DC, 1895.

SECONDARY SOURCES

Books

Ahlstrom, Sidney. A Religious History of the American People. New Haven: Yale University Press, 1972.

Alexander, Roberta S. North Carolina Faces the Freedman: Race Relations during Presidential Reconstruction. Durham: Duke University Press, 1985.

Althusser, Louis. For Marx. New York: Pantheon Books, 1969.

———. Lenin and Philosophy. London: New Left Books, 1971.

Althusser, Louis, and Etienne Balibar. Reading Capital. London: New Left Books, 1970.

Anderson, Eric. Race and Politics in North Carolina, 1872–1901: The Black Second. Baton Rouge: Louisiana State University Press, 1981.

Anderson, John D. The Education of Blacks in the South, 1860–1935. Chapel Hill: University of North Carolina Press, 1988.

Anderson, Perry. Considerations on Western Marxism. London: Humanities Press, 1976.

Appleby, Joyce, et al. Telling the Truth about History. New York: Norton, 1994.

Argersinger, Paul. Populism and Politics: William Alfred Peffer and the People's Party. Lexington: University Press of Kentucky, 1974.

Ash, S. V. Middle Tennessee Society Transformed, 1860–1870: War and Peace in the Upper South. Baton Rouge: Louisiana State University Press, 1987.

Ashe, Samuel A. A History of North Carolina. Raleigh: Edwards and Broughton, 1925.

Ayers, Edward. Vengeance and Justice: Crime and Punishment in the Nineteenth-Century South. New York: Oxford University Press, 1984.

———. The Promise of the New South: Life after Reconstruction. New York: Oxford University Press, 1992.

Baker, Jean. Affairs of Party: The Political Culture of Northern Democrats in the Mid-Nineteenth-Century. Ithaca, NY: Cornell University Press, 1983.

Baker, Paula. The Moral Frameworks of Public Life: Gender, Politics, and the State in Rural New York, 1870–1930. New York: Oxford University Press, 1991.

Barnes, Donna. Farmers in Rebellion: The Rise and Fall of the Southern Farmers' Alliance and People's Party in Texas. Austin: University of Texas Press, 1984.

Barr, Alwyn. *Reconstruction to Reform: Texas Politics, 1876–1906*. Austin: University of Texas Press, 1971.

Barthes, Roland. *Mythologies*. New York: Hill and Wang, 1972.

———. *The Eiffel Tower and Other Mythologies*. New York: Hill and Wang, 1979.

Benjamin, Walter. *Illuminations*. New York: Schocken, 1969.

———. *Reflections*. New York: Harcourt, 1978.

Bernards, Virginia, et al., eds. *Hidden Histories of Women in the New South*. Columbia: University of Missouri Press, 1994.

Billings, Dwight. *Planters and the Making of a "New South": Class, Politics, and Development in North Carolina, 1865–1900*. Chapel Hill: University of North Carolina Press, 1979.

Bisha, K. D. *Western Populism: Studies in an Ambivalent Conservatism*. Lawrence: Coronado Press, 1976.

Blauner, Robert, *Racial Oppression in America*. New York: Harper Row, 1972.

Bleser, Carol, ed. *In Joy and Sorrow: Women, Family, and Marriage in the Victorian South, 1830– 1900*. New York: Oxford University Press, 1991.

Blumin, Stuart M. *The Emergence of the Middle Class: Social Experience in the American City, 1760–1900*. New York: Cambridge University Press, 1989.

Bocock, Robert. *Hegemony*. New York: Tavistock Publications, 1986.

Bode, Frederick A. *Protestantism and the New South: North Carolina Baptists and Methodists in Political Crisis, 1894–1903*. Charlottesville: University Press of Virginia, 1975.

Boggs, Carl. *Gramsci's Marxism*. London: Pluto Press, 1976.

Bordin, Ruth. *Woman and Temperance: The Quest for Power and Liberty, 1873– 1900*. Philadelphia: Temple University Press, 1981.

Boyd, W. K. *The Story of Durham: City of the New South*. Durham: Duke University Press, 1925.

Brandfon, Robert. *Cotton Kingdom of the New South*. Cambridge: Harvard University Press, 1967.

Brantlinger, Patrick. *Crusoe's Footprints: Cultural Studies in Britain and America*. New York: Routledge, 1990.

Brittan, Arthur, and Mary Maynard. *Sexism, Racism, and Oppression*. New York: Blackwell, 1984.

Brown, Hugh V. *A History of Education of Negroes in North Carolina*. Raleigh: Irving-Swain Press, 1961.

Brundage, Fitzhugh W. *Lynching in the New South: Georgia and Virginia, 1880–1930*. Urbana: University of Illinois Press, 1993.

Buck, Solon J. *The Granger Movement*. Cambridge: Cambridge University Press, 1933.

Buhle, Mari Jo. *Women and American Socialism, 1870–1920*. Urbana: University of Urbana Press, 1983.

Buhle, Paul. *Marxism in the United States: Remapping the History of the American Left*. New York: Routledge Chapman-Hall, 1986.

Burton, Orville, and Robert McMath, eds. *Towards a New South? Studies in Post Civil War Southern Communities*. Westport: Greenwood Press, 1982.

Calhoun, Craig. *The Question of Class Struggle*. Chicago: Chicago University Press, 1982.

Callinicos, Alex. *Althusser's Marxism*. London: Pluto Press, 1976.

———. *Against Postmodernism: A Marxist Critique*. New York: St. Martin's Press, 1989.

Canovan, Margaret. *Populism*. New York: Harcourt Brace, 1981.

Carlton, David. *Mill and Town in South Carolina, 1880–1920*. Baton Rouge: Louisiana State University Press, 1982.

Cartwright, Joseph H. *The Triumph of Jim Crow: Race Relations in the 1880s*. Knoxville: University of Tennessee Press, 1979.

Cash, Wilbur J. *The Mind of the South*. New York: Vintage Book, 1960.

Cecelski, David, and Timothy Tyson, eds. *Democracy Betrayed: The Wilmington Riot of 1898 and Its Legacy*. Chapel Hill: University of North Carolina Press, 1998.

Cecil-Fronsman, B. *Common Whites: Class and Culture in Antebellum North Carolina*. Lexington: University of Kentucky Press, 1992.

Centre for Contemporary Cultural Studies. *The Empire Strikes Back*. London: Hutchinson, 1982.

Cheney, John L. *North Carolina Government, 1585–1979: A Narrative and Statistical History*. Raleigh: North Carolina Department of the Secretary of State, 1980.

Cherney, Robert. *Populism, Progressivism and the Transformation of Nebraska Politics*. Lincoln: University of Nebraska Press, 1981.

Clanton, Gene. *Kansas Populism: Ideas and Men*. Lawrence: University Press of Kentucky, 1969.

———. *Populism: The Humane Preference in America, 1890–1900*. Boston: Twayne, 1991.

———. *Congressional Populism and the Crisis of the 1890s*. Lawrence: University Press of Kansas, 1998.

Clark, John B. *Populism in Alabama, 1874–1896*. Auburn: Auburn Printing Company, 1927.

Clinch, T. *Urban Populism and Free Silver in Montana*. Missoula: University of Montana Press, 1970.

Cobb, James B. *Industrialization and Southern Society, 1877–1984*. Lexington: University Press of Kentucky, 1984.

Cott, Nancy. *The Bonds of Womanhood: "Women's Sphere" in New England, 1780–1835*. New Haven, CT: Yale University Press, 1977.

Cox, Oliver. *Caste, Class, and Race: A Study in Social Dynamics*. New York: Monthly Review Press, 1948.

Creech, Joe. *Righteous Indignation: Religion and the Populist Revolution*. Urbana: University of Illinois Press, 2006.

Crow, Jeffrey J., and Robert Durden. *Maverick Republican in the Old North State: A Political Biography of Daniel L. Russell*. Baton Rouge: Louisiana State University Press, 1977.

Crow, Jeffrey J., Paul D. Escott, and Fiona Hatley. *A History of African Americans in North Carolina*. Raleigh: Division of Archives and History, 1992.

Crow, Jeffrey J., and Fiona Hatley. *Black Americans in North Carolina and the South*. Chapel Hill: University of North Carolina Press, 1984.

Cunningham, R., ed. *The Populists in Historical Perspective*. Boston: Heath, 1968.

Dailey, Jane. *Before Jim Crow: The Politics of Race in Post-emancipation Virginia*. Chapel Hill: University of North Carolina Press, 2000.

Daniel, Peter. *Breaking the Land: The Transformation of Cotton, Tobacco, and Rice Culture*. Urbana: University of Illinois Press, 1985.

Davies, Ioan. *Cultural Studies and Beyond*. London: Routledge, 1995.

Davis, Mike, *Prisoners of the American Dream: Politics and Economy in the History of the U.S. Working Class*. New York: Routledge Chapman-Hall, 1986.

DeCanio, Stephen. *Agriculture in the Post-Bellum South*. Cambridge. M.I.T. Press, 1974.

Degler, Carl. *The Other South*. New York: Harper Row, 1974.

———. *Place over Time: The Continuity of Southern Distinctiveness*. Baton Rouge: Louisiana State University Press, 1977.

DeSantis, Vincent P. *Republicans Face the Southern Question—The Departure Years, 1877–1897*. Baltimore: John Hopkins University Press, 1959.

Destler, Chester. *American Radicalism, 1865–1901*. New York: Octagon Press, 1946.

Dirks, N., et al., eds. *Culture/Power/History*. Princeton: Princeton University Press, 1994.

Dittmer, John. *Black Georgia in the Progressive Era, 1900–1920*. Urbana: University of Illinois Press, 1977.

Dobson, J. M. *Politics in the Gilded Age: A New Perspective on Reform*. New York: Praeger, 1972.

Dollard, John. *Caste and Class in a Southern Town*. 3rd ed. Garden City, NY: Doubleday, 1977.

Douglas, Ann. *The Feminization of American Culture*. New York: Alfred A. Knopf, 1977.

DuBois, W.E.B. *Black Emancipation: An Essay toward a History of the Part Which Black Folk Played in the Attempt to Reconstruct Democracy in America, 1860–1880*. New York: Harcourt, Brace, 1935.

Durden, Robert. *The Climax of Populism: The Election of 1896*. Lexington: University of Kentucky Press, 1966.

———. *The Dukes of Durham, 1865–1929*. Durham: Duke University Press, 1975.

Dyson, L. K. *Farmer Organizations*. New York: Greenwood Press, 1986.

Eagleton, Terry. *Criticism and Ideology*. London: New Left Books, 1976.

———. *Walter Benjamin or Towards a Revolutionary Criticism*. London: Verso, 1981.

———. *Against the Grain*. London: Verso, 1986.

———. *Ideology: An Introduction*. New York: Verso, 1991.

Edmonds, Helen. *The Negro and Fusion Politics in North Carolina, 1894–1901*. Chapel Hill: University of North Carolina Press, 1951.

Edwards, Laura. *Gendered Strife and Confusion: The Political Culture of Reconstruction*. Urbana: University of Illinois Press, 1997.

Edwards, Rebecca. *Angels in the Machinery: Gender in American Party Politics from the Civil War to the Progressive Era*. New York: Oxford University Press, 1997.

Ellis, Richard. *American Political Cultures*. New York: Oxford University Press, 1993.

Epstein, Barbara. *The Politics of Domesticity: Women, Evangelicalism, and Temperance in Nineteenth-Century America*. Middletown, CT: Wesleyan University Press, 1981.

Escott, Paul. *Many Excellent People: Power and Privilege in North Carolina, 1850–1900*. Chapel Hill: University of North Carolina Press, 1985.

Escott, Paul, ed. *W. J. Cash and the Minds of the South*. Baton Rouge: Louisiana State University Press, 1992.

Evans, W. McKee. *Ballots and Fence Rails: Reconstruction on the Lower Cape Fear*. Chapel Hill: University of North Carolina Press, 1967.

Femia, Joseph. *Gramsci's Political Thought: Hegemony, Consciousness, and the Revolutionary Press*. Oxford: Clarendon Press, 1987.

Fink, Leon. *Workingmen's Democracy: The Knights of Labor and American Politics*. Urbana: University of Illinois Press, 1983.

Fite, Gilbert. *Cotton Fields No More: Southern Agriculture, 1865–1900*. Lexington: University of Kentucky Press, 1984.

———. *The Farmers Frontier, 1865–1900*. University of Oklahoma Press, 1987.

Flynn, Charles. *White Land, Black Labor, Caste and Class in Nineteenth-Century Georgia*. Baton Rouge: Louisiana State University Press, 1983.

Flynt, J. Wayne. *Dixie's Forgotten People: The Southern Poor Whites*. Bloomington: University of Indiana Press, 1979.

———. *Poor but Proud: Alabama's Poor Whites*. Tuscaloosa: University of Alabama Press, 1989.

Foner, Eric. *Nothing but Freedom: Emancipation and Its Legacy*. Baton Rouge: Louisiana State University Press, 1983.

———. *Reconstruction: America's Unfinished Revolution, 1863–1877*. New York: Harper and Row Publishers, 1988.

Foster, G. M. *Ghosts of the Confederacy: Defeat, the Lost Cause, and the Emergence of the New South*. New York: Oxford University Press, 1987.

Foucault, Michel. *Discipline and Punish*. New York: Vintage Press, 1979.

———. *The History of Sexuality*. Vol. 1. New York: Random House, 1990.

Frankenburg, Ruth. *White Women, Race Matters: The Social Construction of Whiteness*. Minneapolis: University of Minnesota Press, 1993.

Franklin, John Hope. *The Free Negro in North Carolina, 1790–1860*. Chapel Hill: University of North Carolina Press, 1943.

———. *From Slavery to Freedom: A History of Negro Americans*. New York: Alfred A. Knopf, 1967.

Franklin, John Hope, and August Meier, eds. *Black Leaders of the Twentieth Century*. Urbana: University of Illinois Press, 1982.

Fraser, Nancy. *Unruly Practices: Power, Discourse, and Gender in Contemporary Theory*. Minneapolis: University of Minnesota Press, 1989.

Frazier, E. Franklin. *The Negro in the United States*. New York: MacMillan, 1949.

———. *Black Bourgeoisie*. New York: Free Press, 1957.

———. *The Negro Church in America*. 1964. Reprint, New York: Schocken Books, 1974.

Frederickson, George. *The Black Image in the American Mind: The Debate on Afro-American Character and Destiny, 1817–1914*. New York: Harper Row, 1971.

Friedman, Jean E. *The Enclosed Garden: Women and Community in the Evangelical South, 1830–1900*. Chapel Hill: University of North Carolina Press, 1985.

Friedman, Lawrence J. *The White Savage: Racial Fantasies in the Postbellum South*. Englewood Cliff, NJ: Prentice Hall, 1970.

Gaither, Gerald. *Blacks and the Populist Revolt: Ballots and Bigotry in the New South*. University: University of Alabama Press, 1977.

Gaston, Paul M. *The New South Creed: A Study in Modern Mythmaking*. New York: Alfred A. Knopf, 1970.

Gatewood, Willard. *Aristocrats of Color: The Black Elite, 1880–1920*. Bloomington: University of Indiana Press, 1990.

Geertz, Clifford. *The Interpretation of Cultures*. New York: Basic Books, 1973.

Gilmore, Glenda. *Gender and Jim Crow: Women and the Politics of White Supremacy in North Carolina, 1896–1920*. Chapel Hill: University of North Carolina Press, 1996.

Ginzberg, Lori D. *Women and the Work of Benevolence: Morality, Politics, and Class in the Nineteenth-Century United States*. New Haven, CT: Yale University Press, 1990.

Glad, Paul W. *The Trumpet Soundeth: William Jennings Bryan and His Democracy, 1896–1912*. Lincoln: University of Nebraska Press, 1960.

———. *McKinley, Bryan, and the People*. Philadelphia: J. B. Lippincott Co., 1964.

Glucksman, Christine. *Gramsci and the State*. London: Lawrence and Wishart, 1980.

Going, Allen. *Bourbon Democracy in Alabama, 1874–1900*. University: University of Alabama Press, 1951.

Goldberg, Michael L. *An Army of Women: Gender and Politics in Gilded Age Kansas*. Baltimore: John Hopkins University Press, 1997.

Goldfield, Michael. *The Color of Politics: Race and the Mainsprings of American Politics*. New York: New Press, 1997.

Goodwyn, Lawrence. *Democratic Promise: The Populist Movement in America*. New York: Oxford University Press, 1976.

Gourevitch, Peter. *Politics in Hard Times: Comparative Responses to Industrial Economic Crises*. Ithaca, NY: Cornell University Press, 1986.

Gramsci, Antonio, *Selections from the Prison Notebooks*. New York: International Publishers, 1971.

Grantham, Dewey. *The Democratic South*. Athens: University of Georgia Press, 1963.

———. *Southern Progressivism: The Reconciliation of Progress and Tradition*. Knoxville: University of Tennessee Press, 1983.

———. *The Life and Death of the Solid South: A Political History*. Lexington: University of Kentucky Press, 1988.

Greenwood, Janette Thomas. *Bittersweet Legacy: The Black and White "Better Classes" in Charlotte, 1850–1910*. Chapel Hill: University of North Carolina Press, 1994.

Griffiths, D. B. *Populism and Western States, 1890–1906*. Lewiston: Edwin Mellon Press, 1992.

Gutman, Herbert. *The Black Family in Slavery and Freedom, 1750–1925*. New York: Pantheon, 1976.

———. *Work and Culture in Industrializing America*. New York: Vintage, 1976.

Habermas, Jurgen. *Legitimation Crisis*. Boston: Beacon Press, 1975.

———. *The Philosophical Discourse of Modernity*. Cambridge: M.I.T. Press, 1987.

———. *The Structural Transformation of the Public Space: An Inquiry into a Category of Bourgeois Society*. Cambridge: M.I.T. Press, 1989.

Hackney, Sheldon. *Populism to Progressivism in Alabama*. Princeton: Princeton University Press, 1969.

Hahn, Steven. *The Roots of Southern Populism: Yeoman Farmers and the Transformation of the Georgia Upcountry, 1850–1890*. New York: Oxford University Press, 1983.

Hahn, Steven, and J. Prude, eds. *The Countryside in the Age of Capitalistic Transformation: Essays in the Social History of Rural America*. Chapel Hill: University of North Carolina, 1985.

Hair, William Ivy. *Bourbonism and Agrarian Protest: Louisiana Politics, 1877–1900*. Baton Rouge: Louisiana State University Press, 1972.

Haley, John H. *Charles N. Hunter and Race Relations in North Carolina*. Chapel Hill: University of North Carolina Press, 1987.

Hall, Jacquelyn Dowd. *Revolt against Chivalry: Jessie Daniel Ames and the Women's Campaign against Lynching*. Rev. ed. New York: Columbia University Press, 1993.

Hall, Jacquelyn Dowd, et al. *Like a Family: The Making of a Southern Cotton Mill World*. Chapel Hill: University of North Carolina Press, 1987.

Hamilton, J. G. De Roulhac. *History of North Carolina since 1860, History of North Carolina*. Vol. 3. Chicago: Lewis Publishing Company, 1919.

Hanchett, Thomas W. *Sorting Out the New South City: Race, Class, and Urban Development in Charlotte, 1875–1975*. Chapel Hill: University of North Carolina Press, 1998.

Harlan, Louis. *Booker T. Washington: The Making of a Black Leader, 1856–1901*. New York: Oxford University Press, 1972.

———. *Booker T. Washington: The Wizard of Tuskegee, 1901–1915*. New York: Oxford University Press, 1983.

Hart, Roger L. *Redeemers, Bourbons, and Populists: Tennessee, 1870–1896*. Baton Rouge: Louisiana State University Press, 1975.

Haws, Robert, ed. *The Age of Segregation: Race Relations in the South, 1890–1945*. Jackson: University Press of Mississippi, 1978.

Hays, Samuel P. *The Response to Industrialism, 1885–1914*. Chicago: University of Chicago Press, 1957.

Hicks, John D. *The Populist Revolt: A History of the Farmers' Alliance and the People's Party*. Minneapolis: University of Minnesota Press, 1931.

Hirschson, Stanley P. *Farewell to the Bloody Shirt: Northern Republicans and the Negro, 1877–1893*. Bloomington: Indiana University Press, 1962.

Hofstadter, Richard. *The American Political Tradition*. New York: Vintage Press, 1948.

———. *The Age of Reform: From Bryan to FDR*. New York: Random House, 1955.

———. *Anti-Intellectualism in American Life*. New York: Vintage Press, 1964.

Holub, Renate. *Antonio Gramsci: Beyond Marxism and Postmodernism*. New York: Routledge, 1992.

Hunt, James L. *Marion Butler and American Populism*. Chapel Hill: University of North Carolina Press, 2003.

Hyman, Michael. *The Anti-Redeemers: Hill Country Political Dissenters in the Lower South from Redemption to Populism*. Baton Rouge: Louisiana State University Press, 1990.

Ignatiev, Noel. *How the Irish Became White*. New York: Routledge, 1995.

Ingalls, Robert P. *Urban Vigilantes in the New South, 1882–1936*. Knoxville: University of Tennessee Press, 1988.

Jameson, Fredric. *Marxism and Form*. Princeton: Princeton University Press, 1972.

———. *The Political Unconscious*. Ithaca, NY: Cornell University Press, 1981.

———. *Postmodernism, or the Logic of Late Capitalism*. Durham: Duke University Press, 1991.

Janiewski, Delores. *Sisterhood Denied: Race, Gender, and Class in a New South Community*. Philadelphia: Temple University Press, 1985.

Jaynes, G. D. *Branches without Roots: Genesis of the Black Working Class, 1862–1882*. New York: Oxford University Press, 1986.

Jones, Jacquelyn. *Labor of Love, Labor of Sorrow: Black Women, Work, and Family from Slavery to the Present*. New York: Basic Books, 1985.

————. *The Dispossessed: America's Underclass from the Civil War to the Present*. New York: Basic Books, 1992.

Jones, S. *The Presidential Election of 1896*. Madison: University of Wisconsin Press, 1964.

Justesen, Benjamin. *George Henry White: An Even Chance in the Race of Life*. Baton Rouge: Louisiana State University Press, 2001.

Kantowitz, Stephen. *Ben Tillman and the Reconstruction of White Supremacy*. Chapel Hill: University of North Carolina Press, 2000.

Kaye, Harvey, and Keith McClelland, eds. *E. P. Thompson: Critical Perspectives*. Philadelphia: Temple University Press, 1990.

Kazin, Michael. *The Populist Persuasion: An American History*. New York: Basic Books, 1995.

Kelley, Robin D. G. *Hammer and Hoe: Alabama Communists during the Great Depression*. Chapel Hill: University of North Carolina Press, 1990.

————. *Race Rebels: Culture, Politics, and the Black Working Class*. New York: Free Press, 1994.

Kenzer, Robert C. *Kinship and Neighborhood in a Southern Community: Orange County, North Carolina, 1849–1881*. Knoxville: University of Tennessee Press, 1987.

————. *Enterprising Southerners: Black Economic Success in North Carolina, 1865–1915*. Charlottesville: University Press of Virginia, 1997.

Key, V. O. *The Shaping of Southern Politics*. New York: Vintage, 1949.

Kirwan, Albert D. *Revolt of the Rednecks: Mississippi Politics, 1876–1925*. New York: Harper, 1951.

Kousser, J. Morgan. *The Shaping of Southern Politics: Suffrage Restriction and the Establishment of the One Party South, 1880–1910*. New Haven: Yale University Press, 1974.

————. *Colorblind Injustice: Minority Voting Rights and the Undoing of the Second Reconstruction*. Chapel Hill: University of North Carolina Press, 1999.

Kovel, Joel. *White Racism: A Psychohistory*. New York: Pantheon Books, 1970.

Kuhn, Thomas. *The Structure of Scientific Revolutions*. 2nd ed. Chicago: University of Chicago Press, 1982.

Laclau, Ernesto. *Politics and Ideology in Marxist Theory*. London: Verso, 1977.

Laclau, Ernesto, and Chantal Mouffe. *Hegemony and Socialist Strategy: Towards a Radical Democratic Politics*. London: Verso, 1985.

Lasch, Christopher. *The New Radicalism in America, 1889–1963: The Intellectual as Social Type*. New York: Knopf, 1965.

————. *The Agony of the American Left*. New York: Vintage, 1969.

————. *Revolt of the Elites and the Betrayal of Democracy*. New York: Norton, 1995.

Lears, T. J. Jackson. *No Place of Grace: Antimodernism and the Transformation of American Culture, 1880–1920*. New York: Pantheon Books, 1981.

Lefler, Hugh. *North Carolina: Told by Contemporaries*. Chapel Hill: University of North Carolina Press, 1965.

Lefler, Hugh, and Albert Newsome. *North Carolina: The History of a Southern State*. Chapel Hill: University of North Carolina Press, 1973.

Lefler, Hugh, and Alan D. Watson. *The North Carolina Experience: An Interpretive and Documentary History*. Chapel Hill: University of North Carolina Press, 1984.

Leloudis, James L. *Schooling in the New South: Pedagogy, Self, and Society in North Carolina, 1880–1920*. Chapel Hill: University of North Carolina Press, 1996.

Lester, Connie. *Up from the Mudsills of Hell: The Farmers' Alliance, Populism, and Progressive Agriculture in Tennessee, 1870–1915*. Athens: University of Georgia Press, 2006.

Levine, Lawrence. *Black Culture and Black Consciousness*. New York: Oxford University Press, 1977.

————. *Highbrow/Lowbrow: The Emergence of Cultural Hierarchy in America*. Cambridge, MA: Harvard University Press, 1988.

Lewis, David L. *W.E.B. DuBois: A Biography of Race, 1868–1919*. New York: Henry Holt and Company, 1993.

Link, William. *The Paradox of Southern Progressivism, 1880–1930.* Chapel Hill: University of North Carolina Press, 1992.

Litwack, Leon. *Trouble in Mind: Black Southerners in the Age of Jim Crow.* New York: Vintage, 1998.

Livingston, James. *The Origins of the Federal Reserve System: Money, Class, and Corporate Capitalism, 1890–1913.* Ithaca, NY: Cornell University Press, 1986.

Logan, Frenise. *The Negro in North Carolina, 1876–1894.* Chapel Hill: University of North Carolina Press, 1964.

Logan, Rayford. *The Betrayal of the Negro from Rutherford B. Hayes to Woodrow Wilson.* New York: Collier Books, 1965.

Lott, Eric. *Love and Theft: Blackface Minstrelsy and the American Working Class.* New York: Oxford University Press, 1993.

Lukacs, Georg. *History and Class Consciousness.* Cambridge: M.I.T. Press, 1973.

Mabry, William. *The Negro in North Carolina Politics since Reconstruction.* Durham: Duke University Press, 1940.

Magdol, Edward, and J. L. Wakelyn, eds. *The Southern Common People: Studies in Nineteenth-Century Social History.* Westport: Greenwood Press, 1980.

Marable, Manning. *How Capitalism Underdeveloped Black America.* Boston: South End Press, 1983.

Marcuse, Herbert. *One Dimensional Man.* Boston: Beacon Press, 1964.

Marks, S. A. *Southern Hunting in Black and White.* Princeton: Princeton University Press, 1993.

Matthews, Donald E., ed. *North Carolina Voters General Election Returns, by County, for President of the United States, 1868–1960, Governor of North Carolina, 1868–1960, United States Senators from North Carolina, 1914–1960.* Chapel Hill: University of North Carolina Press, 1962.

Marx, Leo. *The Machine in the Garden: Technology and the Pastoral Ideal in America.* New York: Oxford University Press, 1964.

McGuire, Patrick, and Donald McQuarie, eds. *From the Left Bank to the Mainstream: Historical Debates and Contemporary Research in Marxist Sociology.* Dix Hills, NY: General Hall, 1994.

McKenna, G. *American Populism.* New York: Putnam, 1974.

McKinney, Gordon. *Southern Mountain Republicans, 1865–1900: Politics and the Appalachian Community.* Chapel Hill: University of North Carolina Press, 1978.

McLaurin, Melton A. *Paternalism and Protest: Southern Mill Workers and Organized Labor, 1875–1905.* Westport: Greenwood Press, 1971.

———. *The Knights of Labor in the South.* Westport: Greenwood Press, 1978.

McMath, Robert. *Populist Vanguard: A History of the Southern Farmers' Alliance.* Chapel Hill: University of North Carolina Press, 1975.

———. *Populism: A Social History, 1877–1898.* New York: Hill and Wang, 1993.

McNall, S. G. *The Road to Rebellion: Class Formation and Kansas Populism, 1865–1900.* Chicago: University of Chicago Press, 1988.

McPherson, James, and J. Morgan Kousser. *In Region, Race, and Reconstruction.* New York: Oxford University Press, 1982.

Meier, August. *Negro Thought in America: Racial Ideologies in the Age of Booker T. Washington, 1880–1915.* Ann Arbor: University of Michigan Press, 1963.

Meier, August, and Elliot Rudwick. *From Plantation to Ghetto.* New York: G. P. Putnam and Sons, 1960.

Merrill, Horace S. *Bourbon Leader: Grover Cleveland and the Democratic Party.* Boston: Little, Brown and Company, 1957.

Miles, Robert. *Racism.* London: Routledge, 1989.

Miller, William R. *Oklahoma Populism: A History of the People's Party in Oklahoma Territory.* Norman: University of Oklahoma Press, 1987.

Mitchell, Theodore. *Political Education in the Southern Farmers' Alliance, 1887–1900.*

Madison: University of Wisconsin Press, 1987.

Mobley, Joe A. *James City: A Black Community in North Carolina, 1863–1900*. Raleigh: Division of Archives and History, Department of Cultural Resources, 1981.

Moger, Allen W. *Virginia Bourbonism to Byrd, 1870–1925*. Charlottesville: University of Virginia Press, 1968.

Montgomery, David. *The Fall of the House of Labor: The Workplace, the State, and American Labor Activism, 1865–1925*. New York: Cambridge University Press, 1987.

Morgan, Howard W. *From Hayes to McKinley: National Party, 1877–1896*. Syracuse, NY: Syracuse University Press, 1969.

Morley, David, and Kuan-Hsing Chen, eds. *Stuart Hall: Critical Dialogues in Cultural Studies*. New York: Routledge, 1996.

Morrison, Joseph. *Josephus Daniels Says . . . : An Editor's Odyssey from Bryan to FDR*. Chapel Hill: University of North Carolina Press, 1965.

————. *Josephus Daniels: Small d-Democrat*. Chapel Hill: University of North Carolina Press, 1965.

Morton, Richard. The *Negro in Virginia Politics, 1865–1902*. Charlottesville: University of Virginia Press, 1919.

Mouffe, Chantal, ed. *Gramsci and Marxist Theory*. Boston: Routledge, 1979.

Myrdal, Gunnar. *The American Dilemma: The Negro Problem and Modern Democracy*. New York: Harper, 1944.

Nathans, S. *The Quest for Progress: The Way We Lived in North Carolina, 1880–1920*. Chapel Hill: University of North Carolina Press, 1983.

Newby, I. A. *The South: A History*. New York: Rhinehart and Winston, 1978.

————. *Plain Folk in the New South, 1880–1915*. Baton Rouge: Louisiana State University Press, 1989.

Nieman, Donald G. *Promises to Keep: African-Americans and the Constitutional Order, 1776 to the Present*. New York: Oxford University Press, 1991.

Noblin, Stuart. *Leonidas Lafayette Polk: Agrarian Crusader*. Chapel Hill: University of North Carolina Press, 1949.

Nordin, D. S. *Rich Harvest: A History of the Grange, 1867–1900*. Johnson: University Press of Mississippi, 1974.

Nugent, Walter. *The Tolerant Populists: Kansas, Populism, and Nativism*. Chicago: University of Chicago Press, 1963.

O'Brien, Michael. *Rethinking the South: Essays in Intellectual History*. Baltimore: John Hopkins University Press, 1988.

Omi, Michael, and Howard Winant. *Racial Formation in the United States from 1960 to the 1980s*. New York: Routledge, 1986.

Ostler, Jeffrey. *Prairie Populism: The Fate of Agrarian Radicalism in Kansas, Nebraska, and Iowa, 1880–1892*. Lawrence: University Press of Kansas, 1993.

Ownby, Ted. *Subduing Satan: Religion, Recreation, and Manhood in the Rural South*. Chapel Hill: University of North Carolina Press, 1990.

Owsley, Frank. *Plain Folk of the Old South*. Baton Rouge: Louisiana State University Press, 1950.

Painter, Nell Irvin. *Standing at Armageddon: The United States, 1877–1919*. New York: W. W. Norton, 1987.

Palmer, Bruce. *"Man over Money": The Southern Populist Critique of American Capitalism*. Chapel Hill: University of North Carolina Press, 1980.

Parson, Stanley B., et al., eds. *The United States Congressional Districts, 1883–1913*. New York: Greenwood Press, 1990.

Parsons, Stanley B. *The Populist Context: Rural versus the Urban Power on a Great Plains Frontier*. Westport: Greenwood Press, 1973.

Perman, Michael. *Struggle for Mastery: Disfranchisement in the South, 1888–1908*. Chapel Hill: University of North Carolina Press, 2001.

Pollack, Norman. *The Populist Response to Industrial America*. Cambridge: Harvard University Press, 1962.

———. *The Populist Mind*. Indianapolis: Bobbs-Merrill, 1967.

———. *The Just Polity: Populism, Law, and Human Welfare*. Urbana: University of Illinois Press, 1987.

———. *The Humane Economy: Populism, Capitalism, and Democracy*. New Brunswick, NJ: Rutgers University Press, 1990.

Poulantzas, Nicos. *Political Power and Social Classes*. London: Verso, 1968.

Prather, H. L. *Resurgent Politics and Educational Progressivism in the New South: North Carolina, 1890–1913*. Rutherford, NJ: Fairleigh Dickinson University Press, 1979.

———. *We Have Taken a City: Wilmington Racial Massacres and Coup*. Rutherford, NJ: Fairleigh Dickinson University Press, 1984.

Rabinowitz, Harold. *Race Relations in the Urban South, 1865–1900*. New York: Oxford University Press, 1978.

———. *The First New South, 1865–1920*. Arlington Heights, NJ: Harlan Davidson, 1992.

Ransom, Roger, and Richard Sutch. *One Kind of Freedom: The Economic Consequences of Emancipation*. New York: Cambridge University Press, 1977.

Rice, Lawrence. *The Negro in Texas, 1874–1900*. Baton Rouge: Louisiana State University Press, 1971.

Ritter, Gretchen. *Goldbugs and Greenbacks: The Antimonopoly Tradition and the Politics of Finance in America, 1865–1896*. Cambridge: University of Cambridge Press, 1997.

Rochester, Anna. *The Populist Movement in the United States*. New York: International Publishers, 1943.

Rodabaugh, Karl. *The Farmers' Revolt in Alabama, 1890–1896*. Greenville, NC: East Carolina University Press, 1977.

Roediger, David. *The Wages of Whiteness: Race and the Making of the American Working Class*. London: Verso, 1991.

———. *Towards the Abolition of Whiteness*. London: Verso, 1994.

Rogers, William. *The One Gallused Rebellion: Agrarianism in Alabama, 1865–1896*. Baton Rouge: Louisiana State University Press, 1970.

Rosenberg, Carroll Smith. *Disorderly Conduct: Visions of Gender in Victorian America*. New York: Knopf, 1985.

Royce, Edward. *The Origins of Southern Sharecropping*. Philadelphia: Temple University Press, 1993.

Rozwenc, Edwin C., and John C. Malton, eds. *Myth and Reality in the Populist Revolt*. Boston: D. C. Heath and Company, 1967.

Rudwick, Elliott M. *W.E.B. DuBois: Negro Propagandist of the Negro Protest*. New York: Atheneum, 1968.

Saloutos, Theodore. *Farmer Movements in the South, 1865–1933*. Berkeley: University of California Press, 1960.

Saloutos, Theodore, ed. *Populism: Reaction or Reform*. New York: Rhinehart and Winston, 1978.

San Juan, E. *Racial Formation, Critical Transformations: Articulations of Power in Ethnic and Racial Studies in the United State*s. Atlantic Heights, NJ: Humanities Press, 1992.

———. *Hegemony and Strategies of Transgression: Essays in Cultural Studies and Comparative Literature*. Albany: State University of New York Press, 1995.

Sassoon, Ann. *Gramsci's Politics*. New York: St. Martin's Press, 1980.

Saxton, Alexander. *The Rise and Fall of the White Republic: Class Politics and Mass Culture in Nineteenth-Century America*. New York: Verso, 1990.

Schlereth, Thomas, *Victorian America*. New York: Harper Collins Publishers, 1981.

Schwartz, Michael. *Radical Protest and Social Structure: The Southern Farmers' Alliance and Cotton Tenancy, 1880–1890*. New York: Farrar and Rhinehart, 1976.

Scott, Anne Firor. *The Southern Lady: From Pedestal to Politics, 1830–1930*. Chicago: University of Chicago Press, 1970.

Scott, Joan W. *Gender and the Politics of History.* New York: Columbia University Press, 1988.

Shaw, Barton C. *The Wool Hat Boys: Georgia's Populist Party.* Baton Rouge: Louisiana State University Press, 1984.

Sheldon, William D. *Populism in the Old Dominion: Virginia Farm Politics, 1885–1900.* Princeton: Princeton University Press, 1935.

Simkins, Francis. *The Tillman Movement in South Carolina.* Durham: Duke University Press, 1926.

———. *Pitchfork Ben Tillman: South Carolinian.* Baton Rouge: Louisiana State University Press, 1944.

Sims, Anatasia. *The Power of Femininity in the New South: Women's Organizations and Politics in North Carolina, 1880–1930.* Columbia: University of South Carolina Press, 1997.

Sitterson, J. C. *Business Leaders in the Post Civil War North Carolina, 1865–1900.* Chapel Hill: University of North Carolina Press, 1957.

Skocpol, Theda. *Protecting Soldiers and Mothers: The Political Origins of Social Policy in the United States.* Cambridge: Harvard University Press, 1992.

Slotkin, Richard. *The Fatal Environment: The Myth of the Frontier in the Age of Industrialization, 1800–1890.* New York: Anthenum Books, 1985.

Smith, Henry Nash. *Virgin Land: The American West as Symbol and Myth.* New York: Vintage Books, 1984.

Steelman, Lala Carr. *The North Carolina Farmers' Alliance: A Political History, 1887–1893.* Greenville, NC: East Carolina University Press, 1985.

Stover, J. F. *The Railroads of the South, 1865–1900: A Study in Finance and Control.* Chapel Hill: University of North Carolina Press, 1955.

Suggs, Henry L., ed. *The Black Press in the South, 1865–1979.* New York: Greenwood Press, 1995.

Summers, Mark W. *Party Games: Getting, Keeping, and Using Power in Gilded Age Politics.* Chapel Hill: University of North Carolina Press, 2004.

Susman, Warren. *Culture as History: The Transformation of American Society in the Twentieth Century.* New York: Pantheon Books, 1984.

Takaki, Ronald. *Iron Cages: Race and Culture in Nineteenth-Century America.* New York: Oxford University Press, 1990.

———. *A Different Mirror: A History of Multicultural America.* New York: Little, Brown and Company, 1993.

Taylor, John. *Alternative American: Henry George, Edward Bellamy, Henry Demarest Lloyd, and the Adversary Tradition.* Cambridge: Harvard University Press, 1983.

Thompson, E. P. *William Morris: Romantic to Revolutionary.* London: Lawrence and Wishart, 1955.

———. *The Making of the English Working Class.* New York: Pantheon Books, 1963.

———. *The Poverty of Theory and Other Essays.* London: Monthly Review Press, 1978.

Tilley, Nannie May. *The Bright Tobacco Industry, 1860–1929.* Chapel Hill: University of North Carolina Press, 1948.

Tindall, George. *South Carolina Negroes, 1887–1900.* Columbia: University of South Carolina, 1952.

———. *The Emergence of the New South, 1913–1945.* Baton Rouge: Louisiana State University Press, 1967.

———. *The Persistent Tradition in New South Politics.* Baton Rouge: Louisiana State University Press, 1975.

———, ed. *A Populist Reader: Selections from the Works of American Populist Leaders.* New York: Harper Torchbooks, 1966.

Trachtenburg, Alan. *Brooklyn Bridge: Fact and Symbol.* New York: Oxford University Press, 1965.

———. *The Incorporation of America: Culture and Society in the Gilded Age.* New York: Hill and Wang, 1982.

Trelease, Allen. *The North Carolina Railroad, 1849–1871, and the Modernization of North Carolina.* Chapel Hill: University of North Carolina Press, 1991.

Tullos, A. *Habits of Industry: White Culture and the Transformation of the Carolina Piedmont*. Chapel Hill: University of North Carolina Press, 1989.

Volonsinov, V. N. *Marxism and the Philosophy of Language*. New York: Academic Press, 1973.

Watson, Alan. *Onslow County: A Brief History*. Raleigh: Division of Archives and History, 1995.

Wayne, Michael. *The Reshaping of Plantation Society: The Natchez District, 1860–1880*. Urbana: University of Illinois Press, 1990.

Webb, Samuel. *Two-Party Politics in the One-Party South: Alabama's Hill Country, 1875–1920*. Tuscaloosa: University of Alabama Press, 1997.

Weinstein, Allen. *Prelude to Populism: Origins of the Silver Issue, 1867–1878*. New Haven: Yale University Press, 1970.

Wiebe, Robert. *The Search for Order, 1877–1920*. New York: Hill and Wang, 1967.

Williams, Raymond. *Marxism and Literature*. Oxford: Oxford University Press, 1977.

———. *The Sociology of Culture*. New York: Schochen Books, 1981.

———. *Keywords*. Rev. ed. New York: Oxford University Press, 1983.

Williamson, Edward. *Florida Politics in the Gilded Age, 1877–1893*. Gainesville: University of Florida Press, 1976.

Williamson, Joel. *The Crucible of Race: Black-White Relations in the American South since Reconstruction*. New York: Oxford University Press, 1984.

Wood, Phillip J. *Southern Capitalism and the Political Economy of North Carolina, 1880–1980*. Durham: Duke University Press, 1986.

Woodman, Harold D. *King Cotton and His Retainers*. Lexington: University of Kentucky Press, 1968.

Woodward, C. Vann. *Tom Watson, Agrarian Rebel*. New York: Oxford University Press, 1936.

———. *Origins of the New South*. Baton Rouge: Louisiana State University Press, 1951.

———. *The Strange Career of Jim Crow*. New York: Oxford University Press, 1955.

———. *The Burden of Southern History*. Rev. ed. Baton Rouge: Louisiana State University Press, 1968.

———. *American Counterpoint*. New York: Little, Brown and Company, 1971.

Wright, Gavin. *The Political Economy of the Cotton South: Households, Markets, and Wealth in the Nineteenth Century*. New York: Norton, 1978.

———. *Old South, New South: Revolutions in the Southern Economy since the Civil War*. New York: Basic Books, 1986.

Wright, J. E. *The Politics of Populism: Dissent in Colorado*. New Haven: Yale University Press, 1974.

Wyatt-Brown, Bertram. *Southern Honor: Ethics and Behavior in the Old South*. New York: Oxford University Press, 1982.

Wynes, Charles E. *Race Relations in Virginia, 1870–1902*. Charlottesville: University of Virginia Press, 1961.

Zinn, Howard. *A People's History of the United States, 1492 to Present*. Rev. ed. New York: Harper Collins, 1995.

PERIODICALS

Abramowitz, Jack. "The Negro in the Agrarian Revolt." *Agricultural History* 24 (1950): 89–95.

———. "John B. Rayner—Grass-Roots Leader." *Journal of Negro History* 26 (1951): 160–193.

———. "The Negro in the Populist Revolt." *Journal of Negro History* 38 (1954): 257–289.

———. "Agrarian Reformers and the Negro Question." *Negro History Bulletin* 11 (1974): 138–139.

Alvord, Wayne. "T. L. Nugent, Texas Populist." *Southwestern Historical Quarterly* 57 (1953): 65–81.

Argersinger, Paul. "No Rights on this Floor: Third Parties and the Institutionalization of Congress." *Journal of Interdisciplinary History* 22 (1992): 655–690.

Atack, Jeremy. "Tenants and Yeomen in the Nineteenth Century." *Agricultural History* 62 (1988): 6–32.

Atkins, Leah R. "Populism in Alabama: Reuben F. Kolb and the Appeals to Minority Groups." *Alabama Historical Quarterly* 35 (1970): 167–180.

Bailey, K. K. "Southern White Protestantism at the Turn of the Century." *American Historical Review* 68 (1963): 618–635.

Baker, Paula. "The Domestication of American Politics: Women and American Political Society, 1780–1920." *American Historical Review* 89 (1984): 620–647.

Bardham, P. K., and T. N. Srinivasan. "Cropsharing Tenancy in Agriculture: A Theoretical and Empirical Analysis." *American Economic Review* 61 (1971): 48–64.

Beatty, B. "Textile Labor in the North Carolina Piedmont: Millowners Images and Workers Response, 1830–1900." *Labor History* 25 (1984): 485–503.

———. "The Edwin Holt Family: Nineteenth-Century Capitalists in North Carolina." *North Carolina Historical Review* 63 (1986): 511–535.

Beck, John J. "Building the New South: A Revolution from Above in a Piedmont County." *Journal of Southern History* 53 (1987): 441–470.

Beeby, James M. " 'Equal Rights to All and Special Privileges to None': Grass-Roots Populism in North Carolina." *North Carolina Historical Review* 78 (2001): 156–187.

Bell, J. P. "The General Supply Merchant in the Economic History of the New South." *Journal of Southern History* 43 (1951): 37–59.

Bell, John L. "Baptists and the Negro in North Carolina during Reconstruction." *North Carolina Historical Review* 42 (1965): 391–409.

Berry, Mary F. "Judging Morality: Sexual Behavior and Legal Consequence in the Late Nineteenth Century South." *Journal of American History* 78 (1991): 835–857.

Black, P. V. "The Knights of Labor and the South, 1876–1893." *Southern Quarterly* 1 (1963): 201–212.

Bode, Frederick A. "Religion and Class Hegemony: A Populist Critique in North Carolina." *Journal of Southern History* 38 (August 1971): 417–438.

Brady, Marilyn D. "Populism and Feminism in a Newspaper by and for Women of the Kansas Farmers' Alliance, 1891–1894." *Kansas History* 7 (1984/85): 280–290.

Bromberg, Alan B. "The Worst Muddle Ever Seen in N.C. Politics: The Farmers' Alliance, the Subtreasury, and Zeb Vance." *North Carolina Historical Review* 56 (1979): 19–40.

Brown, T. J. "The Roots of Bluegrass Insurgency: An Analysis of the Populist Movement in Kentucky." *Register of the Kentucky Historical Society* 78 (1980): 219–242.

Cantrell, Gregg. "John B. Rayner: A Study in Black Populist Leadership." *Southern Studies* 24 (1985): 432–443.

Cantrell, Gregg, and D. S. Barton. "Texas Populists and the Failure of Biracial Politics." *Journal of Southern History* 55 (1989): 659–692.

Carlton, David. "The Revolution from Above: The National Market and the Beginnings of Industrialization in North Carolina." *Journal of American History* 77 (1990): 445–475.

Carter, Purvis. "Robert Lloyd Smith and the Farmers' Improvement Society Self-Help Movement in Texas." *Negro History Bulletin* 29 (1966): 175–176, 190–191.

Censer, Jane T. "A Changing World of Work: North Carolina Elite Women, 1865–1895." *North Carolina Historical Review* 73 (1996): 28–55.

Chafe, William. "The Negro Problem: A Kansas Study." *Journal of Southern History* 34 (1968): 402–419.

Clevenger, Homer. "The Teaching Techniques of the Farmers' Alliance: An Experiment in Adult Education." *Journal of Southern History* 2 (1945): 504–579.

Cobb, James B. "Beyond Planters and Industrialists: A New Perspective on the New South." *Journal of Southern History* 54 (1988): 45–68.

Crow, Jeffrey. "Fusion, Confusion, and Negroism: Schisms among Negro Republicans in the North Carolina Election of 1896." *North Carolina Historical Review* 53 (1976): 364–384.

————. "Thomas Settle Jr., Reconstruction, and the Memory of the Civil War." *Journal of Southern History* 62 (1996): 689–726.

Crowe, Charles. "Tom Watson, Populists, and Blacks Reconsidered." *Journal of Negro History* 55 (1970): 99–116.

Debray, Regis. "Notes on Gramsci." *New Left Review* (1970): 48–52.

DeCanio, Stephen. "Cotton Overproduction in the Late Nineteenth Century Southern Agriculture." *Journal of Economic History* 33 (1974): 608–633.

Degler, Carl. "Rethinking Post–Civil War History." *Virginia Quarterly* 57 (1981): 250–267.

Delap, Simeon A. "The Populist Party in North Carolina." *Trinity Archives* 14 (1922): 40–74.

Edwards, Laura F. "Sexual Violence: Gender, Reconstruction, and the Extension of Patriarchy in Granville County, North Carolina." *North Carolina Historical Review* 68 (1991): 237–260.

Faulkner, Ronnie. "North Carolina Democrats and Silver Fusion, 1892–1896." *North Carolina Historical Review* 59 (1982): 230–251.

Fields, Barbara Jean. "Slavery, Race, and Ideology in the United States." *New Left Review* 181 (1989): 95–118.

————. "Ideology and Race in American History." In *Region, Race, and Reconstruction: Essays in Honor of C. Vann Woodward*, ed. J. Morgan Kousser and James M. McPherson, 143–177. New York: Oxford University Press, 1992.

Fite, Gilbert. "The Agricultural Trap in the South." *Agricultural History* 60 (1986): 38–50.

Ford, Lacy K. "Rednecks and Merchants: Economic Development and Social Tensions in the South Carolina Upcountry." *Journal of American History* 71 (1984): 294–318.

Fuller, W. E. "The Populists and the Post Office." *Agricultural History* 65 (1991): 1–16.

Gatewood, William. "North Carolina's Negro Regiment in the Spanish-American War." *North Carolina Historical Review* 48 (1971): 370–388.

Gay, Dorothy. "A Crisis of Identity: The Negro Community in Raleigh, 1890–1900." *North Carolina Historical Review* 50 (1973): 121–140.

Gilmore, Glenda. "Gender and Jim Crow: Sarah Dudley Pettey's Vision of the New South." *North Carolina Historical Review* 68 (1991): 261–285.

Going, Allen. "Critical Months in Alabama Politics, 1895–1896." *Alabama Review* 26 (1952): 269–281.

————. "Alabama Bourbonism and Populism Revisited." *Alabama Review* 36 (1983): 83–109.

Goodwyn, Lawrence. "Populist Dreams and Negro Rights: East Texas as a Case Study." *American Historical Review* 76 (1971): 1435–1456.

Green, J. "Populism, Socialism, and the Promise of Democracy." *Radical History Review* 24 (1980): 7–40.

Hackney, Sheldon. "Origins of the New South in Retrospect." *Journal of Southern History* 38 (1972): 191–216.

Hahn, Steven. "Class and State in Post Emancipation Societies: Southern Planters in Comparative Perspective." *American Historical Review* 95 (1990): 75–98.

Hall, Jacquelyn Dowd. "Disorderly Women: Gender and Labor Militancy in the Appalachian South." *Journal of American History* 73 (1986): 354–382.

Hicks, John D. "The Farmers' Alliance in North Carolina." *North Carolina Historical Review* 2 (1925): 162–187.

Hicks, John D., and John Bernhart. "The Farmers' Alliance." *North Carolina Historical Review* 6 (1929): 254–297.

Higgs, Robert. "Railroad Rates and the Populist Uprising." *Agricultural History* 44 (1970): 291–297.

Holmes, William F. "The Demise of the Colored Farmers' Alliance." *Journal of Southern History* 41 (1975): 187–200.

————. "The Southern Farmers' Alliance: The Georgia Experience." *Georgia Historical Quarterly* 72 (1988): 627–652.

————. "Populism: In Search of Context." *Agricultural History* 64 (1990): 26–58.

Hunt, James L. "The Making of a Populist: Marion Butler, 1863–1895." *North Carolina Historical Review* 62 (1985): 53–77, 170–122, 317–343.

Hyman, Michael. "Taxation, Public Policy, and Political Dissent: Yeoman Disaffection in the Post Reconstruction Lower South." *Journal of Southern History* 55 (1989): 48–76.

Ingle, Larry H. "A Southern Democrat at Large: William Hodge Kitchin and the Populist Party." *North Carolina Historical Review* 45 (1968): 179–194.

Jeffrey, Julie R. "Women in the Southern Farmers' Alliance: A Reconsideration of the Role and Status of Women in the Late Nineteenth Century South." *Feminist Studies* 3 (1975): 72–91.

Jolley, H. E. "The Labor Movement in North Carolina, 1880–1922." *North Carolina Historical Review* 30 (1952): 354–373.

Justesen, Benjamin. "George Henry White, Josephus Daniels, and the Showdown over Disfranchisement, 1900." *North Carolina Historical Review* 77 (2000): 1–33.

Kenzer, Robert C. "The Black Businessman in the Post War South: North Carolina, 1865–1885." *Business History Review* 63 (1989): 61–87.

Koch, W. E. "Campaign and Protest: Singing during the Populist Era." *Journal of the West* 22 (1983): 47–57.

Kousser, J. Morgan. "Progressivism for Middle-Class Whites Only: North Carolina Education, 1880–1910." *Journal of Southern History* 46 (1980): 169–195.

Krauss, James O. "The Farmers' Alliance in Florida." *Southern Atlantic Quarterly* 25 (1926): 200–315.

Launius, R. D. "The Nature of the Populists: An Historiographical Essay." *Southern Studies* 22 (1983): 366–385.

Leloudis, James L. "School Reform in the New South: The Woman's Association for the Betterment of Public Schools in North Carolina, 1902–1909." *Journal of American History* 69 (1983): 886–909.

Lemmon, Sarah M. "Raleigh—An Example of the 'New South.'" *North Carolina Historical Review* 43 (1960): 261–285.

Logan, Frenise. "Movement of Negroes from North Carolina, 1876–1894." *North Carolina Historical Review* 33 (1956): 45–65.

———. "The Economic Status of the Town Negro in Post-Reconstruction North Carolina." *North Carolina Historical Review* 35 (1958): 448–460.

Mabry, William. "Negro Suffrage and Fusion Rule in North Carolina." *North Carolina Historical Review* 12 (1935): 79–102.

———. "White Supremacy and the North Carolina Suffrage Amendment." *North Carolina Historical Review* 13 (1936): 1–24.

MacLean, Nancy. "The Leo Frank Case Reconsidered: Gender and Sexual Politics in the Making of Reactionary Populism." *Journal of American History* 78 (1991): 917–940.

Mann, S. A. "Sharecropping in the Cotton South: A Case of Uneven Development in Agriculture." *Rural Sociology* 49 (1984): 412–429.

Mayhew, Anne. "A Reappraisal of the Causes of Farm Protest in the United States, 1870–1900." *Journal of Economic History* 32 (1972): 464–475.

McKinney, Gordon. "Southern Mountain Republicans and the Negro, 1865–1900." *Journal of Southern History* 41 (1975): 495–516.

McLaurin, Melton A. "The Knights of Labor in North Carolina Politics." *North Carolina Historical Review* 49 (1972): 464–475.

McMath, Robert. "Agrarian Protest at the Forks of the Creek: Three Subordinate Farmers' Alliances in North Carolina." *North Carolina Historical Review* 51 (1974): 41–53.

Miller, Floyd. "Black Protest and White Leadership: A Note on the Colored Farmers' Alliance." *Phylon* 33 (1972): 169–174.

Miller, W. R. "A Centennial Historiography of American Populism." *Kansas History* 16 (1993): 54–69.

Mitchell, Herbert H. "A Forgotten Institution: Private Banks in North Carolina." *North Carolina Historical Review* 35 (1958): 24–49.

Mobley, Joe A. "Agrarianism and Populism in Tennessee, 1886–1896: An Interpretative Overview." *Tennessee Historical Quarterly* 42 (1983): 76–94.

———. "In the Shadow of White Society: Princeville, a Black Town in North Carolina, 1865–1915." *North Carolina Historical Review* 63 (1986): 340–384.

Ownby, Ted. "The Defeated Generation at Work: White Farmers in the Deep South, 1865–1890." *Southern Studies* 23 (1984): 325–347.

Parsons, Stanley B. "The Role of Cooperatives in the Development of the Movement Culture of Populism." *Journal of American History* 69 (1983): 866–885.

Prather, H. L. "The Red Shirt Movements in North Carolina, 1898–1900." *Journal of Negro History* 62 (1977): 174–184.

Proctor, Samuel. "National Farmers' Alliance Convention of 1890 and Its Ocala Demands." *Florida Historical Quarterly* 28 (1950): 161–181.

Redding, Kent. "Failed Populism: Movement Party Disjuncture in North Carolina, 1890 to 1900." *American Sociological Review* 57 (1992): 340–352.

Roberts, C., and Robert Higgs. "Did Southern Farmers Discriminate? An Exchange." *Agricultural History* 49 (1975): 441–448.

Rodabaugh, Karl. "The Prelude to Populism in Alabama." *Alabama Historical Quarterly* (1981): 121–152.

———. "Agrarian Ideology and the Farmers Revolt in Alabama." *Alabama Review* 36 (1983): 195–217.

Saloutos, Theodore. "The Grange in the South, 1870–1877." *Journal of Southern History* 19 (1953): 473–488.

Saunders, Robert. "The Southern Populists and the Negro in 1892." *University of Virginia Essays in History* 12 (1966): 7–25.

———. "Southern Populists and the Negro, 1893–1895." *Journal of Negro History* 54 (1969): 240–261.

———. "The Transformation of Tom Watson, 1894–1895." *Georgia Historical Quarterly* 54 (1970): 339–356.

Schlup, L. "Adlai E. Stevenson and the 1892 Campaign in North Carolina: A Conservative Response to Southern Populism." *International Review of History and Political Science* 26 (1989): 16–34.

Shannon, Fred A. "C. W. Macune and the Farmers' Alliance." *Current History* 28 (1955): 330–335.

Sharp, J. A. "Entrance of the Farmers' Alliance into Tennessee Politics." *East Tennessee Historical Society's Publications* 9 (1937): 72–92.

Simkins, Francis. "Ben Tillman's View of the Negro." *Journal of Southern History* 3 (1937): 161–174.

Simms-Brown, R. J. "Populism and Black Americans: Constructive or Destructive?" *Journal of Negro History* 65 (1980): 349–360.

Steelman, Joseph. "Vicissitudes of Republican Party Politics: The Campaign of 1892 in North Carolina." *North Carolina Historical Review* 43 (1966): 430–442.

———. "Republican Party Strategists and the Issue of Fusion with Populists in North Carolina, 1893–1894." *North Carolina Historical Review* 47 (1970): 244–269.

Steelman, Lala Carr. "The Role of Elias Carr in the North Carolina Farmers' Alliance." *North Carolina Historical Review* 57 (1980): 133–158.

Trelease, Allen. "The Fusion Legislature of 1895 and 1897: A Roll Call Analysis of the North Carolina House of Representatives." *North Carolina Historical Review* 57 (1980): 288–309.

Watson, Richard. "Furnifold M. Simmons: Jehovah of the Tarheels?" *North Carolina Historical Review* 44 (1967): 166–187.

Webb, Samuel. "A Jacksonian Democrat in Postbellum Alabama: The Ideology and Influence of Journalist Robert McKee, 1869–1896." *Journal of Southern History* 62 (May 1996): 239–274.

Whitener, Daniel. "The Republican Party and Public Education in North Carolina, 1867–1900." *North Carolina Historical Review* 37 (1960): 382–396.

Woodman, Harold D. "Post–Civil War Southern Agriculture and the Law." *Agricultural History* 53 (1979): 319–337.

———. "Postbellum Social Change and Its Effects on Marketing the South's Cotton Crop." *Agricultural History* 56 (1982): 215–230.

Wright, Gavin. "Cotton Competition and the Postbellum Recovery of the American South." *Journal of Economic History* 34 (1974): 610–635.

THESES AND DISSERTATIONS

Ali, Omar. "Black Populism in the New South, 1886–1898." PhD diss., Columbia University, 2003.

Barnes, B. "Triumph in the New South: Independent Movements in the 1880's." PhD diss., University of Virginia, 1991.

Beck, J. J. "Gentlemen Politicians: A Study of Southern Democratic Congressmen and Senators in the 1890's." Master's thesis, University of North Carolina at Chapel Hill, 1976.

———. "Development in the Piedmont South: Rowan County, North Carolina, 1850–1900." PhD diss., University of North Carolina at Chapel Hill, 1984.

Beeby, James M. "Revolt of the Tar Heelers: A Socio-Political History of the North Carolina Populist Party, 1892–1901." PhD diss., Bowling Green State University, 1999.

Bell, Willard B. "Enigmatic Danger: Populism, Status Anxiety, and the Wilmington Race Riot of 1898." Master's thesis, University of North Carolina at Charlotte, 1999.

Bolton, C. C. "The Failure of Yeoman Democracy: Poor Whites in the Antebellum South." PhD diss., Duke University, 1989.

Bowditch, Mary F. "The North Carolina Railroad Commission, 1891–1899." Master's thesis, University of North Carolina at Chapel Hill, 1943.

Boyette, Robert. "The North Carolina Alliance Legislature of 1891: Harvest Time for the Farmer." Master's thesis, East Carolina University, 1981.

Bromberg, Alan B. "Pure Democracy and White Supremacy: The Redeemer Period in North Carolina, 1876–1894." PhD diss., University of Virginia, 1977.

Cody, Sue A. "After the Storm: Racial Violence in Wilmington, North Carolina, and Its Consequences for African Americans, 1898–1905." Master's thesis, University of North Carolina at Wilmington, 2000.

Creech, Joseph W. "Righteous Indignation: Religion and Populism in North Carolina, 1886–1906." PhD diss., University of Notre Dame, 2000.

Elmore, Joseph. "North Carolina Negro Congressmen, 1875–1901." Master's thesis, University of North Carolina at Chapel Hill, 1964.

Faulkner, Ronnie. "Samuel A'Court Ashe: North Carolina Redeemer, 1840–1894." Master's thesis, East Carolina University, 1975.

———. "Samuel A'Court Ashe: North Carolina Redeemer and Historian, 1840–1900." PhD diss., University of South Carolina, 1983.

Hershman, James. "The North Carolina Republican Party: The Years of Revitalization, 1888–1892." Master's thesis, Wake Forest University, 1971.

Higuchi, Hayumi. "White Supremacy on the Cape Fear: The Wilmington Affair of 1898." Master's thesis, University of North Carolina at Chapel Hill, 1980.

Hild, Matthew. "Greenbackers, Knights of Labor, and Populists: Farmer-Labor Insurgency in the Late-Nineteenth-Century South." PhD diss., Georgia Institute of Technology, 2002.

Hill, Joseph S. "Cyrus Thompson and the Dilemmas of North Carolina Populism." Master's thesis, University of Virginia, 1998.

Holt, S. A. "Time to Plant: The Economic Lives of Freed People in Granville County, North Carolina, 1865–1900." PhD diss., University of Pennsylvania, 1991.

Honeycutt, Adolph. "The Farmers' Alliance in North Carolina." Master's thesis, North Carolina State College of Agriculture and Engineering, 1925.

Hopper, C. M. "Three Dissenting Views of the Nineteenth-Century South: Albion W. Tourgee, Charles W. Chesnutt, and Walter Hines Page." PhD diss., Duke University, 1985.

Hunt, James. "Marion Butler and the Populist Ideal, 1863–1938." PhD diss., University of Wisconsin-Madison, 1990.

Johnson, R. A. "Political Ideology and Political Historiography: Reporting the Populists." PhD diss., University of California, Berkeley, 1981.

Jones, L. A. "The Task Is Ours: White North Carolina Farm Workers and Agrarian Reform, 1886–1914." Master's thesis, University of North Carolina at Chapel Hill, 1983.

Jones, Theron. "The Gubernatorial Election of 1892 in North Carolina." Master's thesis, University of North Carolina at Chapel Hill, 1949.

Kimmel, Bruce I. "The Political Sociology of Third Parties in the United States: A Comparative Study of the People's Party in North Carolina, Georgia, and Minnesota." PhD diss., Columbia University, 1981.

King, William E. "The Era of Progressive Reform in Southern Education: The Growth of Public Schools in North Carolina, 1885–1910." PhD diss., Duke University, 1969.

Larson, Karl. "Separate Reality: the Development of Racial Segregation on Raleigh, North Carolina, 1865–1915." Master's thesis, University of North Carolina at Greensboro, 1983.

Lester, Connie L. "Grassroots Reform in the Age of New South Agriculture and Bourbon Democracy: The Agricultural Wheel, the Farmers' Alliance, and the People's Party in Tennessee, 1884–1892." PhD diss., University of Tennessee, 1998.

McDuffie, Jerome A. "Politics in Wilmington and New Hanover County, North Carolina, 1865–1900: The Genesis of a Race Riot." PhD diss., Kent State University, 1979.

Miller, Bertha H. "Blacks in Winston-Salem, North Carolina, 1895–1920: Community Development in an Era of Benevolent Paternalism." PhD diss., Duke University, 1981.

Muller, Philip. "New South Populism: North Carolina, 1884–1900." PhD diss., University of North Carolina at Chapel Hill, 1971.

Paoli, Donna. "Marion Butler's View of the Negro, 1889–1901." Master's thesis, University of North Carolina at Chapel Hill, 1969.

Piehl, C. "White Society in the Black Belt, 1870–1920: A Study of Four North Carolina Counties." PhD diss., Washington University, 1979.

Redding, Kent. "Making Power: Elites in the Constitution of Disfranchisement in North Carolina, 1880–1900." PhD diss., University of North Carolina at Chapel Hill, 1995.

Reid, George. "A Biography of George H. White, 1852–1918." PhD diss., Howard University, 1974.

Rodriquez, Alicia E. "Urban Populism: Challenges to Democratic Party Control in Dallas, Texas, 1887–1900." PhD diss., University of California, Santa Barbara, 1998.

Roller, David. "The Republican Party in North Carolina, 1900–1916." PhD diss., Duke University, 1965.

Smith, Robert W. "A Rhetorical Analysis of the Populist Movement in North Carolina, 1892–1896." PhD diss., University of Wisconsin, 1957.

Steelman, Joseph. "The Progressive Era in North Carolina, 1884–1917." PhD diss., University of North Carolina at Chapel Hill, 1955.

Thurtell, Craig M. "The Fusion Insurgency in North Carolina: Origins to Ascendancy, 1876–1896." PhD diss., Columbia University, 1998.

Underwood, Evelyn. "The Struggle for White Supremacy in North Carolina, 1880–1930." Master's thesis, University of North Carolina at Chapel Hill, 1943.

Wagner, M. J. "Farms, Families, and Reform: Women in the Farmers' Alliance and Populist Party." PhD diss., University of Oregon, 1986.

Weaver, Garrett. "The Politics of Local Democratic-Populist Fusion in the Election of 1896 in North Carolina." Master's thesis, University of North Carolina at Chapel Hill, 1968.

Weaver, Phillip. "The Gubernatorial Election of 1896 in North Carolina." Master's thesis, University of North Carolina at Chapel Hill, 1937.

Wilkerson-Freeman, Sarah. "Women and the Transformation of American Politics, North Carolina, 1896–1940." PhD diss., University of North Carolina at Chapel Hill, 1995.

Wooley, Robert H. "Race and Politics: The Evolution of the White Supremacy Campaign of 1898 in North Carolina." PhD diss., University of North Carolina at Chapel Hill, 1977.

INDEX